LIVING WITHOUT

PHILOSOPHY

LIVING
WITHOUT
PHILOSOPHY

ON NARRATIVE, RHETORIC, AND MORALITY

Peter Levine

STATE UNIVERSITY OF NEW YORK PRESS

Published by
State University of New York Press, Albany

Printed in the United States of America

For information, address State University of New York
Press, State University Plaza, Albany, N.Y., 12246

Production by Diane Ganeles
Marketing by Patrick Durocher

Library of Congress Cataloging-in-Publication Data

Levine, Peter, 1967–
    Living without philosophy : on narrative, rhetoric, and morality /
Peter Levine.
        p.   cm.
    Includes bibliographical references and index.
    ISBN 0-7914-3897-X (alk. paper). – ISBN 0-7914-3898-8 (pbk. :
alk. paper)
    1. Ethics.   2. Description (Rhetoric)   I. Title.
BJ42.L48   1998
    170–dc21   98-7524
                                                                CIP

10 9 8 7 6 5 4 3 2 1

For Laura

CONTENTS

ACKNOWLEDGMENTS

Portions of Chapter 4 were previously published as "*Lolita* and Aristotle's Ethics," in *Philosophy and Literature*, volume 19, number 1 (April 1995), pp. 32–47. That material is reprinted here by permission of the editors. In Chapter 1, the illustration from *The Philosophical Investigations* by Ludwig Wittgenstein, third edition (translated by G. E. M. Anscombe), © 1953, is reprinted by permission of Prentice-Hall, Inc., Upper Saddle River, New Jersey. Excerpts from *The Annotated Lolita* by Vladimir Nabokov, edited by Alfred Appel Jr., © 1970, 1981 by Alfred Appel Jr., are reprinted by permission of Vintage Books, a division of Random House, Inc.

INTRODUCTION

W hen we want to judge a person, evaluate an institution, consider an action, or choose an overall plan of life, one possible source of guidance is philosophy. In popular culture, the philosopher is a sage who dispenses wisdom to the perplexed. However, most academic philosophers today would not presume to decide actual cases, especially subtle and ambiguous ones. When two leading members of the profession, John Rawls and Jürgen Habermas, recently clashed in print, each vied to show that he was less pretentious than the other about his discipline, and more solicitous of ordinary people's intuitions. Rawls stated flatly: "There are no [normative] experts: a philosopher has no more authority than other citizens."[1]

Philosophy professors teach several standard moral theories to their students, but most do not believe that these theories can settle all difficult cases, nor do they think that conclusive arguments favor one theory over the competition. A typical argument may begin: "If one were a utilitarian –," or "In Kantian terms –." Few philosophers presume to convert their audiences to these general doctrines.

In print, philosophers conduct an abstract and sophisticated debate about issues that often lie far from concrete cases. Sometimes they seem content to analyze the form and structure of moral discourse for purely intellectual reasons, just as number-theorists study arithmetic. But often they have more practical motives. As James Dreier writes: "Moral theory can progress by illuminating the variety of structures and contents that normative schemes can have, improving our map of the overall landscape. Or, it can progress by attempting to reduce the variety of plausible or justifiable options, weeding out incoherent ones or trying to drive us to one spot or another by appealing to our settled convictions."[2]

For instance, students in introductory ethics classes are taught that they can either be concerned about motives or about consequences when they judge actions. If they believe that motives matter most, then they should be attracted to Kant; but if they care more about consequences, then they ought to adopt utilitarianism (or some kindred theory). They are free to choose their basic commitments, as long as they understand these values and apply them consistently. Dreier, like most of his colleagues, respects people's fundamental moral intuitions, but he argues that attention "to conceptual apparatus at the level of metaethics is necessary if we are to find good reasons for choosing among normative theories."[3]

The distinction between motives and consequences has not settled the debate between Kantianism and utilitarianism; it certainly hasn't "weeded out" either theory. Thus philosophers who want to defend one doctrine against the other must look for subtler points of conflict. Rawls achieved something along these lines when he argued that classical utilitarianism "fails to take seriously the distinction between persons, because utilitarians only care how much aggregate happiness exists, not how it is distributed."[4] Rawls's analysis revealed a formal aspect of the theory that forced some believers to abandon it, but only because they had a conflicting prior commitment.

More recently, professional journals have devoted considerable attention to the contrast between "agent-relative" and "agent-neutral" reasons. Thomas Nagel explains: "If a reason [for acting in a certain way] can be given in a general form which does not include an essential reference to the person who has it, it is an *agent-neutral* reason."[5] For instance, maximizing human happiness might be an agent-neutral reason for me to treat other people nicely. Some philosophers doubt that there are genuinely agent-neutral reasons; perhaps everything is only good for someone. Others ask: Can a reason ever be morally legitimate if it is *not* agent-neutral? In other words, must everything I do be good "objectively," or may I pursue objects of value only to myself? Finally, philosophers ask whether the belief in agent-neutral reasons is compatible with utilitarianism, with Kantianism, or with virtue theory. They hope that by deciding what they think about agent-neutral reasons, they can find new grounds for choosing a comprehensive moral doctrine. But the issue of agent-neutrality is perplexing, and so is its relationship to any particular philosophy.

Under these conditions, the taxonomy of moral theories has become a high art. Current journals are full of articles defining consequentialism, deontology, eudaimonism, subjectivism, realism, altruism, welfarism, liberalism, communitarianism, act- and rule-utilitarianism, and other categories into which normative positions can be placed. This discussion resembles the scholasticism of the late Middle Ages in both its merits and its failings. It is a subtle, difficult, and impressive discipline. To outsiders, it looks like hair-splitting, because it has few practical implications. On the other hand, given its point of departure, the questions that it considers may be unavoidable. Once you decide to assess such theories as utilitarianism and Kantianism, you must soon determine what they imply about agent-relative values and similarly abstruse topics.

Meanwhile, applied ethics is mostly a question of clarifying terms, applying accepted standards, and using informal arguments to defend moral positions. Ethicists point out contradictions, call attention to consequences, interpret and apply professional codes, and invoke widely shared values such as autonomy, equality, and utility. When these values conflict, ethicists have no clear and compelling way to rank them. Annette Baier asks, "Can we approve of a division of labor in which the theorists keep their hands clean of real-world applications, and the ones who advise the decision makers, those who do 'applied ethics,' are like a consumer reports service, pointing out the variety of available theories and what costs and benefits each has for the serious user of it?"[6] In fact, some leading moral theorists write about "real-world" issues and influence decision-makers; and some applied ethicists make discoveries that influence theory. Nevertheless, Baier's caricature is more true than false.

Philosophers, it seems, have largely abandoned their proverbial place as sages, counselors, and lawgivers—assuming that they ever tried to fill these roles. In his *Critique of Pure Reason*, Kant described the highest ambition of philosophy: "We must be able, in every possible case, in accordance with a rule, to know what is *right* and what is *wrong*, since this concerns our obligation, and we have no obligation to that which we cannot know."[7] Kant provided one such rule, the Categorical Imperative, but most interpreters (even sympathetic ones) do not now consider it an algorithm that can generate clear and reliable answers to all moral dilemmas.

Not only are most academic philosophers modest about the practical applications of their discipline, but the theories that they hold are endlessly varied. It is difficult to find much in common among Kantianism, utilitarianism, virtue ethics, pragmatism, intuitionism, existentialism, social-contract theory, and natural-law doctrine, especially since each of these theories comes in myriad forms and hybrids. Cora Diamond once intervened in a debate about philosophy and literature with the following warning:

> [the] attempt to take as a starting point a widely agreed
> and inclusive notion of the aim of moral philosophy is

pretty much doomed. No one knows what the subject is; most widely agreed accounts of it depend on suppositions that are not obvious and that reflect particular evaluations and views of the world, of human nature, and of what it is to speak, think, write, or read about the world. The more inclusive an account is, the more likely that it will include what many philosophers would not dream of counting as part of their subject.[8]

It is not clear, then, that "philosophy" constitutes a definable or recognizable approach to moral questions. Perhaps philosophers are in precisely the same position as anyone else when they examine concrete moral problems, having nothing special to contribute except academic freedom and the mandate to consider ethical issues.

Nevertheless, for the sake of argument, I will define "moral philosophy" as follows. In its purest form, it is *an effort to develop general normative principles or procedures that can be defended with arguments and then used to settle at least some concrete cases.* (By "cases," I mean acts, choices, situations, characters, habits, institutions, or plans of life that require moral assessment.) Although Kant's philosophy is too abstract and general to resolve many predicaments, he argues that the Categorical Imperative always forbids lying, suicide, and breaking promises to repay loans. Thus, by his own account, he presents a "moral philosophy." Similarly, the utilitarian command to maximize happiness is notoriously difficult to apply, but there are certain problems (especially questions of economic justice) that have clear utilitarian solutions.

When philosophers deny that general principles can ever settle important concrete cases, they disparage moral philosophy as I have defined it. Similarly, when they doubt that conclusive arguments ever support moral principles, they express skepticism about their discipline. This kind of skepticism has a distinguished history. Aristotle, Hume, Nietzsche, Sartre, and many other philosophers of the past denied that they could resolve concrete cases with clear and demonstrable principles: they even made philosophical arguments in favor of this skeptical conclusion. Still, we can call people "philosophical" to the extent that they generalize, rely on principles or procedures, and use abstract arguments to defend their moral views. Even Aristotle and Hume behaved this way to a certain extent. A person who never does so is not a moral philosopher, even if he or she holds a chair in the subject.

I believe that we can settle moral dilemmas without doing any of the things that I have characterized as "moral philosophy." There is an alternative approach, which is more an art than a science, learned by experience rather than by the apprehension of principles or techniques. It is— to be more specific—a matter of describing particulars in a judgmental way.

A single act can be called many things at once: for example, a case of "squeezing a metal object" might simultaneously be an instance of "firing a gun," "killing a person," and even "a heinous murder." As we move from the "thinnest" vocabulary toward the "thickest" phrases, we find ourselves increasingly committed to value-judgments. Squeezing metal objects is morally neutral; killing someone can be justifiable in certain contexts; but a murder is clearly bad. Thick descriptions support value-judgments, and they are not arbitrary, subjective, or indefensible. In order to know that a particular instance of squeezing a metal object is also a case of murder, we have to describe the event in a broader context, explaining what happened in the light of other events, the participants' psychological states, their other options, the cultural background, and so on. Enough information of this kind can make a simple muscular movement look like a heinous murder—and appropriately so.

Some theorists have argued that any story or concrete description with moral meaning must contain—either implicitly or explicitly—general doctrines or principles. If that were true, then we would have to analyze stories to discover their hidden assumptions, and we would need philosophy to decide whether these assumptions were right or wrong. But I will argue that narratives can carry moral meaning without relying upon general principles at all. In part I of this book, I will describe an actual case of sexual harassment, showing that we can judge the conflicting accounts given by each party without resorting to moral theory. My account of ethical judgment and verification will emerge from this discussion.

By describing acts, characters, political alternatives, and even whole social situations in thick, value-laden ways, people support their beliefs and thus try to convince their fellow citizens. Some descriptions are better than others because they make better sense of the whole array of relevant details; some are superior because they reflect greater experience and discernment. A partial or unobservant description can be revealed as such in public debate. Therefore, our judgments can be verified when one detailed description is measured against its competitors. The appropriate judge of a description is anyone who may be affected by it, and consensus is a sufficient test of moral truth. When (as is often the case) we cannot attain perfect consensus, we must decide whether to let individuals choose freely, to apply majority rule, or to maintain the status quo. In other words, we need *political* rules. The appropriate rules vary from institution to institution, but at their best they enjoy unanimous support within their own domains.

The art of thick description does not invoke general theories or deductive reasoning; it does not apply rules to cases or offer abstract reasons for concrete judgments. Instead, it makes use of narratives and rich, evocative depictions of reality. These techniques are the specialty of novelists, historians, visual artists, filmmakers, literary critics, and preachers—in a word, humanists. This book, then, is an argument for the humanities as a source of moral guidance.

Humanists draw moral conclusions from stories by considering all of their relevant details, describing and redescribing events and characters until they settle on a fitting moral characterization. Although they cannot always agree about concrete cases, they know how to try to persuade other people. Moral theorists, on the other hand, assert that certain rules or principles are *true*—but there is no way to test the validity of abstract normative statements. When philosophers attempt to "ground" their moral doctrines in facts about nature, reason, or human nature, they again make unverifiable claims that give their theories spurious authority.

But this criticism does not discredit all moral theories, because they vary widely in their methods, pretensions, and assumptions. Kant, for example, was fully aware that his ethics could not be verified in the same way that we test ordinary propositions. He held that metaphysical statements generally lie beyond the powers of human reason, but our freedom of the will could be assumed as a "fact *of* reason," in part because all it expressed was "the lawgiving [authority] of reason itself."[9] Perhaps this argument was faulty and Kant simply asserted the truth of an unverifiable hypothesis. But even if I can show that Kant erred in this way (not a modest task), I have not proved the same case against every other moral philosopher. I suspect, for example, that utilitarians and social-contract theorists—purported critics of metaphysics—actually make numerous unverifiable claims about human nature that are ultimately metaphysical. But I would have to make that case against each theorist individually, since they differ in their methods and axioms.

Besides, it is not sufficient to complain that moral theories are unverifiable. This complaint smacks of "verificationism," a doctrine that is itself not subject to proof. Perhaps all moral truths that are worthy of the name lie *beyond* the power of human beings to test them against experience. Perhaps they come from faith, conscience, or pure reason, and this is the source of their dignity. "Metaphysics" is not necessarily a term of abuse. A defender of rhetoric may assume that a speaker's ability to persuade other people under fair conditions shows the moral value of his or her position; thus consensus is evidence of validity. But some people doubt that agreement (or even perfect human consensus) can tell us anything important.

For all these reasons, I will not attempt an epistemological, logical, or metaphysical argument against moral philosophy. Instead, I will show that we can live without it. But even if this is true, it is not obvious that we would be wise to avoid it. Philosophy may not be the only satisfactory source of moral illumination, but perhaps it is an excellent and worthwhile one. In order to make the case against philosophy, I will argue that philosophical habits and propensities are morally dangerous.

Generalization, for example, can blind us to crucial particularities about the concrete events that we encounter. Rules and principles work best to judge schematic cases; applied to the subtle events of real life, they promote simplification, even reductionism. Today, many philosophers concede that some dilemmas are intractable and that some situations are indeterminate. This tactical retreat does not, however, resolve the basic conflict between philosophy and narrative. To the degree that we believe in the problem-solving potential of philosophy, we ought to condemn stories that make human affairs look various and ambiguous. But if these stories faithfully depict reality, then philosophy misleads us by promising clear doctrines of a general nature. It is true that some stories, like philosophical arguments, promote general lessons; but literature is better at depicting recalcitrant details, ambiguous situations, and tragic dilemmas. If we face problems that actually lack clear solutions, then stories can offer us rough but decent answers, and they can help us to cope with the sense of failure that results from acting without solid justification.

If moral theory has an uneasy relationship with literature, it also tends to clash with democracy. We do not need democratic deliberation if we can solve moral problems by applying clear, general principles. On the contrary, to include many untrained citizens in public debates may obscure the truth, especially since non-philosophers often use narrative and rhetoric to defend their positions. Not only does an inclusive, unconstrained public discussion threaten the authority of philosophy, but philosophy can ruin democratic debates. As long as people choose to argue about particular cases, they can deliberate, offering new descriptions, drawing attention to new details, invoking new analogies, and so on. But when people invoke clashing abstract principles, their discussion often ends fruitlessly, for no neutral criterion can help them to choose one principle over the others.

Although moral theory has an uncomfortable place in democracy, rhetoric is at home there. Whether I have shown something persuasively only becomes clear if someone else agrees with me. If *everyone* agrees (and continues to agree over the long term), then there is no significant sense in which I can be called wrong. If stories and thick descriptions are the proper methods for addressing questions of value, then deliberative democracy is indispensable—and the more of it, the better.

Not all philosophers are guilty of generalization, abstraction, and intellectual elitism; but the more "philosophical" one is, the more one risks these failings. Clearly, I could not make a general, abstract case against philosophical proclivities without acting like a quintessential philosopher myself. In the first part of this book, I argue that generalization is morally hazardous as well as unnecessary. That, of course, is a generalization. Perhaps my position doesn't logically refute itself, but it wanders close to paradox.

Fortunately, there is another way forward. Skillful and perceptive works of literature have been written in which philosophers appear as characters. We can judge these characters' approach to life much as we judge the habits and attitudes of other figures in fiction and history. When moral failings are depicted in literature, we must generalize tentatively, for no one is identical to a well-drawn literary character, and no one faces exactly the same circumstances. Still, we can derive moral lessons from stories, finding rough parallels in other books and in life.

Here I have selected literary texts in which philosophers clash with rivals who eschew theory and rely instead on rhetoric or narrative to guide them. For the most part, these philosophers are sympathetically portrayed, not caricatured. For example, Socrates is a major character in this book, but I have omitted Mr. Gradgrind, Dickens's broad parody of a utilitarian. On the other hand, Socrates is an *extreme* example of the type "philosopher"–totally committed to generalization, deductive reason, abstraction, and so on. Thus he and similar characters reveal perspicuously the advantages and pitfalls of the philosophical life.

Several of the works that I examine are dialogues, because the dialogue is an excellent vehicle for presenting a conflict between two or more fundamental methods or styles of argumentation. If one tries to write a treatise about the contest between philosophy and literature, then it will naturally express philosophy's side more favorably: its abstract prose can give no indication of the rhetorical power of literature. On the other hand, a novel or poem about the same conflict may be unfair to philosophy, because it will lack the kinds of rigorous arguments that show philosophy in its best light. In a dialogue, however, each protagonist can exemplify a different mode of reasoning–for there is nothing awkward about one participant offering a deductive argument, and then an opponent telling a relevant story. Meanwhile, the author of the dialogue can show (but not tell) us something about the higher-order question: namely, which style of argument is better.

I begin part II with Plato's *Protagoras*, which describes a debate between Socrates, the archetypical philosopher, and Protagoras, who was a teacher of rhetoric and literature and an opponent of theory. In the *Republic* (607b), Socrates remarks that the quarrel between poets and philosophers is "ancient" or "perennial." Because the two disciplines have such different criteria of truth, it seems impossible to resolve their dispute. But Plato combined philosophy and drama into a single synthetic form, the dialogue, that gave neither side an unfair advantage. For this reason, his works offer valuable insights into the quarrel between moral theory and literature. Next, I turn to Aristotle, who tried to defend a concrete approach to ethics that was based in part upon literature and history. However, his arguments were general and abstract. Thus, in a sense, they violated their own principles. In order to show that he was right, but without accepting his abstract postulates,

I examine an example of morally effective literature that eschews generalization and theory: Vladimir Nabokov's *Lolita*. Nabokov not only demonstrates how one can be a moralist without moral doctrine, but he also reveals the ethical pitfalls of theory.

Plato and Aristotle wrote before the rise of Christianity; and Nabokov placed his characters in a secular, even irreligious setting. But for writers in the Judeo-Christian tradition, religion inevitably influences the form of the debate between philosophy and humanism—although it does not resolve that debate. A Jew or a Christian who admires philosophy can assert that the foundations of religion are general principles (both metaphysical and moral) that can be extracted from scripture with the help of deductive reason. But a religious person who disagrees with philosophers may argue that what matters is the concrete story of the Bible, the imitation of holy figures, and the believer's personal (but untheoretical) relationship with God. Therefore, I examine the quarrel between theory and narrative as it played out in the early Christian church. I then turn to the Christian humanists of the Renaissance, describing their dispute with speculative theologians. I treat Erasmus as the quintessential Christian humanist; but, like Aristotle, he uses abstract principles to attack philosophy. In many cases, Erasmus's principles are unverifiable generalizations about the shortcomings of theory; as such, they refute themselves. However, just as *Lolita* offers a persuasive, concrete embodiment of Aristotle's position, so Erasmus's *Praise of Folly* exemplifies his humanistic approach.

Another Renaissance work that develops similar themes to the *Praise of Folly* is Shakespeare's *King Lear*, which I discuss at the end of this book. This play responds directly to the argument that we should not base ethics upon rhetoric and narrative, because wicked people are sometimes the most skillful practitioners of these "glib and oily arts." In *King Lear*, several characters are persuasive rhetoricians and storytellers even though they are evil. However, the characters who try to tell right from wrong by applying abstract theories manifestly fail in the attempt. In various forms, philosophy proves a serious hindrance to wise behavior. Meanwhile, everyone who watches the play knows perfectly well that Cordelia is Lear's best daughter, that it is wrong to put out Gloucester's eyes and to send Lear into a terrifying storm. We know, furthermore, that the glib speeches of Goneril and Regan—Lear's evil daughters—are insincere, whereas Cordelia's silence is a genuine token of love. We know all of these things not by pure intuition or as a reflex response, but because the play shows them to us as clearly and forcefully as any formal argument. Thus Shakespeare's rhetoric demonstrates the difference between good and evil rhetoric in one concrete case; fiction cleans its own house.

I end with a discussion of Martin Luther King Jr. I argue that King was a humanist in several technical respects. His religious beliefs and methods of interpretation closely resembled Erasmus's, his commitment to democracy had humanistic motivations, and his rhetoric generally employed concrete stories rather than theory. My goal in the conclusion is to show that humanism can be an effective method of political change.

I hope that this book helps to rehabilitate Renaissance humanists and Greek Sophists. The Sophists were brilliant and original teachers, but few philosophers take them seriously. They did not offer a philosophy that could be resurrected today, but rather a potent *anti*-philosophical position that philosophers should treat respectfully. Likewise, the humanists of the Renaissance are widely venerated for their role in reviving ancient culture and for their literary excellence; but philosophers generally disregard their critique of philosophy. I believe that humanists and Sophists have something challenging to say—both to professional philosophers and to anyone who wants to address the moral dilemmas of real life.

PART I

THE ABSTRACT
ARGUMENT

CHAPTER 1

MORAL

JUDGMENT

AN ETHICAL PROBLEM

Teresa Harris was a rental manager for a Nashville, Tennessee company called Forklift Systems, Inc. On October 1, 1987, she quit her job and sued Forklift's owner, Charles Hardy, for sexual harassment. As any storyteller must, she told her tale selectively, mentioning only a few of the countless events and statements that had occurred during her two years of employment at Forklift Systems. She characterized these incidents in strongly negative terms and linked them into a coherent narrative. She thereby supported her claim that a specific crime, sexual harassment, had occurred. Her story gained coherence, in part, because she attributed various incidents to one man who had consistently bigoted motives. Thus she constructed a moral as well as a legal case against Charles Hardy, characterizing him (in effect) as a sexist boor.

Hardy told quite another story. He challenged none of Teresa Harris's important facts, but his selection of incidents, his choice of context, his descriptive adjectives, and his conclusion were all quite different from hers. He testified that he had never harassed Harris; he had merely joked with her and treated her "like one of the boys."[1]

When we make moral and legal judgments, we must often assess actions that come to us in the form of stories. We want to put names on these actions—names (such as "harmless joke" or "offensive slur") that carry moral connotations. In many cases, several stories can be told about the same events. How then should we morally assess narratives? What is the relationship between stories and moral concepts? And how, in general, do ethical claims gain their meaning and justification? Sexual harassment is such a new and controversial moral concept that people often draw radically different conclusions about the same events. Since we are still in the early stages of defining this offense, it provides illuminating examples of moral definition, interpretation, and judgment. But the same problems frequently arise in more settled areas of moral and legal debate.

According to Teresa Harris, the following incidents were relevant to her case. On at least one occasion, Charles Hardy told her to bring coffee to a meeting, although he never asked this of male managers. In the presence of other employees, Hardy several times told Harris: "You're a woman, what do you know," "You're a dumb ass woman," and, "We need a man as the rental manager." Once, in front of several colleagues, Hardy suggested to Harris: "Let's go to the Holiday Inn to negotiate your raise." More than once, he told Harris that she had a "racehorse ass," and could not wear a bikini "because your ass is so big, if you did there would be an eclipse and nobody could get any sun." He also suggested that he and Harris should start "screwing around."

Charles Hardy asked Harris and her female colleagues to remove coins from the front pocket of his trousers. He left objects on the ground in front of his female employees and asked them to pick them up, commenting on their clothes in the process. He often used sexual innuendo in describing his female employees' attire.[2]

Harris testified that she became miserable both at work and at home because of Hardy's behavior. On August 18, 1987, she met with her boss, intending to resign after the meeting (which she secretly taped). As her tapes show, Hardy admitted to making the statements that she had described, but he said that he had meant them as jokes and had not expected them to give offense. He apologized and promised to act better in the future. On this basis, Harris agreed not to resign. However, early the following month, another incident occurred. Harris had just won a contract for Forklift, and Hardy asked her, in the presence of several colleagues: "What did you do, promise the guy at ASI (Aladdin Synergetics, Inc.) some 'bugger' Saturday night?" At this point, Harris resigned and filed her sexual harassment suit.[3]

Hardy did not dispute any of these facts, but he argued at trial that his statements were harmless and that no other employees had taken them seriously. Indeed, according to court papers, "Several [female] clerical employees formerly employed at Forklift testified that Hardy's frequent jokes and sexual comments were just part of the joking work environment at Forklift. They were not offended, nor did they know that plaintiff was offended. Angela Hicks, formerly a receptionist at Forklift, aptly expressed her feelings about comments Hardy may have made about her body. Ms. Hicks jauntily testified, 'lots of people make comments about my breasts.'"[4] Hardy also provided a specific explanation for his remark about negotiating Harris's raise at the Holiday Inn. He said that the company often conducted management meetings at that hotel, so Harris knew that he was joking.

Furthermore, according to papers filed by the defense, Harris "was the only woman who participated in regular, voluntary after-work gatherings in the office, and at these gatherings she drank beer, joked and used coarse language." Hardy said that he and his wife had often socialized with Harris and her husband outside of work. She had waited two years before complaining about his behavior. Even then, she had complained most seriously about alleged discrimination in salary, bonuses, and car allowance—complaints that the court found unmerited. Finally, Hardy stressed that he and Harris's husband were business partners; the collapse of their business relationship was the real cause of her anger at Forklift Systems.[5]

The federal magistrate who was assigned to hear this case listened to both sides, resolved a few minor factual issues, and drew a conclusion. "I believe," he wrote, "that Hardy is a vulgar man and demeans the female employees at his workplace." He offered specific moral judgments about each of Hardy's sexist remarks: "Most of Hardy's wisecracks about females' clothes and anatomy were merely inane and adolescent, such as the running joke that large-breasted women are that way because they eat a lot of corn. Hardy's coin dropping and coin-in-the-pocket tricks also fall into this category. [But] Hardy's comment to plaintiff suggesting that she promised sexual favors to a customer in order to secure an account was truly gross and offensive." Thus the magistrate drew most of the moral judgments that Harris had intended. Nevertheless, he denied Harris's claim that Hardy had committed sexual harassment. "I believe that this is a close case, but that Charles Hardy's comments cannot be characterized as much more than annoying and insensitive. The other women working at Forklift considered Hardy a joker. . . . A reasonable woman manager under like circumstances would have been offended by Hardy, but his conduct would not have risen to the level of interfering with that person's work performance."[6]

Did the magistrate make the correct choice in this "close case"? Did he choose the correct moral characterizations when he described Hardy's behavior as "gross and offensive," but refused to call it "sexual harassment"? Conceivably, the magistrate was guided by precise definitions of such terms. Perhaps he even subscribed to an elaborate moral theory—one that explained why certain acts were acceptable; others, objectionable; and still others, illegal. In his report, he certainly espoused a few general principles, arguing, for example, that offensive conduct is only illegal if it is so bad that it would interfere with the "work performance" of a "reasonable woman manager in like circumstances."[7] On the other hand, the magistrate left most of his important terms undefined, and he offered no comprehensive moral or legal theory. For instance, he did not explain what makes someone a "reasonable woman," nor why it was unreasonable for Harris to be overwhelmed by Hardy's statements. Instead, throughout most of his report, the magistrate simply characterized behavior as "inane," "gross," "annoying," and so on. He based these concrete judgments on the particularities of the case as he described it in his own narrative.

In presenting his version of the story and drawing his conclusions, the magistrate may well have been influenced by the details of each party's presentation: their choice of incidents and descriptive vocabulary. Consider, for example, Teresa Harris's testimony about her reaction to Charles Hardy's offensive behavior:

> The comments about how I looked embarrassed me, but the comments about my ability to do my job and that I was stupid and I was dumb devastated me. I hated walking in there. He embarrassed me. Everybody made fun of me because Charles Hardy did that. And I was supposed to laugh about it, and it wasn't funny. . . .
>
> I cried all the time. I was having shortness of breath. I wasn't sleeping at all. I was drinking heavily. I drank a lot. I would get drunk every night so I would go to sleep so I could get up and go to work the next day, and I hated it. I shook. I would sit in my office and I would shake. I hate it. I just hated it. . . .
>
> I was ugly to my children. My children would call me and I would be ugly to them and I would say terrible things to them and hang up on them. I always did that for Mr. Hardy's benefit because he made remarks to me about that too: "Your kids call all the damn time."[8]

Here Teresa Hardy uses a first-person narrative to describe her own emotional state. She describes the relevant facts in terse sentences, now and then using arresting words like "devastated" and "dumb." She repeats phrases to emphasize them. And she tries to capture the listener's sympathy by portraying herself as a mother who drank and was mean to her children—all because of "Mr. Hardy." (By using his title, she demonstrates an enduringly courteous and respectful attitude.) Her demeanor and tone are not described in the transcript, but we might guess that she was tense, solemn, and self-conscious as she gave her sworn testimony.

All of these things—point of view, vocabulary, sentence structure, tone—constitute rhetoric, which has often had a bad reputation, especially among philosophers. John Locke expressed a classic conviction when he wrote:

all the art of rhetoric, besides order and clearness; all the
artificial and figurative application of words eloquence
hath invented, are for nothing else but to insinuate wrong
ideas, move the passions, and thereby mislead the judge-
ment; and so indeed are perfect cheats: and therefore,
however laudable or allowable oratory may render them
in harangues or popular addresses, they are certainly in all
discourses that pretend to inform or instruct, wholly to be
avoided; and where truth and knowledge are concerned
cannot but be thought a great fault.[9]

The metaphor of rhetoric as a "cheat" is itself a rhetorical trope. Indeed,
literary theorists have argued that no language is utterly devoid of style, tone,
allusion, and metaphor; there is no "writing degree zero."[10] Nevertheless, we
know that particularly clever speakers and good actors can persuade
audiences to condone acts of profound evil, while innocent people are
sometimes condemned merely because their rhetoric is clumsy. Perhaps if
Teresa Harris had made different stylistic choices, she would have won her
lawsuit on first hearing. Therefore, rhetoric alone can seem an unreliable
method of moral judgment, too dependent upon personal skill. Philosophy,
with its promise of rigorous methods and principles, is an attractive
alternative.

THE MEANING OF MORAL WORDS

Moral philosophy—at least in the relatively narrow form that concerns
me—always relies upon general principles or procedures. Some philosophers
believe that anyone who knows the difference between right and wrong has
correct principles in mind, either consciously or unconsciously. For instance,
having pointed out that society lacks "any distinct recognition of an ultimate
standard" of morality, John Stuart Mill claims that, nevertheless, our ability
to act morally "has been mainly due to the tacit influence of a standard not
recognized." This standard, Mill claims, is the principle of utilitarianism,
which "has had a large share in forming the moral doctrines even of those
who most scornfully reject its authority."[11] Kant says much the same thing
about his Categorical Imperative, which (he claims) is an implicit possession
of all rational creatures.[12]

Since our ideas about abstract universals are often jumbled and
contradictory, philosophers sometimes advise us to analyze our opinions in
order to reveal our core abstract beliefs, and then treat these critically,
judging them against the true definitions that philosophy can provide. For
example, Socrates asks Meno: "What do you say that virtue is, you and your

friends?"[13] His intention is to analyze the multiple and contradictory answers of ordinary Athenians until he has arrived at a clear definition by means of dialectic. The ultimate in clarity would be a *single* ethical principle, such as Mill's doctrine of utility or Kant's Categorical Imperative. In fact, a single principle seems necessary, because if there were several valid criteria of moral choice, then we would need a "single-consideration procedure" (in Charles Taylor's phrase) to adjudicate among them when they disagreed.[14] According to many philosophers, a plurality of incommensurable principles would leave us in the situation of the classic tragic hero, unable to choose a morally satisfactory course of action.[15] Kant writes:

> It seems arrogant, egotistical, and . . . dismissive to maintain that there was not philosophy before the birth of [Kant's] Critical Philosophy. . . . But there can surely be only one human reason, considered objectively, and so there cannot be many philosophies: that is, only one true system derived from principles is possible, no matter how variously and often antagonistically people may have philosophized about one and the same subject. So the moralist says with reason: there is only one virtue and one doctrine of virtue, that is, a unified system that unites all the duties of virtue under one principle.[16]

He even says, notoriously, that a "conflict of duties and obligations is unthinkable (*obligationes non colliduntur*)."[17] If two obligations appear to conflict, then a higher principle will resolve the dilemma.

Mill agrees that we need a clear and unified theory of the good in order to make rational judgments; and he attributes this view to all past philosophers:

> From the dawn of philosophy, the question concerning the *summum bonum*, or, what is the same thing, concerning the foundation of morality, has been accounted the main problem in speculative thought. . . . And after more than two thousand years the same discussions still continue, philosophers are still ranged under the same contending banners, and neither thinkers nor mankind at large seem nearer to being unanimous on the subject, than when the youth Socrates listened to the old Protagoras.[18]

Mill then proposes his own theory of the *summum bonum*, a definition of the good in terms of utility. Like Kant and Socrates, he assumes that the ethical value of any concrete narrative can only be seen by comparing it against the general principles that are given by philosophy. Thus Mill states that all philosophers are agreed about one thing: "the morality of an individual action is . . . the application of a law to an individual case."[19]

More recently, William K. Frankena has argued:

> Moral and value judgments imply reasons, and reasons cannot apply in a particular case only. If they apply in a particular case, they apply in all similar cases. Moreover, in order to give a reason in a particular case, one must presuppose a general proposition. If Jones answers your question "Why?" by saying "Because you promised to," or "Because it gives pleasure," he presupposes that it is right to keep promises or that what gives pleasure is good.[20]

If this is true, then we soon have to decide the debate between Kantians (who always forbid promise-breaking) and hedonists (who emphasize pleasure). In order to justify a particular action, we need a principle; and in order to test the principle, we need an overall theory about justice, the good, or fairness. We may also have to decide whether the good takes priority over fairness (or vice versa), and other highly abstract questions.

This approach requires an intermediate step between particulars and principles. Moral rules cannot be applied directly to individual cases any more than scientific laws can tell us how ordinary objects will behave. In science, we must measure phenomena and classify data before we can apply theories to them. For example, Newtonian physics does not explain how my alarm clock will behave—at least not until I have measured its mass, velocity, position, and so on. By the same token, utilitarians cannot simply judge stories; they have to analyze them first to see how much happiness or unhappiness each action has caused. Kantians must classify behavior under general rules before they can test whether these rules are permitted by the Categorical Imperative. Virtue theorists must analyze narratives to see what virtues and vices each character exemplifies. And so on.

Thus it seems that moral theorists who are faced with a concrete story will almost always begin by analyzing it; they will then form moral judgments by applying principles or procedures to the analyzed data. Utilitarians, for instance, would measure the effects of Hardy's sexist statements on the total quantity of happiness in the world, subtracting Harris's misery from his pleasure to produce a figure representing the moral value of his alleged acts. But Harris offered no measurements of her own unhappiness; she told a story. Therefore, utilitarian theory cannot be applied directly to her narrative; first her statements must be replaced with a series of numbers. Ever since Mill, most utilitarians have doubted that precise measurements of happiness are available. Nevertheless, they believe that such measurements would settle moral disputes, if only we could obtain them. The methods of moral assessment that they use are *proxies* for precise measurements.

Kant's moral theory does not involve measurements, but rather correct and precise classifications. His first ethical principle is: "I shall never act otherwise than *so that I could also will that my maxim should become a universal law*."[21] Thus I can only allow myself to harass someone if I could want everyone else to do the same thing in the same circumstances. But no individual can desire to be harassed, since harassment seems to mean some kind of *unwelcome* sexual behavior. (If the behavior were welcome, then it would be a case of "joking" or "flirting.") Since we cannot will that harassment be made a universal law, without willing ourselves to be harassed (which is a contradiction), harassment is immoral. On the other hand, "flirting" or "joking around" with one's co-workers could be made a universal law without contradiction.

Kant analyzes actions by identifying the maxims (subjective principles) of the person who acts. Thus a Kantian would ask whether Hardy behaved according to the principle, "I will harass my female employees," or rather according to the maxim, "I will engage in harmless banter." Hardy's understanding of his own maxim could be incorrect; he could misconstrue the principle that guided his actions. Therefore, we have to decide whether Hardy's intentional behavior constituted harassment, rather than "harmless joking" or some other innocuous category. Harris's rhetoric, on this view, is irrelevant to our moral judgment. To judge her case, we must examine the facts that she and Hardy described, analyzing them to see if they constitute harassment.

Kant's second formulation of the Categorical Imperative would also be relevant to a case of sexual harassment. This formulation requires us to treat other people as ends in themselves, not merely as means to our ends. If we treat people as ends, then we must respect their plans and desires. We might therefore ask whether Hardy's behavior was consistent with Harris's wishes—and she testified explicitly that it was not. But some unwelcome actions (such as punishments) are moral; and some immoral acts are welcomed. Therefore, Kant holds that we treat people as ends only when we respect the purposes and desires that they would have if they were rational. Thus it is not enough to know that Harris happened to dislike Hardy's actions. We would also need to know whether her reaction was rational. If Hardy's maxim was to use people as opportunities for gratification, then (regardless of his victims' reaction) his behavior was wrong. But "treating people like one of the boys" might pass Kant's test, assuming that this really meant treating them as equal and autonomous human beings. Similarly, there is no contradiction between "joking around" with someone and treating her as an end in herself. Thus the question for a Kantian is always one of classification. Did Hardy engage in "harmless banter" or "sexual harassment"?

It seems clear that once people agree to describe an act as "sexual harassment," they will never countenance it, any more than people will approve of actions that they call "murder." Someone may knowingly harass his colleagues, but he will not consider his behavior moral or defensible if he calls it "harassment"; his defense will be to give it another, less disparaging name. Similarly, anything that we call "cruel" is wrong, unless there is some extenuating circumstance. And if all we know about an act is that it causes "unhappiness," we will disapprove of it. Of course, a particular act can be simultaneously described with many such words, and this is one common source of moral confusion.

Philosophers who belong to certain theoretical schools deliberately employ only limited moral vocabularies. For example, Kantians consider questions of pleasure irrelevant to moral duty. Thus, if particular behavior is both "discriminatory" and "pleasurable," Kantians will condemn it, since pleasure does not have any moral weight in their system. Pluralists, on the other hand, maintain that several moral vocabularies can apply at once: something can be simultaneously cruel, an example of harassment, and a source of net pleasure, and all these terms can be morally salient. Pluralism poses a challenge to moral philosophy, because if a theory says, "Never do A," and "Always do B," and something can be both A and B at once, then the theory has failed to provide moral guidance.[22] In fact, Jonathan Dancy argues that pluralism entails a rejection of moral philosophy:

> after the discovery that more than one property is morally
> relevant, we begin to admit a plethora of such properties
> without there being any way of ordering them. When we
> face this plethora honestly, we have to adopt a particularist
> epistemology. . . . As particularists, we give no sense to the
> notion of a property being generally morally relevant, and
> hence we fail to understand the possibility of moral
> principles.[23]

On the other hand, philosophers may be able to reduce their moral vocabularies to a few clear and salient terms, or else find ways to rank or weigh moral words when they conflict. In either case, they can salvage moral principles. For the moment, I simply want to observe that descriptive words can carry strong moral connotations—indeed, they can make moral judgments all by themselves. "Sexual harassment" is certainly one such term. We may deny that it applies in a given case; we may call it an irrelevant or ill-defined category; we may argue that another description is more salient—but if we use the phrase to describe an act, we thereby condemn it. The question remains: when are such terms correctly applied to individual cases?

In many of his dialogues, Plato ascribes to Socrates the view that all words (including moral terms) correspond to clearly definable concepts. For example, Theaetetus, a bright young acquaintance of Socrates, wants to know what "knowledge" is, and—by way of answering this question—he enumerates some examples: the sciences, geometry, and crafts. But Socrates objects to his method:

SOCRATES: But you were not asked, Theaetetus, to say what knowledge is about, nor how many kinds of knowledge there are. You did not wish to count them, but to ascertain of knowledge *what it is*. Or do I speak nonsense?

THEAETETUS: No, you are absolutely right.

SOCRATES: Consider this also. If someone asked, "What is it?" about something trivial and easy, such as clay, wouldn't it be laughable if we answered: "The clay of potters, and the clay of ovenmakers, and the clay of brickmakers"?

THEAETETUS: Yes.

SOCRATES: First of all, it is laughable to suppose that the questioner can get any meaning out of our answer, when we mention "clay" whether it is the dollmaker's or any other craftsman's. You do not suppose that anyone can understand the name of something, when he does not know what the thing is?[24]

According to Socrates, the appropriate method is to "grasp many things with one idea." For example, we would have to understand what defines "knowledge" in general before we could use the term—"naming the many kinds of knowledge with one word."[25] Similarly, in a discussion of virtue, he says:

SOCRATES: For if you remember just now when I replied to you about shapes, we rejected any kind of response that attempts to provide an answer by using terms that are still being sought and are not yet agreed upon.

MENO: We did reject that kind of response, Socrates, and rightly.

SOCRATES: So now do the same, my excellent friend, and while you are seeking to know what virtue is as a whole, do not try to communicate it to anyone in terms of its parts, or by any similar kind of answer, but rather you must ask the same kind of question about it. You may say what you want about virtue, but what *is* it?[26]

In another dialogue, Socrates announces that he has two methods for answering questions of the type, "What is virtue?" Together, the two methods constitute "dialectic." The first method, according to Socrates, is to "collect the things that have been dispersed, seeing them all together in one idea, so that, by marking the boundaries of each idea, we can make clear what it is that we are trying to teach. For example, because of what we said just now (whether well or badly) about the boundaries of the term 'love,' our discussion could at least be clear and consistent."[27] This is the method that philosophers employ when they examine numerous cases of ethical behavior (for example) and declare the common feature to be the essence of justice. They are marking the boundaries of the idea of justice. Socrates' second method is "the reverse [of the other one], in which we can cut things up into ideas, splitting them where their joints lie naturally."[28] Socrates uses this second method whenever he arrives at a definition by dividing things into groups or categories so that, within each group, everything conforms to a common description. He typically asks yes-or-no questions that allow him to assign things to one of two categories. A group of things that cannot be divided any further has a single definition, a single "form." Whether Socrates proceeds by splitting or by marking boundaries, he always arrives at the same result: a definition.

Following Socrates' suggestion, we could analyze Teresa Harris's testimony to discover what "thing" she was describing. This approach would not commit us to any particular metaphysical theory, because moral concepts such as harassment could be real, rational, natural, socially constructed, *or* subjective—all we have assumed is that they are clearly definable. Regardless of our metaphysics, we might ask whether Harris experienced harassment (which is illegal and also violates most ethical theories), or rather meaningless banter, friendly repartee, or harmless joking. Once we have decided what Harris really experienced, we can discuss its ethical value in the light of a moral theory.

This approach is evident in the philosophical literature on sexual harassment. Edmund Wall, for example, writes: "we need a set of jointly necessary and sufficient conditions of sexual harassment capable of capturing all subtle instances of sexual harassment while filtering out (even overt) sexual behavior which is not harassive." For him, "the mental states of the perpetrator and the victim are the essential defining elements." This, then, is his definition:

1. X does not attempt to obtain Y's consent to communicate to Y, X's or someone else's purported sexual interest in Y.
2. X communicates to Y, X's or someone else's purported sexual interest in Y. X's motive for communicating this is some perceived benefit that he expects to obtain through the communication.

3. Y does not consent to discuss with X, X's or someone else's purported sexual interest in Y.
4. Y feels emotionally distressed because X did not attempt to obtain Y's consent to this discussion and/or because Y objects to the content of X's sexual comments.[29]

It is not perfectly clear, on this definition, whether Charles Hardy's actions qualified as "harassment." We would need to know the meaning of such terms as "sexual interest," "benefit," "consent," and "distress." Wall adopts the Socratic procedure of drawing logical boundaries; but to complete the job, he would have to provide more definitions. In order to apply his theory, we would also need detailed information about Hardy's motives. Finally, we would want to know why Wall's definition is morally appropriate. If we agree to his definition, then we will automatically judge cases that fall under it as bad, since no one approves of "sexual harassment." But we are entitled to ask whether he has drawn the correct boundaries of the term.

Likewise, Anita M. Superson offers what she calls "an objective definition of SH [sexual harassment] that accounts for the group harms all forms of SH have in common." Like Socrates, she tries to "grasp many things with one idea." Indeed, she claims that her definition "protects all victims in all cases from even the most subtle kinds of SH, since all cases of SH have in common group harm." She defines sexual harassment as "any behavior (verbal or physical) caused by a person, A, in the dominant class directed at another, B, in the subjugated class, that expresses or perpetuates the attitude that B or members of B's class is/are inferior because of their sex, thereby causing harm to either B and/or members of B's sex."[30] Presumably, this definition either covers or does not cover the case of *Harris v. Forklift Systems*. Again, much would depend upon the meaning of such terms as "dominant," "class," "inferior," "perpetuates," and "harm"—but these words could probably be defined in much the same way that Superson defines "harassment."

Since Superson's definition is quite different from Wall's, we might turn to moral theory to tell us which one to employ. Wall is interested in motives; Superson, in consequences. Wall looks at individual behavior; Superson, at "group harms." Individualism, communitarianism, and consequentialism are prominent features of certain moral theories, so if we tried to resolve the debate between Wall and Superson, we would soon ask the same kind of metaethical questions that distinguish Kantianism from utilitarianism.

Even F. M. Christensen, a strong critic of the idea of sexual harassment, assumes "that if a *term* exists, there must be a corresponding *category* that is both significant (morally significant, in this instance) and well defined." He considers sexual harassment a "*pseudo*-concept" and "fundamentally illegitimate" because it does not refer to a set of things that share any one important feature:

> the indiscriminate lumping of "dirty words" together with
> assault and extortion is a clear example of the sophistry of
> guilt by association; organically linking serious felonies
> with things that are at worst obnoxious causes the latter to
> partake of some of the horror of the former. Similarly, . . .
> the fact that sexuality is the only unifying element in an
> otherwise catch-all category makes sex the focus of
> attention—and hence turns a morally incidental feature into
> the core feature involved.[31]

Christensen sees nothing wrong with "sexual frankness"; he thinks that we are puritanical about it. As a result, he denies that "sexual harassment" is a meaningful moral category at all. He would, however, strongly condemn all instances of "rape," since for him this is a clear and relevant moral category. Similarly, Mane Hajdin "presupposes that the law about sexual harassment . . . ought to provide a workable criterion of demarcation between sexual harassment and those forms of sexual interaction between people who work together that do not constitute sexual harassment." Unfortunately, Hajdin concludes, the current law "makes no real demarcation at all."[32]

It seems that Socratic analysis is alive and well, at least in law and applied ethics. The correct definition of "sexual harassment" is a matter of great concern to ethicists, and when their definitions differ, systematic moral principles are required to help them choose. Deborah Wells and Beverly J. Kracher even appeal to "the natural duty of persons and the natural duty not to harm the innocent" in order to ground their definition of sexual harassment.[33] This is a clear example of a very general principle being used to generate a more specific moral rule. By the same token, Wall's definition of "harassment" shows that he is more Kantian than consequentialist in his metaethical orientation. All of these authors adopt the view of moral philosophy that was shared by Socrates, Kant, and Mill—general rules can settle particular cases, but only once the raw data of narratives have been appropriately categorized.

My own view is that neither abstract principles nor moral definitions of the Socratic kind will get us very far in judging actual cases. I want to advance that argument by criticizing one comprehensive moral philosophy that employs clear definitions: Kantianism. But first I must anticipate an objection—that several major moral systems do not rely on definitions of the Socratic kind.

One such system is utilitarianism. At first glance, at least, it seems possible to observe and measure happiness, and its allegedly empirical status has appealed to some philosophers who think that terms like "harassment," "cruelty," and "injustice" are fatally vague or subjective. The idea that morality should be based upon the maximization of pleasure is proposed by

Socrates in the *Protagoras*.[34] Since a celebration of pleasure seems out of character for Socrates, the best explanation for his strategy is methodological: he wants to replace vague talk about virtues and the good with a single measurable quantity, and pleasure seems a likely candidate. If utilitarians were right, then we could avoid defining categories like sexual harassment. We would simply ask Teresa Harris and Charles Hardy to report how happy or unhappy they felt, examine their stories for possible dishonesty, and then ask whether each person's actions maximized the aggregate happiness.

However, it is unclear how we could measure happiness in a morally useful way. It is difficult enough for one person to compare the precise value of two radically different kinds of happiness—say, the pleasure of ice cream versus that of philosophical contemplation. To measure two people's sensations of happiness on a single scale seems impossible. A purely empirical test could perhaps be devised to measure a physiological response to pleasure, but its results would seem morally irrelevant. Some people might revel in trivial sensations; others might fall into profound depression at minor provocations. We call some feelings "trivial" and "minor" because we do not believe that all sensations of happiness and unhappiness are ethically equal. If utilitarianism really meant the maximization of pleasure-sensations as measured by scientific tests, it would violate our moral intuitions. Indeed, it is difficult to see *any* reason for that kind of utilitarianism, other than its methodological simplicity. A morally relevant account of "happiness" would be more useful—but it would be as controversial as the various existing definitions of "sexual harassment," "the good," and "justice."

Like utilitarians, social-contract theorists avoid arguing about moral categories like sexual harassment. Their approach is to ask what system of rules, rights, and duties would be established voluntarily by autonomous people who were about to form a society. Once these rules were in place, people could decide for themselves what to do about most moral issues. Some social-contract theorists (for example, Rousseau) assert that people outside of society would naturally possess fairly specific concepts of the good. Thus Rousseau and similar philosophers smuggle ideas about moral philosophy into their social-contract doctrines, which are not truly neutral. But contractarians of a liberal bent (Rawls, for example) are genuinely impartial about theories of the good. They concede that people will always hold different and incommensurable conceptions of morality. Since these conceptions are based upon metaphysical presuppositions, it is impossible for people to settle moral disagreements on the basis of evidence. Therefore, liberal social-contract theorists assert that each person should simply be allowed to realize his or her own values to the greatest extent consistent with others doing the same.

Liberal political theorists take philosophy out of the business of defining terms like "sexual harassment." Since I am skeptical of philosophy in general, I sympathize with this move—but it does not solve our problem. Even if there is no philosophical answer to many moral questions, citizens must still decide whether and how to define their terms. Is sexual harassment, for example, a breach of basic liberal rights, or isn't it? Even if it doesn't violate constitutional principles, governments may still want to ban it. Should they? May they? And how should they define it? Contract theory evades these questions, but they require answers.

I have not shown that Socratic analysis is essential to all forms of moral philosophy, but clearly it plays an important role in current debates. In order to show what is wrong with analysis, I want to focus on the example of Kantianism, a general system that employs clearly defined terms. Needless to say, Kant would have been baffled by the phrase "sexual harassment," but he acted like a good disciple of Socrates when he treated *lying* as a clearly defined entity. Since it is absurd and paradoxical to state that everyone should lie, lying cannot be made into a universal principle, and therefore it is intrinsically immoral.[35] We might be tempted to perform the same procedure to determine whether or not *killing* can be made a universal law. The conclusion seems straightforward: no one could will that everyone should kill everyone else. But Kant would probably say that killing in self-defense ought to be treated differently from murder: the first can be made into a universal law, the second not. Thus, for Kant, lying is a thing, but killing is really two things: it is produced by combining cases of justifiable homicide with cases of murder. But if that is true, then why couldn't lying really be the union of two things—fraud and justifiable deception—where one is morally acceptable and the other not?

Indeed, Kant distinguishes between "untruth" (*falsiloquium*) and "lie" (*mendacium*), claiming that an untruth is not necessarily condemnable as a lie.[36] Nevertheless, Kant believes that we face no difficulty in judging particular actions. "A lie is a lie, and is in itself intrinsically base whether it be told with good or evil intent. For formally a lie is always evil."[37] Yet if a particular statement is merely an untruth, and not a lie, then it is excusable. Without contradiction, we can will that everyone should express "harmless false-hoods." Therefore, Kant concedes that we need "the power of judgment sharpened by experience" to tell us how to apply moral laws to particular cases.[38] For instance, our judgment tells us that we ought to describe some homicides as examples of self-defense, and others as murder; some false statements as untruths, and others as lies. After we decide how to categorize a particular act, then we can apply general moral laws to it.

Analysis is undoubtedly a useful cognitive process, but (as Kant concedes) we also have to know how and what to analyze. If someone kills another person with a handgun, then the salient issue is whether murder is permissible, not whether it is acceptable to squeeze metal objects (such as the triggers of guns). Rote analysis can never help us to decide which of these analyses is appropriate or relevant. We also need something like judgment as a guide.[39] For example, to call something "murder" rather than "squeezing a metal object" is an exercise in judgment. Even the decision to isolate an act (firing a gun) as the object of moral assessment is a matter of judgment, since we could have focused instead on characters or institutions. Besides, most acts are so deeply entangled with other events that there are many ways to divide the stream of phenomena into discrete elements. Although judgment is difficult, it often does the whole work of ethics. Once we have decided to focus on an act that we call "justifiable homicide" or "a white lie," then it is a tautology to claim that the act is morally acceptable. But if we had instead described it as "murder" or "fraud," it would have been wrong by definition. In short, our moral conclusions often result automatically from our initial categorization of events, but these categorizations can be controversial.

In his epistemological writings, Kant assigns an important role to judgment, the faculty by which we decide "whether something does or does not stand under a given rule."[40] Further, he notes that we cannot be guided by rules when we use the faculty of judgment, for if there were rules, then we would have to use judgment to know how to apply *them*. Therefore, judgment must be an autonomous faculty, not guided by rules or logic, but capable of being cultivated through examples.[41] Someone is "stupid" (*dumm*) who lacks good judgment; he or she "may understand the universal in the abstract, but cannot distinguish whether a concrete case comes under it."[42] However, Kant does not emphasize or discuss the role of judgment in moral reasoning, noting that judgment is an issue for applied ethics (*Ethik*), whereas he is writing about theory. A theory of law, he writes, "needs as much general instruction (method) as to how we should proceed in judgment as does pure mathematics [i.e., none] for it realizes itself in action."[43] But even if he is justified in treating the issue of judgment as irrelevant to his rather formal project, we still have to discuss it. For if moral judgment is a difficult and necessary mental task, then we have not understood ethics until we have developed an account of it.

Perhaps Kant's silence on this topic results from his theory of language. Like Socrates, Kant believes that, if a term has meaning, there must be a clearly delineated range of cases to which it applies. Correct judgment therefore means recognizing the objective boundaries of the concept—and there is not much more that can or ought to be said about it. A wise person sees boundaries correctly; a fool does not. In cases of ethical judgment, we analyze particular events or situations until we discover general *moral* concepts, such as "lying." Our goal is to determine whether the particular case is covered by a given moral concept—whether it falls within the boundaries of that idea. Thus, for Kant, judgment is just a species of analysis: it is the correct identification of an object's moral essence. For example, while a given act could simultaneously be called "a speech," "an exercise of the larynx," "a mental process," or "a lie," its *moral* essence would be only one of those things. Thus the results of an act of judgment are either true or false; we have either named the correct moral essence of a particular case, or else we have made a mistake.[44]

But, as Wittgenstein shows, there may not be any clear boundary to something like lying or sexual harassment.[45] Starting with a case of clearly objectionable behavior, we can work our way through related hypothetical cases until we arrive at one that is pretty clearly not an example of discrimination. According to Socrates, this latter case must lack some essential quality that the objectionable case possessed; there must be a precise point at which examples of sexual harassment cease. But Wittgenstein believes that we often notice a "family resemblance" among a class of actions, in which the first act shares many qualities with the second, the second with the third, and so on. These acts can legitimately be grouped together as a class and given a name, even though no single essence necessarily runs through all the cases. Instead, a large number of individual cases within a given family often share many common features with many of the other cases, and these myriad resemblances produce an overall idea of similarity that does not depend upon any common denominator. Thus, for Wittgenstein, mere analysis will not allow us to identify a class of objects; and judgment must be a fundamentally different process from analysis.

Wittgenstein's most famous example of a "family-resemblance" word is "game."[46] Considering the vast variety of games, it is very difficult to think of any one attribute that they all have in common. They are not all competitive (consider solitaire and "catch"); not all of them involve scoring or winning; some have no rules (for instance, "horsing around" with a child); and some are not played for enjoyment (think of Pentagon "war games" and Russian roulette). If we declare that all genuine games necessarily involve one attribute (for instance, enjoyment), not only will this assertion contradict the normal usage, but it will also leave the concept undefined, because something that is enjoyable is not necessarily a game. The dictionary resorts to offering a long series of partial definitions, some of which are mutually incompatible: "activity engaged in for diversion or amusement . . . a procedure or strategy for gaining an end . . . a field of gainful activity . . . a physical or mental competition conducted according to rules," and so on.[47] Someone who did not already know how to use the word "game" correctly could hardly learn its meaning from the dictionary.

How then do we use the word "game" to communicate with other people? The answer seems to be that there are hundreds of games, each of which has much in common with many other games, although no one substratum runs through all the examples. Thus the word "game" refers to an area of meaning that is somewhat vaguely bordered and that has no logical criterion marking its limits; but it still has a dense core—or perhaps several adjacent cores—to which we can clearly point. It is like a large and thick forest: we may argue about whether a particular tree near the margin belongs to the woods, but the whole entity is obvious enough. Thus, once people are told that football, chess, bridge, solitaire, lotteries, video games, blood sports, and military exercises are all called games, they can see more or less where the heart of the forest lies. Yet even indisputable examples of games do not all share any common feature.

We can, of course, argue heatedly about whether a particular practice is a game. But the solution to such a debate will not follow analytically from the pure concept of "game," for there is no such thing. For example, a sign on a park gate might say, "No Games." Someone might see the sign and decide that he can still play solitaire; this is not forbidden. A park ranger may then approach and point to the sign, saying, "That's not allowed." In this kind of situation, a dispute about definitions quickly becomes as futile as an argument about whether a particular star belongs to the Milky Way, or whether a certain temperature is "warm." Some words actually *are* vague, and understanding their meaning does not help us to discern their borders. Thus, instead of asking what "game" really means in an abstract sense, the two parties ought to discuss the purpose or use of the regulation. For example: What features of certain games are harmful in city parks? Does solitaire involve these features? What did the town council mean to achieve through its regulation? Who has the authority to interpret park rules? Who is responsible for order in the park? In short, the word "game" has an important *function* or *use* in each social context, but no precise definition or Socratic Form; it is indispensable, yet intrinsically vague.

Discussing a similar example, Wittgenstein tries unsuccessfully to discover what common denominator runs through all cases of "deriving." One instance of deriving occurs when we derive spoken words from written words. Wittgenstein writes:

> [W]e told ourselves that this was only a quite special case
> of deriving; deriving in a quite special garb, which had to
> be stripped from it if we wanted to see the essence of
> deriving. So we stripped those particular coverings off; but
> then deriving itself disappeared.—In order to find the real
> artichoke, we divested it of its leaves. For certainly [this]
> was a special case of deriving; what is essential to deriving,
> however, was not hidden beneath the surface of this case,
> but this 'surface' was one case out of the family of cases of
> deriving.[48]

If Wittgenstein is right about the way that general concepts operate, then when we use terms such as "sexual harassment," we are not referring to logically discrete categories; we are rather alluding to a whole family of individual narratives about acts of discrimination, of which no two may be exactly alike—nor must they all share a common denominator. Even if we define the phrase, we still cannot draw a clear line between harassment and nonharassment, because the definition must depend upon other vaguely bordered, family-resemblance words, such as "unwelcome" and "offensive." We might decide to draw a relatively clear but arbitrary line, in order to help people recognize their legal rights and responsibilities; otherwise, the outcome of lawsuits would be unpredictable and even capricious. However, the limits of sexual harassment could not be drawn by means of general principles (e.g., "Never give offense"), because such principles would always have vague borders. The only way to draw the line would be to provide a long list of specifically permitted and prohibited acts. But this method just reinforces the conclusion that there is no conceptual border to the family of cases that we name with the phrase, "sexual harassment." The same is true of diverse situations that make people happy, and of acts that manifest a given virtue— they do not necessarily have any common denominator.

"THICK DESCRIPTION" AND ASPECT-SEEING

On the other hand, Socrates' objection seems to have some force. How, after all, can we use a word like "harassment," unless we have a clear test in mind to distinguish the cases that constitute harassment from those that do not? Even if "harassment" turns out to have a vague sphere of application, it still must have a clear logical core that gives it its meaning. Otherwise, the faculty (call it "judgment") that allows us to assign particular cases to general categories is a mysterious, illogical, or arbitrary power. But here again, there is a plausible alternative position. In my view, calling something "sexual harassment"—an act of moral judgment—is an instance of what Gilbert Ryle called "thick description."[49] Ryle offers the following example. If I say that someone's eyelids contracted, then I am offering a "thin" description. But if I say that the person winked conspiratorially, then I have "thickened" the description: I have depicted the contracting eyelid *as* something, by placing it in a narrative context. I have not just added more detail to my description; rather, I have offered additional facts that are morally *salient* (in this case, information about intentions and purposes). This is a very common method of judgment; it allows us to assign particular cases to broader categories without having to postulate an essence or common denominator for the general category.

We cannot morally judge the contraction of an eyelid unless we know that it is a conspiratorial wink; therefore, thick description is a necessary precondition for ethical judgment. Moreover, some thick descriptions are sufficient in themselves as ethical claims. For example: "a contracting eyelid" is ethically neutral; "a conspiratorial wink" is ethically dubious (and needs to be assessed in some broader context); but "a signal to his confederate that he was about to betray the hapless child" is ruled unethical from the moment it is so described. One and the same physical act could be described using each of these three phrases; but the last phrase constitutes an ethical argument against the act. By describing events in their contexts, we "thicken" our descriptions and give them ethical content. There is perhaps no clear division between thin and thick descriptions; but "sexual harassment" is a good example of a thick, value-laden term, which we apply to particular actions and statements if we want to make them appear unethical.

Any thick description situates an event within a relatively broad context; and often the most useful kind of context is provided by a narrative. Alasdair MacIntyre suggests an example: someone asks what a man is doing in his garden, and receives one of the following responses: "Digging," "Gardening," "Taking exercise," "Preparing for winter," and "Pleasing his wife." All of these descriptions might simultaneously be true, but each would describe the same event within a different narrative context. If we wanted to emphasize that the man was preparing for winter, then we would situate his actions within "an annual cycle of domestic activity." But we might instead locate his behavior within "the narrative history of a marriage."[50] Certain kinds of evidence might count in favor of particular thick descriptions. For example, we might overhear the woman asking her husband to dig the garden; or he might explain that he was only digging to please her; or she might later express delight at what he had done. In any of these cases, we would be inclined to call the event "pleasing his wife," as well as merely "digging." Thus our interpretation would emerge once we had placed the bare action within a more complicated story. This alone would give us license to call it by a "thick" name.

Describing the same act thinly—for example, by calling it "digging"—would not permit us to judge it: digging, per se, sounds neither right nor wrong. However, all things being equal, pleasing one's wife does sound like a good thing. In order to show that pleasing one's wife was not good in a particular case, we would have to provide an even thicker description of the same event, placing it within an even broader context. If, for example, the husband were digging in the garden in order to please his wife, but her goal was to dispose of a murder victim under the daffodils, then we could describe the man's actions as "burying a corpse," "concealing a homicide," "abetting a felony," and so on. These descriptions—even thicker than the phrase, "pleasing his wife"—give us still firmer grounds for judging his actions.

Narratives and thick descriptions are two different things. Consider: "Boy meets girl, boy loves girl, boy loses girl." This is a narrative—a coherent series of events that takes place over time—but it provides far too little information to support any moral judgment. Conversely, a description can be thick, yet lack a temporal dimension, in which case it is not a narrative. To take an obvious example, the Mona Lisa is a sensitive description of a particular woman; and although the image is famously mysterious, it is thick enough that we can draw tentative conclusions about her character. Walter Pater, for instance, detects "something sinister" in La Gioconda's smile; she knows as much as St. Paul about the sins of the past and the imminence of divine judgment, but she merely smiles. "Hers is the head upon which all 'the ends of the world are come,' and the eyelids are a little weary."[51] Pater is fascinated and attracted by her lack of a past, her indifference to the future, her Olympian disdain for ordinary events, her ironic distance from any and all narratives.

So a thick description can lack a temporal dimension and yet support a moral judgment (or, in this case, a judgment *against* Christian morality). Still, telling stories is a common way to thicken descriptions—and it is a morally effective one. Perhaps we can make judgments on the basis of perfectly timeless thick descriptions, but I cannot think of an example. Even in the case of the Mona Lisa, Pater invents an implied narrative to illustrate his subject's detachment from time and history. "She is older than the rocks among which she sits; like the vampire, she has been dead many times, and learned the secrets of the grave; and has been a diver in deep seas, and keeps their fallen day about her; and trafficked for strange webs with Eastern merchants, and, as Leda, was the mother of Helen of Troy, and as Saint Anne, the mother of Mary; and all this has been to her as the sound of lyres and flutes, and lives only in the delicacy with which it has molded the changing lineaments, and tinged the eyelids and the hands."[52] Pater's moral (or anti-moral) judgment is plausible only if we agree that his narrative describes Leonardo's motionless image. In general, I think, detailed stories are the most effective vehicles for moral argument. In the past, many people depended exclusively on biblical narratives; today, novels and biographies are at least as influential—but we have never stopped telling stories for moral purposes.

In *Harris v. Forklift Systems*, both sides used narratives to support their thick descriptions. Harris called Hardy's actions "sexual harassment." To support this characterization, she told a story about repeated offensive statements that caused her to suffer and ultimately leave her job. But Hardy depicted Harris as an employee who had quit because she was angry when her husband's business relationship with Forklift Systems soured; she then tried to exact revenge through the federal courts. In short, Hardy thickly described Harris's actions as "unwarranted retaliation." Both sides omitted inconvenient facts and emphasized ones favorable to their position. The federal magistrate drew from both accounts to tell his version of the story. For example, he stated: "I am certain that Hardy's business relationship with plaintiff played more of a role in [her] dissatisfaction with her job than [she] admitted." He also found that Harris had "tried to get far too much mileage out of Hardy's comment that they would negotiate her raise at the Holiday Inn. The comment shows Hardy to be a man with a bad sense of humor, but it was not a sexual proposition."[53] The magistrate defended this judgment by emphasizing facts about *context*: there was a "joking atmosphere" at Forklift, and management meetings were often conducted at the Holiday Inn. But the magistrate also found clear evidence of offensive conduct on Hardy's part, and constructed a chronology to show that Hardy's sexist remarks had led directly to Harris's resignation. Thus the magistrate's narrative was more nuanced and complete than either party's, and it supported his subtler thick description. Harris *was* a disgruntled employee, angry in part because of Hardy's treatment of her husband. But her boss was a "vulgar man" who demeaned his female employees—yet without actually harassing them. The magistrate was not necessarily correct in his overall findings (indeed, the Supreme Court forced him to reverse himself); but the only way to argue with him would be to tell another story that supported a different thick description without ignoring any salient facts.

From Ludwig Wittgenstein, *Philosophical Investigations.*

In addition to Ryle's account of thick description and MacIntyre's analysis of narrative, Wittgenstein's notion of aspect-seeing can help to clarify what goes on when we make judgments. Wittgenstein points out that we not only see things, but we often see them as one thing or another. For instance, examining the figure to the left, we can make at least three kinds of statement about it. First, we can say what type of object it is, giving it a name like "image," "figure," or "drawing." Second, we can state facts about the figure, such as the length of the line. Finally, we can describe it or interpret it *as* either a duck or a rabbit. This last case is an example of seeing-as, rather than mere seeing; or interpretation, rather than naming.

These three types of assertion involve different logics, different criteria of correctness, and different degrees of precision. Their differences become clear when we consider how someone would defend each claim in a debate. For example, I might say that the object I see *is* an image, and someone might disagree with me. In that case, I would naturally conclude that we were disagreeing about the meaning of the word "image," since what we both see is clear enough. I would be somewhat surprised by our disagreement, because the *word* "image" seems to be easily defined—or, at worst, to refer to a fairly tight family of objects. Therefore I might reply, "What do you mean by 'image,' if this isn't one?" Whatever my opponent's response, I would expect to be able to clarify my terms, or to change my vocabulary, or to appeal to a dictionary, and thereby to reach agreement. If this failed, then I would conclude that my interlocutor was either blind or insane, because seeing the figure, and naming what one sees, should not be problematic.

In the second case, my goal is to offer facts about the image, such as a measurement of the line. If challenged, I could provide evidence to support my claim. For instance, I could invite my interlocutor to use his or her own ruler to verify my measurement. Ultimately, our disagreement should not be any more problematic than a dispute about the figure's name, although the appropriate method for resolving this dispute is different. However, the third case—seeing the figure *as* something, or interpreting it—is by its nature a more problematic process. If I said that the image looked like a rabbit (or could be seen *as* one), and someone disagreed with me, then I would not conclude that we were using the *word* "rabbit" in different ways, nor that either of us was blind or irrational. Except under unusual circumstances, I would not define my terms, nor would I produce evidence, such as a measurement. Instead, I might offer a "hint," pointing out that the face looks up when it is seen as a rabbit. Or I might point to the ears, eyes, and nose in the image, and then point to similar features in a photograph of a real rabbit. These actions would reveal that interpretation is less certain and less automatic than naming, more an art than a science, and that it requires entirely different techniques. One can defend one's interpretations, but it is rarely helpful to appeal to definitions or measurements.

There are other differences between the logic of seeing and seeing-as. For instance, I can *choose* to see the duck-rabbit as a rabbit, once I know that it can be seen in two ways; thus the logic of seeing-as often implies choice.[54] Seeing-as is a species of interpretation, and in many cases we can *decide* how to interpret something (such as an action or event). The logic of seeing, on the other hand, does not involve the idea of choice, for you cannot help what you see if you open your eyes and look in a given direction. Thus seeing (and perception generally) has a different logical structure from seeing-as and interpretation. Moreover, unlike seeing, seeing-as depends upon the viewer's background. The drawing will only look like a duck to someone who has already seen ducks, and also other drawings. Thus whether the duck-rabbit is seen as a duck is a matter of context. However, when we claim that the duck-rabbit *is* something (e.g., a drawing on paper), then we are implying that the truth of our claim is independent of context; it *is* a drawing whether or not the viewer has ever seen a drawing before.

The difference between these two kinds of assertion is not the result of a metaphysical difference between drawings (on one hand) and representations of ducks (on the other). I am not saying that drawings "really exist" whereas interpretations of them are "merely subjective." One could imagine a situation in which someone interpreted an object as a drawing on paper, having first taken it for a shadow or a crack. Then he or she could plausibly say: "I see it as a drawing." Thus we cannot divide all the things in the world into those items that can be seen, and those that must be seen-as; rather, things belong at various times in one or the other category depending upon the situation. Factual claims and interpretations have different logics or grammars and different criteria of correctness, and it is on these grounds that they must be distinguished.

Aspect-seeing is not merely subjective, nor are all interpretations equally valid. The duck-rabbit really does look like a duck, or at least more like a duck than some other shapes would. There are ways of pointing out the resemblance between the drawing and the species of aquatic bird, even if this resemblance cannot be demonstrated conclusively. A better, more complete description of the duck-rabbit would state that it can look like both a rabbit and a duck, depending on how the viewer interprets it. On the other hand, it really does not look much like a house, and it would be practically impossible to make someone see it as one.

Wittgenstein uses his analysis of aspect-seeing as part of an attack on philosophers, like Socrates, who think that all words must correspond to objects. Wittgenstein once wrote, "I cannot characterize my standpoint better than by saying that it is opposed to that which Socrates represents in the Platonic dialogues."[55] And he gave an idea of what he meant by Socrates' standpoint by providing the following paraphrase of the *Theaetetus*:

> Socrates to Theaetetus: "If you have an idea, must it not be an idea of *something*? – Theaetetus: "Necessarily." – Socrates: "And if you have an idea of something mustn't it be of something real?" – Theaetetus: "It seems so."[56]

Aspect-seeing is a case of language-use in which we have an idea that is *not* an idea of something real. For example, as Wittgenstein notes, a face may look different when we suddenly notice its resemblance to another face–but this resemblance is not a "thing," nor does the face change from one thing to another after we recognize a resemblance. The face remains the same, but it looks like something new; it has been interpreted afresh, and we might (for example) draw it differently.

Someone might try to rescue the theory that all words correspond to things by saying that, when we see the duck-rabbit as a duck, we are seeing a mental image of a duck instead of a mental image of a rabbit. Thus, the word "duck" in the sentence, "I see it *as* a duck," does correspond to a thing: namely, a mental image. But the most accurate picture of the duck that I see in my mind would look exactly like the duck-rabbit on the page.[57] Therefore, seeing the drawing *as* something is not a case of seeing a "thing." It is a case of forming an analogy or an interpretation of the drawing; it is a case of seeing it under a new aspect. Only metaphysicians, anxious to show that all similes and interpretations must "really" be factual claims, find it strange that seeing-as does not work like seeing. Wittgenstein comments, "But how is it possible to *see* an object according to an interpretation? The question represents it as a queer fact; as if something were being forced into a form it did not really fit. But no squeezing, no forcing took place here."[58]

Stating something's identity and interpreting it are simply two distinct procedures, as are seeing and seeing-*as*; and context determines which one we are using at any particular point. For instance, Wittgenstein writes that it would normally be absurd to "say at the sight of a knife and fork, 'Now I am seeing this as a knife and fork.'" "One doesn't 'take' what one knows as the cutlery at a meal *for* the cutlery."[59] However, it would be appropriate to say that something looked like cutlery if the light improved, and what had previously looked like a pattern in the tablecloth suddenly looked like a knife and fork. What something is seen as depends upon the context, including the context of our thoughts and associations. For example, a harmless kitchen knife could suddenly look like a grisly weapon to a murder witness who recalled a suppressed trauma.[60]

Putting together Wittgenstein's ideas about family resemblance and aspect-seeing, MacIntyre's account of narrative, and Ryle's concept of thick description, we can begin to understand what typically happens when we call an action by a morally freighted word, such as "murder," "harassment," or "cruelty." In many such cases, we are not assigning the action to a clearly defined category. Rather, we are interpreting it, or emphasizing its resemblance to other acts, or placing it within a narrative context. These techniques justify the value-laden words that we use to describe it. I do not believe that we always use aspect-seeing and thick description when we engage in moral argument. Sometimes we appeal to abstract moral principles; we charge our opponents with inconsistency or hypocrisy; we cite authority, precedent, or revelation; or we predict consequences from other people's actions that they have not foreseen. Nevertheless, the most difficult moral dilemmas arise when none of these strategies succeeds in producing consensus. Persistent dilemmas arise not only between people of different moral persuasions, but also within our own minds when we are morally uncertain. In such situations, the depiction of a particular act *as* something is often both a necessary and a sufficient method of moral argument.

Consequently, aspect-seeing, thick-description, family-resemblance terms, interpretation, and narrative are all crucial to morality. However, I am not suggesting any precise *limits* for these concepts. I have implied a rough division of discourse into two domains—the realms of theory and interpretation—but I have not attempted to mark their respective borders. In the world of theory, terms are clearly-defined, abstract, and general. Although I have argued that some moral words do not belong to this domain, others may. By the same token, many *non*-moral words may belong to the realm of interpretation. For example, crucial phrases from medicine or engineering or even mathematics might turn out to be family-resemblance terms, requiring thick description to make them comprehensible. All that I have argued so far is that certain terms, such as "sexual harassment," are (in many situations) vaguely defined; they require thick description and aspect-seeing; and they cannot be employed as part of an abstract theory. It seems to me, furthermore, that such terms account for most of our thorny ethical quandaries. In order to decide whether any other concept (moral or non-moral) operates in a similar way to these terms, we would have to examine that concept as it is actually used. No general theory can show us in advance the limits of general theory.

A LEGAL ILLUSTRATION

The best way to understand family-resemblance, thick description, aspect-seeing, and kindred concepts is to look at concrete cases; and my basic example is sexual harassment. The Supreme Court held in 1986 that "unwelcome sexual advances that create an offensive or hostile working environment" constitute unlawful sex discrimination.[61] By defining its terms, the Supreme Court seemed to be following a procedure advocated by Socrates. Apparently, the justices identified a "thing" and then gave it a name. But there is another way to understand what the Court did. Sexual harassment became illegal in America not because anyone discovered a concept to which "injustice" could be predicated. Rather, people first began to see acts of racial discrimination in a negative light, once leaders of the civil rights movement (and others) had told their stories of oppression. Congress responded by banning discrimination in the workplace, but without defining this category precisely. African American plaintiffs then persuaded courts that "discrimination" did not necessarily mean being rejected, underpaid, or fired on account of one's race; a company could discourage minority employees just as effectively by allowing them to be systematically harassed on the job. In these cases, juries found that harassment constituted illegal discrimination.

Next, the Civil Rights Act was amended to cover discrimination against women, and female plaintiffs told courts narratives about harassment that seemed akin to stories of racial discrimination. Therefore, the Supreme Court agreed to make sexual harassment illegal. But the Court's definition was full of vaguely defined terms—"unwelcome," "hostile," "offensive"—that each depended heavily upon context, and that might not have any clear logical core. For instance, all "offensive" acts may not have any one thing in common; they may simply share a family resemblance. In *Harris v. Forklift Systems*, the Supreme Court unanimously reaffirmed its test for deciding whether harassment has occurred. But Justice O'Connor wrote:

> This is not, and by its nature cannot be, a mathematically precise test. We need not answer today all the potential questions it raises. . . . But we can say that whether an environment is "hostile" or "abusive" can be determined only by looking at all the circumstances. These may include the frequency of the discriminatory conduct; its severity; whether it is physically threatening or humiliating, or a mere offensive utterance; and whether it unreasonably interferes with an employee's work performance.[62]

Thus O'Connor was aware that the Court's decision did not precisely define a concept. Rather, the justices tried to influence magistrates and jurors who were going to grapple with similar cases in the future, by enumerating some of the criteria that could properly affect their decisions. Whether a particular situation really was "similar" to the case on which the Supreme Court had ruled was an issue left to juries to decide; it was a matter of judgment. In its first harassment case, *Meritor Savings Bank v. Vinson,* the Supreme Court had found against a company for creating a workplace "so heavily polluted with discrimination as to destroy completely the emotional and psychological stability of minority group members." O'Connor now emphasized that the conditions described in that case "merely present some especially egregious examples of harassment. They do not mark the boundary of what is actionable."[63] The legal border of harassment would have to be set by numerous decisions made in concrete cases; no single concept or standard would define it.

According to O'Connor, behavior that belongs to the family known as "sexual harassment" typically includes certain qualities, although all acts of harassment may not involve any one common denominator. To tell whether a given act constitutes sexual harassment, juries must look at the totality of the circumstances of the case: not because moral and legal judgments are relative to local norms, but because a proper evaluation can only be made if a detailed story is first told. "Sexual harassment" describes a whole narrative, complete with several major characters and a set of intentions, reactions, expectations, and so on. We cannot call an act "harassment" without knowing its full narrative context, any more than we could call a contracting eyelid a conspiratorial wink without knowing that a conspiracy was going on.

Justice Antonin Scalia concurred in this case, but he expressed some illuminating reservations in his concurring opinion:

> 'Abusive' (or 'hostile,' which in the context I take to mean the same thing) does not seem to me a very clear standard [for judging whether behavior constitutes harassment].

> Today's opinion does list a number of factors that
> contribute to abusiveness . . . , but since it neither says
> how much of each is necessary (an impossible task) nor
> identifies any single factor as determinative, it thereby
> adds little certitude. . . . One might say that what
> constitutes 'negligence' (a traditional jury question) is not
> much more clear and certain than what constitutes
> 'abusiveness.' Perhaps so. But the class of plaintiffs seeking
> to recover for negligence is limited to those who have
> suffered harm, whereas under this statute 'abusiveness' is
> to be the test of whether legal harm has been suffered,
> opening more expansive vistas of litigation.
>
> Be that as it may, I know of no alternative to the
> course the Court today has taken.[64]

Scalia worried that the legal definition of harassment depended upon
vaguely defined terms. But he was right to see no alternative to the Court's
ruling, for terms like "sexual harassment" and "negligence" simply have no
real essences, no precise definitions. His anxiety resulted, I suspect, from a
dubious theoretical premise: namely, that general concepts always ought to
have essences. But he was right to see that the law is full of concepts that lack
logical borders, not because we have so far failed to understand these
concepts precisely, but because they actually *are* vague. Scalia was concerned
that the concept of harassment might be even vaguer than that of negligence,
because the presence of harm is obvious in cases of negligence, and not in
cases of harassment. A term with extremely vague borders would be
dangerous in a courtroom; and it may be true that "harassment" has a
somewhat vaguer definition than "negligence." However, I suspect that the
difference in clarity between the two words is only a modest matter of
degree. In many cases of alleged negligence, where the damage sustained is
not merely financial, "harm" may prove as difficult to judge as "hostility."
Therefore, Scalia's decision to concur with the Court's ruling was correct: if
we want to punish harassment, we will have to tolerate a certain degree of
vagueness, because the concept actually *is* vague.

Only after we are familiar with many stories of sexual harassment does
the Court's legal definition of it make sense; only then does it have a clear
purpose. As Wittgenstein writes, "We may say, only someone who knows
how to do something with [a thing] can significantly ask a name."[65] And
Stephen A. Dinan argues:

> like the law, universal moral standards have meaning or
> normative content only in their applications, both past and
> future. Rather than confuse the meaning of those moral

standards, the history of their "application" or discernment
in concrete situations makes it possible for the moral agent
to understand what those standards demand here and
now. For what the past application of moral standards has
taught the moral agent is neither an abstract definition of
moral goods nor a set of universal moral rules, but rather,
a way of seeing each new situation in the light of past
applications. . . . What is seen by the virtuous and
intelligent moral agent is an *analogous* likeness [cf. family
resemblance] between a proposed action and other
responses to moral situations in the past.[66]

Along similar lines, John Wisdom discusses an actual case in which the
opposing counsel were agreed about all the facts, but disagreed as to whether
the actions of a certain bank official should be called "negligent" or not.
Wisdom observes that the arguments of the two lawyers are not like chains
of propositions, adding up to a proof. Rather, they consist of a "presenting
and re-presenting of those features of the case which *severally co-operate* in
favour of the conclusion, in favour of saying what the reasoner wishes said,
in favour of calling the situation by the name by which he wishes to call it.
The reasons are like the legs of a chair, not the links of a chain." This
analogy helps to illustrate the cumulative nature of thick description, which,
unlike logical argument, does not rely on a sequence of propositions linked
by valid inferences, so that a single invalid move destroys the whole
argument. (Nor, however, can an ethical argument be called definitive just
because it happens to be logically flawless.) Wisdom concludes:

Whether a lion with stripes is a tiger or a lion is, if you
like, merely a matter of the application of a name.
Whether Mr. So-and-So of whose conduct we have so
complete a record did or did not exercise reasonable care
is not merely the application of a name, or if we choose to
say it is, then we must remember that with this name a
game is lost and won and a game with very heavy stakes.
With the judges' choice of a name for the facts goes an
attitude, and the declaration, the ruling, is an exclamation
evincing that attitude. But *it is an explanation which not only
has a purpose but also a logic*, a logic surprisingly like that of
"futile", "deplorable", "graceful", "grand", and "divine."[67]

Wisdom suggests that the use of an evaluative adjective like "negligent"
or "graceful" is not a matter of comparing the relevant events against an
independent definition or standard of Carefulness or Grace. Rather, the use

of these words is justified only if we are able to offer a thick description that depicts the relevant events in a particular moral or aesthetic light. Wisdom provides examples of several such descriptions, which are designed to illustrate the kinds of argument that can change someone's view of a case, even when all disputants are agreed about the facts. For example, if someone does not see a piece of music as beautiful, I might ask him to listen to it again, to concentrate on certain motifs, to recognize an overall structure, to compare the work to another. When he first listens to the piece, he already hears everything that I hear, so I am not introducing new facts; I am rather "presenting and re-presenting . . . those features of the case which *severally co-operate* in favour of the conclusion." The same kind of reasoning might be useful if I were trying to advise a friend about whether or not to continue a romantic relationship. The friend often knows every fact that I know, but a stressing of selected episodes, a linking of events into selected narrative chains, a comparison to other relationships—these things can be persuasive. In short, as Dancy writes:

> The man who provides reasons is not so much providing evidence for his ethical judgement as trying to show his audience how he sees the situation. He supposes that to see it his way is to join in with his judgement about what is right and wrong; so if you do come to see it his way you will agree with his ethical judgement, but by giving his reasons he is not *arguing* for that judgement, in the way in which adherents of moral principles might suppose.[68]

ARISTOTLE'S VIEW

A similar conception of moral argument plays a role in Aristotle's ethics. Aristotle argues that philosophical theory is appropriate in domains where certainty is possible, but not in ethics, because human behavior is too complex and variegated to be subject to general rules. "It is obvious that practical wisdom is not deductive knowledge," he writes, because human situations do not conform to rules like those in mathematics; each situation is unique.[69] Practical wisdom, he continues:

> is the opposite of intelligence [*nous*, the faculty used in philosophical thought], for intelligence is about definitions [literally, boundaries], about which there can be no argument, while practical wisdom is of the particular thing, of which there is no deductive knowledge, but rather perception—not (that is) perception by one of the senses,

but the sort of perception by which we perceive a triangle
in a set of mathematical figures."[70]

Thus judging something to be good or evil is like finding a triangle in a
complicated network of lines—or, to use Wittgenstein's example, seeing an
intricate geometrical figure *as* two interpenetrating hexagons."[71] These are the
kinds of things that cannot be proved, but can sometimes be pointed out,
much as someone could point out that the duck-rabbit looks like a duck.
They are interpretations, rather than deductive arguments or definitions. To
arrive at such interpretations, we use what Kant calls "judgment sharpened
by experience," and not pure analytic reason.

If there are no systematic rules to explain human behavior (cf.
Nichomachean Ethics 1110b10), then learning to interpret, judge, and predict is a
matter of experience. Aristotle writes:

> young people can become geometers and mathematicians
> and wise in such things; but they do not appear to have
> practical wisdom. The reason is that practical wisdom is of
> particular things, which become familiar through
> experience, but a young person is not experienced, for it is
> the length of time that makes one experienced. . . . Thus it
> is necessary to attend to the undemonstrated sayings of
> those who are experienced and older or people of practical
> wisdom not less than to proofs. For since experience has
> given them an eye, they see straight. (1142a13-17;
> 1143b12-13)

If someone wanted to teach a young person practical wisdom, the best
method would not be to inculcate general principles, but to provide
numerous examples, such as those that are collected in canons of literature
and history. Wittgenstein essentially adopts the same position:

> Is there such a thing as "expert judgment" about the
> genuineness of expressions of feeling?—even here there are
> those whose judgment is "better" and those whose
> judgment is "worse."
>
> Correcter prognoses will generally issue from those
> with better knowledge of mankind.
>
> Can one learn this knowledge? Yes; some can. Not,
> however, by taking a course in it, but through "*experience.*"
> — Can someone else be a man's teacher in this? Certainly.
> From time to time he gives the right *tip.* — This is what
> "learning" and "teaching" are like here. — What one

acquires here is not a technique; one learns correct judgments. There are also rules, but they do not form a
system, and only experienced people can apply them right.
Unlike calculation-rules.[72]

A judgment about the genuineness of someone's feelings is just one
example of the kind of work that we must do when we make moral
evaluations. Since it is not a matter of applying general rules or theories, it
does not promise certainty. On the other hand, reflecting on experience
makes us better at the art of judgment, and the particular details that emerge
in a story (such as the one that Harris told) can help us to judge with greater
assurance.

Aristotle does not deny the importance of rules and generalizations in
the realm of ethics, but (he says) they must be like the flexible rulers used on
Lesbos, which bend to meet the shape of the stone (1137b30). Rules are
deemed true not because they conform to the essence of the situation, nor
because they derive from true general maxims, but because they have
hitherto proved useful as shortcuts, substitutes for the process of detailed,
value-laden description that Aristotle calls *phantasia*. Martha Nussbaum writes
that *phantasia* is "the interpretative, selective element in perception, in virtue
of which things in the world 'appear' (*phainetai*) to the creature as a certain
sort of thing."[73]

Despite Aristotle's commitment to the concrete particular and to aspect-
seeing, there is also a place for universal concepts in his ethical thought, and
particularly in the workings of what he called the practical syllogism
(1147a25ff.). A practical syllogism consists of a major premise (e.g., "All
strawberries are good to eat"), a minor premise ("This is a strawberry"), and
a practical conclusion ("I'll eat it"). Major premises are, by definition,
universals—they take the form "*all* x's are y"—and Aristotle seems to believe
that we must always have such universals in mind before we can act.
However, universals can either be very general and abstract or else rather
concrete. For example, the following is a universal maxim that is also highly
concrete: "When waiting to use a cash machine, do not try to observe the
identification number of the person using the machine." This maxim takes a
universal form, because it covers *all* cases of a certain type. However, the
class of cases that it covers is very narrow, and therefore the concrete image
that comes to mind when we read the maxim is very similar to all the actual
cases to which the rule applies. This is roughly what I mean by saying that
the maxim is concrete. By contrast, the maxim to treat other people as ends
in themselves is not only universal, but also abstract—it is very hard to
picture. It is not clear how general and abstract Aristotle's major premises
are: they could be about things like cash machines and strawberries, or they
could be much broader. For example, the most important major premise of

all could be a version of Mill's utilitarian principle or Kant's Categorical Imperative.

The history of moral philosophy has been dominated by a debate about which single, abstract, major premise should have ultimate authority; this is what Mill means when he reflects that all philosophers have sought the *summum bonum*. In general, philosophers have believed that narrow syllogisms must be replaced with broad ones before moral conclusions can emerge. For example, someone might say: "All acts in the workplace that subject another person to undesired advances constitute sexual harassment; Hardy subjected Harris to undesired advances in the workplace; therefore, he committed sexual harassment." That seems to be a valid syllogism, but it does not prove that what Hardy did was wrong. Thus, a Kantian might point out that this first syllogism fits neatly inside a broader one: "All acts that treat another person as a means are wrong; sexual harassment treats another person as a means to someone's pleasure; therefore, sexual harassment is wrong." By nesting one syllogism inside another, we can proceed toward a grand theory of ethics. If this is what Aristotle meant, then I cannot enlist him for my cause, for his ethics would depend upon abstract axioms.

However, Aristotle explicitly denies that ethics is a deductive system (1139b18ff.). Moreover, on purely logical grounds, he criticizes the idea of a single, universal good (1096a12–1097a14). On the other hand, he does seem to hint at a single abstract principle when he argues that "Syllogisms about practical matters have a major premise of the form 'The end and highest good is such-and such—whatever it may be'" (1144a31–33). That formulation leaves the *summum bonum* very vague, but Aristotle defines it more clearly when he claims that happiness must be "the first principle, since all the other things that we do, we do for its sake" (1102a2–3). Thus, for Aristotle, there seems to be one major premise that underlies every practical choice, which we might express as, "All things that bring about happiness are good." But happiness means acting in conformity with virtue (1098a16–19); the various virtues are distinct and incommensurable (1096b24); and consequently no general guidance can be derived from the maxim that we ought to pursue happiness, which is an empty truism (1097b22). Even the maxim that we ought to pursue any *particular* virtue is of no use unless we add the phrase, "in the right way and . . . time, and the other qualifications" (1104b26–27). But that makes the maxim tautological: obviously a virtue is good if we exercise it at the right time and place, but we need a way of judging what particular behavior is appropriate (1109a29). Likewise, Aristotle concedes that his maxim that we should always obey a mean between excess and deficiency is not helpful as a major premise. For "although the statement is true, yet it is not at all clear" (1138b25–26).

Therefore, the real content of Aristotle's ethics emerges when he discusses *minor* premises. "In practical reasoning," he explains, "the universal has more general application, but the particular is more true" (1107a30–31). He argues that we derive beliefs about concrete particulars—that is, minor premises—by means of a process that sounds a great deal like thick description or aspect-seeing. For example, he notes that a tragedy can show that a particular character is noble by means of the plot, without stating this conclusion explicitly.[74] The idea that someone is noble could provide the minor premise of a practical syllogism. We would reason as follows: "It is right to admire a noble person; Homer has shown us that Achilles was noble; therefore, it is right to admire him." It seems to me—and I think Aristotle would agree—that the minor premise does all the work in this syllogism.[75] Obviously, we ought to admire noble people: that maxim is self-evident, but also empty. The interesting question is: Who is noble?[76] This is where Aristotle turns to *phantasia* for guidance, and to the thick descriptions that are provided by poetry, rhetoric, history, and other genres. Meanwhile, the major premise is merely a formal aspect of moral reasoning, and it provides no useful guidance.[77] As Aristotle notes: "That is why people who do not know general principles can be more successful than those who do know them" (1141b16). General principles provide little guidance, so one can possess them and still be a fool (1147b10ff.). It is the minor premise that counts—for example, "Achilles is noble," "Hardy harassed Harris"—and these can be controversial even when everyone agrees about the facts. We cannot argue about such premises by means of deductive reasoning, but we can support our judgments with value-laden descriptions or stories.

OBJECTIONS TO RHETORIC

When Teresa Harris told her story of sexual harassment to the federal magistrate, she did not provide a theory, even implicitly, but she did offer thick descriptions, stories, and Aristotelian minor premises. Thus her testimony was an example of rhetoric, which (as I have said) enjoys a generally bad reputation among philosophers.

Why do some people prefer theory to rhetoric? Annette Baier believes that modern philosophers yearn for the certainties that were once provided by religion. When theological principles generate practical rules, they connect abstract truth to real-world advice in a comforting fashion. Baier writes: "it may be nostalgia for this theory-linked practical guidance that prompts philosophers today to construct moral theories, fairly elaborate systems of norms with the less general linked to more general principles."[78] Nostalgia is not a very good reason to build theories or to disparage rhetoric. However, Baier's critical hypothesis is difficult to substantiate, because most modern philosophers do not *consciously* yearn for the Age of Faith. Besides, religion involves rhetoric and narrative as well as theology.

Bernard Williams observes that some philosophers have metaphysical reasons to favor moral theory over rhetoric: they believe that the true world is the one seen *sub species aeternitatis*, the world of abstract and general facts. But some people who do not share Spinoza's belief in a timeless reality beyond the phenomena nevertheless argue that narrative and rhetoric are morally inferior to theory. Williams writes, "For many, it is as if reason itself drew ethical thought in the direction of theory and systematization."[79] To make moral judgments *without* general reasons seems irrational, and to offer reasons that don't link together systematically seems illogical.

One of Borges's narrators observes: "To think is to forget a difference, to abstract, to generalize."[80] In fact, thinking is often just the opposite process; it means recalling differences and focusing on particulars. But strong defenders of philosophy associate the abstract kind of thinking with reason, and the particular kind with rhetoric. They argue, furthermore, that bare rhetoric appeals to our emotions, and not to our reason. Judgments unguided by general rules are said to be capricious and erratic, motivated by feelings rather than principles. Thus Socrates claims that rhetoric and poetry move the passionate part of our souls; but dialectic speaks to our reason.[81] He believes, further, that most people's emotions make slaves of their reason. Therefore, he says, "it is not necessary for the would-be orator to concern himself about what is just or good behavior, nor about what kind of people are just or good either by nature or upbringing. For no one in the law courts cares at all about such truths, but only about what is calculated to persuade."[82] Socrates even claims—with false modesty—that he has no capacity for rhetoric at all, but can only speak dialectically, using logical analysis as his tool.[83]

Since his day, Romantics and other friends of the emotions have counterattacked, claiming that poetry and rhetoric give access to the truths of the heart, which are more valuable than those of the head. Finally, some modern philosophers—notably Nietzsche and his disciples among contemporary literary theorists—have been happy to announce that *all* statements are purely rhetorical, that there are no true or false claims, and that we are always guided by the will because dispassionate Reason is a fiction. Nietzsche mocks the "whole idea of rating the passions: as if it were right and normal to be led by reason—while the passions are abnormal, dangerous, half-animal; and besides, their end is nothing but an inordinate desire for pleasure." He adds: "Passion is devalued . . . as if it were the moving force only inappropriately, rather than necessarily and always." He then defines "reason" as a mere "condition of relations among passions and desires."[84] If this is correct, then reason can give no access to truth, and all propositions about the world are *merely* rhetorical. "What then is truth? A mobile army of metaphors, metonymies, anthropomorphisms. . . . Truths are illusions about which it has been forgotten that they are illusions."[85] For Nietzsche, all propositions are tropes of the will, and no beliefs are true.

This kind of argument is taken by some contemporary thinkers as a liberating discovery, an escape from Socrates' dedication to rationality and truth. Nietzsche is supposed to have succeeded in decoupling names from the "things" that they were previously believed to describe; he is said to have undermined the correspondence theory of truth. But what Socrates and Nietzsche share is a belief that rational language—if it exists at all—is merely a set of factual propositions that correspond to the real world. Such a language is considered desirable (by Socrates), undesirable (by Romantics), or impossible (by Nietzsche); but in any case it is assumed to be the essence of rational discourse. In a certain way, Nietzsche is just as metaphysical as Socrates.

The later Wittgenstein, however, refuses to view propositions that correspond to facts either as predominant or as especially reasonable parts of language. He describes numerous other uses of language that are equally effective in allowing one person to communicate with another. This approach avoids the distinctions between rational and emotional discourse, rhetoric and dialectic. After all, tears may communicate as effectively and accurately as formal propositions. It used to be thought that reason and the passions had different seats in the soul, emerged from different faculties, or otherwise acted like competing homunculi within the self. However, what we actually observe is a series of opinions, reactions, attitudes, utterances, and decisions emerging from a person, some of which are more overtly emotional than others. A test that attempted to distinguish the rational statements from the emotional ones by assessing tone of voice, style of argument, or heart-rate would not work, because a completely absurd statement can be uttered in a matter-of-fact voice while a belief that is perfectly consistent with logic can be howled maniacally into the wind.

Alternatively, we could assert—just as a matter of definition—that rational statements are always theoretical, while metaphor, analogy, and thick-description are irrational forms of discourse. Then, unless a statement could be rephrased as a theory (or as the application of a theory to a particular case), it would not be rational. But this definition begs the question; it gives us no reason to *favor* "rational" discourse over other forms of argument that are often more persuasive. It seems better to call a statement "reasonable" if it is intended to persuade other people without coercion. Under such a definition, the distinction between emotional and rational discourse seems irrelevant: sometimes a calm aspect can win favor in a public dispute, but at other times a fiery demeanor is more effective. Nevertheless, we can differentiate between statements that work well in public deliberation and those that are too subjective or inchoate to produce any kind of consensus. The latter are not inferior (for we sometimes value them on aesthetic or spiritual grounds), but they cannot help us to resolve ethical controversies. (I will return to the topic of moral consensus in chapter 2.)

Another reason to be wary about rhetoric is that we may not judge people fairly or equally if we listen to them tell their stories; we may happen to *like* some people better than others. Teresa Harris appealed to the federal magistrate partly by portraying herself as a nice person: as a mother who tried to treat her children kindly, and as an employee who just wanted to do her job. Meanwhile, Charles Hardy took pains to depict Harris as a drinker who used coarse language. But one might say that their characters were irrelevant to the basic question at hand: namely, whether sexual harassment actually occurred. After all, if an unappealing or nasty person were harassed, we might want her case to be treated precisely in the same way as that of a congenial and virtuous person.

An unpleasant victim would find it difficult to depict the events that befell her as awful, since we might not be as upset when we imagined her suffering. This seems to be a drawback of rhetoric. Yet we can adjust in such cases, often by imaginatively substituting some other victim—even ourselves—in her place. Thus I might ask: "How would *I* have felt if I went through what she says that she suffered?" Such thought-experiments can help to compensate for our irrelevant personal attachments and aversions.

In any case, such feelings are not always irrelevant. I see no reason to dispute the judgment that an act of violence against an admired person is more deplorable than the same act committed against an offensive individual. But in a *legal* context, we restrict the power of juries to make judgments on the basis of victims' characters. The reason for this decision is not an abstract principle that crimes are equally bad no matter whom they affect. Rather, social purposes (such as deterrence) are best served if we punish crimes severely even when the victims are abominable—even when we feel that "they deserved it." Further, juries would be excessively powerful if they could decide cases on the basis of their sympathy for various protagonists. Although the most satisfactory conclusion to a particular case would perhaps take personalities into account, there is also the risk that a jury might assess characters improperly, for there is nothing definite or inevitable about acts of judgment. Along these lines, David Hume writes:

> Were men . . . to take the liberty of acting with regard to the laws of society, as they do in every other affair, they wou'd conduct themselves, on most occasions, by particular judgments, and wou'd take into consideration the characters and circumstances of the persons, as well as the general nature of the question. But 'tis easy to observe, that this wou'd produce an infinite confusion in human society, and that the avidity and partiality of men wou'd quickly bring disorder into the world, if not restrain'd by some general and inflexible principles. . . . 'Twas, there-

> fore, with a view to this inconvenience, that men have . . .
> agreed to restrain themselves by general rules. . . . These
> rules, then, are artificially invented for a certain purpose,
> and are contrary to the common principles of human
> nature, which accommodate themselves to circumstance,
> and have no stated invariable method of operation.[86]

Common law precedents are less "general and inflexible" than statutes, but they still make jury decisions somewhat predictable. No doubt, many jurors disregard the principle of impersonality, but they are told to obey it; and if they are obedient, they may try to compensate for their sympathies by substituting imaginary protagonists in place of the real ones: this is what "impersonality" means in practical terms. Then, at the sentencing stage, the judge is permitted to consider the characters of both the victims and the defendants. This seems a wise compromise, for it allows judges to adjust the outcomes of cases in the light of their concrete interpretations of the particular stories. For example, if a judge views a convicted felon as naive or contrite, then he or she can reduce the sentence. Thus—at least in theory—the legal system takes into account both the social requirement of impersonality and our ethical need to form concrete judgments about particular cases by telling value-laden stories about them.[87]

THE SUFFICIENCY OF JUDGMENT

The various examples that I have cited in this chapter are intended to show that judgment, rather than abstract reasoning, is the crucial process that we use to make moral decisions. By "judgment" I do not mean, with Kant, the application of laws to particular cases. Instead, I mean an act of interpretation that describes something *as* something else, without relying (even covertly or implicitly) upon clear, general definitions. We cannot think about facts unless they are somehow described and interpreted. If a description is strongly value-laden, then it will generate an appropriate moral response. If, on the other hand, the description is morally ambiguous, then no abstract principle will allow us to judge it. For example, we cannot decide whether a particular act violates a moral principle that forbids harassment, until we have interpreted it as harassment. And once we have described it that way, then we can judge it without principles.

W. D. Ross writes in his *Foundations of Ethics* (1939), "I never seem to be in a position of not seeing directly the rightness of a particular act of kindness, for instance, and of having to read this off from a general principle—'all acts of kindness are right, and therefore this must be right, though I cannot see its rightness directly.'"[88] Ross is an intuitionist, who believes that we can see moral truth instantly and automatically—"by direct insight." I believe, in contrast, that truth often emerges only after a laborious process of thick description, and that we can verify or criticize such descriptions. Nevertheless, I agree with Ross that an examination of the particular case is all that we need; we do not have to apply general moral principles.

It is true that certain kinds of theoretical knowledge are useful for moral evaluation. For example, someone could examine a beautiful piece of new furniture and not see anything morally wrong about it until he or she learned a general rule: namely, that the harvesting of tropical hardwoods destroys indigenous cultures and ecosystems and causes widespread suffering. In this kind of situation, theoretical knowledge teaches us something about a particular act and its relationship to kindness, rightness, and other moral categories. Yet the theory does not teach us what kindness *is*, nor that we ought to value it (nor do we require a definition or a justification of kindness in order to act right). Rather, the theory tells us something factual about the concrete results of our actions. We then picture those results, sympathizing with their victims, and conclude—without the aid of moral principles—that what we are doing is unkind.

Ross assigns moral authority only to the judgment of particulars; but he still claims value for general moral principles, which, he asserts, can be "recognized by intuitive induction as being implied in the judgements already passed on particular acts."[89] Thus, for Ross, particular judgments have the greatest truth value, yet general principles can be derived from them, much as scientific laws can be derived from experiments. These general principles rest upon particular judgments, but they are both useful and valid in themselves. Once they have been tested against concrete moral judgments, they can be employed to solve dilemmas.[90]

Like Ross, Hume argues that moral judgments are fundamentally *particular*: "the mind restrains not itself by any general or universal rules; but acts on most occasions as it is determin'd by its present motives and inclination. As each action is a particular individual event, it must proceed from particular principles." We judge the morality of actions and events much as we judge the quality of wine or music: we automatically feel sentiments of pleasure and pain. Ethical judgment, Hume says, "proceeds entirely from a moral taste." Nevertheless, we cannot rely on particular judgments alone—it would be too cumbersome for us to judge each action separately, and we would be prone to hasty or biased conclusions. "'Tis necessary, therefore, to abridge these primary impulses, and find some more general principles, upon which all our notions of morals are founded." For Hume, moral principles are rough generalizations that we derive from our particular sensations of pleasure and pain. In turn, they may influence our sensations: "*General rules* create a species of probability, which sometimes influences the judgment, and always the imagination."[91]

For a pure moral theorist, like Kant, nothing about a concrete case can tell us whether a moral principle is valid; the validity of moral doctrines is universal, and is given by pure reason. Therefore, the process of judging examples plays no role in choosing the right moral principle. Kant writes: "One cannot damage morality more than by seeking to borrow it from examples. For each example that is set before me must itself be judged first by principles of morality, whether it is worthy to be a primary example, *i.e.*, to serve as a model, but in no way can it dependably provide the conception of [morality]."[92] Thus, according to Kant, if we are faced with a conflict between moral theory and our intuitions about a particular case, we must ignore our intuitions. But philosophers in the tradition of Hume and W. D. Ross believe that we should use moral examples roughly as scientists use experiments. Nature is complex and heterogeneous; huge numbers of causal relationships are always at work in any situation. Nevertheless, scientists have discovered that theories can be developed and tested if systems are artificially simplified to allow only a few variables. Analogously, simplified moral examples can be tested quite readily against our concrete judgments.

Thus, for instance, the theory of utilitarianism can be tested by means of an example: we might imagine one unhappy but innocent person being executed without a trial in order to maximize the net happiness of a society. This seems wrong, so we are led to reject utilitarianism (at least in its rudimentary form), replacing it either with a rival theory, or else with a subtler version of utilitarian doctrine—perhaps one that assesses the consequence of *rules* rather than discrete actions. The reasonableness of this method seems to contradict Aristotle's view that ethics cannot be theoretical, since moral situations are too complex. Nature is tremendously complex, yet scientists have achieved great understanding by forming hypotheses and testing them with carefully contrived experiments. In the moral sphere, an analogous process might ultimately produce an ornate moral theory, filled with compromises and subclauses. Nevertheless, it would be a theory.

Still, even this moderate defense of theory—which preserves an important role for judgment—gives too much weight to abstract principles. An experimental method assumes that we can judge each example and then treat all similar cases alike, thus employing general rules. However, the moral judgments that we make about particular situations are, in most instances, controversial. This is true, at least in part, because several principles can be often applied to the same case with conflicting results. Therefore, except in the most obvious cases, the important debate occurs at the level of concrete moral judgments, not generalizations. In science, a theory usually predicts events that will occur under selected circumstances; therefore, it can be tested. But since moral judgments are not predictions, they generally remain *con*tested. Further, even if we agreed on a single concrete judgment about a particular case, it would take another act of judgment to determine which situations were "similar" to it. If this similarity were a matter of family resemblance, then no abstract principle could be used to determine the scope of our moral judgment; rather, each case would have to be judged on its own. But that just means that principles play a negligible (or merely formal) role in moral discourse about genuinely controversial cases. Judging particulars is the fundamental process.[93]

Ross's method of salvaging principles is to invoke *prima facie* rules. For example, cruelty may not be immoral in every case, but it is wrong "on its face" or "at first glance." A similar approach employs *ceteris paribus* clauses, so that cruelty is condemned "all things being equal." We might also speak of things being wrong *pro tanto*—"as far as that goes." Such clauses are used with good effect in science, where natural laws are rarely (if ever) true unless we interpret them as *ceteris paribus* generalizations. Thus gravity always pulls objects toward earth, but it can be counteracted by other forces in particular instances. It seems to me, however, that moral "forces" work in quite a different way.

Consider again the *Harris* case. The very fact that Charles Hardy made sexual jokes to an employee appears, under the circumstances, to require justification. His jokes had a negative moral "force," and he can only be excused if we consider this force to be negligible under the circumstances. Are we to conclude, then, that joking is *ceteris paribus* wrong? This is implausible, because sometimes joking has the opposite moral force, actually contributing to the value of a particular statement. Even a sexual joke told to an employee could be praiseworthy if it "broke the ice." It is not that the inherent dubiousness of joking has been counteracted in such cases; on the contrary, joking is what makes some behavior good (under the right circumstances). So we seem to be able to say, with equal validity, that joking is *ceteris paribus* wrong and *ceteris paribus* right. The same is true of many other categories.

The problem is that most particular acts are deeply embedded in their immediate contexts, so that nothing is gained by analyzing them abstractly. The best we can say is that it is more often good than bad to make jokes. Even if true, this statement does not work like a *ceteris paribus* law in science, for it has no explanatory power. It is a mere *ex post facto* generalization, a kind of statistical hypothesis.[94] Words like "cruel" are less controversial, because they almost always describe condemnable behavior. But what such words gain in moral force they lose in clarity. What, after all, constitutes cruelty in any particular case? I will concede that cruelty is *pro tanto* wrong, but I consider this a tautology that can solve no actual moral problem.

I can now explain why I do not accept the most influential philosophical methodology of recent decades: "reflective equilibrium." Rawls argues that we may begin to theorize about justice by canvassing our "considered convictions." "For example," he writes, "we are confident that religious intolerance and racial discrimination are unjust. We think we have examined these things with care and have reached what we believe is an impartial judgment not likely to be distorted by an excessive attention to our own interests. These are provisional fixed points which we presume any conception of justice must fit."

Meanwhile, we may propose "reasonable and generally acceptable" rules that ought to guide people's deliberations about principles of justice: for example, that "no one should be advantaged or disadvantaged by natural fortune or social circumstances in the choice of principles." These rules turn out to be sufficiently restrictive that only certain conclusions can emerge from any fair deliberation. Thus, on one hand, we can move from our considered convictions about things like racial discrimination toward more general moral principles. At the same time, we can deduce general principles of justice from pure procedural rules that seem intuitively fair. We then check our results against our initial convictions, and vice versa. Whenever we find discrepancies,

> we have a choice. We can either modify the account of the [procedural principles] or we can revise our existing judgments, for even the judgments we take provisionally as fixed points are liable to revision. By going back and forth, sometimes altering the conditions of the contractual circumstances, at others withdrawing our judgments and conforming them to principle, I assume that eventually we shall find a description of the initial [deliberative] situation that both expresses reasonable conditions and yields principles which match our considered judgments duly pruned and adjusted. This state of affairs I refer to as reflective equilibrium.

Because moral principles can be tested against considered judgments— and vice versa—Rawls believes that his position deserves to be called a *theory*. "It is a theory of the moral sentiments," he writes, "setting out the principles governing our moral powers, or more specifically, our sense of justice. There is a definite if limited class of facts against which our conjectured principles can be checked, namely, our considered judgments in reflective equilibrium."[95]

Note, however, that Rawlsian equilibrium develops between very general principles of justice and *fairly* general principles, such as: "it is wrong to discriminate on the basis of race." Such precepts are generalizations from something that Rawls does not discuss, namely, concrete judgments. In fact, nearly everyone now agrees that racial discrimination is wrong, but people argue about whether this means that we should pay reparations, establish remedial quotas, institute affirmative action, enforce a color-blind legal system, or pay compensation to *whites* who have allegedly suffered as a result of affirmative action. Again, people disagree about whether "discrimination" always means refusing to hire or admit someone, or whether officials can discriminate by making an environment unpleasant, or by failing to recruit candidates of a certain race. And they argue about whether a particular environment is "unpleasant" or a recruitment effort is "appropriate." We can answer these questions in concrete situations without first developing a comprehensive theory of racial discrimination, let alone a theory of justice. We can listen, instead, to conflicting thick descriptions of particular behavior, and draw conclusions. The moral principle that forbids racial discrimination is a rule-of-thumb generalization from particular cases, too general to provide guidance except in extreme situations. It is an Aristotelian major premise.

Thus Rawls leaves no space in his system for concrete judgments. But he does say something interesting about why we sometimes have to adjust our moral intuitions to conform to broader principles:

> considered judgments are no doubt subject to certain irregularities and distortions despite the fact that they are rendered under favorable circumstances. When a person is presented with an intuitively appealing account of his sense of justice, . . . he may well revise his judgments to conform to the principles even though the theory does not fit his existing judgments exactly. He is especially likely to do this if he can find an explanation for the deviations which undermines his confidence in his original judgments and if the conception presented yields a judgment which he finds he can now accept.[96]

For instance, someone might hear legal testimony or read a novel and draw conclusions that were biased by racial (or other) prejudice. Perhaps a theoretically derived principle would help that person to revise his or her original judgments.[97]

Indeed, moral rules can draw our attention to features of particular cases that we would otherwise ignore. In part, this is true because they employ thick, morally consequential, descriptive words. Often, it is not a theoretical argument or a rigorous definition that causes us to change our minds about a concrete case, but the very use of a word like "discrimination." As such, rules and principles are not normally effective, because people can easily adjust them to fit their more specific prejudices. Think of all the Christians who have read the Sermon on the Mount, yet exploited and oppressed their African American neighbors—without any sense of dissonance. The Golden Rule is too vague to determine behavior.

We sometimes revise our judgments of particulars after we have applied abstract principles; but more typically, we change our minds when we hear other people describe the same concrete situations in different terms. This will not happen unless the procedures of discussion are reasonably fair—a topic to which I will return in chapter 2. For example, if some views are censored, or if some people are excluded from the conversation, then prejudiced judgments may go unchecked. Thus we need rules of procedural fairness, but they are not nearly stringent enough to generate a Theory of Justice.

When Rawls discusses intuitions, he means opinions about general rules; and many people have such opinions. For example, if someone asks me, "Do you think that motives matter, or consequences?" I will express a personal, intuitive preference for motives. Philosophers often rely on such general intuitions as a guide, since it is difficult to construct *arguments* for abstract metaethical positions. However, I am not sure that my own general intuitions have any clear or reliable relationship to my beliefs about particular cases. In real life, I find motives, consequences, characters, principles, and circumstances all relevant to varying degrees. Philosophical debates force me to choose among these approaches, but my choice hardly matters when I consider real problems, most of which are ambiguous, entangled with other cases, susceptible to multiple interpretations, and tinged with emotion.

Typically, philosophers examine hypothetical cases that can readily be addressed with moral theory, and that can be fully described in a few sentences.[98] These are the kinds of moral dilemmas that Lawrence Kohlberg, a psychologist who studied moral development, used to put before children and young adults. For example, he used to ask: Should a man steal a drug in order to save his wife's life, if he cannot afford it?[99] It does not make much difference in this case what kind of relationship the man has with his wife, what community they live in, what kind of person she is, or who the druggist is. The relevant details can be summarized very rapidly, and abstract principles (the inviolability of property, the sanctity of life, utility, etc.) can easily be tested against our intuitions.

Yet this is not the sort of situation that often arises in ordinary life, nor is it a very controversial case for mature adults. (Indeed, Kohlberg's conclusion is that all genuinely mature people favor stealing the drug. In such a schematic case, the value of life *clearly* trumps that of property.) On the other hand, the kinds of dilemmas that we actually face in ordinary life cannot be adequately summarized in a few sentences. Instead of comparing property against life in schematized, artificial situations, we typically face questions of the following type: Should I break up with my lover? Or marry her? How should I make my child happy and secure? What should I do about a troublesome employee?

These questions cannot be answered unless a great deal of context and detail is first provided; and even then it is extremely difficult to arrive at general principles on the basis of concrete judgments. Consequently, such questions are largely absent in philosophy books, but they are the mainstay of fiction, history, and poetry. This indicates, I think, that thick description and narrative are the relevant methods to use in addressing such issues, and that abstract theory is largely irrelevant. We may benefit from tentative generalizations and rules-of-thumb, but the discipline of moral philosophy promises much more ambitious methods and concepts. As such, it is not helpful—either as a source of practical guidance or as a component of moral education.

CHAPTER 2

AGREEMENT

THE IDEAL OF CONSENSUS

In the last chapter, I argued for a broad account of valid ethical argument that makes room not only for logical inferences but also for aspect-seeing, thick description, and narrative. On the other hand, there are also limits to what qualifies as an ethical argument; not just any method that produces agreement can be called moral. If I hope to persuade someone to do what I want, I can use threats or orders, and under the right circumstances, these methods would work. But no one would say that my approach was ethical. Whatever else they are, ethical arguments are attempts to persuade others without the use of coercion, deception, or intimidation; they are efforts to gain sincere, unforced agreement. Further, when we seek the uncoerced agreement of others, we cannot achieve success by merely stating our personal desires and interests; we must instead claim that the proposed action is in the common interest. Such claims are ethical; they deal with what "ought" to be done. If a proposed action only benefits me, and I want to persuade others to agree to it, then I must make a disinterested claim.

Needless to say, I may make a valid ethical argument, yet fail to achieve agreement because others are not interested in acting ethically. For example, I might say that something ought to be done, and others might respond that they simply do not *want* to do it. But in that case, they have failed to respond ethically. Although they may win the argument by gaining the most votes or otherwise achieving the result they desire, they will not be able to demonstrate that their position was right. If we want to know what view is ethical, then we must ask which position would gain agreement in a fair discussion that remained directed at achieving consensus.

This account of ethics describes the logic of ordinary sentences in which someone says, "We ought to do X," rather than simply demanding it or forcing others to do it. It is a pragmatic account, because it measures the ethical validity of a claim by its real effectiveness in gaining agreement under fair conditions.' Thus a pragmatist theory of ethics treats ethical validity as relative to practical success, but it requires practical success of a particular kind. The winners of a political struggle are often ethically wrong; all that their success "proves" is that they had the most power. But the winners of a fair discussion that remains focused on achieving consensus are ethically right, and right by definition.

For Kantians, an ethical claim must appeal to abstract duty, and not just to the interests and desires of all involved in a discussion. Rousseau argues, along similar lines, that citizens must listen only to reason, and not to their inclinations; that they must concern themselves exclusively with general rules, not particular facts or rights; and that they must collectively determine the general will, not the aggregate will of all.' Thus a valid ethical claim is one that says: "We ought to do X because it is right." On the other hand, according to Kant and Rousseau, it would be ethically invalid to say: "We ought to do X because we can all agree to it; it is in everyone's interest." But from a pragmatic perspective, an argument is just an effort at persuasion that works if it achieves agreement, and an ethical argument is one that achieves agreement without the use of force, deception, or intimidation. Therefore, it does not matter to a pragmatist whether an ethical argument relies on an abstract notion of duty or appeals to everyone's interests. But it *is* essential that we consult everyone who is going to be affected, that the discussion is conducted fairly, that information is freely made available, that conditions of equality obtain within the conversation, and that force of any kind is ruled out.

Efforts to persuade by means of disinterested claims are frequently combined with appeals to self-interest. Moreover, appeals to self-interest are often disguised as ethical claims. In many cases, we decide what we want, and then we make an argument for it that appears disinterested. However, such an argument is only likely to work if our self-interest happens to correspond to the common good (in which case, so much the better), or if the discussion is flawed by a lack of information, by deception or coercion, or by a shortage of time, skill, or effort. In such cases, we get away with making our self-interest *appear* to be the common good.

In real life, a few institutions (such as juries and Quaker meetings) require consensus as a condition for action, but these are exceptional. Most policies are decided without unanimous consent, for the following reasons. First, a requirement to achieve consensus does not serve the interests of people who have more than average power: they would rather dictate policy to their fellow citizens. Since power is distributed unequally, the ideal of consensus often has powerful enemies. But this just means that it cannot be made the guiding principle without a struggle.

A more fundamental problem arises when children, animals, or the mentally disabled are involved. It is unclear exactly which creatures are morally competent; but most kindergarten teachers (for instance) would not seek their students' unanimous consent before establishing a curriculum. Nor do we ask dogs to assent to house-training. On the other hand, many societies have excluded women from moral deliberation, claiming that only men are competent to think about such important matters. So clearly the boundary of a moral community can be set in a wrong place—with terrible results. But this does not mean that there should be no limits at all. And since many of our important moral decisions affect small children or other creatures who lack the ability to deliberate competently, we often must act without consensus.

A third problem is that the ideal of consensus can violate norms of diversity and pluralism. If a whole community reaches consensus, then many individuals must have joined a single conversation and reached the same conclusion. This is easy if everyone in the group thinks alike; but people actually differ greatly in values, interests, and even styles of argument. To force them to participate in a single conversation with one agenda and one set of rules may be the only way to create consensus—yet it often requires coercion, which violates the consensus principle. Thus Iris Marion Young argues: "The ideal of the civic public exhibits a will to unity, and necessitates the exclusion of aspects of human existence that threaten to disperse the brotherly unity of straight and upright forms, especially the exclusion of women." In a truly inclusive public, she writes, "consensus and sharing may not always be the goal, but the recognition and appreciation of differences, in the context of confrontation with power."[3] I believe that my account of valid argument is expansive enough to include stereotypically feminine—or feminist—modes of discussion. But Young's general point holds: the search for consensus requires everyone to play by common rules; and even if these rules are highly flexible and tolerant, some people may feel excluded.

In any case, if we require consensus as a condition for action, this does not mean that people will attempt in good faith to achieve unanimous consent. Those participants who are satisfied with the status quo may filibuster, refusing to accept any change of policy. They will have an arbitrary advantage over their opponents who seek change. Similarly, juries must deliberate until they reach unanimous verdicts. Nevertheless, a particular juror can abandon efforts to persuade his colleagues or to listen to their arguments—as long as he does not mind a mistrial. In other situations, people who have abundant time or resources may refuse to deliberate in good faith, knowing that their opponents will have to surrender first. Thus to require consensus can have perverse results: it can produce agreements that do not actually satisfy some parties.

Finally, it takes a long time for most groups to reach consensus, even if they sincerely want to deliberate toward a common position. Given this practical constraint, no society or organization of any complexity can resolve all of its controversies by reaching consensus.

In the absence of consensus, one option is simply to accept disagreement—and this is perfectly acceptable in many cases. For example, people who have chosen one career can often agree with their colleagues about the basic values that their profession embodies. But we do not expect *everyone* in society to deliberate together until they agree that one career is the best of all, because it embodies the very highest values. In all likelihood, they would never reach consensus, because no one vocation *is* the best. If I have the ability to select my career, then I should choose it only after serious deliberation; but I can still be a pluralist about such matters, conceding that there is no one correct choice for everyone.

If friends find themselves unable to agree about an issue, they can stop discussing it. When a voluntary association fails to reach consensus, it can peacefully disband. But certain kinds of disputes cannot be left unresolved, because they affect everyone. If we do not reach consensus about such matters as the proper distribution of wealth in society, then some people will be left unhappy and will only comply under coercion. Thus, for example, we must often employ the coercive power of the judicial system to settle conflicts among individuals. Similarly, democratic societies that cannot agree about important social and economic questions sometimes resolve them with votes— either referenda or bills passed by elected legislatures. And people who refuse either to accept or to debate widely accepted norms sometimes resort to disobedience: a coercive tactic that may incite a coercive response from the state.

These uses of power are necessary because consensus is a utopian ideal. But we prefer consensus to coercion, so we call power "legitimate" only insofar as it approximates the results of a genuine agreement. For example, a government that answers to the majority of voters does not produce consensus, but at least it satisfies many people; and if we limit its power by granting minorities explicit rights, then we can prevent the excesses of majority tyranny. Experience teaches us what procedures best approximate the results of discussions in which everyone really seeks consensus, without resorting to force or filibusters.

Instead of achieving consensus, tolerating disagreement, or allowing the government to settle disputes coercively, we could turn to the market. Market mechanisms are capable of deciding how various objects and activities should be valued and distributed, whether they should be saved or consumed, and what people should produce with their labor—all questions of great moral importance. Furthermore, the market is highly efficient and rational, at least under certain definitions of "rationality." But market mechanisms often produce different results from those that deliberating citizens would choose if they reached consensus. This is true, first of all, because people enter the market arena with varying amounts of wealth. Markets operate on the principle of one dollar, one vote, thereby serving the interests of the wealthy to a disproportionate degree. Thus poor people are not likely to accept market outcomes unless obedience to the market is coerced.

Furthermore, even if everyone can bid the same amount at first, wealth tends to accumulate over time when market mechanisms are allowed to operate freely. And even if property somehow remains equally distributed, the logic of a market differs in important ways from that of consensus-seeking deliberation. For example, I might argue that no one should use a particular chemical that harms natural ecosystems, and perhaps I could persuade everyone else to agree with me. But if the chemical is available for sale, then I may purchase it despite my misgivings, knowing that my tiny consumption of this substance has negligible effects on the environment, whereas my decision to forego it would be a meaningless sacrifice. Everyone else may act in the same way, even though they would all agree to a binding resolution to ban production of the chemical. Our aggregate patterns of production and consumption frequently produce results that we would not support in a public discussion.[4]

In a public forum where the aim is to seek consensus, people speak (albeit sometimes hypocritically) about the common good or general principles of fairness and desert. As long as the discussion is fair and open, there is a good chance that the strongest argument can prevail. But in a market system, no one has the opportunity to articulate general principles. Instead, individuals act to maximize private utility. Thus it is not surprising that public deliberation and market transactions produce significantly different results (or that wealthy people often prefer market outcomes to democratic decisions).

To summarize the argument so far: Consensus is a sufficient test of truth and a normative ideal. But it is impractical because of external constraints and internal paradoxes. The three major alternatives to consensus—disagreement, coercion, and the market—are morally inferior, but necessary because we cannot consistently act with unanimous consent. The question, then, is how to achieve consensus as often and as widely as possible.

This is partly a political matter. People make decisions every day about whether to pursue consensus or to use coercive methods. For example, I can either try to resolve a dispute through discussion, or I can resort to violence.

Assuming that the latter option is blocked, I can still sue my opponents. Similarly, I can either argue with my fellow citizens about moral principles, or else try to force a vote in Congress. Thus police departments, courts, legislatures, and similar institutions can make a great deal of difference to me as I decide whether or not to seek consensus. If, for example, lawsuits are won most of the time by the most expensive lawyers, then wealthy people will often litigate instead of discussing their differences privately. Similarly, if the better funded political candidate almost always wins elections—and if private interests can underwrite election campaigns—then there is not much incentive for wealthy people to deliberate fairly. Thus such matters as civil procedure and campaign financing partly determine how much consensus can be achieved in a society as a whole. The more fair we make our political processes, the more deliberation can occur outside of formal politics.[5]

We must also decide which issues are subject to consideration by courts and legislatures. For example, the separation between church and state has been justified, in part, as a way to encourage public deliberation about spiritual matters.[6] If Congress could "establish" one religion, then the sect with the greatest power might try to settle questions of faith in the political arena. The establishment clause, however, prevents government intervention in religion, thus forcing people to try to *persuade* their fellow citizens about religious truth. Americans will only belong to a single religion if they happen to reach spiritual consensus, so successful religious rhetoric must seek voluntary agreement. People cannot threaten their religious opponents; they must instead argue that everyone should believe as they do, giving reasons for their position.

In short, barriers to government intervention can leave space for public deliberation and the search for consensus. Civil libertarians use this reasoning to support freedom of religion and expression; but some conservatives apply the same argument in the economic arena. Claiming to oppose coercion, they try to ban economic regulation and limit plaintiffs' ability to file civil lawsuits. But if the government and courts cannot intervene in the economic realm, then there will be a strong bias toward the status quo—even if it is unpopular—since a perfect public consensus is virtually impossible to achieve. (Indeed, the separation of church and state prevents rapid change in spiritual matters, much to the distress of religious partisans who want to enforce their will on other people.) In general, if we permit regulatory action by the state, we encourage people to resolve their differences coercively, not to seek consensus. But if we block government action, then we arbitrarily favor the status quo—serving only some people's interests. Thus state institutions should be carefully designed to maximize the possibility of real consensus without preventing innovation.

The ideal of consensus also imposes a positive obligation: to create forums in which people can discuss moral issues freely and on an equal basis.

Such forums do not come into being automatically. Although people some-times talk seriously with strangers in casual situations, constructive discussions usually require institutional support. In particular, the institutions of civil society—schools, clubs and fraternal organizations, churches, mosques, and synagogues—are valuable sites for dialogue. These organizations are not always tolerant, open, or egalitarian; but at their best they can provide the spaces in which true consensus is built. Unfortunately, civil society is regularly threatened by both government and market institutions, so it must be deliberately cultivated and protected.

CONSENSUS AND MORAL THEORY

If consensus can be obstructed by unfair political processes and a weak civil society, it can be hindered just as seriously by an excessive reliance on moral philosophy. Moral theories often make claims about truth that are not subject to verification. Thus, when people differ in their philosophical commitments, their debates almost always end in stalemate.

For example, if a proponent of abortion rights and an opponent of abortion are motivated by contrasting opinions about the status of the fetus, then there may be no way to mediate this conflict. A fetus may be a person with potential to grow into an adult, or it may be a potential person, not yet bearing rights. Personhood is not an empirical concept that can be identified in a laboratory; it is a metaphysical idea. And since metaphysical ideas are not subject to verification, a genuine impasse may result. In fact, I am inclined to think that any statement about the point at which personhood begins is meaningless, because it is not subject to constructive debate; and this means that the question of abortion is one for which there is no philosophical answer.

However, we could discuss the morality of particular abortions without deciding the metaphysical status of abortion in general. In that case, we would reject the claim that abortion is always wrong (since it is murder), for this belief is based upon the metaphysical theory that the fetus, although it does not look or act like a human being, nevertheless has a human identity. Similarly, we would reject the theory that abortion is always completely unproblematic—just like an appendectomy—for this view seems to arise from the equally metaphysical idea that (since a fetus is *not* a human being) it is just a valueless mass of tissue. Indeed, we would avoid making any moral judgment whatsoever about abortion *in general*—for each abortion is different. We would only assume that terminating a pregnancy is usually a matter for serious reflection.

One could argue that only a woman who is actually considering an abortion has the right to judge it morally. I believe that "moral standing" has to be considered case by case: someone who judges his neighbors' private behavior may be nosy or presumptuous, but someone who doesn't care about a close friend's moral choices enough to assess them may be callous. It all depends upon the circumstances. In any event, a woman who is considering abortion requires a method of moral judgment, and concrete description will do the job. On one theory, even she has no duty even to reflect about abortion, for the fetus completely lacks moral significance; but this seems to violate our intuitions about the seriousness of conception. For example, if someone has a miscarriage, no one would tell her that she has simply lost a mass of tissue that she can replace in a few months.

On the basis of the rather minimal assumption that abortion is a weighty matter, we could try to judge individual cases according to their particular circumstances. If we knew a full story about the conditions under which a woman had become pregnant, her options, her plans, and her motivations, then we could defend a thick description of her abortion. For instance, to abort might be a courageous act if the pregnancy were coerced or accidental and the woman wanted to terminate it in order to protect a defensible plan of life. (Imagine, for example, that she had a worthwhile career, involving an element of service to others, which a child would interrupt; and that she doubted her ability to be an excellent mother.) At the opposite extreme, a couple might choose to forgo contraception for mere reasons of convenience, and then the woman might have an abortion because she wanted to delay pregnancy until a more convenient time. In the latter case, the couple's actions would reveal a certain carelessness and frivolity.[7]

Of course, there would be many cases lying between these two extremes, each of which would have to be judged individually. Since it would be impossible to judge such cases according to rules, it would be unwise to make abortion a matter for laws and governments to regulate. But the possibility of moral consensus remains open as long as participants agree to discuss particular cases in their immediate contexts, using "thick" terms to describe them. As soon as someone insists on applying moral theories to general categories—especially ones, such as "human life," that are clearly metaphysical—agreement becomes impossible. Thus moral theory is the enemy of consensus; and our duty as participants in democratic deliberation is to attend to particular cases.

MORAL RELATIVISM

A more fundamental problem for the consensus ideal is presented by some versions of moral relativism. I have argued that we often make and defend moral judgments by "thickly" describing particular facts, and that agreement about such judgments is a sufficient test of truth. But it is remarkable how variously people can view the same facts. For example, in 1993, a

German anti-fascist group created a documentary—consisting only of speeches by Nazis—that was intended to show Nazism as a palpable evil. But the film became a popular recruiting device for neo-Nazi organizers, who obviously saw its thick descriptions differently. Examples like this have persuaded some people to believe that ethical judgments are relative and that rational consensus is impossible.

To say that moral judgments are "relative" implies that they are relative *to* something. They could, for example, arise automatically from our personal experiences, so that people with different backgrounds would inevitably disagree, and no moral consensus could ever emerge. Indeed, if a woman who had been sexually harassed and a man who had been accused of harassment both read the transcript of *Harris v. Forklift Systems*, they might well judge the facts differently. More subtly, people's beliefs about gender roles, industrial workers and managers, and feminists might color their responses to the case; and in general the opinions of women and men might be quite different. If we could rely on moral theory, then we might hope for ethical judgments that did not involve bias. However, absent theory, there can be no neutral, perspectiveless judgment of a particular case.

Yet this skeptical point should not be pushed too far. Even if our prior experiences somewhat affect our interpretations of concrete facts, the facts also have power to move us, especially when they are presented in coherent narrative form. To the extent that people allow generalizations to color their judgments, they are prone to bias; and we cannot completely avoid generalizing. Further, when we consider someone else's story, we sometimes fasten onto analogies from our own lives that may not be entirely relevant or typical. This is especially likely when our experiences have been traumatic, which is why sexual harassment victims and perpetrators might make poor jurors in a harassment case. But—to varying but significant degrees—most of us can attend to the particularities of other people's stories, assuming that we choose to do so.

We can also imagine, more or less accurately, how we—or those close to us—would feel in similar situations. For example, many employees of Forklift Systems, Inc. testified that their boss's sexist statements were just inoffensive jokes. However, "David Thompson, a former employee of Defendant, testified that he would not tolerate Charles Hardy talking to his wife as Charles Hardy talked to Teresa Harris at Forklift."[8] Apparently, the thought-experiment of imagining his wife in Harris's place helped Thompson to focus on the reality of her situation.

The federal magistrate in *Harris* acknowledged that people would respond to alleged acts of harassment differently, depending upon their background expectations and moral beliefs. For example, he wrote, most women employees understood Hardy's statements as ordinary jokes—but Harris, "as a management employee, was more sensitive to these comments than clerical employees, who it appears were conditioned to accept denigrating treatment."[9] It is possible that the magistrate was simply wrong about the clerical workers' reaction; even though they had left Forklift, they might still be afraid to testify against Charles Hardy. In any case, "conditioning" should not be understood as a mechanical process: moral judgments don't emerge automatically from people's backgrounds. Certainly, "conditioning" is not irreversible. Once the clerical employees at Forklift saw a former colleague win a Supreme Court case against their boss for sexual harassment, they may have begun to scrutinize behavior that once seemed normal or inevitable. If so, they would have benefitted from the broader sense of possibilities that Harris enjoyed as a middle-class woman.

Thus the insight that people are influenced by their background experiences does not mean that they are immune to testimony, or mechanically "conditioned" to respond in any particular way. However, another form of moral relativism suggests that people who belong to different *cultures* cannot reach moral consensus, because our cultural identity determines our responses to particular cases. But "culture" can be defined in many ways, and only some definitions lead to moral relativism. For example, if a culture is a perspective from which we view the world—a *Weltanschauung*—then everything must appear differently to people who have different vantage points. In that case, it would be impossible to persuade someone from an alien culture to join us in making a particular moral judgment, because such judgments would be relative to the viewers' perspective. Only by destroying cultural difference could we create consensus. But I see no reason to assume that all members of a culture always view every situation from the same inevitable vantage point. The variability and flexibility of our perspectives is shown by the fact we see things differently at different times; and sometimes we can *choose* how to see them. Besides, many people belong to several cultures at once. And even within each culture, points-of-view vary—sometimes so greatly that it is difficult to assign individuals to a particular culture with any certainty. Therefore, I suggest that the metaphor of culture as a perspective is misleading.

Similarly, if cultures are interpreted as collections of axiomatic beliefs and principles, then rational debate may appear impossible, because people from different backgrounds will presuppose different axioms. This theory assumes that particular judgments are relative to implicit, abstract generalizations. Indeed, some cultures endorse abstract theories, some of which are openly metaphysical. For instance, Catholicism can perhaps be called a culture, and the Catholic Church espouses the doctrine of the Trinity, the immortality of souls, the Immaculate Conception, and so forth. But the fact that some cultures endorse metaphysical theories does not show that all concrete judgments emerge from such abstract premises, nor are cultures mere collections of axioms.

Wittgenstein offers a better metaphor to understand the building-blocks of culture: "language-games," which are sets of more or less precise rules that guide us when we communicate. For instance, when Teresa Harris testified in court, she tried to show that she was extremely upset because of her employer's actions. If she convinced the magistrate about her past emotional state, then (she thought) he would have to declare Hardy's actions "sexual harassment." These were the rules of the language-game as she understood them. She simultaneously participated in many other games. For instance, when she said, "I cried all the time," she followed the rule that the subject belongs before the verb in an English sentence. At the same time, she alluded to the game in which we sympathize when we see tears.

A "culture" is a large set of such language-games. Whenever people say or do anything, they participate in many games at once. Altogether, we know how to play "countless" games; and "this multiplicity is not something fixed, given once for all; but new types of language, new language-games . . . come into existence, and others become obsolete and get forgotten." When two language-games seem to conflict, we can often devise new ones to bridge the gap. As a result of this process, which is repeated endlessly throughout history, "[o]ur language can be seen as an ancient city: a maze of little streets and squares, of old and new houses, and of houses with additions from various periods; and this surrounded by a multitude of new boroughs with straight regular streets and uniform houses."[10] If Wittgenstein is correct, then a "culture" is not a homogeneous, distinct entity that determines our thoughts and judgments, but rather a vaguely bordered, loosely structured, constantly evolving set of conventions. In a sense, everyone belongs to a different culture, since everyone is familiar with a somewhat different set of language-games. Under these conditions, cultural difference does not block communication, although people who want to communicate across great cultural distance must be creative and patient.

A third version of moral relativism suggests that people use phrases such as "sexual harassment" in different ways, and there is no way to settle disputes in such cases. Thus, for example, R. W. Beardsmore writes: "When an action is defended or condemned by characterizing it as integrity, greed, adultery, suicide, and so on, we are usually forced to conclude that an ultimate justification has been offered. [Such concepts] bring the chain of reasons given in an argument to an end."[11] To call something "adultery" simply is to condemn it. However, we know that such words are used differently by different people: for instance, suicide is a sin within Catholic morality, but an act of courage for ancient Stoics and Japanese samurai. Even adultery might be a good thing for a troubadour, singing of courtly love. According to Beardsmore, a word like "suicide" gains its moral coloration solely from its cultural context. So, for a Catholic, "it would be quite superfluous . . . to add that this action is wrong. Suicide is one of the ways in which a Catholic can do wrong."[12] A collection of such basic, morally laden words constitutes a "morality," of which Catholicism is one example.[13] Between distinct moralities, there can be no argument.

But it is not true that a Catholic must cease arguing when someone else (say, a member of the Hemlock Society) disagrees that suicide is wrong. The Catholic's language is not "merely relative" to his or her moral scheme, so that no one outside the Church could possibly come to agree with its position. On the contrary, Catholics can characterize suicide as a desecration of God's creation, a sign of cowardice or despair, an act of reckless abandonment, and so on. Some of these thick descriptions rely on factual claims (e.g., God created us); others take agreed-upon facts and set them in particular social or narrative contexts; but none necessarily brings the argument to an end. And while the Catholic discusses the sin of despair in the context of a narrative of redemption, his opponent can redescribe suicide as an act of freedom or dignity. They may never reach agreement, but their differing moral outlooks do not prevent them from arguing rationally about particular cases.

Wittgenstein argues that statements are only intelligible as part of language-games, and that particular language-games can only exist in specific cultural or social settings. Thus, like Beardsmore and other relativists, Wittgenstein recognizes the role of context in shaping our moral judgments. But he understands context in a way that does not lead to moral relativism. For him, the crucial term is a "form of life," which is the environment in which a language-game functions.[14] Again, an example can show what he means. Teresa Harris's case against Forklift Systems passed through several stages of appeal until at last it reached the Supreme Court. The higher courts had to resolve one basic question: What criterion should be used to assess allegations of harassment? In other words, they had to select a language-game to play. For example, is a woman harassed if she feels so distressed by sexual behavior that she cannot do her work? Can she claim harassment only if a reasonable person in her position would feel equally upset? Should the standard be the reaction of a reasonable *woman*, rather than a reasonable person? Or should the court simply determine what behavior is so obnoxious as to create a hostile workplace, regardless of anyone's subjective reaction to it? Each of these approaches was proposed during the appeals process.

Wittgenstein shows that the answer to this question is not a factual one. No language-game is more true to the real definition of "harassment" than any other, but each inhabits a different social context or form of life. For instance, if plaintiffs must only show that their distress is genuine, then highly sensitive people will prevail relatively easily in harassment lawsuits. Indeed, it will be impossible to show that any plaintiff is *unduly* sensitive. Thus sexual harassment lawsuits will be common and often successful (although women who happen to have very thick skins will rarely be able to show that they were harassed). As a result, behavior in the workplace will change dramatically—whether for good or ill.

If, instead, the relevant criterion is the response of a "reasonable person," then courts must decide how such a person would respond. For one thing, they will have to ask whether reasonable people tolerate behavior that is customarily accepted. Acceptance of prevailing conditions could be taken as evidence of reasonableness—but that approach would protect obnoxious behavior as long as it was common. Choosing to consider the reasonable *person*'s response to alleged harassment, instead of concentrating on the reasonable victim, also has social consequences. Men's conceptions of acceptable behavior may differ markedly from those of women who have been harassed. Thus one judge wrote: "Unless the perspective of the reasonable victim is adopted, courts . . . [will] sustain ingrained notions of reasonable behavior fashioned by the offenders, in this case, men."[15] Finally, courts could ignore victims' responses altogether and simply decide what environments they considered "hostile." In that case, some women would be harassed even though their employers' behavior never actually bothered them.[16]

Each of these language-games works: it leads courts to ask questions for which there are fairly precise answers. Each game also contributes to a different society—one that is more or less adaptable, egalitarian, and litigious. Finally, each game would produce different results in different social contexts. For example, what is "reasonable" changes over time. Thus, as Wittgenstein tells us, games belong within broader "forms of life." We can argue about which context, which *Lebensform*, we prefer, but not by showing that one corresponds more closely to the true definition of Justice. Rather, if we do not like a society, then we must thickly describe it as sexist, litigious, puritanical, or unfair. Such descriptions help to guide us as we select which language-game to use; and the language-game we use tells us how to define "harassment." Thus there is no philosophical answer to the question "What is harassment?" But there are political answers—best supported by thick descriptions—which can lead over time to consensus.

PHILOSOPHY AND LIBERATION

In defense of philosophy, it is often said that any culture's traditional stories may promote prejudice, constrain choice, and prevent change, whereas philosophical doctrine is liberating. Moreover, unless we can attain a detached perspective by reflecting theoretically, we may be unable to invent *new* stories that challenge the prejudices of our culture. In a chapter entitled "The Necessity of Platonism," Eric Havelock argues that Plato opposed oral poetry because it encouraged listeners to identify too deeply with tragic heroes. Poetry since Homer "had merged the personality [of both heroes and listeners] with the tradition, and made self-conscious separation from it impossible." Socrates began philosophy by asking "the poets what their poems said. The poets are his victims because in their keeping reposes the Greek cultural tradition. . . . Here was the tribal encyclopedia, and to ask what it was saying amounted to a demand that it be said differently, non-poetically, non-rhythmically, and non-imagistically."[17]

As well as interrogating the keepers of traditional values, philosophers can also apply principles (such as freedom or equality) with radical effects, sweeping away all beliefs that serve the status quo. When we think of this kind of critique, we may recall Socrates, rejecting myth and dying for his conscience; or Luther, nailing his incendiary theses to the cathedral door; or Marx, criticizing bourgeois society from the transcendent position provided by dialectic.

But if Socrates was a leading force in the "enlightenment" of fifth-century Athens, so was his rival, Protagoras. According to legend, both men were prosecuted on the same charge: impiety. Even if this isn't literally true, Protagoras did criticize traditional stories and political arrangements; he was a religious skeptic and a democrat. Similarly, Erasmus agreed with Luther about the need for civil and ecclesiastical reform, although he refused to leave the Catholic Church. And Martin Luther King Jr. achieved more liberation in the United States than any Marxist critic. Protagoras, Erasmus, and King were not philosophers: they were quintessential humanists, skeptical about theory, but willing to use stories and rhetoric strategically against the prejudices and institutions of their time. They adopted traditional myths selectively, and they made up their own fables with satirical and subversive effects.

Thus there are at least two routes to liberation: philosophy and humanism. In favor of philosophy, we can cite its conceptual radicalism, its ability to cast aside all beliefs except those that comport with some fundamental principle, such as Socrates' logic, Luther's conscience, or Marx's dialectical materialism. But there are also points to be made against philosophy as a critical tool. The same stringent reasoning that can so easily discredit the status quo may also undermine subversive arguments. It is very difficult to develop political methods, to design social alternatives, or to tell liberating stories that meet the tests of theory. Therefore, pure philosophers find it hard to create positive political programs, especially ones that can appeal to broad constituencies. Bernard Williams writes:

> Theory looks characteristically for considerations that are very general and have as little distinctive content as possible, because it is trying to systematize and because it wants to represent as many reasons as possible as applications of other reasons. But critical reflection should

> seek for as much shared understanding as it can find on
> any issue, and use any ethical material that, in the context
> of the reflective discussion, makes some sense and
> commands some loyalty. . . . Theory typically uses the
> assumption that we probably have too many ethical ideas,
> some of which may turn out to be mere prejudices. Our
> major problem now is actually that we have not too many
> but too few, and we need to cherish as many as we can.[18]

If we have relatively few ethical ideas today, it is partly because critical theorists have unmasked most of the traditional ones as ungrounded. This is not necessarily a route to liberation, because some inherited stories and moral judgments are critical and subversive.

Because of his logical rigor, Socrates probably had no positive views at all, just a critique of inherited dogma. Luther had no grounds for criticizing injustice, unless an institution or belief happened to violate his principles of personal religious conscience and "faith alone." Indeed, he supported the German nobility in their ruthless suppression of the peasant revolt, and he promoted anti-Semitism. Protagoras and Erasmus, on the other hand, were skeptical about moral theory, but Protagoras advised Pericles and wrote democratic constitutions; Erasmus satirized war, advocated peaceful dialogue with Islam, and promoted education for women and the poor. These were radical positions in their time.

Michael Walzer explicitly rejects Martin Luther as a critical hero, observing that he was "brutal and intolerant." But Walzer draws a more general conclusion: "I want to deny that the critical enterprise is best understood with reference to its heroic moments." It is possible, he argues, to condemn greed, cruelty, lust, and oppression by devising a "correct ideological position"—theoretically justified, comprehensive, and universal in its application. This can be done, however, "only in a minimalist way, responding to the grossest and most offensive injustices. But critics also respond to ordinary injustice, and they respond in detail, thickly and idiomatically. . . . [We] ought to understand this effort less by analogy with what philosophers do than by analogy with what poets, novelists, artists, and architects do." Vernacular criticism is "an activity of the many, not the special task of the few"; and it is often more effective than "high philosophical or theological argument."[19]

Williams and Walzer hint at a final complaint. Philosophers who manage to design positive programs of their own are often schismatic and doctrinaire. This is because their principles—being clear and rigorous—support limited outcomes. For example, although Socrates had no positive program, his student Plato drew the blueprint of a totalitarian state, managed by properly instructed philosophers. By the same token, there is much in

Marx's method that leads to dogmatism, even though Marxists are not *necessarily* doctrinaire. Absolute skepticism and narrow dogmatism are not the only outcomes that can result from theoretical reflection: some philosophers adopt more moderate methodologies or find reasons in favor of pluralism. Still, these are perennial dangers, and humanism avoids them.

DEMOCRACY OR THE MARKET?

I have argued that differences in background and culture make agreement difficult, but they do not block it altogether. However, some people object to the ideal of consensus on different grounds. A true consensus is a meeting of the minds, achieved in a fair and equal discussion. Jürgen Habermas links this concept to democracy:

> [T]here is one form of political decision-making according to which all decisions are supposed to be made equally dependent on a consensus arrived at in a discussion free from domination—the democratic form. Here the principle of public discourse is supposed to eliminate all force other than that of the better argument, and majority decisions are held to be only a substitute for the uncompelled consensus that would finally result if discussion did not always have to be broken off owing to the need for a decision.[20]

Habermas (along with John Dewey) has inspired a school of political philosophers who defend democracy *epistemically*: they claim that democratic procedures produce a kind of (normative) knowledge that is not available by any other means.[21] But this school has been attacked by theorists who believe that market exchange, not democratic debate, is the mechanism by which all values are established. Barbara Herrnstein Smith, for example, is eloquent in her condemnation of Habermas as a utopian dreamer. Habermas's theory, she writes, is "quite sublime (and, as such, apparently necessary to ground his view of the alternate possibilities of human society) but also quite empty."[22] His approach, she says:

> reflects what appears to be a more general recurrent impulse to dream an escape from economy, . . . to create by invocation some place apart from the marketplace—a kingdom, garden, island, perhaps, or a plane of consciousness, form of social relationship, or stage of human development—where the dynamics of economy are . . . altogether suspended, abolished, or reversed.

Herrnstein Smith recognizes the moral advantages of democratic debate over market exchange: for example, citizens in a democracy are roughly equal, whereas the market operates on a principle of one dollar, one vote. However, she calls the market "inescapable."[23] On her theory, material goods, status, glory, comfort, art, and even "terms divine" are all exchangeable and constantly exchanged in a process of barter that establishes all forms of value.[24] "For," she argues, "we always live in a market."[25] She parodies "humanist" critics of the market (who want to treat democracy, art, and love as sequestered from economic exchange), calling them "the counterparts of the priestly agents of any society who preside over the demarcation of spheres of value, establish the classification of certain objects as sacred, and protect them from the forces of 'nature.'"[26]

A similar model has been employed to explain many forms of discourse and evaluation: for example, Lars Engle reads Shakespeare's sonnets as an effort to raise the market value of the poet's beloved.[27] If Herrnstein Smith and others are correct that the market mechanism is universal and inevitable, then their theory has several important consequences for ethics. First, it means that Habermas's goal of fairness is more or less utopian: wealth and power will always dominate, and no value-judgments are ever legitimate in Habermas's sense. Whenever anyone values anything (a legal right, a painting, another human being), this is always the result of market forces. Even when poor people value things, they still think in language that has resulted from past economic exchanges, all of which were influenced by wealth and power. Thus there is no such thing as an authentic (let alone an objective) evaluation.

Second, Herrnstein Smith's theory makes democratic debate super-fluous. A democratic model suggests that people must deliberate in common about values that pertain to the public sphere. However, if everything—material goods as well as love, beauty, truth, status, and rights—has a market price, then aggregate utility or average utility can be maximized without public participation in politics. (The ideal mechanism for utility-maximization might be a free market, a panel of experts, a computer algorithm, or a regulated market; but it is unlikely to be a public debate.) Meanwhile, on a personal level, people can make rational choices that maximize their own totals of status, happiness, love, and so on. If, on the other hand, such diverse values are not mutually commensurable, then no rational measuring method can make moral decisions for a community—nor for a human being. If some things have no price, then people will have to *discuss* how to organize their common lives. Instead of calculation, they can perhaps use rhetoric to describe admirable individuals and societies, showing that good people and communities possess diverse values in harmonious proportion. Thus, if Herrnstein Smith is wrong, democracy and rhetoric are indispensable; but if she is right, then a so-called democracy is really just a screen for market forces, and rhetoric is the mere offering of a bid in a universal market wherein everything has a price.

Long before Barbara Herrnstein Smith, Adam Smith asserted that commodity exchange—or "the propensity to truck, barter, and exchange one thing for another"—was "common to all men."[28] Some modern economists have gone so far as to say that the exchange of commodities, aimed at maximizing participants' utility, is an *a priori* principle of all social systems, whose presence or absence cannot be shown by observation.[29] Like these neoclassical economists, Herrnstein Smith considers the universality of markets to be axiomatic. However, it is not at all clear that every existing system for making evaluations really is an exchange-market. Indeed, among anthropologists, there is a lively debate between "formalists" (who assert that all social systems are formally markets) and "substantivists" (who treat markets as just one cultural structure among others).[30]

Foreign and Western examples are offered to support both the formalist and substantivist positions. For instance, substantivists assert that in the Trobriand Islands of the Western Pacific, home of the Massim people, a principle of gift-giving replaces that of exchange.[31] Within a Massim village, each man is responsible for providing for his sister's or mother's husband's family, *gratis*, and another group of in-laws provides for him.[32] In addition, on a very large scale throughout the islands, men provide various objects to each other as gifts, especially certain necklaces and bracelets which are highly prized. Each type of jewelry moves around the islands in only one direction, and there is no direct exchange of equivalent goods, although everyone can expect to receive valuables in due course. The tokens are in constant motion, because holding them for a long time gives one a bad reputation.[33] The fact that no exchange occurs is stressed by the participants, who know what barter is because they barter certain other goods.[34]

If this practice (called Kula) were fundamentally a system of commodity exchange, then there would have to be a means of enforcing contracts, or people would give each other smaller gifts than they received until the average value of all gifts approached zero.[35] Furthermore, the Massim cannot be motivated by mere economic utility, since their system of gift exchange involves great labor and danger (they must travel long distances on the open sea in canoes), yet the net result of the exchanges is the uncoerced redistribution of objects, some of which have no practical purpose.

Attempts have been made to assess the Kula as a disguised market, in which *status* is exchanged for material goods of equivalent value.[36] But Kula gifts are ranked, such that big necklaces and bracelets "trump" small necklaces and bracelets, which "trump" whalebone spatulae, which "trump" yams. That means that no number of small bracelets can ever reciprocate for a gift of one large necklace; they do not have a price, since a price is a value-ratio between two commodities.[37] This system of ranking is standard in non-commodity systems; Claude Lévi-Strauss even understood marriage as a gift of the highest-ranked offering: a woman.[38] In order to assimilate ranking systems to the market mechanism, we would have to posit an extremely high—but never acknowledged—price for some goods.

The Kula may seem exotic, but in fact it closely resembles our own tradition of giving gifts to each other on birthdays. Like the Massim, we expect to get comparable gifts from those to whom we dispense presents, but there is no mechanism of coercion, nor is there a direct hand-to-hand exchange or a public reckoning of the gifts' relative value. If participants were simply trying to maximize their wealth, then they would not participate at all or at best they would try to give less than they received, resulting in a collapse of the system. In fact, there are several reasons why gifts are "redundant" from the perspective of pure economic utility: in many cases, they are chosen so that they will be seen as non-utilitarian; they often bring no benefit to the recipient since he or she has had no hand in choosing them; and frequently they give *no one* any net benefit since they are reciprocal.[39] Joel Waldfogel, an economist, has calculated that gifts exchanged in the United States every year are "worth" $4 billion less to their recipients than their market price, because people do not particularly like or need the goods that are chosen for them.[40] But the money-value of a gift is not supposed to be calculated by the recipient. Indeed, the sphere of gift-exchange in our culture is carefully distinguished from that of money-exchange. While we have to buy many of the things that we offer as gifts, it is considered rude to sell them once received. Similarly, while we might reciprocate for a dinner invitation by giving a dinner party of our own, we would not offer money in return. In some other societies, one-way exchanges and differentiated spheres of exchange are central, whereas in our market-dominated society they are relatively peripheral.[41]

Of course, a formalist can describe gift-exchange as a market process in which status or love is traded for material goods of equal value. Indeed, Herrnstein Smith, following Pierre Bourdieu, interprets gifts just this way.[42] The flexibility of her economic metaphor suggests that the substantivist and formalist positions may be more like languages than theories. A language, such as French, can be used to state many propositions as well as their precise opposites, so in itself it is neither provable nor refutable. A theory, on the other hand, is subject to being tested against evidence. Since it appears that both formalists and substantivists can describe any conceivable phenomenon in their own language, their accounts are unfalsifiable, and neither can be endorsed as more true than the other. If, for example, in a certain society, no one *ever* trades land for labor, or even conceives of such an idea, then a formalist can simply describe this situation as the result of an extremely high transaction cost imposed by the culture. If people would rather die than sell their land, then the formalist can conclude that they have put a higher money-value on land than on life. On the other hand, if one day the entire world became thoroughly committed to a unified market mechanism, then substantivists still would not have to concede that everything had "really" been a commodity all along.

Despite the fact that neither language can be refuted, each has different ramifications for ethics. As noted above, a formalist account, which describes everything as a market, encourages us to address moral questions by trying to maximize the aggregate value of "commodities" (including love, gifts, freedom, etc.); but this is impossible if some things are not subject to exchange. Indeed, gifts, works of art, love, titles of nobility, and political rights all have evident value in some contexts, but we do not normally understand them as commodities. If we did, then they would cease to exit for all practical purposes. For example, we define gifts partly in contrast to market exchanges, claiming that they are voluntary, complimentary, and so on. If someone tries to weigh the value of one gift against another, or treats a gift as a payment for friendship, then this defies the spirit of gift-giving and leads us to believe that no gift exchange, properly speaking, has occurred. A title of nobility, too, loses its meaning if it can be sold. The point of a hereditary aristocracy is that nobles possess their honor by birth, regardless of wealth; if their titles are for sale, then they immediately lose their traditional meaning (as has happened at various points in history). Similarly, we distinguish love from prostitution and merely hedonistic sexual relationships by denying that it is a mere exchange of services or money. We define a work of art partly by saying that it has permanent, unique, and inherent value, and so we deny people at least the moral right to destroy art-works that they own, although they can sell them for money.[43] Finally, we say that we have a system of inalienable rights only if we subscribe to a moral structure that cannot be compromised at any price.

The dispute between formalists and substantivists is somewhat like the argument between philosophers and humanists. Neither debate can be settled with a definitive argument that employs evidence or an *a priori* deduction. However, people can live according to either position. For instance, an individual can act as if everything has a value-ratio, or else as if no cost can be assigned to certain "priceless" goods. Similarly, people can obey moral doctrines, or else they can draw guidance from concrete stories. Each of these approaches can be depicted in a positive or negative light in a literary text. Therefore, in the following chapters, I will discuss concrete examples of contests between people who treat everything as exchangeable commodities, and other people who deny that some objects have prices. I will address this contest at the same time that I discuss the debate between philosophy and humanism, because there is a certain affinity between formalism and philosophy, and also between substantivism and humanism. If goods like love and freedom have no value-ratio, then no rational art of maximization can be employed to solve our moral dilemmas. In the absence of such an art, individuals may make moral decisions by describing their own lives as coherent narratives that encompass incommensurable values. At the same time, communities can decide moral questions of common interest by means of democratic debate. After all, a democracy, unlike a market, can make choices among alternatives even when no aggregate value can be calculated.

Thus I hope to show (rather than prove) that it is better to act as if not every value is subject to market exchange. This assumption creates space for Habermas's democratic ideal, because it suggests that the market mechanism is not universal.

Apart from democracy, another form of life that is consistent with pragmatism is the system of common law, with its high premium on narrative and its strictly pragmatic use of general principles. Finally, the humanities are clearly consistent with pragmatism, because they teach us how to interpret narratives and descriptions offered by other people: a necessary precondition for reaching ethical consensus. Within the humanities, many kinds of interpretation are practiced (and legitimately so), but pragmatism puts a particularly high premium on efforts to discover an author's intentions. While this is only one valid way of interpreting a text, it is similar to the kind of interpretation that we must carry out when we want to reach agreement with someone—for in that case, we need to know what he or she is *trying* to say. In general, the arts and humanities are important vehicles for thick description, aspect-seeing, and narrative; and these, in turn, are the most pragmatically effective methods of moral argument. That is why self-described "humanists," at least since the Renaissance, have usually favored moral education through literature, and have opposed theoretical moral philosophy.[44]

This concludes my sketch of an alternative, non-theoretical approach to ethics. My goal has been to show that concrete descriptions, weighed by a deliberating public, are all that we need to form moral judgments. For reasons that I have already suggested, my approach cannot be proved superior to Kantian, utilitarian, or other philosophical systems of morality. First, these systems are not inconsistent or empirically false, and they are so diverse that no single argument can rebut them all. Second, an abstract, general, deductive argument against the spirit of philosophy would violate its own conclusions. Finally, none of the reasons that support my view are self-evident or amenable to proof—not the belief in concrete truth over abstraction, nor the commitment to consensus, nor pragmatism and verificationism. Therefore, the remainder of this book is devoted to a series of concrete episodes in the quarrel between moral philosophy and humanism, which are designed to show what cannot be argued: that the humanities are superior.

CONCRETE ILLUSTRATIONS

A P H I L O S O P H E R

E N C O U N T E R S   A

H U M A N I S T

SOCRATES AND PROTAGORAS

In Plato's dialogue entitled *Protagoras*, the quintessential philosopher, Socrates, clashes with the ideal humanist, Protagoras. Apparently, Plato realized that it is difficult to discuss the conflict between philosophy and humanism impartially, for if we use deductive arguments, they often favor moral philosophy, but if we use narratives and "thick" descriptions, they generally support humanism. Nevertheless, he wanted to decide what role philosophy ought to play in public and private life. Thus he could not simply ignore the contest between philosophy and the humanities; yet he was too honest and acute (or perhaps too ambivalent) to approach the issue with the methods of just one side in the quarrel. Instead, he worked out a profoundly illuminating stylistic synthesis, the Socratic dialogue, which incorporates elements of logical argument while simultaneously presenting *characters* whose methods and values can be judged morally.

In discussing Protagoras, I am primarily interested in the character who appears in Plato's dialogue—the "literary Protagoras"—even though Plato based this character on a real man. I am interested in the literary character because the dialogue (which is probably mostly fiction) provides a suggestive illustration of the perennial contest between philosophers and humanists. However, since the historical Protagoras was very famous—perhaps the most famous intellectual of his time—Plato must have expected his readers to know what this man believed and wrote.¹ Thus Plato's dialogue is not fully comprehensible unless we know a certain amount about the historical Protagoras. For centuries, scholars have debated the parallel question of the "historical Socrates," which is one of the thorniest issues in the history of ideas. But since Socrates did not write anything, Plato probably expected his audience to read his dialogues without much prior knowledge of Socrates' beliefs. Protagoras's works, on the other hand, were widely read. Thus a full understanding of the dialogue requires at least a sketchy idea of what the historical Protagoras argued.

Unfortunately, none of Protagoras's works survive, and all of his extant aphorisms and remarks come to us as quotations contained in other authors' works; thus we have no idea about their original context, and we cannot even be certain that they are accurately attributed to Protagoras. However, we do know that Protagoras was a Sophist, and we possess some general information about the Sophists' social role and theoretical orientation. By profession, they were paid teachers of rhetoric. They also studied history and literature, probably because they viewed these disciplines as repositories of moral, practical, and stylistic examples. As part of this project, they wrote some of the earliest books of literary criticism.² In addition, they studied grammar and philology (Protagoras may have discovered grammatical moods and gender);³ and some even devised whole philosophies of language.

What defined them as a movement, however, was their profession as teachers. In Plato's dialogue, the character Protagoras describes his pedagogical method as follows:

> The works of the best poets are set before [children] to read on the classroom benches, and they are compelled to learn them thoroughly; and in these works are displayed many warnings, many detailed narratives and praises and eulogies of good men of ancient times, so that the boy may desire to imitate them competitively and may stretch himself to become like them.⁴

This passage probably gives an accurate description of a Sophistic classroom, if only because Protagoras was a famous teacher whose methods were widely known. Besides, the same approach to education survived for centuries and continued to be associated with self-styled Sophists even in the Roman period. In the first century B.C., Plutarch offered a conventional Sophistic defense of history, arguing that historical narratives could—in and of themselves—have educative effects. Without providing any theory of the good, he said, history could offer moral instruction. "Virtue, by the bare statement of its actions, can affect men's minds so as to create at once both admiration of the things done and desire to imitate the doers of them."⁵

Against the Sophists, Socrates argued that a theory of the good was always necessary if people were to know whether an individual act that was described in a narrative was worthy of praise or contempt. In the *Phaedrus*, he remarks, "no one will ever be able to speak about anything appropriately, unless he has sufficient knowledge of philosophy."[6] This is a classic philosophical position, held later by Kant, who wrote: "Imitation finds no place at all in morality, and examples serve only for encouragement, *i.e.*, they put beyond doubt the feasibility of what the law commands, they make visible that which the practical rule expresses more generally, but they can never authorize us to set aside the true original which lies in reason, and to guide ourselves by examples."[7]

Socrates, as presented by Plato, sought to know the "true examples" of goodness and virtue that were available only by means of pure reason. But most Sophists appear to have been skeptics about metaphysics and moral theory. Thus, for example, Protagoras wrote a book called the *Antilogiae* (*Contrasting Arguments*), in which he probably attempted to undermine the discipline of philosophy by offering arguments on both sides of each question.[8] A frequently repeated story reports that he was expelled from Athens for agnosticism.[9] In a fragment that survives, he wrote: "Concerning the gods, I cannot know either that they exist or that they do not exist, for there are many obstacles to knowing: the obscurity of the subject and the shortness of human life."[10] From this remark, it sounds as if he thought that deductive arguments could neither prove nor disprove religion. Experience, on the other hand, was relevant to religious questions—but any single person had too little experience to judge whether the gods existed. It is possible that Protagoras proceeded to offer arguments either for or against the existence of gods, based on the cumulative experience of human beings as recorded in history.

A few other aphorisms have survived that are securely attributable to Protagoras. First, he is famous for claiming that "man is the measure of all things."[11] (By contrast, Socrates remarks in the *Laws*: "For us, *God* will be the greatest 'measure of all things'—much more than some 'man' of whom they talk."[12]) Protagoras's man-is-the-measure doctrine could have several meanings. In the *Theaetetus*, Socrates interprets it to mean that each person is the sole arbiter of truth: thus, whatever anyone thinks, is right.[13] Socrates also attributes to Protagoras a secret metaphysical doctrine that allegedly underlies this extreme relativism: there is no objective truth, because everything is flux and becoming. Thus there are no "things," only descriptions, beliefs, and interpretations, and these are subjectively imposed. However, Protagoras is not present to defend himself, and there is no independent reason to believe that he intended to offer a metaphysical claim like the one that Socrates attributes to him. (The fact that Socrates calls it a "secret" doctrine implies that Protagoras never published it.) Metaphysicians, believing that all ideas have a metaphysical foundation, have consistently tried to show that humanists must be implicitly committed to some metaphysical theory. That is why Socrates thinks that Protagoras is a secret metaphysician of flux, who possesses an image of the universe as an ebbing and flowing body of water.[14] But I doubt that Protagoras held any esoteric cosmological or ontological view at all.

Clearly, he was some kind of skeptic, but skepticism can take at least two contrasting forms. The first moment of skepticism occurs when someone denies a belief that speculative philosophers have previously affirmed: for example, the existence of a free will, causality, things-in-themselves, the self, God, the soul, the objective world, or truth. Socrates accuses Protagoras of this kind of skepticism regarding truth, things-in-themselves, and objectivity. But the second moment of skepticism occurs when a skeptic criticizes the *denial* of metaphysical theories, claiming that refutations are just as dogmatic as assertions. This kind of skepticism is often called Pyrrhonism, after Pyrrho of Elis, a Hellenistic philosopher who distrusted all speculative beliefs, both positive and negative. Since Pyrrhonists doubted the validity of arguments both for and against metaphysical theories, they set aside the problems of traditional philosophy and turned to more practical concerns. They mainly addressed these practical questions through the medium of a "Ciceronian" dialogue, that is, a debate in which no conclusion is reached, but the participants discuss practical questions by giving long rhetorical speeches—full of examples and analogies—that can help to incline the reader toward a view of the *probable* truth. Pyrrhonists doubted not only the validity of dialectic, but also the testimony of experience. However, they thought that probable truth could emerge if people pooled their experiences in search of consensus.

Sextus Empiricus, a Pyrrhonist of the Roman period, accused Protagoras of holding the dogmatic version of skepticism:

> He says then that matter is in flux. . . . He says also that the reasons (*logoi*) of all appearances are present in the matter, so that the matter is capable, insofar as it depends on itself, of being all things that appear to all people. . . . Thus, according to him, man is the criterion of all things, for all things that appear to men also are, and all things that do not appear to any man are not. We see then that he asserts dogmatically that matter is flux and that the reason of all appearances is present in it, even though these are obscure issues about which we [the Pyrrhonists] suspend judgment.[15]

Sextus probably attributed dogmatic views to Protagoras because of what Socrates had said in the *Theaetetus.*[16] In my view, the literary Protagoras is more like a Pyrrhonist: that is, someone who suspends judgment about theoretical issues. Likewise, when the historical Protagoras offered contrasting answers to philosophical questions, he may have wanted to induce suspension of judgment, rather than defending any metaphysical theory of his own—even a metaphysics of flux. According to Seneca: "Protagoras asserts that it is possible to argue equally well on either side of any question, including the question whether both sides of all questions can be argued."[17] If this was the gist of Protagoras's *Antilogiae*, then the result would have been an abandonment of all philosophy, not a dogmatic form of skepticism.

Similarly, when Protagoras said that "man is the measure of all things," he probably did not mean that things *are* just as each person sees them. Instead, he may have meant that human beings and their experiences are the only standard or criterion of truth. But since people differ in their opinions, their judgments must be reconciled somehow, and Protagoras may have advocated a process of comparing opinions to produce probable truth. In the *Theaetetus*, after Socrates dismisses his metaphysical interpretation of Protagoras's man-is-the-measure doctrine, he makes a second effort to elucidate Protagoras's meaning. This time he makes the Sophist's doctrine sound pragmatic and also plausible. Socrates (describing Protagoras's position) says that a sick man may find something sour that a healthy man finds sweet. Neither person is correct, for things are objectively neither sweet nor sour. However, a doctor has real wisdom, for he can *move* a man from the state of being sick to the preferable condition of being well. Likewise, nothing is objectively better or worse for a state, but a Sophist (as political counselor) can help people to change their political situation into one that seems better to them as a group.

Paraphrasing Protagoras, Socrates says, "For whatever *seems* to be just and beautiful to each city, *is* such for that city, as long as the city considers it so; but the wise man causes the good—rather than that which is evil for each in each situation—to be and to appear."[18] Note that the protagonist in this sentence is the "city," not any individual; thus truth is a product of social agreement. There appears to be an inconsistency between the first and second parts of this formula: according to the first clause, anything that seems good, is good; but then it turns out that a wise person makes what actually is good seem so. This inconsistency disappears if we assume that what is good is only identifiable as such if it succeeds in satisfying public opinion over the long term. Then the foolish person is the one who persuades people to adopt a wrong course of action, but—if the policy is wrong—then the error of their ways will soon become clear to them. In short, the test of wisdom is pragmatic: the wise person produces enduringly popular results by promoting policies that are good insofar as they seem good over time.[19] Protagoras was active in politics: he taught many prominent politicians and wrote a constitution for the new panhellenic city of Thurii.[20] He was said to be of humble origin and a close advisor to Pericles, so he was probably a democrat. Thus he may have believed that truth was a product of democratic discussion, aimed at consensus.

In another phrase that is securely attributable to Protagoras, he said that one should "make the lesser reason [*logos*] stronger." In Aristophanes' parody of the Sophists, *The Clouds*, a character called the Wrong Reason actually engages the Right Reason in a brawl.[21] Many contemporaries seem to have thought that Protagoras wanted to play devious, "sophistical" games in which the wrong argument was made to look right by the force of rhetoric. Aristotle explained: "And for this reason men were justly offended by Protagoras's promise, for it is a falsehood and not a truth, but only an apparent probability. And it belongs to no art except rhetoric and competitive debate [eristic]."[22] But it is important to note that Aristotle, even though he was hostile to Protagoras, never suggested that the Sophist had wanted to make *false* arguments appear true. Rather, Protagoras wanted to support arguments (i.e., make them stronger), but without proving them to be absolutely true. He operated in the realm of rhetoric, but did not deny that some arguments could be made stronger than others. The best *logos* was the one that appeared strongest of all after efforts had been made to support every alternative view. Thus Protagoras favored eristic—competitive argument—not as a game, but as a pragmatic method of seeking the most probable truth.[23]

If rational claims are ones that emerge with logical rigor from axiomatic principles, then no dialogue is necessary; a single philosopher can determine what is right in the privacy of his or her study. This would be the case if Kantian or utilitarian moral philosophers were right: moral truths would result from the application of general maxims to specific cases. But if morality is a matter of aspect-seeing, then pure logical argument will not suffice, and something else must take its place. Protagoras probably favored the humanities as an alternative to dialectic and a source of moral truth. It is almost certain that he taught his students the art of convincing others by exposing them to history, literature, literary criticism, and rhetoric. Thus Protagoras envisioned truth not as lying "out there" in some non-human realm, but as emerging from a continuous process of discussion in which people sought to persuade each other to see things *as* they saw them. Above all, people could try to persuade others of their moral vision by producing new works of literature and history, by making speeches laced with literary and historical examples, and by offering interpretations of poems and events. This, he thought, was the most pragmatically effective way to make the lesser logos stronger. At best, the process of comparing *logoi* might lead to the formation of a consensus, after adequate and well-informed discussion. As a result of this consensus, policies might emerge that would make the condition of the state *seem* better to its members—and this was all that Protagoras promised.

THE DIALOGUE
OPENING

Like many of Plato's works, the *Protagoras* is actually a dialogue within a dialogue. In the opening lines, Socrates is asked by an anonymous companion where he has been all morning. The companion assumes that Socrates has been pursuing the "very charming" Alcibiades. No, Socrates replies, he has discovered a "much fairer love"–Protagoras of Abdera, with whom Socrates has just had an encounter. So beautiful was Protagoras's intellect that it made Socrates completely forget Alcibiades, whom he describes entirely in physical terms. Socrates then proceeds to relate what happened between him and Protagoras.

This opening draws attention to the status of the work as a piece of literature narrated by one of the participants.[24] The narrator (Socrates) may not fully understand his fellow characters, his views may differ from those of the author, and he may not always give a fair account of what took place. This, then, is not going to be an abstract philosophical tract; it will be a drama, full of vivid characters and narrated from a contingent, immanent perspective. Since Socrates later attacks literature, perhaps he would not approve of the dialogue in which he appears. We are warned that Socrates and Plato are not identical, and that the conflict between Socrates' philosophical position and the dramatic nature of Plato's writing is a potential issue for the dialogue.

Socrates begins relating the day's events by saying that he was awakened before dawn by a young man named Hippocrates, who wanted to tell him some exciting news: Protagoras had just arrived in Athens. Hippocrates wanted to rush off to see Protagoras immediately, hoping that Socrates would introduce him to the great man. Socrates pointed out that it was still nighttime and much too early to go visiting; so they waited for a few minutes, conducting a philosophical discussion to pass the time. Hippocrates' zeal to meet Protagoras indicates that the Sophist is a famous, charismatic, and popular teacher. However, Plato depicts Hippocrates' enthusiasm humorously, thus encouraging us to consider the possibility that Socrates might actually be the better educator. The stage is set for a battle over Hippocrates' soul, waged between the most prominent Sophist of the day and the man whom Plato credits with founding rigorous philosophy.

Plato's choice of the name Hippocrates may be deliberate. The original Hippocrates (this young man's famous namesake) was a legendary founder of medicine. One of the works that was attributed to the physician Hippocrates describes the early doctors as follows: "They did not want to look on the naked face of luck (*tuchē*), so they turned themselves over to method (*technē*). As a result, they are released from their dependence on luck, but not from their dependence on *technē*."[25] Laszlo Versényi asserts that this

Hippocratic work was "unmistakably influenced by Protagoras."[26] Just as physicians promised to combat the bad luck of illness with their scientific techniques, so Protagoras may have claimed to teach a method for handling luck in moral and practical affairs, Likewise, Socrates' philosophical method, which is supposed to free us entirely from contingency, is a central theme of the *Protagoras*. Socrates' *technē* is a method for measuring the objective value of actions and objects, so that we can make correct moral decisions free from all randomness and luck. Near the end of the dialogue, he says: "the art of measurement [*metrikē technē*] would invalidate the effect of mere appearance and, showing the truth, would finally cause the soul to abide in peace with the truth, and so save its life" (356d). Socrates' metaphor of measuring suggests that the true value of everything is comparable on a single scale. Therefore, anyone who knows how to measure objective value can maximize the moral quality of his or her actions in a perfectly rational way. Anyone who holds Socrates' view must abandon the love of individual people, because erotic or romantic love means devotion to a particular person, that is, devotion that is not exchangeable for any other value at any cost.[27] At the beginning of the dialogue, therefore, Socrates deliberately eschews the particular love of Alcibiades in order to discuss a general, abstract calculus of value. Protagoras, on the other hand, seems to reject the metaphor of measurement and the idea that all goods are mutually commensurable. Thus the basic issues to be addressed in the dialogue are as follows. First, is there a *technē* that can help us to make ethical decisions securely, universally, and with rigor? And second, who posseses the better technique for overcoming luck, Socrates or Protagoras?

Socrates begins his attack on Sophism as he waits with Hippocrates for dawn to break. Socrates asks the young man what he expects to learn from Protagoras. If someone wanted to learn sculpture, Socrates says, he would study with Pheidias; but what can a young man learn from a Sophist? Hippocrates is embarrassed by the obvious answer: that he would learn to be a Sophist. In the classical period, Sophists had a dubious reputation and an ambiguous social status.[28] Socrates therefore rescues Hippocrates with another suggestion. What one can gain from a Sophist, he says, is an education that "suits a freeman and a layman" (312b). Sophists offer improvement for the soul, rather than specialized knowledge; they make their students into better people and better citizens. But Socrates is concerned that Hippocrates may not know in advance how to judge Protagoras's wares. If you want to buy a horse, you must first examine it to make sure it is sound. But education for the soul is a more important—and riskier—matter. Once ingested, a piece of knowledge immediately takes its irreversible effect, even if the recipient decides he would rather not accept the treatment after all.

Socrates sets the terms of his argument with Protagoras on ground best suited to his methods. Prior to any ethical education, he implies, is a true understanding of the good. Any ideas that Protagoras imparted would be either good or evil, depending upon their relation to abstract moral truths. If philosophical analysis revealed that Protagoras was teaching good ideas, then Hippocrates should study with him; otherwise, he should shun the treatment. Thus, before anyone studies under Protagoras, he should first learn the skill that Socrates practices: philosophy. Socrates' analytic method has already reduced Hippocrates to confusion; and he plans to use it also against Protagoras. He plans to analyze Protagoras's methods to determine their consistency and correspondence to the Good as revealed by philosophy. Many centuries later, Kant showed his Socratic bent when he argued that examples can never serve as a source of moral truth, because we first need an accurate moral *theory* against which to judge any example. Otherwise, we might try to teach someone what the Good was by using concrete cases that happened to be evil. Examples belong to the realm of *tuchē*, but philosophy has a *technē*.

In general, Socrates believes that correct use of dialectic, rather than age or experience, is the criterion of wisdom. Even the slave-boy in the *Meno* possesses native insights about geometry (85c). Similarly, Socrates often claims that a rigorous argument can reveal truth, whereas mere human opinion can err. However, at the end of his discussion with Hippocrates, he concludes that he cannot decide for sure whether Sophists are good or bad for the soul: this question lies beyond the reach of his dialectic. Therefore, he decides to go with Hippocrates to visit Protagoras, giving two reasons for this risky decision. First, Protagoras and the other Sophists are old, whereas he and Hippocrates are "too young to decide such matters" (314b). Second, Protagoras is not alone, but is accompanied by many other Sophists at Callias's house. Thus, when it comes to the metaquestion of whether moral issues should be addressed with humanistic or philosophical methods, Socrates at least initially gives a humanistic response. Like Protagoras himself (cf. 320c), Socrates asserts that age, experience, and majority opinion are criteria of truth–but only when the question is whether to rely on philosophy rather than experience and human consensus. At least so far, Socrates seems to agree with Plato, for Plato uses a humanistic vehicle, the dialogue, to address the conflict between philosophy and humanism. However, when Socrates actually encounters Protagoras, he will use his dialectical methods to criticize the Sophist's humanism.

Socrates and Hippocrates are still talking philosophically when they arrive at the house where Protagoras is staying. Socrates does not tell us the topic of their conversation, but they apparently reach agreement. At last, a eunuch slave opens the door, sees the two men talking, and slams it shut again, mumbling, "Ha! Some Sophists! He's busy" (314d). Upon finally gaining entrance to the house (which belongs to Callias, the richest man in Athens) the visitors see Protagoras strolling back and forth accompanied by numerous admirers, who hang on his every word. Distributed around the house are many of the most important thinkers of the day, engaged in their separate intellectual specialties; the scene looks like Raphael's "School of Athens." Protagoras, the ethical thinker, takes pride of place before mathematicians, historians, physicians, philologists, and others.

In describing this scene, Socrates quotes several times from book XI of the *Odyssey* (Odysseus's journey to the underworld) to suggest that Callias's house is very much like Hades. Socrates compares Protagoras to Orpheus, who charmed his way safely out of hell. He likens Hippias (another major Sophist) to Herakles, whose image sat in Hades while he frolicked in Elysium. Finally, he compares Prodicus (a rather pedantic grammarian) to Tantalus, who is eternally "tantalized" in hell by food and water that moves away from his grasp.[29] No doubt, some of these allusions constitute recondite jokes about particular Sophists and Sophistical schools. Overall, however, Socrates has a serious purpose in setting a symbolic scene for the dialogue. For example, the comparison of Hippias and Herakles is significant, because Hippias is a teacher of "calculation, astronomy, geometry, and music" (318e). These are theoretical or mathematical disciplines that use dialectic rather than thick description. Thus, like Herakles, Hippias only *appears* to live among the shades; he is really in heaven communing with the Forms. Similarly, the analogy of Protagoras and Orpheus suggests that Protagoras is not a permanent resident of Sophistic hell; he knows his way around, but he still belongs to the world of the living. Thus he and Socrates may be able to find common ground, for Socrates too is a temporary visitor to the realm of the Sophists: his true methods belong outside Callias's door.

The fact that the doorkeeper is a eunuch may represent the banishment of erotic love from the Sophists' domain. After all, the Sophists' relationship with their students was indiscriminate and mercenary; Socrates has already called them "merchants" (313d).[30] The transition symbolized by the door is obviously an important one, because Socrates behaves in a noticeably different way once he moves inside. Outside, he engages in the kind of discussion that is typical of early Platonic dialogues: he cross-examines Hippocrates in order to undermine the young man's assumptions so that he may begin to think. This is not a competitive form of argument: no one wins. Inside the door, however, Socrates proposes and defends theses in an unusually competitive, even underhanded, way—that is, in the style that is usually attributed to Sophists.[31] Thus the dialogue describes a foray by one philosopher into the hellish territory of the Sophists, and it shows him acting in a somewhat compromised manner, as a sort of half-Sophist. But that is perhaps fair, since he has implied that Protagoras is a half-philosopher.

The description of the Sophists inside Callias's house is neither wholly admiring nor completely critical. The fact that the slave has already had enough of Sophists at dawn suggests that they are something like a cult: they are so obsessed with Protagoras's teaching that they have come to see him in large numbers when most ordinary people are still asleep. The setting underscores their political influence: later in the dialogue, Hippias the sage will point out that the wisest men in Greece are gathered together in the most glorious household of the greatest city in the hellenic world—and he is right.[32] Another index of the Sophists' political importance is the presence at Callias's house of several leaders of the next generation, including Critias and Alcibiades. This generation saw Athens defeated and tyranny victorious; so the effect of the Sophists' teaching is obviously questionable. If Protagoras really made people better citizens, Plato seems to be asking, then why did his students destroy the Periclean state in which citizenship flourished best? This is exactly the kind of "argument" that a Sophist or humanist would use: it sets an intellectual movement in its historical context it order to show it *as* dangerous. Therefore, despite the fact that Plato is a disciple of Socrates and not of Protagoras, he still uses Protagoras's methods to depict their quarrel.

Socrates now approaches Protagoras and introduces Hippocrates as a young man of talent and political ambition. Protagoras seems wary of Socrates and slightly defensive. Without provocation, he gives a speech defending Sophism as an "ancient *technē*," and identifying many of the greatest Greek poets, musicians, and even gymnasts of the past as Sophists (316d).[33] Homer, Hesiod, and Simonides, he says, were secret Sophists, afraid to bear the title publicly because of the odium attached to it; whereas he (Protagoras) is more honest and dares to advertise his profession openly. Thus Protagoras identifies his version of Sophism as a self-conscious and self-reflective form of the humanistic tradition that Homer founded.[34]

Protagoras offers to speak with Socrates about his teaching methods. But Socrates says that he believes that Protagoras would rather hold forth in front of an audience, so he asks everyone to gather and listen to Protagoras's speech. It is difficult to tell whether Socrates is really trying to please Protagoras by assembling an audience, or whether he hopes to embarrass the Sophist publicly with his dialectical skills. The historical Protagoras apparently believed that the validity of an argument lay in its capacity to produce consensus; so he would have good reason to desire an audience. On the other hand, Socrates might want to imply that his method, too, can convince the many, although this is not his criterion of truth. In any case, Socrates begins the conversation over again so that everyone can hear. The purpose of his visit, he repeats, is to introduce Hippocrates, who "would be glad to hear what will really happen to him if he associates with you. That is all we have to say."

Protagoras directs his response to Hippocrates: "Young man," he says, "if you associate with me, on the day that you first converse with me you will be able to return home a better person, and better on the second day than the first, and each day after that you will grow ceaselessly better" (318a). Socrates politely replies that he is not surprised: Protagoras is old and wise, and anyone would be better off who was exposed to his knowledge. But, Socrates asks, what does Protagoras's wisdom consist in? What is the content of his teaching? Protagoras answers that he teaches "good counsel about domestic matters—how best to administer a household—and also about civic matters: how to speak and act most powerfully in the affairs of the state" (318e–319a). Protagoras thereby avoids answering Socrates' question exactly as asked. Socrates wanted to know the *content* of the Sophist's teaching (i.e., his philosophy, or what he believes), but Protagoras describes his pragmatic goal: the making of persuasive citizens. If Protagoras possessed a theory of the good, then being educated under him would be a simple and brief process; the student would just listen as he articulated his theory. Thus one would not grow "ceaselessly better" by studying under him; the whole process would be over and done with quickly. Socrates wants Protagoras to announce his theory, so that it can be debated. However, Protagoras does not claim to possess a theory of the good; rather he promises to fashion skillful citizens, a process that inevitably takes time. Socrates asks whether he means that he teaches the art of politics. Protagoras assents.

Socrates now states the thesis that he will defend through most of the dialogue: virtue, he says, cannot be taught. He supports this assertion by pointing out that everyone is allowed to argue in the assembly about moral matters, without being taught by experts in the "political *technē*," whereas no one can claim expertise in shipbuilding (for example) until he has had tuition under a master shipbuilder. This thesis puts Protagoras in an apparently difficult position. On one hand, he could say that virtue must be taught by an expert, just like shipbuilding, in which case no one who lacked a Sophist for a tutor could be a decent citizen. But this conclusion sounds implausible: Achilles and Theseus never had the advantage of a Sophistic education, yet they knew what virtue meant. Besides, this view would be undemocratic, and might get Protagoras into trouble in Periclean Athens. Alternatively, he could admit that many people understand virtue without professional assistance— but then his own services would appear worthless.

Protagoras asks Socrates whether he would like to hear an answer in the form of a *mythos* (story), told by an older man to a younger, or whether he would prefer to continue the dialectical exchange. Socrates leaves the choice up to Protagoras, who opts to tell a story. Just by making this decision, Protagoras has already said something important about his methods. As a Sophist, he prefers to *show* people what he has learned as a man of worldly experience, rather than engaging in an *a priori*, logical exchange. The historical Protagoras expressed his skepticism about philosophy in his published works. In Plato's dialogue, he appears to be taking a position similar to that of Aristotle, namely: (1) moral questions deal with particulars, not abstract universals that can be understood through dialectic; (2) moral argument is a matter of aspect-seeing, not logic; and therefore (3) the opinion of more experienced people is valuable even if it is not backed up with arguments, just because their experience makes them able to perceive things better.[35]

This, then, is already an answer to Socrates. What teaches people to be better citizens is experience in interpreting the world. People gain this experience on their own as they grow into adults. However, more experience than a person could ever gain on his own is contained in the literary heritage of Greece, as exemplified by such "Sophists" as Homer and Simonides. Protagoras, a man of great worldly experience and an expert on poetry, possesses more experience than a young man like Hippocrates. Hence Hippocrates (and even Socrates) would be able to learn something by studying with Protagoras, who would show them what Homer and the other poets saw as they interpreted, imagined, and described concrete human actions.

THE "GREAT SPEECH"

However, Protagoras does not lay out this position in abstract terms, as I have. Instead (and more usefully), he *shows* the efficacy of Sophistic methods by telling a story. Given his pragmatic orientation, Protagoras probably believes that the proof of his method is in the pudding: if his view is right, then his story ought to *work* as a tool for convincing his audience, including even Socrates. Therefore, without attempting to lay out an abstract position for Socrates to refute, Protagoras plunges immediately into his story. However, he says that he has an abstract position that he could present, if Socrates demanded it; he simply prefers to exemplify that position by telling a story. If asked for his implicit position, he would (I think) attack abstract philosophizing, as he did in his published works. Thus Protagoras would have good reasons to resist the abstract, generalized analysis of his position that I provided above. At best (to use Wittgenstein's metaphor), this analysis could serve as a ladder to climb up beyond abstract arguments, after which he should throw away the ladder.

Protagoras's "Great Speech" is a creation story, borrowed (with original additions) from Greek myth.[36] In the beginning, the Titan Epimetheus gave all the animals except man means of defending themselves: shells, claws, or quick feet. Man had nothing—no "capacities"[37] at all—until Prometheus recognized the mistake and provided people with knowledge of the arts and the making of fire. They then "discovered, by means of their *technē*, articulate speech and names,"[38] as well as religion, agriculture, and crafts (322a). If human beings had no capacities at all until they were given culture, then they *were* nothing without it. Protagoras says that Epimetheus had left man *acosmētos*: unorganized, unarranged, or unprovided. The Greek word means the opposite of "cosmos," which is a comprehensible order formed out of chaos. Thus one fairly clear implication of Protagoras's story is that there is no "human nature" that can be appealed to as a foundation for philosophical theories, and no coherent essence of humanity that is more fundamental than the diverse beliefs, techniques, and experiences of concrete human beings. If true, this idea would have dire consequences for Socrates, who is always trying to arrive at universal definitions of things like "man."

According to Protagoras, early human beings possessed religion and practical arts, but they did not know how to get along with each other, so they fell into fratricidal conflict. Prometheus had wanted to give them political wisdom, but this was hidden away in Zeus' citadel, where he could not venture. Fortunately, Zeus, fearing that the human race would perish, ordered Hermes to bring shame and justice to human communities (322c). Hermes asked whether these qualities should be given to only a few people. Zeus replied, on the contrary, that everyone should possess them; and those who didn't should be killed as enemies of the peace. Protagoras concludes that it is right for everyone to participate in peaceful political deliberations, even if their endowments of Promethean skills and virtues happen to be unequal.[39] This is a basic principle of democracy: the assumption that people with different types or amounts of aptitude and education nevertheless possess equal political rights. Protagoras, after all, believes that moral and political questions have no correct answers that can be deduced by means of a specialized intellectual process, such as Socrates' dialectic. To practice medicine or to navigate a ship requires study of the relevant Promethean disciplines; but the truth about moral questions can only be ascertained as a result of an inclusive dialogue. The right answer *just is* the one that seems best to everyone, so everyone must be able to participate in political discourse.

Somewhat later in the dialogue (323b), Protagoras asserts that everyone always claims to be on the side of justice in an argument, whereas people do not falsely claim to be able to play the flute. This observation provides further support for Protagoras's distinction between Prometheus's arts and Zeus's justice. It also reveals his understanding of the logic of democratic debate, in which participants must always state their own selfish interests in terms of general justice or universal interests, if they hope to achieve consensus. This is how they make the weaker argument stronger. The historical Protagoras apparently believed that the argument that appeared strongest of all at the end of a competitive debate was the best one, so he may have thought that a democratic argument in which everyone *pretended* to seek justice was an excellent means for discovering what justice actually required.

At the end of the dialogue (361d), Socrates compares himself to Prometheus, saying that he admires that god and that he tries to use Promethean virtue continually in his own life. In fact, Socrates resembles

Prometheus is several respects. First, Prometheus was punished for distributing the arts (as well as fire) to mankind; similarly, Socrates was forced to drink hemlock for disseminating the incendiary art of dialectic to Athenians. Second, Prometheus stole the wisdom of practicing arts from Hephaestos and Athena; likewise, Socrates derives knowledge from the divine realm of the Forms by means of dialectic. Finally, Prometheus defies the will of the Olympian gods, and Socrates' philosophy undermines the authority of religion. "Prometheus" means "forethinker"; the verb *promethein* means "to think ahead." When Protagoras first meets Socrates, he says, "You are right, Socrates, to exercise forethought [literally, to prometheanize] on my behalf" (316c).[40] But Protagoras's story implies that it is not enough for us to possess Promethean intellectual skills. Despite Prometheus's ability to steal specialized arts from the gods, he could not gain access to political wisdom. People who possess specialized arts and yet lack political skill inevitably fall into anarchy. Responding to human beings in a state of fratricidal conflict, Zeus distributed justice and political wisdom; and these are the same skills that Protagoras now teaches. In general, Protagoras resembles Zeus: he is a fatherly figure, distinguished, old, powerful, universally respected, and wise. Thus the myth seems to imply that Socrates/Prometheus is a useful character, but that Protagoras/Zeus is indispensable. Socrates, of course, disagrees with this conclusion, arguing that his Promethean skill of measurement allows us to integrate our lives and communities into rational wholes: it is the ultimate form of political wisdom. In any case, Louis Bodin correctly emphasizes the pragmatic nature of Protagoras's point of view: "Under the guise of the *principle* and the *law* of Zeus, what Protagoras opposes to Socrates-Prometheus, to his techniques and his θεîα μοîρα [divine providence], is the proclamation of the conditions judged necessary by man in order that man can live in society, and therefore live smoothly: it is truth about man according to man."[41]

Protagoras's creation myth may seem to be a kind of social-contract doctrine, similar to the ones that Socrates outlines in the *Crito* and the *Republic*. Some of the other Sophists probably held social-contract doctrines as well.[42] These theories treat justice as a natural fact, by suggesting that humans, in a state of nature, would inevitably choose to obey specific laws. But Protagoras forestalls this interpretation of his story, saying that people "do not suppose that virtue is by nature, or something automatic, but a thing that is taught and that is gained by taking pains" (323c). Human beings turned out as they did because Epimetheus happened to make an initial mistake; Prometheus failed in his effort to remedy his brother's error; and then Zeus decided to teach people a form of wisdom that he could have kept to himself. In short, our origins are *contingent*, and so is our continued survival as a species. Zeus began the process of political education, and now we continue it, in each generation, through a combination of punishments and lessons. In the beginning, Zeus need not have decided to educate mankind, and any generation of humans might fail to educate its children. So there is nothing natural or inevitable about political virtue, but nevertheless it is a good thing to teach if we want to prevent anarchy of the kind that befell several Greek cities during Plato's lifetime. Protagoras (characteristically) refers to a literary work, *The Savages* by Pherecrates, to show how awful life would be if Greeks forgot to teach their children virtue.

Protagoras says that moral education takes place every day from birth to death. Parents, nurses, and tutors constantly tell a young child what is—and is not—just, noble, or pious; if the child does not heed them, they punish him. (Protagoras was probably the first thinker in Western history to argue that punishments are only valid as a form of education, never for revenge.) Later, the child is turned over to a schoolmaster, who enlarges his field of moral vision by exposing him to historical and literary texts. Just as his mother tells him that his own acts are good or bad, so the schoolmaster describes the deeds of heroes and villains as noble or base. The method remains the same, but the scope of experience grows larger. Finally, once the child is done with school, he continues to be taught morality by the city's laws, which incorporate the experience of past generations, and evolve to encompass the values of the present. Therefore, Protagoras concludes, knowledge of virtue is universal among Greeks, not because it is inborn, but because the mechanisms for teaching it are so widespread and pervasive. Can virtue be taught? You might as well ask (Protagoras says) whether Greek can be taught. The teachers of language are the same as those of virtue: the entire society. And yet, since virtue comes through experience, some people may be more knowledgeable about it than others, and that is why Protagoras's students "get their money's worth and even more" from him (328b). Protagoras concludes his myth by stating that the following three propositions are all true at once: (1) virtue must be taught; yet (2) virtue is universal among Greeks; yet (3) Sophists are valuable as teachers of virtue. Protagoras's position emerges not out of an *a priori* argument, but out of his "myth" and his detailed description of current social practices.[43]

SOCRATES' DIALECTICAL RESPONSE

Socrates says that he is charmed almost out of his wits by Protagoras's speech. At first he does not realize that Protagoras has finished speaking—for a story, unlike a deductive argument, does not have to end at any particular point; there is no QED.[44] Socrates describes his mental state in words that Milton echoed (*Paradise Lost* VIII.2–3): "So charming left his voice, that I the while / Thought him still speaking; still stood fixed to hear."[45] But, according to Socrates, beguiling speech is dangerous, for it can inculcate false beliefs.

And he believes Protagoras's position to be logically false. He says that there is "one tiny obstacle" in Protagoras's position that he is *sure* the great man will clear up, since he has explained so much already (328e). In fact, Socrates intends to use this "tiny" logical difficulty to undermine Protagoras's entire position; so Socrates' praise is ironic. He says that Protagoras is better than such great rhetoricians as Pericles, who refuse to engage in question-and-answer but respond to every critical question with another long speech, "like great copper caldrons that reverberate at length when they are struck" (329a–b). Protagoras, in contrast, is capable of dialectic as well as beguiling rhetoric. Therefore, says Socrates, he would now like to engage in dialectic in order to discuss the "tiny obstacle" that he has identified in Protagoras's speech. The trap has been set, and Protagoras must walk into it unless he wants to admit that he is not very good at dialectic.

Socrates now asks how the various virtues (justice, piety, self-control) are related to each other. Are they, for example, parts of one thing, or different names for the same thing? In other words, Socrates wants to reveal the metaphysical referent signified by the word "virtue." Protagoras has used that word, so, according to Socrates' theory of language, he must implicitly believe that "virtue" *is* something: either a unitary concept that can be better defined, or else the union of several ideas, in which case it should be analyzed into its components. Protagoras, playing along, says that all the virtues are one thing; but, in response to further cross-examination, he adds that they are all one in the way that many facial features can be part of one face. Socrates, however, wants to suggest that all the virtues are actually synonymous—that Virtue is the abstract universal that the various virtues reflect. If this is true, then Protagoras's speech contains an error, for it assigns a different (and contingent) origin to each virtue. Socrates proceeds to lead Protagoras through three dialectical "proofs," meant to demonstrate, respectively, the *identity* of justice and piety, of wisdom and self-control, and of self-control and justice. Having (allegedly) established these equations, Socrates can conclude that all the virtues are one. If so, then they could not have been given to man at different times and by different deities (one a Titan, the other an Olympian). Furthermore, if all the virtues were identical, then it would be easy to see how the good might be known *a priori*; it would be a single principle implicit in all of our genuinely ethical actions—one that we would recognize instinctively and that philosophers could clarify by means of analysis. Thus Socrates would be right and Protagoras would be wrong: there would be no need for an education in virtue.

This is the logical kernel of Socrates' first proof:

1. Assume that no virtue is like any other (this is to be refuted).
2. Justice is like being just.
3. But holiness is not like being just (from 1).

4. Therefore, holiness is like being not just.
5. Therefore, holiness is like being unjust.
6. But it is inconceivable that holiness is unjust.
7. Therefore, holiness and justice are like each other.
8. Therefore, proposition 1 is false. QED.[46]

As Socrates lays out this argument, Protagoras assents to every step, but he complains several times about the method. At one point, instead of answering "yes" to one of Socrates' questions, he says, "If you like—what difference does it make?" (331c). But Socrates refuses to accept this conditional answer and extracts a "yes." At another stage, Protagoras remarks that things must be more complicated than Socrates is making them seem; nevertheless, he continues to cooperate with the dialectical investigation. But even on Socrates' own terms, the logic of the argument is dubious. Reducing his proof to its skeletal form allows us to see how weak it is (e.g., in the transition from steps 4 to 5, which is an outright error), and how dependent it is upon questionable axioms. No such paraphrase of Protagoras's Great Speech would be fair to the original, because its "beguiling" descriptions are essential to its content. But it seems fair to paraphrase Socrates' arguments, because he holds that logic is a matter of pure content, independent of its rhetorical form. However, such analysis makes Socrates' position appear untenable.

For his third proof—the demonstration that self-control and justice are identical—Socrates uses a different method. He begins to outline a theory that "the good" is one thing, and that therefore justice and self-control must be identical, because they both seek the good. Before he can express this view in so many words, he notices that Protagoras is "getting agitated and preparing for a contest and marshalling his forces for a reply" (333e). Given his chance, Protagoras responds that there is no such thing as the good in-itself, only individual things that are good *for* various species; and he enumerates some examples. This is Protagoras's famous pluralism, used as a rebuttal of Socrates' moral absolutism. According to Protagoras, there is not one common denominator—"the good"—by which the good of all things can be measured; their value is rather contextual and relative to many scales of measurement. For example, Protagoras might say that, even in theory, it is impossible to weigh the value of poetry against that of good nutrition. If this is true, then Socrates' philosophical method would be unable to tell us what is right to do in every case, for some ethical dilemmas would involve incommensurable values.[47]

A DEBATE ABOUT METHOD

But the argument quickly changes focus. Socrates, protesting a "bad memory," complains that Protagoras has outlined his position in a long speech. He demands shorter answers, in other words, dialectical cross-examination, which must be as free as possible from rhetoric. Protagoras says that he is famous for his long speeches, and that is how he intends to proceed. Socrates says that since *he* cannot engage in a rhetorical competition, he will have to leave. This is a shame, he says, because Protagoras is capable of both kinds of discourse, whereas he, Socrates, is only able to speak dialectically. Callias, the host, intercedes, trying to persuade Socrates to stay. Socrates protests his embarrassing inability to make orations. "If you desire to hear Protagoras and me," he says, "you must ask him to answer briefly and keep to the point of the questions, as he did at first; if not, how can there be any dialogue? I was under the impression that there is a difference between coming together to have a dialogue, and making a public speech" (336a–b).[48]

In fact, Protagoras's last speech was not more than two hundred words long. But Protagoras did raise numerous points and examples before Socrates could respond to each one. Dialectic requires a subject to be analyzed down to its atomic propositions; each one is then assessed separately. But Protagoras's descriptive method demands a more continuous style. Thus Socrates and Protagoras are not merely squabbling about how to compete fairly; they have arrived at a substantial methodological difference. Philosophers like Socrates do not believe that real, human discussions are an ideal forum for discovering truth: they are too contingent, too dependent on the participants' skill, too random in their direction, and too vulnerable to rhetoric. Since philosophers must leave the realm of pure ideas to rejoin ordinary humans in their "cave," they must be willing to engage in real discussions.[49] But, as far as possible, contingency should be banished from these discussions by the introduction of a rigorous method: dialectic.

Plato chose to write naturalistic dialogues instead of abstract philosophical tracts, but this may have been because he wanted to help his readers make the transition from ordinary talk to philosophical speculation, which is free of human contingency. He experimented with dialogues that were more or less contingent in their form. For instance, the first book of the *Republic* is ruined as a piece of dialectic by the obstreperous behavior of the Sophist, Thrasymachus, who refuses to engage in logical disputation with Socrates. Once Thrasymachus leaves, the dialogue becomes a kind of lecture by Socrates: this is much more satisfactory as a way of setting out a complex theoretical argument, but much less successful from a literary point of view. Furthermore, Thrasymachus's departure seems to symbolize Socrates' inability to persuade Sophists by means of dialectic. Even theoretical discourse is dependent for its success upon the kind of audience that one faces—one's listeners must be committed in advance to the sovereignty of abstract reason. Conversely, Sophists like Protagoras cannot persuade Socrates by means of eloquent speeches, for Socrates demands logical rigor, and he will walk out as quickly as Thrasymachus if his standards of argument are not met. Thus

Plato knew that it was difficult to weigh Socrates' abstract arguments against Protagoras' eloquence without begging all of the important questions.

Most modern readings of the *Protagoras* interpret it as a dialectical work about virtue, which investigates how virtue is defined and whether it can be taught.[50] But this interpretation describes what Socrates wants the dialogue to be, and not what it actually is. Initially, the encounter between Socrates and Protagoras is a dispute between two methodological approaches to ethics, one dialectical and the other humanistic. In keeping with *his* outlook, Socrates tries to make the encounter into a dialectical argument about virtue; but Protagoras resists this move, and with some success. Ancient readers were aware that the dialogue was primarily a debate about method; and this aspect of the work was frequently imitated. For example, in his *Tusculan Disputations*, Cicero deals explicitly with the conflict between dialectic (*disputatio*) and rhetoric (*oratio*). Cicero's questioner, unsatisfied with the argument that Cicero has made against the fear of death, asks for a longer *oratio* that might help convince him. But Cicero, echoing Socrates, maintains that the proper method is to demand yes-or-no answers to brief theses that are logically linked.[51] Nevertheless, the *Disputations* fails to reach a sure conclusion, and the question about method recurs throughout, just as in the *Protagoras*. In both cases, the form in which the work is presented is a mixture of philosophy and rhetoric, mirroring the substantive issue at stake.

The argument of the *Protagoras* continues when Alcibiades describes Socrates' forte as the "give and take of argumentation," while Protagoras (he says) is good at "making a speech at such length that most of his hearers forget the question at issue." This is not fair to Protagoras, as Critias points out; and several other speakers try to effect a reconciliation. In the end, Socrates tries a blatant trick, suggesting that Protagoras should conduct the dialectical cross-examination, while he, Socrates, responds. In other words, he implies that the problem is not a conflict between two methods of argument, but simply a disparity in skill that can be remedied by handicapping Protagoras. He describes their difference in methods quantitatively, rather than qualitatively, as if what distinguished their speaking styles was simply the *number* of words that each used.[52] A numerical difference could be assessed by means of Socrates' *technē* of measurement. However, a quantitative account of the conflict between philosophy and humanism seems to miss the point; there is a crucial methodological difference at stake. Nevertheless, Protagoras is forced to agree to Socrates' suggestion about how to proceed, since it receives widespread approval. Socrates says that there will be no need for a judge to ensure that Protagoras is playing by the rules and asking properly dialectical questions—*everyone* can judge together.

Socrates has successfully won the many over to his side. For Protagoras, consensus is the criterion of truth, but Socrates has persuaded the audience to consider only the degree to which each side is playing by his rules.[53] This is what they are to arrive at a consensus *about*. Nevertheless, Protagoras still has a card up his sleeve: he suggests that "ability in poetry is the most important part of education," and that this ability allows the reader to distinguish ethically "correct" works from "incorrect" ones (339a). Thus Protagoras proposes to continue talking about virtue, and to adopt Socrates' dialectical style, but to make literature and literary interpretation the subject of their discussion. In this way, Protagoras presumably hopes to inject some elements of humanism back into an otherwise dialectical conversation. More specifically, he suggests that they should interpret a poem by Simonides, his "Eulogy to Skopas," because this contains a discussion of virtue. Socrates says there is no need for Protagoras to recite the poem; he has not only read it, but memorized it and made a study of it. They proceed to interpret the poem.

SIMONIDES AND THE PROBLEM OF CONTINGENCY

Simonides' "Eulogy to Skopas" only exists as quoted by Socrates and Protagoras in this dialogue, and there is no independent evidence that the fragments they quote are correct or ordered as in the original; they are certainly not complete.[54] But the following is the text of the eulogy as it is quoted in fragments by Protagoras and Socrates during their debate:

To become a truly good man is difficult: 1
Built without a blemish, square in feet and hands and mind.
[. . . .]

And although it comes from a wise man, it does not ring true to me,   3
The saying of Pittacus that: "It is hard to be good."
A god alone has this excellence; and a man cannot help but be evil   5
If he is overpowered by calamity, and impotent.
For if things go well, all men are good,
But all are evil in adversity,
And those whom the gods favor are most likely to act nobly.

Therefore, I will never throw away a portion of my allotted life   10
Seeking a futile hope, something that cannot be:
A man wholly without fault among us who take fruit from the
    broad earth.
But if I find one, I will send you the good news.
I applaud all those, and love them
Freely, who merely commit no atrocity; for even the gods   15
Never battle against necessity.
[. . . .]

for I am no lover of censure;   17
I am satisfied if
Someone is less than good, but not too incompetent –
If he knows the law that benefits the community–   20
A sensible man. Such a man I will never
Reproach. For the race of fools
Is boundless;
And everything is beautiful in which no outright atrocity is mixed.

There is good reason to suppose that Plato's original audience would have known this poem by heart, and recognized it as soon as they read its opening line quoted in the *Protagoras*. After all, in the dialogue, Protagoras, Socrates, and Hippias are all ready to offer detailed interpretations of the poem at the drop of a hat, and no one else who is listening asks that the work be recited. In his *Nicomachean Ethics*, Aristotle also alludes to the "Eulogy of Skopas": further evidence that the poem and Simonides' perspective on ethics were widely known (1124a3–5). So, by having Protagoras bring up Simonides' work, Plato introduces into the dialogue a whole alternative perspective on ethics that is immediately recognizable to his audience.

In some respects, Simonides' perspective is as far removed from that of Socrates as possible. From the beginning of the *Protagoras*, we know that Socrates possesses a method or art (*technē*) for solving moral dilemmas by means of pure reason, and thereby avoiding contingency. However, this approach to ethics is radically inconsistent with Simonides' point of view. Socrates assumes that there is always just one right thing to do in any case, and that this choice is made clear by his philosophical method. Later in the *Protagoras*, Socrates takes up the case of someone who is "overcome by desire," and therefore fails to do what reason demands. He argues that this is actually impossible: humans beings always do what they think is right, but they sometimes make mistakes in calculation because they lack a rigorous philosophical method. The young Socrates who is depicted in the *Protagoras* already possesses such a method, so he correctly chooses the intellectual stimulation provided by Protagoras over the contingent, sexual stimulation of Alcibiades' company. The older Socrates depicted in the *Symposium* has cultivated his philosophical art to such a degree that he is impervious to both wine and sex: no matter how much he drinks, his behavior is not altered in the slightest. And Socrates spends the very last minutes of his life engaged in teaching and philosophical speculation, without showing any signs of fear or resentment. He knows what is right to do in any situation, no matter how desperate, and he simply does it with equanimity. One of Socrates' essential doctrines is that a just man can never be unhappy, for happiness *is* justice.[55] A just man is unaffected by fate and necessity, for there is always one just choice in any situation; and by doing the best thing, the just man is perfectly happy. In *The Republic*, Socrates describes for Adimantus the proper way to respond to bad luck:

> "Custom, I suppose, teaches that it is noblest to be as still as possible in times of misfortune and not to be vexed, because it isn't obvious what is good and evil, and it isn't useful to take things hard, and nothing in human life is worth great trouble, and to feel distress is an obstacle to that which we need to come to our aid as quickly as possible."
>
> "What are you referring to?" he said.
>
> "Deliberation," I replied, "about the things that have happened. As in a throw of the dice, we should reckon our affairs according to the results, as reason proves to be best, rather than grasping at the calamity like children and wasting time wailing, and should always accustom the soul to engage as quickly as possible in healing and correcting what has fallen and is unsound, eliminating dirges [threnody] with the art of healing." [X.604b–d]

No matter what situation arises, however tragic or unlucky it may seem, we always face a moral problem that we can solve; we can always do what is best. Although bad luck may reduce our prosperity, our longevity, our health, and our status, it cannot affect our morality. In any situation, we can be perfectly moral by doing whatever reason demands. Similarly, Kant says that reason demands just one action in any situation, and those who do the right thing are free from necessity. Freedom of the will, for Kant, just means acting according to the dictates of reason; and no unresolvable conflict among duties can even be imagined.[56] Likewise, Mill believes that there always exists a choice that maximizes happiness; and Rousseau argues that there is one objectively right choice, which corresponds not to subjective desire but to the "general will." This belief is an essential ingredient of the metaphysical tradition in ethics.

But this rational or philosophical response to calamity is, according to Socrates, impossible for those who think in a "poetic" fashion. Poetic descriptions often make situations look genuinely tragic—that is, sufficiently horrifying as to paralyze us, and devoid of any rational solution. For Socrates, poetic "dirges" are childish; and maturity means a rational art of calculation.[57] But Simonides (whose surviving works include several "Threnodies") thinks that it is impossible to be a perfectly good person, because necessity rules human affairs and makes us imperfect. Not only prosperity and health, but even moral worth is completely contingent upon good fortune: "a man cannot help but be evil / If he is overpowered by calamity . . . . And those whom the gods favor are most likely to act nobly" (lines 5–9). This is not just a cynical view of human nature. Simonides even believes that the gods never battle against necessity (line 15), so he seems to be saying that, in principle, there is no escape from contingency. In another fragment, he writes: "For even those who were born in olden days, demigod sons of lordly gods, did not grow old without toil, nor envy, nor danger."[58]

It is unclear why Simonides believes that necessity is inescapable, but one good reason would be a lack of faith that there is always one right choice, a correct decision demanded by reason. Anyone who believes in tragedy thinks that some situations have no satisfactory solution. Simonides has precisely this tragic perspective, which is most evident in his "Dirges." For example: "All things come to one terrible Charybdis / even great virtues and wealth" Or: "There is no evil / that men should not expect, for in short order / god turns everything upside-down."[59] Nevertheless, Simonides says that he finds beauty in lives that are not truly infamous. One function of his poetry is to make tragic situations appear beautiful. Perhaps this is the meaning of his aphorism: "In necessity even harshness is sweet."[60] The theme of his eulogy to Skopas is the glory of a human life that is lived *as well as possible* in a world of inescapable necessity.

Plato is deeply aware of the conflict between a tragic and a philosophical outlook; he even has Socrates ban tragedy from the ideal republic. Not only a tragic view of life, but also a commitment to pluralism would rule out Socrates' belief that there is always one right thing to do in any case. A tragic view rests on the assumption that some situations are *true* dilemmas in which no choice is good. And pluralism assumes that some values are not mutually commensurable—there is no common coin with which to compare them—so reason cannot always tell us which good to choose. Plato presents Socrates as a literary character who is almost supernaturally immune to contingency, who has brought his life under the control of a philosophical *technē* that allows him to measure the true worth of any choice. But in the process, Socrates has lost sight of the complexity and tragic struggle that is celebrated by Simonides; his life is in some ways sterile. The ideal republic that Socrates describes has struck many readers as an anti-Utopia because of its totalitarian banishment of contingency and pluralism; and the realm of ideas in which the philosopher dwells seems to some a poor substitute for the tragic beauty of real human life as celebrated by Simonides.

The contrast between Socrates and Simonides invokes the perennial conflict between an active and a contemplative life. Socrates advocates making one's life as simple as possible, so as to avoid entangling contingencies. Even faced with a complex dilemma, the philosopher is always able to do the right thing, because he can measure the situation and determine the best course of action. But given a choice between a complex or simple life, Socrates always follows the course of minimum complexity. If one's life involves financial, familial, erotic, and civic ties all at once, then difficult moral choices are bound to arise. These dilemmas can be solved by philosophy, but trade-offs may be required. Therefore, in order to maximize the overall ethical quality of his decisions, Socrates sheds as many contingencies as he can, including money, politics, erotic love, and most of his family obligations, seeking instead to lead an essentially contemplative existence. Since he believes that all important knowledge is of the Forms, and that we know them *a priori*, he does not think that experience is a necessary precondition for wisdom; rigorous introspection and logic will produce better results, and these activities are compatible with a purely ascetic, contemplative life. Simonides, on the other hand, celebrates a life that is lived actively, amid contingency, and with benefit to the community. Likewise, Protagoras apparently believes that wisdom comes through experience, especially the experience of facing complex and knotty moral dilemmas. Both his pragmatic stance and his activities as a political advisor suggest that the historical Protagoras preferred the *vita activa* to the path of Socratic withdrawal.

The dispute between these two visions of the good life cannot be decided by a philosophical argument, because dialectic is only sovereign for those who believe in the possibility of a life guided by philosophy. In other words, to *argue* for the sovereignty of philosophy is to load the dice in favor of the contemplative life. Later in the *Protagoras*, Socrates therefore offers a "thick description" of the ascetic life, trying to make it appear beautiful. Simonides takes precisely the opposite position in his "Eulogy to Skopas," which is a celebration of contingency and the active life. Plato's own view on the matter is disguised, for he presents Socrates to us as the perfect contemplative philosopher, but he never tells us in his own words whether he finds Socrates' life admirable. This is a matter to be decided by aspect-seeing, so no abstract statement would carry persuasive force.

Simonides' perspective is not identical to "humanism" as I have been using the term to describe Protagoras' methods. But his perspective is at least highly compatible with humanism. For, in the absence of an *a priori* correct choice in any situation, moral dilemmas must be faced by methods other than moral philosophy; and one alternative source of wisdom is poetry, which can help us to depict one choice as more attractive than another in a difficult situation, although without dialectical certainty. Poetry can also find beauty in the plight of human beings who must make tragic choices between two unpalatable decisions.

Protagoras invokes Simonides' poem, but it seems to me that he does not make it work as well as he could for his own position; he treats it as a kind of philosophical text, and a flawed one at that. By failing to quote any lines (and perhaps stanzas) in which Skopas is described, Protagoras and Socrates make the "Eulogy to Skopas" appear more abstract than it probably was. The success of the original poem would have depended upon its portrait of a particular man who was necessarily less than perfect, but still admirable. But Protagoras is perhaps not wholly at fault in mistreating the poem, for Socrates has established rules to govern the debate that require Protagoras to ask dialectical questions—and dialectic is inappropriate to literary interpretation. First, Protagoras asks Socrates whether the poem is "beautiful" and "correct" (339b). Socrates says that it is. Protagoras then asks whether a good poem can contain a contradiction; when Socrates denies this, Protagoras points out an apparent inconsistency between lines one and four of the poem. In line one, Simonides says that it is difficult to become good; but in line four, he says that he disagrees with the aphorism that it is difficult to be good. Protagoras's intention is to use cross-examination to reveal an error in Socrates' judgment, and he is rewarded with partisan cheering that makes Socrates "feel faint, as if I had just been hit by an excellent boxer" (339e).

As narrator of the dialogue, Socrates confesses that he now tries to buy some time in which to invent a response by turning to Prodicus, an expert on etymology. This stratagem demonstrates that, despite all disclaimers, Socrates is good at tactical maneuvering in real-life debates. He asks Prodicus about the origins of the words "being" (*emmenai*) and "becoming" (*genesthai*). Socrates wants to make Simonides' poem appear consistent by arguing that the poet considered it hard to *become* good, but easy to remain so once goodness was attained. This is a notably poor reading of the poem, for Simonides clearly indicates that it is impossible either to be or to remain purely good—that is, free from necessity.

Protagoras responds: "The ignorance of the poet would be great, if he said that it was easy to hold onto virtue, since everyone knows that this is the most difficult thing of all" (340e). Thus, according to Protagoras, Socrates has removed the inconsistency from the poem by means of a logical distinction between being and becoming, but he has made it sound implausible; the consensus of wise people is against the moral that Socrates finds in the poem. Socrates again turns to Prodicus, and elicits from him the theory that the word "difficult" (*chalepos*) in the poem actually meant "evil" in Simonides' Doric dialect. Thus, in the poem, Simonides disagrees with Pittacus's aphorism because he takes it to mean an absurdity: "It is evil to be good." Protagoras finds this reading incredible; and, on reflection, so does Socrates, who says that Simonides cannot have meant "It is evil to be good," for he also says that gods alone are good. Since confusion has ensued from Protagoras's effort to apply dialectic to a poem, Socrates asks whether he may instead lay out a reading of the entire poem in some detail. Presumably, he has cooked up this reading during his etymological discussion with Prodicus.[61] Although Socrates is violating his own rule that the discussion must remain dialectical, no one complains, and he proceeds.

Socrates now says that in Sparta and Crete, there is an esoteric tradition of wisdom that is embodied in the pithy sayings of sages like

Pittacus. One of these sayings is that it is difficult to be good. Socrates construes Simonides as rebutting this aphorism by claiming that the difficulty is not to be good, but to be perfect: "built without blemish, square in hands and feet and mind." According to Simonides, it is not merely difficult, but actually impossible, to be perfect.[62] Socrates says that this may be true, in part, because "to be" means to remain permanently in a given state, yet experts in individual arts and crafts are always overcome by bad luck sooner or later. Even doctors and other intellectual specialists—who are "good" because of what they know—inevitably forget their knowledge over time. Everyone (Simonides, Socrates, and Protagoras) agrees that specialized, Promethean arts do not guarantee durable goodness. Therefore, Simonides favors a moderate kind of civic virtue, which can serve in place of Pittacus' unrealistic standard of perfection. His goal is to avoid outright antisocial behavior, and to build a political system in which *satisfactory* results can generally be achieved. Socrates does not state his response to this view immediately, but he prepares the ground for it. He will argue later that there is one supreme Promethean *technē*, the philosophical art of measuring objective value, that allows us to escape luck permanently and decisively.

Socrates implies that the debate between Pittacus and Simonides is an ancient version of his own quarrel with Protagoras. Pittacus used the same style of speaking, *brachylogia* (terse speech), that Socrates claims for himself. He was a philosopher, not a Sophist. Further, according to Socrates, Pittacus's wisdom was best understood and appreciated in Sparta and Crete. These states were known for their heroic asceticism, their "laconic" style of speech, their xenophobia, their distaste for public debate, and their total-itarian opposition to pluralism and contingency. We might imagine that these traits resulted from anti-intellectualism, or even from downright ignorance. However, Socrates asserts that the Spartans and Cretans were actually wise, but they kept their wisdom to themselves. In effect, they were much like the citizens of Socrates' ideal republic, and their rulers were like his philosopher kings. Indeed, Pittacus was a tyrant, but a benevolent one. As a philosopher, he knew what was objectively best for his subjects, so they had no need for democratic debate.

By contrast, Simonides argued in public; he defended a pragmatic or realistic approach to ethics; he was a cosmopolitan; and he debated competi-tively, trying to beat Pittacus and thereby enhance his own reputation.[63] Unlike the ancient Spartan sages, he had a reputation for wordiness and digression.[64] Ancient tradition held that he was the first poet to charge money for his works, and that he was very interested in wealth.[65] Both accusations were later made against the Sophists. As a professional writer of odes, Simonides' job was to make his subjects appear noble. Therefore, like a Sophist, Simonides did his best to make the lesser *logos* stronger, as when he praised men (including Skopas) who were evidently flawed. In one extreme case, he even accepted a fee to praise a client's mules, calling them "daughters of storm-footed horses."[66] Thus his role was "economic"—clients paid him to improve the posthumous reputation of their relatives (or pets), and his fee presumably equalled the increase in status that his encomia produced. According to Cicero, Simonides once wrote an ode in praise of Skopas that also contained many tributes to Castor and Pollux. Skopas threatened to pay Simonides only half of the prearranged fee, since these deities had received half of the poet's adulation (but Skopas was immediately struck dead for impiety).[67]

In his cosmopolitanism, his competitiveness, his pragmatism, his commitment to rhetoric, and his fee-taking, Simonides resembled Protagoras, who earlier in the dialogue claimed him as a Sophistic forebear (316d). Further, like Protagoras, Simonides was a particularly successful teacher, an epistemological skeptic, and a pioneer in the study of language.[68] Simonides was a friend of the democratic leader, Themistocles, just as Protagoras was Pericles' friend. He was also an associate of Pausanias, the Spartan reformer who was persecuted by conservatives.[69] Thus, like many humanists, Simonides may have been a democrat.[70] In addition, he admired representational art (another typical humanist attribute), saying: "Painting is silent poetry; poetry is painting that speaks."[71] His literary forte was the creation of moving, naturalistic, "pathetic" images. Quintillian, following Catullus and other classical authorities, said that Simonides' "chief excellence is his ability to arouse compassion, so that some prefer him in this respect to all other authors."[72] Based on Simonides' surviving fragments, it appears that he was, indeed, a moving poet. Thus (to summarize), Simonides participated in a competitive process of praising and damning people through naturalistic poetry, out of which a public estimate of their worth could emerge. His belief in the democratic, deliberative process may account for his statement that "the city teaches man."[73]

Socrates, on the other hand, argues that people and things have real, inherent value that can be known by pure reason. Consequently, the worth of an object or a moral choice is not established by the mere act of describing it; and competitive, rhetorical debate is both dangerous and unnecessary. We can now see that Simonides, Protagoras, the Sophists, most poets and artists, and Athenian democrats all belong to a single humanistic movement, over which Zeus presides as Protagoras's patron and the god of Justice.[74] Opposing them are Pittacus, Socrates, esoteric philosophers, and the ancient Spartans and Cretans, who are alligned with Prometheus.[75] No wonder Socrates thinks that the quarrel between poetry and philosophy is "eternal" (*Republic*, 607b)— it can be traced back from the classical present to the archaic past, and even further, to the primeval struggle between Titans and Olympians.

Although Socrates' interpretation of Simonides' ode is implausible in places, he speaks eloquently and makes the poem appear relevant to his debate with Protagoras. On the other hand, he fails to advance the discussion of virtue. Protagoras had tried to show his mettle by catching Socrates in a purely logical inconsistency; Socrates escaped the trap by means of a skillful exercise in literary criticism; but by that time, the original point was lost. Socrates might say that points *typically* get lost in real conversations that lack dialectical rigor. The fault would then lie with Protagoras, who introduced a poem into the discussion, thereby making it necessary for Socrates to offer lengthy speeches and a historical narrative. In short, Socrates was forced to become a humanist in order to provide a persuasive reading of the poem—but the result (he implies) was a waste of time. Socrates believes that he has struck a blow against literature by his very success in offering a literary interpretation. He argues that the poem embodies Protagoras's point of view—but also that there is no point to arguing about literature. He remarks:

> I leave it to Protagoras to do whatever he pleases; but if you are willing, Protagoras, let's refrain from lyrics and odes, because I would like to reach a conclusion about the questions that I asked you at first, seeking the solution with you. For it seems to me that conversation about poetry is too much like the wine-parties of superficial and vulgar people. These people—since they are too uneducated to entertain each other with their own voices and ideas while they drink—pay a fee for flute-players, hiring for great sums another's voice (the flute's), and entertaining each other with this voice (347b–d).

Kant argues that to act as directed by reason makes us free and autonomous, whereas to act for any other cause makes us heteronomous creatures of contingency.[76] Similarly, according to Socrates, the "vulgar" people who rely on poetry are heteronomous and subject to luck, for they have hired another person to do their talking for them. The word that I have translated as "vulgar" (*agoraios*) is derived from *agora*, the town square and public forum of a Greek city-state. The word connotes someone or something (presumably distasteful) that might be found in the *agora*; but it also alludes to the political realm, and consequently some classical authors used the word positively. Thus Socrates' rhetoric is subtly antidemocratic, as well as anti-poetic. Against his image of a vulgar wine-party, Socrates contrasts a description of an orderly, rational discussion, in which contingency (symbolized by wine) has no effect. He says:

> But where the drinkers are noble, virtuous, and well-educated, you will see no flute-players, nor female dancers and harpers, but they are capable of entertaining themselves on their own and with their own voices, without

> nonsense and childish games, speaking and listening in
> turn according to a plan, even when they are drinking a
> lot of wine. (347d–e)

It is almost as if Socrates were describing his own behavior (years later) in the *Symposium.*[77]

So far, Socrates' "argument" against poetry has consisted in a skillful deployment of similes; it is an exercise in aspect-seeing, intended to make poetry seem vulgar and philosophy appear noble. Socrates then remarks that interpreting literature is futile, because the poet is never present to answer, so any reading is as reasonable as any other. He says that noble people "need no alien voice, not even that of poets, whom you cannot question about what they are saying; people bring them in as allies, some saying that the poet intends one thing with his words, others something different, and the point that is being discussed can never be settled conclusively" (348e). Socrates' first two (implausible) interpretations of the poem by Simonides are perhaps intended to support this point about the indeterminacy of literary criticism. By offering a more plausible interpretation, and then making this appear useless and "vulgar," Socrates wins his argument with Protagoras, for he persuades the company that they ought to turn the discussion back to pure dialectic. Socrates says that the best people, instead of pursuing a futile and vulgar discussion of poetry, "talk with each other, offering and testing their own arguments. And it seems to me that it is better to imitate these people, you and I, setting aside the poets and conducting the conversation according to our own ideas, seeking the truth and testing each other" (347e–348a).

This speech convinces the audience, and ends the "humanistic" section of the dialogue. Instead of understanding virtue by imitation of literary classics (as Protagoras had suggested), the company decides to imitate an ideal philosophical conversation. But Socrates gains his victory over poetry by rhetorical means, not by setting forth a philosophical argument. Moreover, the poem of Simonides remains in the background as an alternative view, compatible with Protagoras's humanism and unrefuted by Socrates' philosophy.

DIALECTICAL CONCLUSION

When Socrates finishes his speech, Alcibiades takes his side and accuses Protagoras of cheating by refusing to answer dialectical questions. Socrates then flatters Protagoras by calling him a good and experienced man, with whom dialectical conversation is uniquely rewarding. Between them, they persuade Protagoras to accept a Socratic approach to the discussion. Socrates then tries to restore the dialectical rigor of the conversation by asking once again whether all the virtues are one. This was the metaphysical question that he had been discussing when Protagoras created a diversion by introducing poems and long speeches (although the point of Protagoras's speech had been to show that all the virtues are *not* one). The discussion had become un-philosophical, but Socrates now struggles to restore it to its ideal, dialectical form. His thesis that all the virtues are one serves to buttress his philosophical position against the rival claim of pluralism, which holds that different ends are not always commensurable, so there may be no *technē* that can tell us what to do in all situations.

Protagoras has a new answer to Socrates' question: wisdom, self-control, justice, and piety are all one, he says, but courage is something else, because a person can be courageous in acting unjustly or impiously. Socrates offers an initial response that depends upon the following logical structure: (1) knowledge is confidence, (2) confidence is courage, and therefore (3) knowledge is courage. Protagoras rapidly demolishes this argument on purely logical grounds. Socrates' second attempt to prove that courage equals knowledge requires several pages of exposition. He wants to begin this intricate argument with an axiom: pleasure equals the good. However, Protagoras says that this claim needs to be investigated. Socrates therefore backs up even further and suggests a new starting point: people, he says, always seek pleasure, and therefore pleasure must be the good. This thesis is often called "eudaimonism." John Rawls argues that the fundamental assumption behind eudaimonism is the idea that all goods are mutually comparable; they can be measured on a single scale, which the eudaimonist calls "happiness." According to Rawls, hedonism "attempts to show how a rational choice is always possible, at least in principle."[78] In contrast to this view, Rawls (like Protagoras) argues that there is not always one morally correct and rational choice. Only in the *Protagoras* does Socrates adopt a view that seems so close to hedonism, or the unequivocal embrace of pleasure. But if the real issue in the dialogue is the conflict between Socrates' *technē* and Protagoras's pluralist vision, then perhaps Socrates adopts eudaimonism largely as a way of getting around pluralism. In other words, what attracts him to eudaimonism is its promise of a single scale on which all goods can be measured, and the most plausible scale is that of happiness.

Socrates suggests that "the many" disagree with the thesis that people always seek the good; they believe that someone can know what is good, but still do the wrong thing because he or she is overcome by pleasure. Socrates believes that there is no such thing as being overcome by pleasure when one is pursuing the good, in part because he has defined the good *as* pleasure. Protagoras agrees with Socrates that the many are wrong, but he wants to know why it is worth even discussing their beliefs, since they "just say any random thing" (353a) Protagoras believes that the truth is whatever everyone believes *once* they have discussed matters rationally and with full information;

he is actually less interested in ordinary, unreflective public opinion than is Socrates.[79] But Socrates promises that the truth will emerge from his refutation of the commonly held view that people can be overcome by pleasure. Socrates always begins with ordinary opinion and then analyzes it until truth emerges, for analysis—rather than synthesis or judgment—is the heart of his dialectical *technē*.

Socrates' refutation of the view that people can be overcome by pleasure essentially consists in the theory that, when people appear to seek pleasure rather than the good, they are actually seeking an immediate pleasure rather than a deferred one. In other words, their error comes not from choosing pleasure over the good, but in failing to measure correctly: they take a distant pleasure to be "smaller" than a more immediate one, through an illusion of perspective. Things are good or evil (i.e., pleasurable or afflicting) in themselves, but people rely on perspectival appearances, and are thereby misled. Socrates' philosophical "science of measurement" promises to provide true measurements of the things in themselves; this is the essence of his "metaphysics of morals."

There are several ways to criticize this position. For instance, someone could say that things are not good or evil in themselves, but that their value depends upon context; or that some things have value that cannot be measured against other things, for they are mutually incomparable. Protagoras was just beginning to express the view that value is relative to context when Socrates complained that his speeches were too long, and the discussion then turned to Simonides' poem. So Socrates is never challenged in his assumption that the value of all things can be measured by a single standard. This assumption serves as the foundation of his "proof" that courage equals knowledge.

In the last section of the dialogue, the conversation at last becomes perfectly dialectical. Socrates asks simple questions that demand yes or no for an answer; each question is logically linked to the next. After Protagoras obediently answers seventeen of these questions, the conclusion that courage is knowledge seems to emerge. Once it is clear that he is going to lose the argument, Protagoras at first refuses to answer Socrates' questions. At last he says: "It is very contentious of you, Socrates, to make me answer." But, being a man of grace, he states "very reluctantly" that courage has been proved to equal wisdom, and then he praises Socrates' skill in disputation. Socrates' successful argument takes the following form:

1. Cowardice means having ignoble fears.
2. Ignoble fears result from ignorance.
3. The coward is fearful because of ignorance.
4. But, by definition, the coward is fearful because of cowardice.
5. Therefore, cowardice is ignorance.
6. Therefore, (by inversion) courage is wisdom.

By "proving" that courage is wisdom, Socrates is supposed to have completed his argument that all the virtues are one, and thereby refuted Protagoras's Great Speech, in which the virtues were treated as plural. However, it is clear that many of Socrates' logical steps are controversial at best. The individual propositions mostly follow from his core philosophical assumption: his view that a rigorous, theoretical method (*technē*) can show us the correct moral choice in any situation. For example, this is why Socrates believes that ignoble fears result from ignorance: anything that results from reason is–by definition–right and noble. Thus the difference between a coward and a prudent person is that the latter is guided by reason, and has correctly measured the situation at hand. He is not misled by the way things appear, but knows how they really are. Socrates' *a priori* metaphysics is profoundly opposed to Protagoras's pragmatism, which depends upon the thesis that man is the measure of all things; for Socrates, things have an objective, non-empirical moral measure. Socrates appears to have won the argument in favor of a metaphysics of morals, but it is not at all clear that he deserves the victory. His logic is assailable on numerous grounds; he has left Simonides' tragic perspective unrefuted; and he has persuaded Protagoras to argue dialectically only by using non-dialectical methods, such as his caricature of literature as a vulgar wine party.

Moreover, there is an irony to the dialogue's conclusion. Socrates says:

> It seems to me that the end of the argument is accusing us and mocking us as if it were a human being; and if it had a voice, it would say, "You are strange, Socrates and Protagoras: you, the one who was saying earlier that virtue cannot be taught, are now eager to contradict yourself, trying to show that all things are knowledge, including justice, prudence, and courage, which is the best way to show that virtue is teachable. For if virtue is something other than knowledge, as Protagoras was trying to say, then clearly it could not be taught; but if it appears to be knowledge as a whole, as you are claiming, Socrates, then it would be remarkable if it weren't teachable. But Protagoras, who suggested that virtue could not be taught, is now eager to show that it is anything other than knowledge, and in that case it is not at all likely to be teachable." (361a–c)

Actually, the structure of the dialogue is as follows. First, Protagoras, in his "Great Speech," claims that virtue is teachable, and that literature is the best means of moral education. Then he and Socrates engage in a methodological dispute, pitting literature against philosophy. Finally, Socrates shows that virtue is teachable, but only by means of philosophy.[80] Thus it seems to me that Socrates and Protagoras are each quite consistent, but they have different definitions of "knowledge" and of "teaching." For Protagoras, virtue can be taught by imparting experience in the form of narratives and examples, which he might call "knowledge." But his notion of knowledge is purely experiential. Socrates, on the other hand, thinks that true knowledge is *a priori*, and if this is right, then virtue can never be learned through experience.[81] Nevertheless, Socrates is capable of educating people in an idiosyncratic way: he draws dialectical conclusions out of his interlocutors as if the conclusions had been there all along—which must be the case if all knowledge is *a priori*. In the *Theaetetus*, he likens his skill to midwifery, explaining that he has no wisdom of his own—only the ability to extract knowledge out of his interlocutors through question-and-answer. "The many beautiful things that they bring forth have been discovered by themselves from within themselves. But god and I are the cause of the delivery."[82] This is why Socrates is eager to make Protagoras explicitly admit, against his will, that courage is knowledge. Protagoras thinks that Socrates is just being an unmerciful winner; but it is essential to the Socratic method to allow the interlocutor to state the intended conclusion himself, since it comes from within and is *a priori*.

Socrates points out that he and Protagoras still have to decide whether or not virtue can be taught, and he suggests proceeding methodically this time, by first asking what virtue *is*. But Protagoras is in no mood for any more rounds of argument with Socrates. He states that he is not of a base nature and is therefore not envious of Socrates' skill; he is willing to acknowledge its excellence. But he would rather talk about something else. Socrates says that for his part he should really leave, since he is late for a prior appointment—and so the dialogue abruptly ends.

WHO WINS THE DEBATE?

In considering Plato's intentions for the dialogue, most readers have assumed that Socrates is supposed to be the victor over Protagoras. I have suggested some reasons to doubt this assumption. First of all, Socrates' dialectic is full of logical errors, and his conclusions are therefore unconvincing. Michael Gagarin has even argued that the weakness of Socrates' dialectic is meant to show Protagoras as the preferable figure.[83] Socrates also fails to deal at all with Protagoras' pluralism or Simonides' tragic vision. But if someone recognized Socrates' mistakes and concluded from them that dialectic itself was inadequate, Socrates would accuse this person of "misology," or prejudice against reason. In the *Phaedo*, Socrates tries to sustain his disciples' commitment to dialectic after several efforts at philosophical argument have failed. We must not, he says, give up philosophy altogether just because of such failures. Socrates tells his followers that misanthropy arises when we believe in people and then become disillusioned with them: we begin to hate humankind in general. Similarly:

> when someone believes in the truth of an argument without basis in the *technē* of reasoning, and then after a short while believes it to be false, whether it actually is or not, and then another and another—and most of all, as you know, those who spend their time with contradictory arguments [*antilogikous logous*], they end up thinking they are the wisest men [*sōphotatoi*], and that they alone have perceived that there is nothing sound or stable either in things or in language, but that all things act as if they were in the Euripus [a treacherous tidal channel], spinning up and down and never staying anywhere for any time.[84]

In this passage, Socrates clearly refers to the Sophists, and particularly to Protagoras. When he mentions "contradictory arguments," he alludes to Protagoras's book entitled *Antilogiae*; and when he describes a doctrine of flux, this sounds like the view that he attributes to Protagoras in the *Theaetetus*: namely, that "nothing is in itself according to itself, but it is always *becoming* for someone, and 'being' is totally meaningless."[85] Thus, according to Socrates, anyone who doubts that absolute truth can be attained by *a priori* arguments must believe that there is no stable reality at all, only appearance and change.

Socrates accuses misologists not only of holding an implicit metaphysics of flux, but also of being intellectually dishonest. Like Thomas Hobbes, Socrates believes that when reason is against a man, he will often be against reason. In the *Phaedo*, Socrates says that it would be "pitiable" for someone to give up on dialectic just because he had so far failed to discover "an argument which is true and certain and capable of being observed."[86] The *Protagoras* ends without Socrates' discovering a "true and certain argument," and it breaks off for contingent reasons (Protagoras's fatigue and Socrates' prior engagement). Nevertheless, it would be a deplorable thing to infer from this that no valid and true argument could *ever* be discovered, given more time and better techniques. Many of Plato's dialogues end in a similarly inconclusive fashion: the *Phaedo* actually stops when Socrates dies. Moreover, Plato often presents failed arguments that improve as the work progresses. For instance, Socrates' first argument that justice equals courage is refuted by Protagoras, but he then provides a better (although still flawed) argument. So the message seems to be that Socrates cannot give us access to perfect *a priori* truth, for he is still a man of contingency and has not attained perfection. However, rather than becoming misologists because of Socrates' failure, we should continue his project, making our conversations ever more perfectly dialectical and improving our techniques, until truth is at last in our grasp. The word "philosophy," after all, means love of wisdom, not the possession of it; and Socrates is the perfect philosopher not because he knows the truth, but because he is the ideal lover of truth, who never succumbs to misology.

Thus we should not conclude from the weaknesses of Socrates' arguments that Plato prefers Protagoras's method. But another reason to doubt that Socrates is supposed to be the victor is the fact that the dialogue is written in a literary form, complete with irony, rhetoric, and value-laden descriptions, and is thus more in line with Protagoras's methods than those of Socrates. However, Plato may have intended to help his readers make a transition from ordinary, "vulgar" conversation—as represented by Protagoras' stories and digressions—to Socrates' pure dialectic, which takes over near the end of the dialogue. This interpretation would explain Plato's use of literary techniques without assuming that he ultimately favored literature.

Socrates' most sustained attack on literature and the other representational arts is contained in the last book of the *Republic*, where he also presents an elaborate *mythos* of his own. A brief examination of this section is relevant to the question of who "wins" the *Protagoras*. In the *Republic*, Socrates says of mimetic poetry: "such things are like a mutilation of the intelligence of the listeners—those who do not have the antidote of knowing what such things really are" (X.595b). Poetry is bad insofar as it shows the concrete world from a particular perspective, but it is bad only for those who lack a philosophical understanding of poetry, which Socrates is able to provide. Socrates is opposed to metaphor and aspect-seeing, but he is willing to accept rhetorical language that is really just a paraphrase or instance of some true metaphysical proposition.

After declaring his intention to attack poetry, Socrates immediately states in shorthand his theory of the Forms, for his core metaphysical ideas are what lead him to denounce narrative. "I suppose," he says, "that we are accustomed to posit one Idea for the many particulars to which we apply the same name" (X.596a). This is a restatement of Socrates' fundamental metaphysical principle that any name must correspond to a single logical entity. For example, Socrates notes that there are many tables and couches; "but there are, I suppose, just two Ideas for these objects, one of the couch and one of the table" (X.596b). He further notes that when a craftsman makes a table or a couch, he keeps his mind on the Idea or Form. In more ordinary language, we could say that the craftsman is guided by the definition of a table or couch when he designs a particular piece of furniture.

According to Socrates, the Form of a couch is everything that a couch *must* be; it contains no contingency or particularity. An ordinary couch, on the other hand, is particular and concrete, and all of its specific characteristics (e.g., color, size, and shape) are extraneous to its identity as a couch. A concrete, particular couch seems to change shape as we view it from different perspectives. This appearance of change is just an illusion created by human perception, but it is inevitable in the world of mere phenomena. On the other hand, the form of a couch—or the couch in-itself—would be subject to no such perspectival relativism: we apprehend it by means of abstract speculation, not by using our senses. At the other extreme, an artistic representation of a concrete couch would be purely perspectival: it would depict an object *as seen* only from one angle, using merely human eyesight. It would therefore be "three steps removed from reality" (X.599a).

When Socrates mentions the example of an artisan who can make representations of anything, his interlocutor, Adimantus, exclaims: "A marvelous Sophist!" (X.596c–d). Adimantus thinks of the Sophists in this context because they were proponents of the representational arts, and because their own rhetorical skills were mimetic. Socrates says that painters and other representational artists do not really make things; instead they merely create "the appearance of them, but not the being and the truth" (X.596e). He argues that the proper response in dealing with poetry is to analyze it until its essential factual claims are revealed—and these usually turn out to be disappointing. He calls imitation "a childish pastime, not to be taken seriously"; and he claims that *trompe l'oeil* painting "is little better, as a calamity for our nature, than witchcraft, conjuring, and many other such arts" (X.602b, e). Thus, as in the *Protagoras*, Socrates tries to make poetry and painting appear base and "ungentlemanly." He states that mimetic artists should never be allowed in a well-governed state (X.605b). And he argues that "measuring and numbering and weighing" are the best antidotes to those arts that mislead us by playing on the frailties of our senses. Measuring is a function "of the rational part of the soul," the faculty that tells us what a couch *really* is, rather than what it looks like from one contingent position (X.602e–f).

Socrates' denunciation of the mimetic arts in book X of the *Republic* is intertwined with a discussion (reminiscent of the *Protagoras*) of contingency and the possibility of unhappiness. For Socrates, the just man can never be unhappy, because he knows the proper "measure" of any situation, and can therefore always choose to do a right and rational thing. This is the chief reward for studying philosophy; it is the benefit of using one's measuring and numbering faculties to discover the nature of things. By contrast, the mimetic arts show things in perspective, relative to the vantage point of the viewer, and so they do not provide us with satisfactory solutions to all dilemmas. In Protagoras's formula, they take man to be the measure of all things. Thus (in the *Republic*, as in the *Protagoras*) Socrates combines the topic of literature or art with the question of unhappiness; and he sees the methods of literary authors as dangerous to the well-ordered state or soul. After denouncing poetry for a few more pages and referring to "the ancient (or eternal) quarrel between poetry and philosophy" (X.607b), Socrates ends the *Republic* by telling his own elaborate and deeply rhetorical story, the Myth of Er. But this is a story about the essential rationality, harmoniousness, and order of the universe. It is a kind of countermyth, a rhetorical statement against tragedy, told with one eye on the Form of the Good. Thus for Socrates, aspect-seeing has its place, but only to demonstrate the supremacy of philosophy.

The doctrine of the Forms is at once metaphysical, aesthetic, and ethical. On several occasions, Socrates tries to prove that the Forms exist and that they are the most genuinely real things. But he also tries to show that they are the most beautiful and best part of existence, and that a life devoted to their contemplation is the happiest life. He makes his metaphysical point through purely dialectical argument; but his aesthetic and ethical judgments are harder to support with logic. Therefore, he often turns to value-laden descriptions, and even to myths, to make the case that the Forms are ideal. In other words, Socrates often makes use of the very literary techniques that he also attacks—but only in order to make the case against literature. Similarly, in the *Protagoras*, Plato cannot argue for the superiority of Socrates' *technē* to Protagoras's humanism, but he can try to show it in dramatic form.

Some philosophers in the ancient world surpassed even Socrates in their hostility to literature. For example, Colotes, an Epicurean, apparently posed the following question to the dead Socrates: "If you wished to impart to us a conception of the heavenly realms and reveal the condition of souls, why . . . did you not do so in a simple and straightforward manner, instead of defiling the very portals of truth with imaginary character, event, and setting, in a vile imitation of a playwright?"[87] Perhaps Plato would respond to this criticism by saying that he wrote dialogues—and Socrates told mythical stories—only in order to show the ultimate superiority of philosophy to literature.

Thus there are good reasons to suppose that when Plato wrote the *Protagoras*, he meant to show Socrates' methodology in a better light than Protagoras's, despite Socrates' failure to discover absolute truth. It would be "misology" to despair about philosophy just because Socrates failed to reach a certain conclusion in the dialogue. However, it would be equally foolish to dismiss humanism because of Protagoras's defeat. The sudden conclusion of the dialogue suggests that Socrates and Protagoras *could* continue their discussion. Plato invites us, if nothing else, to continue the "perennial" debate.

But he also implies something else: that the proper tribunal in which to judge the rival claims of philosophy and humanism is a public discussion—one in which rhetoric and narrative predominate. If we want to decide whether Socrates' way is better than Protagoras's, we must examine how each man actually operates; and that means describing them in a "thick," judgmental way and then deciding where we stand as individuals and as a community. Plato's contribution to our deliberation is, and must be, a literary one. In the end, we may choose philosophy, at least to some extent and for some purposes. But our method of reaching that conclusion will have to be humanistic rather than philosophical. Thus Plato indicates that an inclusive, rhetorical, democratic, public dialogue is ultimately sovereign.

CHAPTER 4

INSTRUCTIVE

TRAGEDY,

ANCIENT AND

MODERN

ARISTOTLE ON TRAGEDY

At least since the time of Socrates, many philosophers have argued that stories gain their value—if they are valuable at all—by encapsulating or exemplifying general truths in concrete form. Since philosophers can know these truths directly, fiction and history are inferior to philosophy, except perhaps as tools for moral instruction. This position harmonizes well with the view, also common among moral philosophers, that moral truth is ultimately a matter of theory. For if truths in the moral realm are laws, maxims, or doctrines, then stories can (at best) offer instantiations or illustrations of these doctrines.

At the opposite end of the spectrum is the position that narrative is an autonomous form and a rival of philosophy, capable of carrying moral meanings that are not subject to philosophical paraphrase. Intimations of this latter view appear in Aristotle's *Poetics*. Its opening phrase promises a manifesto against the Socratic doctrine of literature, for it announces that the work will be "about poetry in itself and its various forms, and the capacity that each has."[1] By contrast, Socrates had treated poetry as a potential vehicle for philosophy, and not as a genre "in itself." Aristotle asserts that poetry has its own form and function, and that it reflects a natural impulse in human beings, namely, to imitate nature and to draw pleasure and knowledge from such imitation (1448b4ff.). If something has a form proper to itself, then for Aristotle it has inherent merit: realizing a form is a good thing. Similarly, if it reflects a natural human impulse (in moderation), then it has *prima facie* value (*Nicomachean Ethics*, 1149b4–5). Thus the good human life can include poetry, defined as imitation with words, as long as the urge to imitate is balanced against other natural impulses. Indeed, imitation is one of the few endeavors that Aristotle dignifies with the word "*diagōgē*"–"rational activity," that for which the enlightened person lives.[2]

Further, Aristotle asserts that poetry ought to realize its natural form to the greatest possible extent, aiming toward unadulterated imitation. He praises Homer for rarely speaking in his own voice as a narrator, which can undermine a poem's imitative effect; unlike some authors, Homer always lets his characters speak for themselves (*Poetics* 1460a5). In terms used by high-school English teachers, Aristotle believes that literature ought to *show* us what it wants to communicate, and not *tell* us. He knows that "imitation is not [merely] transcription," and that descriptive or narrative prose can contain meaning, even if the text never mentions abstract ideas.[3]

Aristotle notes that a well-constructed tragedy is not haphazard; it unifies a series of actions into a rational plot-line. Each incident flows into the next for a reason (1450b21ff.); closure is reached; and the qualities of pity and fear are impressed upon the whole structure of the work (1453b10). To some extent, these criteria are aesthetic; for example, since the use of imitation to incite pity gives us pleasure, the tragic author should impress pity upon the structure of the play (1453b1). But the dramatist's goal of coherent representation has an ethical, as well as an aesthetic, function. A good play presents a series of potentially inchoate events in a comprehensible order so that they leave a certain impression. We know from the *Nicomachean Ethics* that Aristotle views moral argument as a matter of perceiving and describing people and their actions so as to portray them as noble or evil.[4] This is just what a playwright does. For example, a tragedy is a coherent, rational frame-work for ordering events—so harmonious, in fact, that Aristotle compares it to a living organism, in which all the parts cooperate toward a common end.[5] By showing that a tragedy can be discerned within the complex history of a family, the tragedian passes judgment on the characters (for a tragedy is a lamentable thing that happens to a sympathetic person). Similarly, if a satirist makes fun of someone, this means showing that the target of the satire is incompetent, foolish, or evil—and that too constitutes a moral argument. In short, good poetry is the imitation of nature by means of a comprehensible story that incites selected emotions.[6] These emotions—such as the pity and fear that are normally induced by tragedy—serve an ethical function, because they authorize and encourage certain actions and prevent others. Further-more, they have a rational basis, because a story is a form of argument that must be taken as seriously as a logical deduction.

According to Aristotle, any representation in words or images teaches us about the thing represented;[7] and in the case of drama, what is represented is human action under conditions of grave ethical uncertainty. We can imitate the playwright's methods of representation when we face dilemmas of our own, learning about our lives by telling coherent stories about ourselves that produce specific emotions and judgments. Thus the playwright demonstrates a technique that we can use for ethical purposes. In addition, we sometimes notice analogies between events in literature and events that we experience ourselves.

For Aristotle, only a belief about a concrete particular (i.e., a situation that we can actually envision or experience) is genuinely true in the realm of ethics. Any generalization about a multitude of cases is a distortion insofar as the cases actually differ from each other.[8] Furthermore, we do not judge particular cases by applying moral doctrines or definitions to them. "Such arguments have some validity, but truly the decision lies in the facts of life and deeds; for the authority lies in these."[9] Moral truth emerges from the concrete facts when we describe them "thickly," portraying them as part of a meaningful narrative. We make them appear either noble or base by the way that we describe them. Thus, we ultimately gain the authority to judge only if we have perceived the particular case in careful, value-laden terms. "For . . . such matters depend upon the particular circumstances, and the decision lies with perception."[10]

On the other hand, we must also generalize, because real life does not grant us the opportunity to tell coherent stories about every issue that confronts us. The advantage of literature over history is that its examples can be contrived so as to permit a greater degree of generalization without distortion. This is roughly what Aristotle means when he states that "poetry tends to express the universal," and is therefore preferable to history (*Poetics* 1451b1ff.). History is, for example, "what Alcibiades did and experienced"– something highly particular and unrepeatable–whereas tragedy represents *typical* scenarios of betrayal, moral conflict, and so on (1451b10). Fictional stories are valuable partly because we can recognize salient features in them that seem to apply to a wide range of cases; this allows us to forego deliberating afresh about every situation.

On Aristotle's account, poetry is superior not only to history, but also (in some respects) to moral philosophy. For one thing, philosophy cannot arouse emotions in most people, because only the particular case can incite an emotional response.[11] Besides, poetry works better than philosophy as a method for describing good and evil characters, which is a necessary precondition for judging actions–either our own actions or other people's. Aristotle notes: "If by chance someone placed ethical [*ēthikas*] speeches in a row, even supposing that they were well made both in style and intelligence, he still would not make a tragedy that was nearly as effective as one which, however weak it was in these respects, still had a plot and a rational ordering of events" (1450a29ff.).

When Aristotle mentions "ethical speeches," he does not primarily mean dialogue *about* values or moral beliefs; instead, he means speeches that reveal character (*ēthos*). Thus, at one level, Aristotle simply means that we cannot represent characters without showing them in action by means of a plot; merely having them state what they believe or desire is not as effective. However, the Greek word *ēthikos* also means "ethical" in our modern sense; for the portrayal of characters as good or evil by means of a rationally ordered plot serves an ethical function—it communicates values.[12] In fact, Aristotle believes that almost all works of poetry necessarily portray characters in moral terms: "Since imitators imitate people doing things, it is necessary that these people be either noble or base, for characters [*ēthē*] almost always follow one of these models, everyone differing in respect to evil or virtue" (1448a1).

We often recognize that some of the characters in a story are noble, but not by applying a definition of "nobility" to them (Aristotle offers none in the *Poetics*). Rather, we see that they have been described or presented in an admiring spirit—for example, as good yet realistic characters who suffer grave misfortunes (Aristotle's definition of a tragic hero). Thus the emotion-inducing descriptions of literature teach us something about virtue; they help us to see what is noble as opposed to base.[13]

Aristotle famously stressed the importance of plot in revealing character and producing emotion. I suspect that this emphasis resulted in part from his quarrel with Plato, for Plato apparently believed that people always do what they believe is right (vice is just a matter of miscalculation), and therefore we should be able to assess people's characters by analyzing what they believe.[14] Aristotle, on the other hand, thought that people can sometimes err despite their moral beliefs, and therefore we must assess their actions, not their statements—"for it is our choice of good or evil that makes us what we are, not our opinion about it."[15] Hence plot is an essential tool for ethical description. Furthermore, the genres of literature known to Aristotle (epic, tragedy, and comedy) primarily used plot to reveal character. Today, however, we have experience with genres in which character is largely delineated not by plot, but by other means. For example, the rhetoric used by a first-person fictional narrator can tell us something about his or her character—even something that the narrator would prefer not to reveal. Thus Aristotle's analysis should be broadened: plot is just one of many literary techniques that can help to depict characters in such a way as to incite emotions with an ethical character.

Aristotle states that the two emotions that are always induced by tragedy are fear and pity. Further, tragedy always brings about a *katharsis* of these emotions (1453b10). The term "catharsis," in Aristotle's philosophy, is often thought to mean purgation, the process of removing an emotion in order to achieve psychological peace. However, some scholars suggest on philological grounds that it should rather be translated as "clarification." They argue that an audience gains cathartic pleasure not by purging itself of an emotion, but by learning about the sentiment in question.[16] For example, when an audience pities Oedipus, this is because they identify with him,[17] and they thereby realize that they too are vulnerable to misfortune. In this way, they learn something about themselves. Therefore, Isaiah Smithson reads Aristotle as arguing that, although tragedies do not exemplify general moral ideas, they do always capture a kind of metaprinciple of ethics: "The universal truth that members of the audience learn and relearn through the catharsis brought about by *Oedipus Tyrannus* and all tragedy is that life and action have moral aspects, and that at any time circumstances may force them into a position in which their character is assessed."[18]

I believe that this is true; but it is not the whole story. As Smithson says, we identify with the protagonist of a tragedy and thereby come to feel pity for him and fear for ourselves. Thus we learn a valuable lesson: that we may face situations in which our own characters will be assessed. But more specifically, tragedies help us to see *for whom* we should feel pity and under which circumstances.[19] A sensation of pity for someone is a moral response that authorizes certain kinds of actions; and it is quite a different response from contempt, censure, or loathing. Deciding when to feel one of these emotions instead of another is a basic moral issue; and tragedies persuade us to feel pity rather than other sentiments because of their very structure. Thus a tragedy is an "argument" that we should pity a particular person, and a satire might provide a counterargument. Although we (and the people we know) are not precisely the same as the characters whom we see on stage, we can at least imitate the dramatist's methods of representation by telling our own tragic or comical stories about the events of our lives.

In addition to pity and fear, tragic drama can also induce other feelings. For example, Aristotle praises Agathon's plays for being "philanthropic" as well as tragic (1456a21); and *philanthropia* is a virtuous emotion, closely related to pity.[20] When Agathon's plays communicate a spirit of philanthropy, this is not because the author or any of his characters asserts (even implicitly) a maxim, such as "love all of your fellow human beings." Rather, according to Aristotle, Agathon seems to feel compassion toward his characters, which is revealed by the way that he depicts them. Unfortunately, we know much less about Aristotle's analysis of satire and comedy than about his theory of tragedy, for his work on comedy has been lost. But we can probably infer that comedy inspires ethical emotions that are roughly opposite to those induced by tragedy: not compassion, pity, or fear, but rather derision, ridicule, and scorn. These emotions are equally valid under the right circumstances, and equally important as part of a person's moral repertoire.

OBJECTIONS TO ARISTOTLE

Aristotle's position is attractive; but, like any theoretical attack on theory, it suffers from several basic weaknesses. First, there is an apparent problem of circularity: Aristotle's criticisms of generalization seem themselves to be generalizations. This circularity can perhaps be tolerated by asserting that one set of general doctrines—Aristotle's—is valid. But this solution only raises a more serious dilemma, namely, that it is impossible to justify or verify Aristotle's general claims. For example, his postulate that only the particular is true in ethics was explicitly denied by Plato, Kant, and others; and it is difficult to see a way to resolve their dispute, since perennial metaphysical questions are at stake, such as the ontological relationship between universals and particulars. For Plato, what is "really real" is the abstract Form, so he would find Aristotle's commitment to concrete cases unsatisfactory. For Kant, only the universal has authority, so he would repudiate Aristotle's allegiance to specific narratives. Thus any conflict between philosophical theory-building and concrete storytelling must end in a stalemate. Still, we have to act, and that means making a decision about which approach to employ—in itself, an ethical dilemma.

If we try to argue for the philosophical or the literary approach to ethics, the argument will either beg the question by assuming that abstract reason is the highest authority, or else make unverifiable claims about the superiority of literature (such as the claims that Aristotle made). A more promising method, it seems to me, is to use concrete, particular cases to argue for an approach that stresses the concrete and the particular. While this approach by no means avoids the problem of circularity, at least it gives more content to the Aristotelian view. If the concrete cases convince someone who is well-informed and open-minded, then they have offered a good argument.

A further reason to offer a concrete example of morally effective literature is that this may remedy a weakness in Aristotle's position. Aristotle lays heavy stress on the idea that tragedy has a form and a harmonious organization that naturally produce pity and fear. Just as a plant produces seeds and replicates itself, so a tragedy generates two specific emotions in its audience. Indeed, spectators feel fear and pity because they realize that the events in a story constitute a tragedy, which is a recognizable form. In Aristotle's period, there were very few extant literary genres, and these had emerged gradually, as if without human design. Thus it was possible for him to envision tragedy, comedy, and epic as natural phenomena with inherent goals and consequences. Today, however, we recognize an enormous diversity of genres and numerous works that are generically unclassifiable; furthermore, we know that some genres are deliberate creations of individual authors or schools. Thus we cannot rely on the idea that tragedy, for example, "naturally" produces pity and fear, if we hope to explain the relationship between certain plays and certain emotions. On the other hand, it is unlikely that any single theory could explain how every work of art produces its own range of emotions. But a reading of one text can reveal how a particular book produces specific emotions that are both morally relevant and rationally justified by the "argument" of the work.

NABOKOV'S MODERN TRAGEDY

Many literary works effectively communicate values without didacticism. In particular, some books: (1) describe concrete events in such a way as to incite particular attitudes or emotions without being paraphrasable as a series of general doctrines, and (2) simultaneously criticize philosophy, but without resorting to theory as a method of criticism. An especially radical example of this kind of work is Vladimir Nabokov's *Lolita*, which parodies general moral principles, but nevertheless has ethical meaning built into its very structure. Thus Nabokov provides support for Aristotle's position without repeating or endorsing Aristotle's generalizations, and without meeting Aristotle's precise criteria for a "tragedy." In fact, *Lolita* looks at first like the very opposite of a paradigmatic Greek tragedy: it seems to celebrate vice, not virtue; the events described are hardly typical or even plausible; the narrator freely inserts his judgments into the narration; and the characters are not noble. However, these surface differences conceal a basic similarity: like tragedy (in Aristotle's formulation), *Lolita* incites ethically justified emotional responses in the attentive reader, and thereby teaches us some subtle lessons about moral behavior.

Nabokov famously detested the "novel of ideas"—especially those of Thomas Mann and Dostoyevsky. In a 1969 interview, he explained: "By 'ideas' I [mean] of course general ideas, the big, sincere ideas which permeate the so-called great novel, and which, in the inevitable long run, amount to bloated topicalities stranded like dead whales."[21] And he told another interviewer: "As an artist and scholar I prefer the specific detail to the generalization, images to ideas, obscure facts to clear symbols, and the discovered wild fruit to the synthetic jam."[22] *Lolita*, the story of a man's rape of a twelve-year-old girl, could perhaps be read as an allegory of "general ideas," such as selfishness, objectification, or coercion. But a warning not to read it that way is clearly posted at the beginning. The "Foreword," by a fictional psychologist, John Ray Jr., Ph.D., stresses "the ethical impact [that] the book should have on the serious reader." For, he explains: "in this poignant personal study there lurks a general lesson; the wayward child, the egoistic mother, the panting maniac—these are not only vivid characters in a unique story: they warn us of dangerous trends; they point out potent evils. 'Lolita' should make all of us—parents, social workers, educators—apply ourselves with still greater vigilance and vision to the task of bringing up a better generation in a safer world."[23]

Everything about this passage warns us to shun Dr. Ray's method of reading: the Ph.D. appended self-importantly to his name, the reference to "social workers" and "educators," and the mischaracterizations of Lolita, Charlotte, and Humbert, none of whom behave in the novel as they are described here. Ray relies on a "personal communication" from Dr. Blanche Schwarzmann (black-and-white-man) to tell him that at least 12 percent of American males "enjoy yearly" the pederastic pleasures indulged in by Humbert (p. 5).

Ray and his colleagues seek to simplify and classify human behavior, viewing everything in the monochrome statistics of a Kinsey report. The name John Ray recalls the seventeenth-century British naturalist, who devised an influential system for classifying insects—Nabokov's favorite non-literary pastime (p. 326, note). The fictional Dr. Ray Jr. wants us to categorize Humbert as species: pederast; genus: sex maniac; family: egoist; order: sinner; class: human being. Nabokov was proud of his work in classifying insects, although he said that "certain crusty lepidopterists have criticized my works on the classification of butterflies, accusing me of being more inter-ested in the subspecies and the subgenus than in the genus and the family."[24] But he did not treat the human characters in his novels like classifiable insects; he was not interested in reading a "poignant personal study" as a mere example or instantiation of a broader theory. To do so would mean imitating the fictional John Ray, clearly a figure of fun for Nabokov.

So, if we must not attempt to classify Humbert, how *should* we approach the story? Nabokov wrote to Edmund Wilson: "When you do read *Lolita*, please mark that it is a highly moral affair and does not portray American kulaks."[25] Nabokov could, of course, have been wrong about the ethical value of his own novel; but his comment suggests that it is worth examining the book for moral purposes. *Lolita* is Humbert's confession, or a piece of testimony in his own defense.[26] He sometimes addresses "the ladies and gentlemen of [a] jury," sometimes "the reader"; and he asks explicitly for their (or our) forgiveness and understanding. We have to decide whether to grant what he asks, in part by deciding whether he has told us the whole truth. Perhaps there is no such thing as the whole, neutral, impartial truth in any situation, and certainly not in a novel by Nabokov. On the other hand, a careful, critical sifting of the text produces numerous clues about events that Humbert does not mention directly; it also reveals other perspectives on the events that he does report. In fact, at least two parallel stories can be recon-structed: one for Humbert's evil double, Clare Quilty, and one for Lolita herself.

Quilty appears throughout the book under a dizzying array of aliases and disguises. Almost at the end of the book, we finally learn that he has been shadowing Humbert all along, and at that point we can identify at least a few of the forty or more places in the novel where he has already appeared, usually under some kind of pseudonym.[27] In this way, we can reconstruct the outlines of a story with Quilty as protagonist, to rival Humbert's story. We can do the same for Lolita, revealing some new facts about her, but also coming to understand the events of the novel from her perspective.[28] This procedure will reveal how cruelly Humbert has behaved. An interviewer once remarked that he had found Humbert "touching." Nabokov replied, "I would put it differently: Humbert Humbert is a vain and cruel wretch who manages to *appear* 'touching.' That epithet, in its true, tear-iridized sense, can only apply to my poor little girl."[29]

Humbert uses an array of rhetorical techniques to gain our sympathy.[30] For example, he chooses to mention only certain events, trying to turn them into a coherent narrative that shows his character in a good light. Any narrative must select its incidents, and Humbert chooses carefully in order to defend himself; but he fails to control the presentation completely. Hints of other, more damning stories emerge between the lines. In order to spot these hints, we must resist Humbert's version of the narrative—which, at least initially, is entirely selfish and biased—and read critically on the principle that other characters in the book also have interests, desires, emotions, and stories to tell.[31] Thus full understanding of the story is dependent upon an ethical stance; it is an exercise and an epitome of ethical behavior. It requires us to act justly toward Lolita, and we can learn from this experience.

Humbert's self-defense begins in the first pages of the novel, where he recalls that his mother was killed when he was just three years old, and her death deprived him of warmth and love (p. 10). Furthermore, he says that he had a romance with a young girl when he was just thirteen, but that she died of typhus. "I am convinced," he adds, "that in a certain magic and fateful way Lolita begins with Annabel. . . . [T]he ache remained with me, and that little girl with her seaside limbs and ardent tongue haunted me ever since—until at last, twenty-four years later, I broke her spell by incarnating her in another" (pp. 13–15). So Humbert does not hesitate to employ two conventional defenses—the unhappy childhood and the lingering trauma.

However, another interpretation of his overall story emerges in a passing remark. Humbert recalls: "At first, Annabel and I talked of peripheral affairs," namely, "the plurality of inhabited worlds, competitive tennis, infinity, solipsism, and so on" (p. 12). Each of these terms reoccurs in the novel, and in ways that reflect upon the others. The problem of "solipsism" prefigures Humbert's later use of Lolita for his own purposes (for instance, his treatment of her as a mere reincarnated Annabel). At one point, he even boasts that Lolita "had been safely solipsized" (p. 60) by his fantasies. The concept of the infinite reemerges when he explains his sexual perversion by observing: "it may well be that the very attraction immaturity has for me lies . . . in the security of a situation where infinite perfections fill the gap between the little given and the great promised—the great rosegray never-to-be had" (p. 264). Yet this vision of infinity is thoroughly solipsistic; it pays no heed to the twelve-year-old object, the "little given." Lolita's forte is competitive tennis, but Humbert admits that his abuse of her breaks her spirit and thus prevents her from becoming a star (p. 232). Even the "plurality of inhabited worlds" is more than a random preoccupation of two "intelligent European preadolescents," for Humbert shows us *his* world in the novel; but if we want to know what really happened, we must remember that there are other perspectives too, including the world as inhabited by Lolita.[32]

Mention of "infinity" and "solipsism" may seem to conjure up the great, general ideas that Nabokov detested in literature. But "infinity" is Humbert's concept, his excuse for nympholepsy, and the novel can be read as a parody of his selfish use of transcendent abstractions. As for the solipsism that becomes an issue in the novel, this is not a theory presented or criticized by Nabokov (e.g., "Nothing exists or is important except myself"). Nor can we derive any very useful general maxim from the story. An injunction not to be a moral solipsist would be fairly empty and self-evident, like the advice not to be wicked; what matters is to decide what constitutes solipsism. In this case, the spirit of Humbert's narrative is inherently solipsistic, and this flaw prevents us from knowing all the relevant facts about him and Lolita, unless we transcend his perspective. The fact that we can gain information by challenging his solipsistic presentation proves that his account is biased. Thus his solipsism is not a theory or a belief; it is a feature of the text. Nabokov does not offer an account of solipsism; rather, he describes a particular person in such a way as to reveal him as a solipsist. This is what Aristotle meant when he said that an ethical story describes a particular thing *as* something by setting it in a narrative context.

Humbert's next line of defense is to argue that the prohibition on sex with young girls is culturally relative, that it was absent in ancient Israel, Egypt, Polynesia, and other places. Therefore, all such norms are arbitrary. "I soon found myself maturing amid a civilization which allows a man of twenty-five to court a girl of sixteen but not a girl of twelve" (p. 18). True: but Humbert does not *court* Lolita, he rapes her; and anyone who tries to interpret the story from her perspective will not be impressed by his abstract arguments about alien cultures. Cultural relativism is a perennial issue for moral philosophy, but Nabokov shows us something that philosophy could never definitively tell us, namely, that Humbert is an evil man, and that his excuses about the contingency or relativity of moral values are irrelevant. Stated as a proposition, this conclusion is empty or tautologous: it merely condemns evil without telling us in general what is right and wrong. (Similarly, after Aristotle states his doctrine that the right principle is the mean between excess and deficiency, he concedes: "So stated, this proposition is true, but not instructive" [*Nicomachean Ethics* 1138b25–26]. Excess is obviously excessive; deficiency is self-evidently deficient.) Therefore, philosophers have tried to establish theories that objectively and precisely discriminate between good and evil. Whether this project is viable remains an open question. But Nabokov's concrete method of argument bypasses such abstract difficulties: it is clear that Humbert's actions are evil, and this conclusion follows from the details of the text, not from any theoretical position of Nabokov's.

Other hints of Humbert's selfishness emerge in the early chapters: for example, when he remarks a propos of his wife that "matters of legal and illegal conjunction were for me alone to decide, and here she was, Valeria, the comedy wife, brazenly preparing to dispose in her own way of my comfort and fate [by leaving him for another man]" (p. 28). For Humbert, "matters of conjunction" are always for him to decide, and other people's activities and desires are merely ways to dispose of his comfort and fate. Humbert even recalls that "the gloom of another World War had settled on the globe when, after a winter of ennui and pneumonia in Portugal, I at last reached the States. In New York, I eagerly accepted the soft job fate offered me; it consisted mainly of thinking up and editing perfume ads" (p. 32).

Thus, for Humbert, the slaughter of tens of millions in the Second World War is remarkable largely for its "gloom" and the inconvenience that it causes him; the solution is a soft job in New York. So too, when Humbert's potential landlord in America greets him with the news that his home has just burned down, he thinks: "All right, his house would have to be completely rebuilt, so what? Had he not insured it sufficiently? I was angry, disappointed, and bored." His disappointment arises in part because he knows that a twelve-year-old girl lives across the street from the destroyed building where he was to live (p. 36).

Here I am selecting episodes from Humbert's narrative with the deliberate aim of making him look as bad as possible; in many ways, he is a charming and sympathetic character. Some critics have even argued that Humbert is the victim in the tale; and Lolita, a cruel seductress.[33] I think that this estimation is radically, troublingly wrong, but it demonstrates that Humbert's narrative can be persuasive. Nevertheless, my purpose is to read against the grain of Humbert's defensive narrative—and this method proves its worth once he encounters Lolita, the nymphet across the street. He moves into her house instead of the burned one, and ultimately marries her mother as part of a stratagem to remain close to his love-object. Before describing one of their important early moments together, Humbert writes: "I want my learned readers to participate in the scene I am about to replay; I want them to examine its every detail and see for themselves how careful, how chaste, the whole wine-sweet event is if viewed with what my lawyer has called, in a private talk we have had, 'impartial sympathy.' So let us get started. I have a difficult job before me" (p. 57).

He certainly does have a difficult job before him, if his goal is to present the next scene as wine-sweet and chaste. The bare facts are damning: he tries to feel "the hot hollow of [Lolita's] groin" on the pretext of examining a bruise; and she rebuffs him, wiggling and squirming. But these facts are related with much lyrical context, as the living room fills with "implied sun" and "supplied poplars" and "deep hot sweetness." Humbert observes before he makes his move that the softly singing Lolita "had been safely solipsized" (p. 60). In fact, her thoughts and desires are concealed beneath the lyrical solipsism of Humbert's prose; and Humbert is transformed in his own mind from a "sad-eyed degenerate cur" to "a radiant and robust Turk, deliberately, in the full consciousness of his freedom, postponing the moment of actually enjoying the youngest and frailest of his slaves" (p. 60). This is how Humbert envisions the moment; but to Lolita—"who crie[s] with a sudden shrill note in her voice" when he touches her (p. 61), the events must appear quite different. Perhaps there is no such thing as "impartial sympathy"; but if we at least give equal weight to Lolita's version of the events, then Humbert's account appears self-serving to an extreme.

Despite "the insatiable fire of [his] venereal appetite," Humbert boasts that he intends "to protect the purity of that twelve-year-old child" (p. 63). He contrives a plan to knock her out with sleeping pills and then fondle her in her sleep, "operating only in the stealth of the night, only upon a completely anesthetized nude" (p. 124). Reciprocal love is not a part of Humbert's solipsistic plans. After a scene of surreptitious masturbation, he remarks: "What I had madly possessed was not she, but my own creation, another, fanciful Lolita—perhaps, more real than Lolita; overlapping, encasing her; floating between me and her, and having no will, no consciousness—indeed, no life of her own" (p. 62).

On the night when his lust is first consummated, Humbert discovers that Lolita is not a virgin, and presents this as another fact relevant to his defense: "Sensitive gentlewomen of the jury, I was not even her first lover" (p. 135). Furthermore, it is she who suggests that they perform the "stark act of love," Humbert's euphemism for what she calls "doing it" (p. 133). But in the morning, Humbert feels "as if I were sitting with the small ghost of some-body I had just killed." Lolita calls him a brute, and points to a "squashed squirrel" on the road as an apparent analogue to her own situation (p. 140). Humbert knows why she feels as she does, despite her advances to him, and he confesses the reason in the last sentence of Part One: "At the hotel we had separate rooms, but in the middle of the night she came sobbing into mine, and we made it up very gently. You see, she had absolutely nowhere else to go" (p. 142). She knows that he desires her and believes that he has killed her mother (p. 286). Thus she feels herself completely at his mercy.

Humbert imagines how he would use paintings to illustrate their first night together, mentioning all kinds of lyrical and fantastic details, including "a tiger pursuing a bird of paradise" and a "sultan . . . helping a callypygean slave girl to climb a column of onyx." ("Callypygean," according to Alfred Appel's note, means "having shapely buttocks.") But, characteristically, Humbert lets another, more damning image sneak into view among all the others: "There would have been a fire opal dissolving within a ripple-ringed pool, a last throb, a last dab of color, stinging red, smarting pink, a sigh, a wincing child" (pp. 134–35). The wincing child is all but hidden among Humbert's fabulous jungle creatures, but she is there to be spotted nonetheless.

Part Two of the book begins with a long description of Humbert's life with Lolita, intended to show Humbert in a good light. After mentioning an occasion on which he brought Lolita and a friend iced drinks, he explains: "I itemize these sunny nothings mainly to prove to my judges that I did everything in my power to give Lolita a good time" (p. 163). But in the same paragraph, Humbert describes Lolita playing with a jump-rope, and then concludes: "whereupon, flashing a smile to the shy, dark-haired page girl of my princess and thrusting my fatherly fingers deep into Lo's hair from behind, and then gently but firmly clasping them around the nape of her neck, I would lead my reluctant pet to our small home for a quick connection before dinner" (p. 164).

Those fatherly fingers firmly clasping the reluctant Lo's neck tell a story far different from the one that Humbert wants to project; but they are buried amid pages of diversionary material. We also learn (if we are attentive to details) that Humbert denies Lolita her coffee "until she ha[s] done her morning duty" (p. 165); that she never "vibrate[s]" under his touch (p. 166); that he bribes her; that she accepts his money in the hopes of escaping from him (pp. 184–85); and most poignantly, that she weeps "in the night—every night, every night—the moment I feigned sleep" (p. 176). Dolores Haze is dolorous indeed; she is not the Latin temptress whom Humbert conjures up with his private nickname, Lolita. She is a four-foot-ten victim of child abuse. Yet, to repeat, these hints of Lolita's perspective are dropped only *inter alia*; they have to be strung together into a coherent picture against Humbert's intent.

He loves to watch children leaving school from the safety of his car. But "This sort of thing soon began to bore my easily bored Lolita, and, having a childish lack of sympathy for other people's whims, she would insult me and my desire to have her caress me while blue-eyed brunettes in blue shorts . . . passed by in the sun" (p. 161). A "childish lack of sympathy for other people's whims" is Humbert's precise but inadvertent self-description. He never literally rapes Lolita, but no ethical scruples prevent him: rather, "because of the very nature of love's languor, I could not obtain [pleasure] by force" (p. 164). Yet she considers herself to have been raped on their first night together (p. 202). When Humbert does mention "purely ethical fears and doubts," these turn out not to be ethical at all, but rather selfish and practical: he is afraid of being caught (p. 105). He and Lolita quarrel, but we are granted only fragments of "her wild words (swell chance . . . I'd be a sap if I took your opinion seriously . . . Stinker . . . You can't boss me . . . I despise you . . . and so forth)" (p. 171). On another occasion, she says "unprintable things" (p. 205)–unprintable only because they would undermine Humbert's case. If they were unmentionable because they discussed lewd matters, then the whole book would be unprintable.

While all this is going on, Humbert is being shadowed by his double, the playwright Clare Quilty, who also desires Lolita. Humbert loses Lo to Quilty, and finds her again only after she has escaped this second pervert and finally begun a life of reciprocated love and motherhood in the squalor of an Appalachian mining town. Humbert hints that he is going to kill Lolita; but again he misleads us. Upon seeing her, he doesn't murder her, but instead experiences an epiphany, understanding his own behavior from her point of view for the first time. He realizes that he loves her as she is, a pregnant, "hopelessly worn" adult of seventeen (p. 277). When she says that she would prefer Quilty to Humbert, Humbert sympathetically supplies the words that she omits: "*He* broke my heart. *You* merely broke my life." (p. 279). He recognizes that "even the most miserable of family lives was better than the parody of incest" that he had offered her (p. 287).

He recalls that he once overheard her saying that the worst part of death is loneliness; and with this recollection, he suddenly realizes that she might have something profound to say: "that I simply did not know a thing about my darling's mind and that quite possibly, behind the awful juvenile clichés, there was in her a garden and a twilight and a palace gate" (p. 284).[34] In fact, we have reason to believe that Lolita is a remarkably witty, resilient, resourceful child; Nabokov once said that he only admired Pnin more among all the characters in all of his novels.[35]

After his epiphany, Humbert kills Clare Quilty (who, lacking any remorse, is Clearly Guilty[36]), and then experiences one more transcendent moment, when, high above a mountain town, all he can hear are children at play: "and then I knew that the hopelessly poignant thing was not Lolita's absence from my side, but the absence of her voice from that concord" (p. 308). "Had I come before myself," he adds, "I would have given Humbert at least thirty-five years for rape, and dismissed the rest of the charges" (p. 308). It is now possible to imagine that Humbert's testimony has not been a defense in the usual sense. Rather, he may have acted as a "very conscientious recorder" (p. 72) of his mental states as they occurred, displaying "retrospective verisimilitude" (p. 71)–in order to damn himself. If this is true, then his ultimate change of heart is a genuine conversion that deserves our respect. He may in the end play the role of "educator" that he falsely claims earlier in the narrative (p. 91). In that case, his story serves as an exercise in solipsistic description, but laced with just enough clues about the truth that we should be able to transcend his selfish perspective in order to see correctly.

Whether Humbert *deliberately* damns himself is a question that bears on his defense; if he means his story to show his past actions as evil, then he demonstrates true repentance at the end of the novel. It is difficult to know whether his repentance is sufficiently self-conscious and self-critical to absolve him.[37] One reason not to exculpate him is that his own, quasi-theoretical statements about the purpose of *Lolita* verge on immoralism. For example, late in the book, Humbert offers the following justification for his story:

> Unless it can be proven to me . . . that in the infinite run it does not matter that an American girl-child named Dolores Haze had been deprived of her childhood by a maniac, unless this can be proven (and if it can, life is a joke), I see nothing for the treatment of my misery but the melancholy and very local palliative of articulate art. To quote an old poet:
>
> > The moral sense in mortals is the duty
> > We have to pay on mortal sense of beauty. (p. 283)

It sounds as if Humbert wants to justify his book by arguing that, even if it is completely immoral, it nevertheless contains beauty, which provides some consolation. The "local palliative" of art is designed to diminish his own pain, which is caused by guilt. In the last paragraph of the book, he again cites "the refuge of art," adding: "And this is the only immortality you and I may share, my Lolita" (p. 309). But that refuge does no one any good except Humbert: Lolita is dead, and we can gain no obvious moral or therapeutic benefits from Humbert's efforts to assuage his own guilt through literature. Indeed, this invocation of infinity and immortality seems typical of the old, solipsistic Humbert.

Further evidence for Humbert's immoralism emerges during his last meeting with Lolita, when he finally learns the true identity of Quilty. At that moment, he recalls: "everything fell into order, into the pattern of branches that I have woven throughout this memoir with the express purpose of having the ripe fruit fall at the right moment; yes, with the express and perverse purpose of rendering . . . that golden and monstrous peace through the satisfaction of logical recognition, which my most inimical reader should experience now" (p. 272).

Humbert believes that he has exercised so much control over the story that he can generate selected emotions in his readers, including a kind of catharsis (using the word to mean "relief" or "purgation") that emerges when we solve the puzzle of the Quilty subplot. This catharsis is golden, but also monstrous; it is an aesthetic pleasure that we derive from a story about the misery of a child. The same could be said about Humbert's use of lyrical language and fascinating imagery thoughout the book: they afford us an ethically dubious kind of enjoyment. Humbert's statement, then, is a parody of Aristotelianism: the tragedy of Lolita brings us cathartic pleasure because of the artifice of its teller, and specifically because of the reversal of plot (in Aristotle, peripeteia) that affords us "satisfaction" through sudden "logical recognition."[38] As Socrates observed, spectators often feel purged when they watch a tragedy, even though the hero may be blind, miserable, and damned. Similarly, Humbert believes that we can gain monstrous satisfaction from *Lolita*, even though its heroine is exploited and dolorous. Humbert, with his references to the refuge and palliative of art, seems to endorse this immoral version of Aristotelianism.

NABOKOV'S INTENTIONS

But this is only Humbert's defense of his story; Nabokov claims higher value for *his* art–and in particular, for his creation of Humbert as a fictional character. In the afterword ("On a Book Entitled *Lolita*"), Nabokov discusses the purposes of fiction in essentially different terms from those that Humbert uses:

> There are gentle souls who would pronounce *Lolita* mean-
> ingless because it does not teach them anything. I am
> neither a reader nor a writer of didactic fiction, and despite
> John Ray's assertion, *Lolita* has no moral in tow. For me a
> work of fiction exists only insofar as it affords me what I
> shall bluntly call aesthetic bliss, that is a sense of being
> somehow, somewhere, connected with other states of
> being where art (curiosity, tenderness, kindness, ecstasy) is
> the norm. (p. 315)

At first, this sounds like a defense of art-for-art's sake and a repudiation of any ethical role for fiction. But it is important to note that "art," in Nabokov's formulation, entails such ethical attitudes as tenderness and kindness. Even curiosity is a virtue; for example, Humbert should have been more curious when a barber prattled on about his son the baseball player, for then he would have realized that the son was long dead, and that the barber was trying to share his grief.[39] As Richard Rorty notes (discussing the barber): "Suddenly, *Lolita* does have a 'moral in tow.' But the moral is not to keep one's hands off little girls but to notice what one is doing, and in particular to notice what people are saying. For it might turn out, it very often does turn out, that people are trying to tell you that they are suffering."[40] I am not sure that Nabokov wanted to generalize about how people "very often" act; but it is true that we must listen to the characters in his books who try to say that they are suffering; otherwise, we're liable to miss what is going on. Understanding his novels requires curiosity, tenderness, and kindness (and ecstasy emerges only from such understanding). Thus Nabokov's approach is not immoral or amoral; he just wants to distinguish his own work from "topical trash or what some call the Literature of Ideas," as epitomized by Balzac, Gorky, and Mann (p. 315). To avoid the didacticism of a Thomas Mann does not require the pure aestheticism of a decadent; the "local palliative of articulate art" is (in part) the achievement of a redemptive moral sensibility. Nabokov's book has ethical content, but no mere "moral in tow"—nothing like the generalized messages that are sometimes transmitted in didactic fiction.[41]

In the novel itself, the art-for-art's-sake approach is just as much a target of ridicule as the trite moralism of John Ray. For example, Quilty is an aesthete, who first appears under the alias "Aubrey McFate" (p. 52); he later reappears as "Aubrey Beardsley [of] Quelquepart Island" (251). The original Aubrey Beardsley was a fin-de-siècle decadent, whose last name also graces the town of Beardsley, where Humbert and Lolita live: a decadent spot filled with Freudians, whose inhabitants are overly solicitous of the loathsome pederast aesthete Gaston Godin.[42] Humbert remarks that he needs Godin for his defense, for Humbert looks better in comparison (p. 183).

But if all of this represents evidence in favor of the idea that Nabokov despised pure aestheticism, we must remember that the evidence is presented by Humbert, and not directly by the author.[43] Besides, there are also facts suggesting the contrary: that the author of *Lolita* was actually a pure aesthetic immoralist. For example, Quilty's collaborator and biographer is "Vivian Darkbloom," an anagram for Vladimir Nabokov, suggesting that Nabokov is on Quilty's side, a friend of the dissolute aesthete. On the other hand, perhaps the word "darkbloom" indicates that Vivian is Nabokov's wicked twin (or perhaps, like some aesthetes, Nabokov *likes* flowers of evil). Further, although I have observed that Nabokov defines "aesthetic bliss" in partly moral terms in the afterword, there are reasons to doubt that the "real" Nabokov is speaking even here. The essay begins: "After doing my impersonation of suave John Ray, the character in *Lolita* who pens the Foreword, any comments coming straight from me may strike one—may strike me, in fact—as an impersonation of Vladimir Nabokov talking about his own book" (p. 311). That disclaimer leaves us on shaky ground—not that the terrain would have been much firmer without it. Then, half a page later, Nabokov writes that he got the idea for *Lolita* in 1939 or 1940 when he read about an ape in the Jardin des Plantes in Paris. This is an evocative story, alluding to Edgar Allan Poe (whose "Annabel Lee" is a leitmotif in the novel), but it cannot be the whole truth, since a version of the *Lolita* plot appears in Nabokov's Russian novel *The Gift* of 1934–37.[44] So perhaps nothing in the afterword can be taken at face value.

When Nabokov was asked directly why he wrote *Lolita*, he replied: "It was an interesting thing to do. Why do I write any of my books, after all? For the sake of pleasure, for the sake of the difficulty. I have no social purpose, no moral message; I've no general ideas to exploit, I just like composing riddles with elegant solutions."[45] This quotation repeats Nabokov's attack on didacticism, but it also seems to move further, toward a pure formalism that denies any concern for ethics. Of course, there is no reason to think that Nabokov was being "himself" when spoke to BBC reporters in 1962, any more than when he wrote an afterword to his book, or any more than when he put words in the mouths of fictional characters who resembled him, including both Humbert and Quilty. Nabokov once said: "What I really like about the better kind of public colloquy is the opportunity it affords me to construct in the presence of my audience the semblance of what I hope is a plausible and not altogether displeasing personality."[46] This is hardly a guarantee of sincerity.

Furthermore, in the same 1962 interview in which Nabokov described himself as a pure aesthetic formalist, he also explained why he put so many cruel characters in his novels: "they are outside my inner self like the mournful monsters of a cathedral façade—demons placed there merely to show that they have been booted out. Actually, I'm a mild old gentleman who loathes cruelty."[47] Thus, despite his claim of immoralism, it appears that Nabokov was a kind of moralist after all: for it is possible to read his novels, including *Lolita*, as a demonstration of how *much* he despised cruelty.[48] As if these statements were not confusing enough, Nabokov gave yet another formulation of his own ethical role in a public lecture:

> There is, however, one improvement that quite unwittingly a real writer does bring to the world around him. Things that commonsense would dismiss as pointless trifles or grotesque exaggerations in an irrelevant direction [e.g., Humbert's perversion?] are used by the creative mind in such a fashion as to make iniquity absurd. The turning of the villain into a buffoon is not a set purpose with your authentic writer: crime is a sorry farce no matter whether the stressing of this may help a community or not; it generally does, but that is not the author's direct purpose or duty.[49]

In other words, *Lolita* has ethical value, but just by chance, and Nabokov is not much interested in that aspect of his work. This pronouncement about the relationship between art and ethics does not seem to me to be perfectly consistent with the other statements quoted earlier. In the final analysis, the "real" Nabokov may be a chimaera, not because it is always impossible to know what any author means, but because Nabokov is so deliberately and consistently deceptive. It certainly seems unwise to criticize him on the basis of his theoretical declarations, or to take his occasional statements about the artist's access to "infinity" and "immortality" as literal metaphysics.[50]

In any case, regardless of Nabokov's theoretical stance toward fiction, his novel tells its own story.[51] It seems to me that Nabokov does produce "articulate art," and specifically, art that articulates sentiments of "curiosity, tenderness, kindness, [and] ecstasy." In order for us to read the book along these lines, we have to adopt an essentially ethical stance, seeking (as Humbert should have sought all along) to understand Lolita's perspective as well as his own. This stance proves its worth pragmatically, for it produces demonstrable facts about the story. Thus reading *Lolita* is an ethical exercise, and one that can help to train us in the art of behaving well: for ethical behavior is often a matter of understanding the interests and needs of our fellow human beings. On the other hand, *Lolita* will not yield obvious morals or maxims. But then, as Aristotle argued, doing the right thing is often not a question of knowing what is right in general, but of possessing techniques or skills, such as the interpretive skill that fiction teaches us.

Nabokov could perhaps be criticized for producing a work of potential ethical value that is so subtle as to encourage entirely the wrong reactions in some normally astute readers. For example, Robertson Davies argues that Nabokov's theme "is not the corruption of an innocent child by a cunning adult, but the exploitation of a weak adult by a corrupt child."[52] Page Stegner writes: "But readers who are able to transcend their socially conditioned response to sexual perversion . . . find in Humbert's story something that is touching and most un-comic in the destructive power of his obsession. For Humbert Humbert is not a monster; he is not simply grotesque and absurd. Unlike Rousseau, whose confession his sometimes resemble, Humbert evokes our sympathy and pity."[53] Lionel Trilling calls Lolita, "perpetually the cruel mistress; even after her lover has won physical possession of her, she withholds the favour of her feeling." Trilling even accepts Humbert's defense: "Perhaps his depravity is the easier to accept when we learn that he deals with a Lolita who is not innocent, and who seems to have very few emotions to be violated."[54]

Nabokov's turn away from didacticism has a price: he can easily be misinterpreted. This is an especially serious charge if we accept Aristotle's argument for literature over philosophy: namely, that stories can induce intended emotions in a way that abstract theory cannot. If the real effect of *Lolita* was to provide Lionel Trilling with aesthetic pleasure at the expense of an (admittedly imaginary) twelve-year-old girl, then perhaps we would be better off with abstract theories. Better no emotions than the wrong ones, as Socrates might say. As I noted in chapter 2, people's prior experiences and general beliefs influence their concrete moral judgments. Trilling and his contemporaries were accustomed to the battle between aesthetic freedom and Victorian sexual mores; taking the side of freedom, they read *Lolita* as a critique of Puritan America. However, their liberal values did not include much concern for victims of sexual abuse. Consequently, they were blind to demonstrable features in the text of *Lolita*, some of which I have indicated here. Surely I too have overlooked many salient features, but these can be emphasized by other critics. The debate about the moral meaning of a text never ends, but some readings are evidently mistaken.

Nabokov's own distress at the inappropriate readings of his book is apparent in the afterword (written in 1957), and in his letter to Edmund Wilson, in which he implores Wilson to read it as a "highly moral affair." I think, therefore, that it would be unfair to blame Nabokov for an egregious failing on the part of a particular subculture of reviewers, especially since his ability to respond was circumscribed. Since his novel had "no moral in tow," there was nothing clear and general that he could say to encourage a correct reading, without falsifying and simplifying his own work. To declare that Humbert is bad would have been like announcing that *Lolita* contains parodies of Poe, Bizet, and Rousseau (among others). Just as Nabokov assumed that his readers were literate, so he relied on their moral sensitivity. If he had revealed either the literary or the ethical machinery of his novel, he would have spoiled the effect. Nor could he make interpretation too easy without undermining the book's function as a moral exercise. The best he could do was to write an afterword in which he emphasized the role of "tenderness, kindness, and ecstasy" in the novel, and in which he selected certain scenes as especially important: scenes in which ethical sensitivity plays a central part (p. 316).

Thus, strange as it may seem, *Lolita* (the famous dirty book) meets Aristotle's criterion for excellent, edifying fiction. In return, Nabokov's novel supports Aristotle's position, showing by example how morally effective pure literature can be, assuming that it reaches a sensitive audience. At the same time, Nabokov satirizes the generalizing approach that has been common among moral philosophers. Philosophical generalizations per se are not Nabokov's target: Plato, Kant, the utilitarians, and other moral theorists are absent from the pages of *Lolita*. But Freudianism *is* the object of his ridicule— Freudianism conceived as a reductive approach that classifies human behavior and explains it all in terms of one or two principles, instead of understanding people in their indissoluble particularity. Humbert denounces "the scholastic rigmarole and standardized symbols of the psychoanalytic racket" (p. 285); and in the afterword, Nabokov concurs: "I detest symbols and allegories (which is due partly to my old feud with Freudian voodooism and partly to my loathing of generalizations devised by literary mythists and sociologists)" (p. 314). Geoffrey Green writes that Nabokov "sustained the grandest and most extravagant contempt for psychoanalysis known in modern literature."[55] This contempt resulted in part, Green suggests, from Nabokov's belief that Freud was a "demonic monomaniacal champion of one interpretation for all situations."[56] Since Nabokov celebrated the idiosyncratic, unclassifiable, inexplicable detail, he considered Freud his mortal enemy.[57] It would be crude to call moral philosophers, such as Kant and J. S. Mill, "monomaniacal champions of one interpretation for all situations"–but these theorists did propose unitary principles that allegedly underlay all moral action.

Freudians make several appearances in *Lolita* itself. First they try to cure Humbert of melancholia, diagnosing him as "potentially homosexual" and "totally impotent"; but he heals himself by discovering that "trifling with psychiatrists" can be an "endless source of robust enjoyment" (p. 34). He fools his doctors completely, conceals his nympholepsy, and actually prolongs his stay in the sanatorium because he gains so much pleasure from misleading these reductive theorists of the human psyche. Humbert encounters Freudians again when he is lectured by Lolita's principal and teachers, the staff of Beardsley School. Their fixation on anal and genital zones and their desire to prepare "students for mutually satisfactory mating and successful child rearing" sounds almost more obscene than Humbert's private fancy (p. 195).

John Ray and the Freudians in *Lolita* are generalizers, and their generalities are not only satirized, but also shown to be manifest failures when it comes to assessing Humbert. For instance, despite their sophisticated obsession with sex, the Freudians at Lolita's school think that Humbert is an "old-fashioned Continental father" who is "making a princess" of his Lolita (pp. 193–94). Anyone who tries to read *Lolita* along reductive psychoanalytic lines risks missing the point of the book and becoming a posthumous butt of Nabokov's wit.

Nabokov, who remarked that he did not like Plato,[58] might have adopted the same contemptuous attitude toward anyone who tried to devise a simple theory (either normative or explanatory) to cover all human behavior. He certainly criticized Marxists, in part for this reason. Marxists and Freudians were the most influential "philosophers" of the mid-twentieth century, if "moral philosophy" means the creation of theories to cover human action. Nabokov's satire of such projects cannot provide a definitive argument against moral theory in general, nor a conclusive defense of Aristotle's position. He did, however, contribute to the perennial quarrel between philosophy and literature by showing that ethical content can be contained in pure fiction, and by presenting theory-builders as fools. This technique of describing people as something by means of a narrative was precisely the method that Aristotle advocated for ethical argument. Thus Nabokov's *Lolita* counts as an argument against moral theory.

CHAPTER 5

RELIGION VERSUS
THEOLOGY

METAPHYSICS IN RELIGION

In Plato's dialogues, Socrates advocates living according to Truth and Justice as they are revealed by theoretical reason. For him—as for many moral philosophers—normative principles ultimately rest upon "a general account of what there is, including fundamental, fully general statements." This is John Rawls's definition of "metaphysics."[1] Perhaps some moral theories are not metaphysical; but metaphysics involves philosophical habits and attitudes to an extreme degree. Metaphysicians prefer *a priori* arguments to human consensus, certainty to ambiguity, and absolute generality to particular context and detail. It is not difficult to find "fundamental, fully general statements" in most moral theories, certainly including Kantianism and utilitarianism. Therefore, if it is right to use metaphysics in ethics, then my antitheoretical position in wrong.

Today, when people appeal to metaphysical principles or absolute moral standards, they usually do not draw these ideas from secular philosophy. The names of Plato and Aristotle, Locke and Kant are sometimes invoked because of the authority that they seem to bear, but the specific doctrines that are associated with these names rarely have much influence in shaping cultural values or public policy. However, metaphysical views are far from irrelevant in our culture. On the contrary, they play an important role in debates about abortion and euthanasia, the death penalty, animal rights, and other issues. For example, when someone says that a fetus has a right to life because it possesses the essence of a human being, that is a metaphysical claim, as is the claim that a fetus is only potentially a human being. But such ideas are much more likely to come from religion than directly from secular philosophy. After all, although most Americans do not read Plato or Kant, 40 percent go weekly to church, where they may hear, among other things, metaphysical doctrines propounded.[2]

In general, to be religious is often thought to require a commitment to abstract principles of a metaphysical kind: beliefs about the cosmos, God, and the soul that cannot be given by experience, but are so basic and general that they must be taken on faith or perhaps inferred by pure reason. For example, the Nicene Creed (A.D. 325) lists some characteristic religious beliefs:

> We believe in one God, the all-governing father, maker of all things visible and invisible, and in one lord Jesus Christ, the son of God, born of the Father as the only-born, namely born of the essence of the father, God from God, light from light, true God from true God, begotten, not made, of the same essence [*homoousion*] as the Father, through whom all things came to be both in heaven and on earth; who for us human beings and for our salvation descended and was incarnated, becoming human, suffered and rose again on the third day, ascended into heaven, and will come to judge the living and dead.
>
> And we believe in the HOLY SPIRIT.
>
> The Catholic and Apostolic Church anathematizes those people who say that there was a time when the Son of God was not, and that before he was born he was not, and that he came to be out of nothing, or that he is of another essence [*hypostasis*] or substance [*ousia*], or that he is a creature or changeable or mutable.[3]

The Creed is saturated with the vocabulary of Greek philosophy and is explicitly metaphysical. For example, the question, whether Christ was made within time or begotten before time, is an *a priori* one, because no answer could be given by experience. Not even a direct *mystical* experience, such as a vision, could tell the recipient whether Christ was born before time, as the Creed asserts, for even a mystical experience would have to take a spatiotemporal form. Only if a supernatural figure appeared in a vision and announced the explicit proposition that "Christ was born before all time" could an experience help to justify this doctrine—and even then the experience per se would not show that the metaphysical doctrine was true; it would merely show that the celestial speaker had authority to utter metaphysical truths. Thus Martin Luther, who was skeptical about metaphysics, remarked: "I saw that the Thomist opinions, whether they be approved by pope or by council, remain opinions and do not become articles of faith, even if an angel from heaven should decide otherwise."[4] The beliefs of subscribers to the Nicene Creed are thoroughly *a priori* and unrelated to experience, even experience of a mystical or supernatural kind. This does not make their beliefs wrong, but it means that people must believe in metaphysics before they can affirm the Creed.

I have already cited several passages in which Kant argues that we cannot know what is right from mere *examples* of moral action; we must first understand morality in general. Similarly, Kant holds that the truths of Christianity are *a priori* and that even the stories found in the Bible can only be understood if they are analyzed to reveal their harmony with the Idea of the Good. Arguing for a radically metaphysical approach to religion, he writes:

> Even the Holy One of the gospels must first be compared with our ideal of ethical perfection, before one can know Him as such; likewise He says of Himself: Why do you call me (whom you see) good; no one is good (the model of Good) but the one God (whom you do not see). But from where do we have the concept of God as the highest good? Solely from the Idea, which reason draws *a priori* from the concept of ethical perfection, and which it ties inescapably to the concept of free will.[5]

Since, according to Kant and others, religion relies on *a priori* doctrines of a general character, my attack on metaphysics as a source of moral guidance might seem to deny the authority of religion—even to be atheistic. But, although religion is frequently expressed or interpreted in metaphysical terms, it does not necessarily have anything to do with metaphysics. On the contrary, a venerable, devout, and orthodox tradition of Jewish and Christian thinkers have been radical *anti*-metaphysicians, holding that "faith" means a personal relationship with (or experience of) the divine, and that theorizing about God is not just fruitless, but actually impious.

For example, Luther argues that Eve and Adam sinned by beginning to think *about* God—specifically, whether God was to be obeyed—instead of merely worshipping God; this is the original human sin. In Luther's *Lectures on Genesis*, he considers the argument that sin is justified, because without it, there can be no consciousness of God's mercy. This argument, he claims, is used by some Christians to excuse sin; they say, "If our unrighteousness commends the righteousness of God, then I will proceed to sin confidently."

But Luther condemns such reasoning as "philosophical"—as "metaphysics, or rather hypermetaphysics." It is metaphysical because the subject asks about God's abstract relationship to us, instead of merely experiencing that relationship. If a sinner experiences his relationship to God as personal, then he will never contrive an excuse for sin, because obviously God (as a good father) will be upset when he sins. Rather than excusing sin on the ground that human unrighteousness brings forth divine mercy, "you [must rather] become unrighteous when you *feel*, acknowledge, and confess that you are truly a sinner and say: 'I have sinned. Forgive me.'"[6]

A metaphysician might respond to Luther by claiming that any utterance of this kind relies upon a general metaphysical view. To say "Forgive me" to God *implies* that there is some kind of divine being who "really exists" and whose relationship to creation we can know to some degree, although we may not understand all of its mysteries. (Even to speak of mysteries implies that there is some truth about God's abstract nature, although it may be concealed from us.) However, by the same token, a metaphysician may also claim that to act requires a belief in an objective world, that to talk requires a belief in other minds, that to care about things in the future requires a theory of continuous personal identity, that to make moral judgments depends upon a theory of the free will, and so on. On the other hand, it is clear that we can live normal lives without holding such doctrines; and so we may have a relationship with God without ever doing what Luther condemns: "disputing about God" (*disputare de deo*).[7]

Analogously, consider two people who are old friends. One of them becomes convinced by philosophers' attacks on the self, and so begins to doubt that there is any such thing as a continuous human subject that underlies or causes our actions. Despite this skepticism, his relationship with his friend does not change at all: he still cares about her, still respects her, still has a pretty clear understanding of her likes and dislikes, still fondly recalls their past experiences together and looks forward to future events. We could conclude from these facts that the man really does not believe in the skeptical attacks on the self that he has articulated; he must maintain that the human subject exists, for he treats his friend as one. But that would be strange: we would be denying that the man believes an argument that he can state cogently and that he (along with many other people) heartily endorses. Surely it is better to say that his attitude toward metaphysical questions, such as the existence of the human subject, has no bearing on his friendship, for that is not a matter of theory. Rather, the friendship consists of concrete memories, anticipations, worries, hopes, judgments, and so on. Similarly, the faith of a religious person is a relationship with God that is sustained over time; and the believer's general theory of the cosmos has little to do with it. To have faith, people must experience God, fear God, love God, hope to embrace God—but they do not have to articulate a theory of God.

This means, further, that a representation of God or Jesus in scripture, art, poetry, or music does not merely hint at some transcendent, ineffable, abstract quality, such as Love or Goodness—for one cannot have a relationship with Love, and to give it the name "Christ" is to make a merely semantic point. Rather, a representation of God or Jesus is a hypothesis about the literal experience of a divine *person* under a certain aspect, from a certain point of view, and at a certain moment. To the extent that a religious picture is a metaphor, what it refers to is not an abstract, metaphysical proposition, but rather a concrete experience.

My emphasis on the literal meaning of scripture (and of other religious representations) may seem to align me with protestant fundamentalists, who hold the Bible to be "literally true"—that is, inerrant. In fact, biblical interpretation raises two separate issues. One question concerns the nature of biblical *truth*: Is scripture infallible, or can it be tested against outside evidence? The second question concerns the kind of *meaning* that Bible stories contain: Are these stories instantiations of abstract doctrines, or are they concrete narratives, from which we must learn by analogy and imitation? Either answer to the first question is compatible with either response to the second. For the purposes of this book, I am interested only in the nature of biblical *meaning*; I want to argue that Bible stories (like most stories) are meaningful because of their literal, concrete content, and not because they support metaphysical doctrines. This view is compatible with the doctrine that the Bible is inerrant, but it is equally compatible with the theory that scripture is fallible.

Ever since Socrates, philosophers have discovered that when they ask people whether they believe in an objective world, being, the self, and so on, most people reply in the affirmative rather than the negative. But when philosophers ask foolish questions, it is not surprising that they receive foolish answers. Somehow, affirming that the objective world exists seems better than denying it; but people are rarely offered a third option, which is to reply that the question is meaningless, since there is no way to decide the issue if two people offer opposite answers. Furthermore, the metaphysical questions that are asked have varied through the centuries. For example, no one asked classical Greeks whether they believed or disbelieved in a free will, for there was no word for "will" in their language. Yet they thought fruitfully and constantly about choices, actions, and moral responsibilities. Similarly, if a philosopher asks religious people whether God exists, most will say "Yes," and many may even affirm complex abstract doctrines about God's existence, such as the doctrines of the Nicene Creed. But the same people may also affirm the existence of consciousness, the self, and the free will: all doctrines that have come under intense philosophical attack, and that were absent in earlier periods.

Modern skeptics about metaphysics typically say that there are no meaningful answers to questions about the existence or nature of God, because no hypothesis about the divine could be verified by experience. At first glance, this seems to imply atheism: since verifiable propositions cannot be made about God, there is no sense to the phrase "God exists." But the same kind of skepticism would apply equally well against atheism, for the theory that the cosmos is *not* directed by a divine intelligence is no more empirically verifiable than the opposite view. For these reasons, A. J. Ayer (making a typical, if crude, case against metaphysics) claims to be neither a theist, nor an atheist, nor even an agnostic, for agnostics say that they do not know the answer to the question, "Does God exists?" whereas Ayer thinks that there *can be* no answer to this question.[8] I think that Ayer is right to demand that propositions be verifiable, although I have offered somewhat different reasons for this attitude, as well as a broader account of verification (see chapter 1). However, Ayer is disingenuous in claiming that he is not an atheist; at the very least, he is profoundly irreligious. He accepts most empirical statements made by scientists, historians, and others as verifiable, but he denies that an empirical religious statement can ever make sense. Thus he deposits scripture, liturgy, and prayer into the same junk pile of senselessness to which he also consigns the "pseudo-propositions" of Hegelian metaphysics. Specifically, Ayer holds that anyone

> who asserts that he is seeing God is saying not merely that he is experiencing a religious emotion, but also that there exists a transcendent being who is the object of this emotion; just as the man who says that he sees a yellow patch is ordinarily saying not merely that his visual sense-field contains a yellow sense-content, but also that there exists a yellow object to which the sense-content belongs. And it is not irrational to be prepared to believe a man when he asserts the existence of a yellow object, and to refuse to believe him when he asserts the existence of a transcendent god. For whereas the sentence "There exists here a yellow-coloured material thing" expresses a genuine synthetic proposition which could be empirically verified, the sentence "There exists a transcendent god" has, as we have seen, no literal significance.[9]

In fact, the man's statement that "there exists a yellow object to which the sense-content belongs" is completely metaphysical and is not subject to verification (nor is it the kind of statement that anyone but a philosopher would "ordinarily" make). In claiming that the sense-data "belong" to a non-sensible object, the man is asserting a realist position, and if someone else made the contrary claim that the world only contains sense-data, then there would be no way to resolve their dispute.[10] If ordinary statements about colored things always imply that there is an objective world to which sense-content "belongs," then ordinary language must always depend upon metaphysics—for this is a metaphysical doctrine. Therefore, Ayer would be condemning us to silence by arguing that metaphysical claims have no meaning. If this were true, then every time I said something like, "I want you to read this book," I would be asserting a belief in the human subject ("I"), free will ("want"), the existence of other minds ("you"), and the existence of an objective, non-sensible world ("this book"). But, on the contrary, we can sensibly talk about such matters without committing ourselves to realism, idealism, solipsism, determinism, or any other metaphysical doctrine. If, for example, I say that there is a book in my hand, other people can test this claim for themselves without being either idealists or realists. In the same way, we can perhaps experience divinity or believe that other people have had such experiences without asserting anything about the place of God in an abstract map of the cosmos. Just as we can preserve ordinary language about the world without engaging in metaphysics, so we may preserve faith but deny theology.

THE NON-METAPHYSICAL ROOTS OF JUDEO-CHRISTIAN RELIGION

This would mean, not creating some radical new kind of religion, but returning to the roots of Judaism and Christianity. The ancient Jewish religion consisted initially of direct experiences of God through miracles and prayer; traditional rites and laws; and the Hebrew scriptures. The scriptures, in turn, contained concrete narratives, laws, and works of prophesy. None of this explicitly involved metaphysics. The Jewish Bible, like the body of Greek myth, simply told a series of stories about human beings and their interaction with a character, God, about whose metaphysical status little or nothing was said. It was clear that God did things, including making the world; but whether he was inside or outside of time, immanent or transcendent, omnipresent or located in heaven, immutable or subject to change, of the same order of being as ours or a different one—these things were never stated. There were a few utterances that later served as grist for the metaphysician's mill, such as the words from the burning bush, "I am what I am" (Exodus 3:14); but in general, the Bible lacked what could be called a theory of God. For example, as Jaroslav Pelikan notes: "In Judaism it was possible simultaneously to ascribe change of purpose to God and to declare that God did not change; for the immutability of God was seen as the trustworthiness of his covenanted relation to his people in the concrete history of his judgment and mercy, rather than as a primarily ontological category."[11]

Pelikan is referring to two problematical verses from the same chapter of the First Book of Samuel. God first says, "It repenteth me that I have set up Saul to be king" (1 Sam.15:11). But a few lines later it is written that "the Strength of Israel [i.e., God] will not lie or repent, for he is not a man, that he should repent" (1 Sam. 15:29). Thus God is described both as changing and unchanging. Sophisticated theologians could perhaps work out a subtle doctrine to resolve this apparent contradiction (e.g., God is outside of time, and therefore changeless, but he manifests himself to us as a changing phenomenon in order to fulfill his plan). On the other hand, it seems clear that the biblical text itself is not even slightly interested in such metaphysical issues. God is a character in the Bible, a player in the history of Israel, albeit a much more powerful player than any of his human subjects. And a character in a story can be both unchanging—in the sense of faithful to his covenant—as well as changeable in his moods and emotions. As the Strength of Israel, he upholds his promises; as a character with strong emotions, he can repent himself. It is only when the text is interrogated in a metaphysical way that the apparent contradiction arises, for if God is an omnipotent, sempiternal being, an unmoved mover, then talk of his repentance seems strange. The theory that God and Christ cannot be incited to passion by mere human affairs was affirmed universally by early Christian theologians, and was ultimately derived from Aristotle.[12] I have already cited the Creed, which states: "The Catholic and Apostolic Church anathematizes those who say that . . . the Son of God is a creature or changeable or mutable." If Christ (or, a fortiori, God) is unchangeable, then he cannot be moved to any emotion, including repentance, because of human actions. But for someone who is either innocent of metaphysics or skeptical about it, the scriptural reference to a repenting God presents no difficulty.[13]

Christians added to the Jewish legacy a new series of narratives about Jesus and his disciples, a new book of prophesy, and a set of letters written by specific Christians to other Christians about matters of law, ritual, and interpretation. With some exceptions, little of this new structure was any more metaphysical than the Jewish scriptures had been. For example, Jesus provides a trenchant and ingenious interpretation of the Hebrew Bible, but not an analysis of the Socratic kind, that is, not an investigation that reveals the metaphysical status of God. Jesus interprets God's relationship with human beings as one of love, shared suffering, and redemption, but he does not propose (for example) that God is truly real while human beings are dependent for their being upon him, nor that God is inside or outside of time, transcendent or immanent.

Nor, for that matter, do the gospels generalize much from Jesus' particular situation to tell us explicitly how we should lead our lives. Jesus represents more than just an example of moral excellence like the ones that Protagoras might find in Homer—for he is the Son of Man—yet he faces concrete problems that are not the same as those that trouble us, so we must mimic him by a process of analogy, and not by merely applying general rules to our own situation. In other words, rather than offering a philosophy, the gospels propose a concrete example of unparalleled virtue from which we are to learn by comparison. The nature of Christ is never argued for nor even explicitly stated (except perhaps in the opening verses of John, discussed below); it is rather shown, by means of a story and numerous allusions to the prophesies of the Hebrew Bible. Indeed, even Jesus seems to learn his true nature gradually, as it is manifested to him by his deeds and their relation to prophesy. Finally, Jesus rarely states general, abstract truths, but (like Protagoras) prefers to teach by means of parables or stories.

At one point, after Jesus has "taught [the multitude] many things by parables" and he is alone with his disciples, they ask him to explain what he meant by the Parable of the Sower. "And he said unto them, Unto you it is given to know the mystery of the kingdom of God, but unto them that are without, all these things are done in parables: That seeing they may see, and not perceive; and hearing they may hear, and not understand; lest at any time they should be converted, and their sins should be forgiven them" (Mark 4:11–12).[14]

Jesus then proceeds to explain his parable as an allegory of the kingdom of heaven. Thus it might seem that Jesus' method of teaching is "philosophical" after all–his parables, although concrete stories, refer to general, abstract meanings that he *could* impart to the multitude, except that he chooses to encode his doctrine in allegories, "lest . . . they be converted." The apparent cruelty of that strategy is mitigated by the fact that everyone can now read the gospels, so we are all counted among the disciples who have access to Jesus' encoded doctrine. So perhaps Jesus means to say that he does not want the multitude to be converted *yet*, for once he is widely believed to be the Messiah, he will be killed. On that interpretation, the only purpose to Jesus' use of allegory would be *temporary* secrecy. If it were not for political contingencies, his doctrines would be better taught in straightforward, abstract, propositional language. For: "[Jesus] said unto them, Is a candle brought to be put under a bushel, or under a bed? and not to be set on a candlestick? For there is nothing hid, which shall not be manifested; neither was anything kept secret, but that it should come abroad" (Mark 4:21–22).

Thus there is an element of secrecy in Jesus' teaching, but I do not believe that he holds general, abstract doctrines that he translates into allegories in order to conceal them. For one thing, Jesus' private explication of the Parable of the Sower, while more general than the parable, is still a narrative of sorts and not a theoretical statement. Compare the first part of the parable (left) with Jesus' private interpretation of it (right):

Behold, there went out a sower to sow;	The sower soweth the word.
And it came to pass, as he sowed, some fell by the way side, and the fowls of the air came and devoured it up.	And these are they by the way side, where the word is sown; but when they have heard, Satan cometh immediately, and taketh away the word that was sown in their hearts.
And some fell on stony ground, where it had not much earth; and immediately it sprang up, because it had no depth of earth;	And these are they likewise which are sown on stony ground; who, when they have heard the word, immediately receive it with gladness;
But when the sun was up, it was scorched; and because it had no root, it withered away. (Mark 4:3–6)	And they have no root in themselves, and so endure but for a time: afterword, when affliction or persecution ariseth for the word's sake, immediately they are offended. (Mark 4:15–17)

Jesus' explanation certainly gives some guidance about how the parable should be read. But he translates his story about a sower into another story about people who are converted and then wander astray. As interpreted, the parable speaks of "the word," but there is no reason to think that this refers to the Logos of the Stoics and the Neoplatonists (i.e., a rational principle underlying the cosmos); it rather means the news about God as relayed in Scripture. If we hope to find in Jesus' explanation of his parable answers to general metaphysical or theoretical questions, then we seek in vain. For instance, theologians have often asked whether humans are endowed by God with freedom, or whether our fate is predetermined. Jesus' parable could be read by a theologian to reveal the latter view, for the seeds do not choose where they fall. But surely the parable should not be interpreted so mechanically, as a theological theory dressed up in allegorical clothes, so that each detail of the story corresponds to some abstract truth. Jesus is not dealing with the question of free will versus determinism; such abstract issues are foreign to his concrete and practical style. He is rather using an agrarian metaphor to warn his rustic audience about some everyday human pitfalls, such as the error of receiving the word of God too glibly. They are to compare his story of the sower to the story of their own lives, which is the method we often use to draw ethical guidance from narratives.[15]

The Gospel of John is the most "philosophical" of the four: it lacks much of the action of the other versions and contains some abstract theological claims stated by John in his authorial voice. The famous Prologue (1:1–5) has sometimes been interpreted as a reference to Stoic metaphysics, which postulated the Logos as a rational cosmic principle:

> In the beginning was the Word, and the Word was with God, and the Word was God.
> The same was in the beginning with God.
> All things were made by him; and without him was not anything made that was made.
> In him was light, and the light was the life of men.
> And the light shineth in darkness; and the darkness comprehended it not.

These verses stand out from the New Testament in general, and even from most of John's Gospel. "The Word" is used here, apparently, to mean a cosmic, generative principle; but this technical usage is not repeated anywhere after verse 14. Once John has finished his cosmological or metaphysical Prologue, he begins to tell a story filled with concrete signs of Jesus' role as Messiah. Thus the Anchor Bible commentary notes: "In the estimation of some, the Prologue has little to do with the substance of the Gospel but represents the phrasing of the Christian message in Hellenistic terms to catch the interest of Greek readers."[16] If that reading is correct, then an anti-metaphysical Christian could say that the content of John's Gospel lies in the story that it tells; and his Greek-style metaphysical gloss, while not theologically *wrong*, is lacking in content because it is impossible for us to grapple with its concepts and no evidence could be given to show that they are true. If the Prologue originated as a hymn or devotional poem (as most scholars now affirm), then perhaps it should be read not only as an appeal to Greek metaphysicians, but also as a kind of incantation that does not exactly say anything comprehensible, but rather deliberately states something *in*comprehensible in order to underline the majesty of the gospel narrative. John means that this is not just going to be a moving story about a man; it must be treated as authoritative and holy. A Christian anti-metaphysician can agree to imbue the Gospel narrative with unique authority without affirming the literal content of a cosmological proclamation like the one that appears in the Prologue—for these verses turn out to have no comprehensible content at all.

While the Prologue is unusually metaphysical for a New Testament passage, at the same time it is less metaphysical than it could have been. The Anchor commentary notes:

> The description of the Word with God in heaven is remarkably brief; there is not the slightest indication of interest in metaphysical speculations about relationships

> within God or in what later theology would call Trinitarian processions. The Prologue is a description of the history of salvation in hymnic form, much as [Psalm 78] is a poetic description of the history of Israel. Therefore, the emphasis is primarily on God's relation to men, rather than on God in Himself. . . . The Prologue says that the Word was; it does not speculate *how* the Word was, for not the origins of the Word but what the Word does is important.[17]

The story of what the Word does is the story of the Old and New Testaments. In general, the Gospel of John is much more interested in showing Jesus as a character in a story—thereby giving concrete manifestations of his power and glory—rather than speculating about the nature of his being. According to John, Jesus speaks to his disciples on the night when he is to be betrayed, and says: "These things have I spoken unto you in proverbs: but the time cometh, when I shall no more speak unto you in proverbs, but I shall shew you plainly of the Father" (16:25). In fact, it seems that the apostles receive the plain truth after the resurrection when they accept the Holy Ghost (20:22). But what they learn is not a secret doctrine or proposition; rather, they *see* the resurrected Jesus, who bids them to be at peace. In this way, Jesus fulfills his promise to "*shew* you plainly of the Father."[18] Thus John's Gospel is predominantly about showing, not telling; and abstract statements of doctrine are not its essence.

One modern scholar detects in the gospel of John an imitation of forensic testimony: John wants to demonstrate that Jesus was the Messiah by retelling the story of his life with appropriate commentary and references to Old Testament prophesy.[19] John ends his gospel (but for the coda of chapter 21) with the story of Doubting Thomas, to whom Jesus proves his resurrection in a tangible fashion—he offers Thomas his hand. Jesus says: "Thomas, because thou hast seen me, thou hast believed: blessed are they that have not seen, and [yet] have believed" (20:29). This is surely meant for the reader, who cannot touch Jesus' resurrected hand, but can read about it in John's Gospel. John concludes: "And many other signs truly did Jesus in the presence of his disciples, which are not written in this book: But these are written, that ye might believe that Jesus is the Christ, the son of God, and that believing ye might have life through his name" (20:30–31).

CHRISTIANITY ENCOUNTERS GREEK PHILOSOPHY

Thus Judaism and Christianity initially took the form of concrete stories, laws, rituals, traditions, and direct or vicarious mystical experiences.

But Christians and Jews lived in the Hellenistic world, writing in Greek for a Greek-influenced audience, and so they soon encountered a basic cultural presupposition: namely, that any moral or spiritual value inherent in a story must arise because the story refers to an abstract theory that could be stated in plain propositional language. Because of this presupposition, the early Christians often tried to uncover the general truths (cosmological, moral, spiritual, and ontological) that were allegedly contained in the narratives of their tradition. For example, when the Bible mentioned God, they sometimes asked what this meant about the structure of the universe, e.g., Was it guided by the Word as a rational generative principle?

Within the New Testament itself, there is already some evidence of an encounter between Christianity and classical metaphysics. Paul is described as disputing with Stoics and Epicureans at Athens (Acts 17:18), but he does not interpret his religion in their terms; on the contrary, he tries to persuade them that a certain Unknown God whom they have been worshipping is actually the Judeo-Christian deity (17:23). The Prologue of the Gospel of John can be read as influenced by Stoicism, but, as noted above, this is an isolated and enigmatic passage. In general, the New Testament is remarkably free of speculation about God and Christ and the metaphysical interrelation between them: it describes their *emotional* relationship in some detail, but it does not venture a guess as to whether Jesus is one with the Father in form or essence or matter, or any such view. On the other hand, the Bible asserts that there is just one God, yet it also depicts Christ and the Holy Spirit as divine. Therefore, it seemed to Greek-influenced Christians that they had to resolve the problem of the Trinity. Unless a subtle metaphysical doctrine were contrived to explain the three persons as one, the scriptures would seem to contain a contradiction. Debates about the nature of the Trinity (which is not mentioned at all in the New Testament) were conducted in explicitly metaphysical terms, using Aristotelian language of substance and essence, and were so fierce that they led to civil wars, schisms, and massacres. But the authors of the New Testament had not faced the trinitarian problem, because they had not asked metaphysical questions.

Some of the Church Fathers recognized that scripture did not address such issues, but they accounted for this silence in various ingenious ways. For instance, Tertullian (ca. 160–230) wanted to argue that God had created matter out of nothing. He conceded that Genesis did not address this issue at all, but he claimed that this was because the answer was so obvious. If God were coeternal with matter, as Aristotle had falsely argued, then Genesis would have explained this dubious view explicitly so as to prevent error.[20] Tertullian claimed to be an implacable enemy of pagan philosophy; he answered his own questions—"What has Athens to do with Jerusalem? What has the Academy to do with the Church?"—by asserting that the holy scriptures were perfectly sufficient and that Christians had no need of guidance from philosophers.[21] However, he also wrote an entire philosophical treatise on the soul, in which he even "commission[ed] the Stoics to help me" in making the case that the soul is a corporeal substance.[22] In the introduction to this work, he describes the appropriate role of philosophy for a Christian. He begins by attacking metaphysics in a way that makes him sound almost like Wittgenstein. He writes: "But a Christian needs only a little to arrive at knowledge of [the soul]. For what is certain can always be stated in a few words; and one must not ask beyond where one can discover answers; for the Apostle prohibits questions about the infinite. Man must not find more than what he learns from God; but what he learns from God, is all."[23] (Cf. Wittgenstein: "What we cannot speak about we must pass over in silence."[24])

That would be the whole story for Tertullian—there would be no need for a Christian *De anima*—except for one thing: the existence of heresy. Tertullian writes: "And if it were not the case 'that there must be heretics . . . that they which are approved may be made manifest' (1 Cor. 2:19), then it would be unnecessary for us to argue about the soul with philosophers, who are (so to speak) the patriarchs of heretics."[25] But unfortunately, heretics have adopted philosophical doctrines about the soul and have used them for nefarious purposes. Therefore, it is necessary for Christians to articulate an orthodox theory of the soul; and they must derive this doctrine from pagan philosophy, since Scripture is silent about theoretical matters. Tertullian hates philosophers, ridiculing them for their failure to agree about metaphysical matters and stating sarcastically that "the Holy Teaching certainly made a great mistake to come forth in Judea and not in Greece [whose squabbling philosophers he has just described]; and Christ certainly erred when he sent forth fishermen as heralds rather than sophists."[26] Nevertheless, Tertullian finds it necessary to draw on Stoic metaphysical teachings in order to refute the heretics. Thus even this most anti-Greek and anti-philosophical of all the theologians assumed that questions about the metaphysical status of the soul were essential to an orthodox understanding of the Bible. To him it seemed indisputable, if unfortunate, that basic religious questions could only be answered by means of philosophy.

The appropriation of Greek philosophy for Christianity was encouraged by developments in pagan thought after the classical period. Later Greek and Roman philosophers read their myths allegorically, showing that all the apparently ignoble behavior of the gods was only figurative, and that the ultimate meaning of the stories pointed toward a neuter, singular, incorporeal concept of the divine. So Aristotle already held that the gods of Olympus were just popularized, figurative versions of his unmoved mover,[27] and the pagans Longinus and Plotinus, writing during the early years of Christianity, proposed elaborate, allegorical, Platonic readings of Homer.[28] Meanwhile, Jews who lived in the Greek diaspora began reading the Hebrew scriptures as allegorized versions of classical philosophy. For example, Philo of Alexandria (ca. 20 B.C. – A.D. 50), "first reduces classical wisdom to anonymous conceptual form, and then, by reading scripture allegorically, presents that wisdom as the true, underlying meaning of scripture."[29] This became standard procedure for early Christians, notably Clement of Alexandria, Origen, Basil, and Eusebius. Meanwhile, pagan philosophers were sometimes converted to Christianity because they understood it as platonism in a new concrete guise.

According to Werner Jaeger, Gregory of Nyssa (A.D. ?331–?396) "insisted that even the historical books of the Old Testament were to be understood . . . as transparent illustrations of great metaphysical or ethical truths."[30] In his commentary on the Song of Songs, Gregory offers a typical Hellenistic idealist defense of art, claiming that when someone looks at a painting, "he does not linger over the colors painted on the tablet; he beholds instead only the form which the artist has shown." Similarly, Gregory says, when we read the Song of Songs, we must not concentrate on the "mouth, kiss, myrrh, wine, bodily limbs, bed, maidens, and so on," but rather on the forms which these concrete images indicate, namely, "blessedness, detachment, union with God, alienation from evil, and likeness to what is truly beautiful and good."[31] Jews and Christians, unlike some pagans, affirmed that their myths (even the Song of Songs) were literally true; but, like pagan philosophers, they could assert that the allegorical level of interpretation was much more important than the literal—"for the letter killeth, but the spirit giveth life" (2 Cor. 3:6).

In his book *On Christian Doctrine*, Saint Augustine lays out perhaps the most systematic argument for the position that scripture should be read for its hidden metaphysical doctrines. He argues that Bible stories and metaphors always refer directly to general truths "which are elsewhere stated very plainly."[32] According to Augustine, some words are signs that refer directly to things in the world; but some words are signs that refer to other signs which, in turn, refer to things.[33] Augustine is certain that the meaning of any word is its reference to a "thing"; thus he says that even verbs and adverbs must refer to things, or else they would be meaningless.[34] But those words that primarily refer to other words, and only indirectly to things, are called metaphors; and proper understanding of a metaphor means recognizing what "thing" it ultimately refers to.[35] For instance, in the Song of Songs, Solomon sings to his lover: "Thy teeth are like the flock of sheep that are even shorn, which came up from the washing; whereof every one bear twins, and none is barren among them" (Cant. 4:2). Augustine believes that Solomon must be referring to the faithful servants of God, who have rid themselves of worldly cares, been baptized, and borne the fruit of twofold charity (i.e., love of God and man).[36] Solomon put this straightforward fact into metaphorical language, but his metaphor can be accurately and fully paraphrased in plain words. According to Augustine, the usual motive for stating facts in metaphorical language is that they are more moving in this form. But the duty of the reader is always to analyze metaphors until general truth reemerges. And a simple test can be used to decide whether biblical passages are literal or figurative: whatever does not literally describe virtuous behavior must be a metaphor.[37] Since a carnal love song would not be virtuous, the Song of Songs must be an allegory.

Above all, Augustine warns against reading metaphors and stories literally. For example, if someone read the Song of Songs literally as a man's love poem to a woman, this would be a "carnal" reading and a sign of "miserable slavery of the soul"; it would mean being "satisfied with signs instead of things, and not being able to elevate the eye of the mind above corporeal creation to drink in eternal light."[38] He believes that rhetoric has a legitimate place as a means of persuasion, for God ordained the rules of eloquence and chose to use them in dictating scripture.[39] On the other hand, rhetoric is potentially obfuscating and always dangerous. The Lord sometimes uses metaphors as a way of making his meaning difficult to understand, thus reducing man's pride.[40] But no such license is granted to humans, who should always "say wisely what they cannot say eloquently, rather than speaking eloquently but without wisdom."[41] For even the Apostle Paul says: "But though I be rude in speech, yet not in knowledge" (2 Cor. 11:6).

If an audience already knows what is right to do, then eloquence can be used to exhort them into action. But if they do not know what is right, then "of course first they are to be instructed, then moved."[42] In other words, a sober statement of moral truth must precede any use of rhetoric. Similarly, at the beginning of the *Protagoras*, Socrates tells Hippocrates to study philosophy before learning the dangerous art of rhetoric from a Sophist. On the other hand, Jesus *never* teaches his doctrine in plain words, but always uses parables, even when he is explaining to his disciples how the parables are to be read. His method is therefore closer to Protagoras's than to that of Socrates and Augustine.

Augustine represents the archetype of a theologian: not only does he interpret scripture analytically and contrive abstract doctrines, but he also explains why these techniques are necessary, referring to a general theory of language. This theory is so characteristic of metaphysics that Wittgenstein uses Augustine as an explicit target in the opening sentences of his *Philosophical Investigations* (I:i). But some of Augustine's Christian contemporaries have been called "humanists," because they emphasized not speculative theology, and not allegorical analysis, but rather the literal interpretation and representation of scripture. In other words, instead of examining the Bible to see what it says implicitly about the abstract nature of God, they primarily treated God, the patriarchs, the prophets, Jesus, and the apostles as characters with whom living relationships could be established, and about whom concrete interpretive questions could be asked. Why, for example, did God destroy civilization with a flood and then agree to a second covenant with his people? Why did Jesus consort with tax-collectors, inn-keepers, and prostitutes? Early Christian authors wrote homilies, or sermons that encouraged people to imitate Jesus and the prophets. For similar reasons, they wrote inspirational lives of the saints. They depicted Bible stories in visual form, representing the appearance and expression of the characters at each point in the narrative, revealing thematic unities and allusions in the text, and stressing selected episodes in order to make moral or spiritual points. They translated the Bible into the vernaculars of the time, worrying endlessly about how to convey its *literal* meaning in new languages. And they experimented with the imitation of Christ, developing new forms of life (such as monasticism) that were supposed to allow people to act as Christ would. These are all excellent ways to provide moral and spiritual guidance without having to appeal to abstract arguments or general rules.

Some early Christian authors showed a manifest lack of interest in metaphysical issues. Given an ethical question—whether to devote one's time to metaphysics or to the direct imitation of Christ—they chose the latter alternative. For example, Saint Jerome was extraordinarily learned about literature and rhetoric, but it seems that he was both unschooled and uninterested in philosophy.[43] One of his most important models was Apollinarus, bishop of Laodicea, who (as a modern scholar writes), "had little use for either the niggling examination of words popular in some circles or the imaginative allegorism favoured in others. Rather he exerted himself to bring out in all its width and depth what his author was trying to say."[44] Jerome's greatest achievement was a translation and commentary on the Bible, which served as a kind of interpretation of its literal meaning, achieved by rendering it into another language. Jerome lived just when rival creeds were being endlessly debated, but he showed no interest in such abstract statements of belief. "Every day a creed (*fides*) is demanded of me, as if I had been baptized without faith (*fides*). I confess whatever they want: it doesn't satisfy them. I sign: they don't believe."[45]

On the other hand, to my knowledge, no early Christian author developed a consistent *attack* on metaphysics, nor did anyone promote a purely rhetorical approach to religion. Tertullian denounced the pagan philosophers, but (as already noted) he assumed that important religious questions could only be settled philosophically. Jerome showed a lack of interest in philosophy; however, his response was not to deny that theological questions had merit, but to defer to theologians, especially Augustine, to solve these problems.[46] Indeed, he saw himself as the scourge of heretics who held metaphysical views (especially concerning the Trinity) that were denied by the Church, even though he showed little interest in developing orthodox doctrines himself.

ASCETICISM AND ICONOCLASM

Thus proponents of Greek-style theory won a complete victory in the early Church at the level of ideology: they convinced everyone that it would be necessary to import classical metaphysics into the Judeo-Christian tradition if that tradition were to become self-conscious and rational. However, this does not mean that all Christians actually lived according to their explicit pro-philosophical ideology; on the contrary, many showed a kind of inarticulate resistance to theory. The ancient battle between the humanities and philosophy continued in the early Church, for although philosophy's authority was acknowledged in theory by everyone, when it came to deciding how one should live, the purely Socratic approach to life remained controversial.

In chapter 3, I argued that the debate between the Sophists and Socrates was closely related to two other disputes: first, between the active and contemplative life; and second, between defenders and opponents of the imitative or mimetic arts. Socrates, as he is depicted in the *Protagoras*, favors the contemplative or simple life over an active, engaged existence. He believes in contemplation because he thinks that pure thinking, without experience, can produce useful results. Also, since he believes that there is one correct moral choice in any situation (even though some situations require us to make moral trade-offs), he proposes a simplified life that minimizes such compromises and allows us to maximize the morality of our decisions. The Sophists, on the other hand, believe that we must participate in life in order to know anything, since knowledge comes from experience. Further, they doubt that there could be an abstract method for deciding what is morally right in all cases, so instead they advocate participating in real public discussions about political and ethical matters; that way, a public consensus can emerge. But this means living an engaged life. Similarly, Socrates denies the value of imitative art, because it represents concrete particulars from contingent perspectives, whereas metaphysics deals with the things in themselves. But the Sophists defend illusionistic painting and sculpture on the grounds that they present concrete situations from a deliberately chosen perspective, and are therefore useful devices for moral argument.

Both of these debates gained, rather than lost, potency during the early Christian era. Hermits and monks experimented with radically simplified contemplative lives, ascetic beyond the wildest dreams of any Stoic; but some Christians opposed this withdrawal from the world, even to the point of persecuting monks. Simultaneously, a bitter dispute broke out over the role of mimetic Christian art, with Iconoclasts taking the position that all illusion was blaphemous, and anti-Iconoclasts defending the role of icons and other religious pictures. Although the Iconoclasts were defeated as a political force after several episodes of outright civil war, the early Church remained highly suspicious of illusionism.[47]

The anti-representational stance in early Christianity influenced every aspect of the culture, and can perhaps best be shown by means of an example from the plastic arts. The church of San Apollinare in Classe in Ravenna was decorated around A.D. 549, when Ravenna was the political and cultural capital of the Western Roman Empire, and Western Europe was passing from classical to medieval civilization. In the apse of the church is a huge mosaic in the Byzantine style, depicting San Apollinare in awesome and somber majesty. Like most Byzantine works, the mosaic is remarkable for its lack of "realism": there is no foreshortening, no perspective, no use of light and shadow. The picture lacks an earthly setting and a definable context. San Apollinare is a purely conventional figure, without personality, and he is accompanied by twelve identical stylized sheep. Any illusion of reality is further disrupted by the Latin letters that identify the saint by name.

Sixth-century Ravenna, despite being the capital of the Western Roman Empire, was a fairly barbarous place. The self-styled emperor, an Ostragoth named Theodoric, was rumored to be illiterate; it was said that he signed documents using a stencil.[48] So it might appear that the mosaics in San Appolinare lacked naturalism because the artisans of the day were ignorant of classical techniques such as linear perspective. If so, then the artisans of Ravenna must have lost these skills in just a few generations, for the nearby Mausoleum of Galla Placida, decorated about 100 years earlier than San Appolinare, contains mosaics that are skillfully naturalistic. For example, a depiction of the "Good Shepherd" in the Mausoleum shows Christ tending a flock of sheep. Each animal is posed differently—in itself a realistic touch and one that gives the artist a chance to show his virtuosity at foreshortening. Shadows, which appear to be cast by a hypothetical sun to the viewer's rear left, serve to make the forms appear solid and corporeal. Christ sits in a fairly naturalistic position, and the entire hillside is angled back in such a way as to form an entirely believable pictorial space, which appears at the same time to have been arranged like a stage-set for the convenience and enjoyment of the viewer. Christ strokes the muzzle of a sheep, surely a gesture designed to involve the viewer emotionally in the scene as well as to comfort him or her with a concrete manifestation of the Good Shepherd's love. The mosaic looks a little bit like the apse picture from San Appolinare, except that life has been miraculously breathed into it.

The departure from naturalism took place quickly in Ravenna, but not as a result of any catastrophe: the city was safe and prosperous between A.D. 450 and A.D. 550. Nor did the turn away from naturalism produce a decline in aesthetic standards, for the apse mosaic in San Apollinare is majestic and awe-inspiring. Rather, the ambandonment of mimesis in early

Christian art was consistent with an important strain in the philosophy or ideology of the era. There was, first of all, the biblical prohibition against graven images. Moses says that the Lord told him to admonish the people of Israel, "lest ye corrupt yourselves, and make you a graven image, and similitude of any figure, the likeness of male or female, the likeness of any beast that is on the earth" (Deut. 4:16–17). The biblical prohibition against graven images was interpreted by many of the Church Fathers in the light of Socrates' attack on mimesis. After all, Socrates would presumably have disliked the naturalistic mosaic in the Mausoleum of Galla Placida, which depicts individual sheep *as* they would be seen by a human being standing in one particular place. Worse, the mosaic depicts Christ–whose being is divine–in earthly perspective. But Socrates might have had less to say against the mosaic in San Appolinare, which depicts stylized figures that are, to the greatest extent possible, perspectiveless. Short of destroying icons, many early Christians sought to make their art non-realistic, so as to avoid creating "graven images." If a saint or Christ was portrayed without naturalism and labelled in words, then the resulting picture would be more like an abstract statement than a mimetic image.

According to Ernst Gombrich, the "Byzantine icon is not conceived as a free 'fiction'; it somehow partakes of the nature of Platonic truth."[49] And Walter Lowrie writes:

> It is no disparagement of early Christian art to say that it did not aim at sensuous beauty, least of all when depicting the human form. . . . This cannot be explained as an impoverishment of artistic talent; for, if this were the explanation, so sudden a relapse would be unprecedented in the history of art. No, it does not represent a rustifica-tion; for it is manifest that early Christian art purposefully and consistently suppressed the features characteristic of classic art in all times. The classic interest in ground and background disappeared, together with everything tangible, three-dimensional, or plastic–but not space itself, which became free space, space *an sich*, i.e., an infinite or meta-physical space, which is not merely an optical phenomenon. This is an expression of a new meaning and purpose in art.[50]

Lowrie's generalizations about early Christian art aptly describe the mosaics of San Appolinare; and his thesis has been reaffirmed by more recent scholarship.[51] However, the realistic pictures in the Mausoleum of Galla Placida have more in common with the naturalistic spirit of the gospel narrative, which is supposed to be Christianity's foundation.

THE CONSOLATION OF PHILOSOPHY

In A.D. 524, right in the middle of the transition from naturalistic to abstract Christian art, a distinguished citizen of Ravenna named Boethius wrote one of the most influential works for the Middle Ages, an attack on narrative and mimesis called the *Consolation of Philosophy*. This book was translated by, among others, King Alfred, Chaucer, and Queen Elizabeth I; it was a staple of medieval education. It is worth examining closely because it puts the case for religious metaphysics concisely and powerfully, and it does so without prejudicing the issue by merely using the dialectical methods of a philosopher; it is also a work of literature, which contains moving concrete descriptions and narrative prose. Like Plato, Boethius uses rhetoric, thick description, and narrative to argue *against* these techniques, by making a life that is guided by poetry appear contemptible.

Furthermore, if an important strand in Western religious tradition is ascetic, pro-metaphysical, and anti-humanistic, then Boethius is one of its most important sources. Not only was Boethius present and writing just as naturalism disappeared from the visual arts, but he was also an exact contemporary of St. Benedict, the chief architect of ascetic, contemplative monasticism in the Latin West. Boethius grew up at a time when Chistian participation in civic life was widely valued; education in the West was exclusively literary and rhetorical; and the visual arts still preserved the classical tradition of naturalistic representation.[52] But Boethius helped to found a culture that prized asceticism, abstract theology, and non-naturalistic art. As well as introducing some specific scholastic doctrines, he also helped to establish theology as the queen of the sciences, arguing that the true theological method is the application of metaphysics to religious issues. Thus he helped to make theology sovereign over faith, the arbiter of orthodoxy and the most reliable guide for the perplexed. Even after scholasticism faded, this conception of religion remained—and still remains—highly influential in many denominations.

Although the current consensus holds that Boethius was a devout Catholic, he nevertheless wrote a consolation of *philosophy*, not a confession of faith, and explicit references to Christian doctrines are notably absent from it.[53] Henry Chadwick concludes that it is "a work written by a Platonist who is also a Christian, but it is not a Christian work."[54] I am inclined to say something slightly different: it is a classic statement of the view that what is important about religion can best be known by means of theoretical analysis. Today, many Christians who would dismiss "philosophy" as secular would still agree with Boethius that the most important thing in life is *disputare de deo*. In its purest form, this attitude renders unnecessary human experiences of God as recounted in scripture, revelation, etc. It can even encourage an author like Boethius to drop all references to any particular religion, although he almost certainly believed in the literal truth of the Christian Bible.[55]

In addition to serving as an important official at the court of Theodoric, Boethius was also a prolific philosopher, who set himself the project of translating into Latin all the works of Plato and Aristotle, with a commentary that would synthesize their ideas. He never got very far in this task, but he did write several important theological tracts, which offered answers to traditional problems (e.g., free will and the nature of the trinity) by applying philosophical vocabulary and concepts. Boethius's life was cut short in 524, when he was imprisoned and then brutally killed by Theodoric. His *Consolation* depicts himself as a character, awaiting death in prison. Lady Philosophy arives in his cell and teaches him a Socratic attitude toward suffering: in essence, that a just man can never be unhappy.

Boethius's secondary theme (also Socratic) is the superiority of philosophical speculation to narrative. The *Consolation* depicts Boethius as a character who moves from sorrow and self-pity at his own worldly misfortune, to a recognition that, from the perspective of the infinite, his worldly state means exactly nothing. Lady Philosophy's argument consists almost entirely of a series of changes of vantage point, each of which is intended to be inclusive of the last, and each more objectively true. The subjective is inevitably cloaked with that "fog" that rises from false opinion (I:6p),[56] while the otherworldly perspective of the Divine is objectively and timelessly true. Meanwhile, the form of the book moves deliberately from poetry to philosophy, from highly rhetorical, emotional, and subjective verse to detached speculative prose. The book alternates prose and poetry sections; at first, the verse sections are many and lengthy, but they gradually give way to didactic prose. Thus, in the *Consolation*, the abandonment of worldly perspective is deliberate and carefully orchestrated, a gesture in favor of philosophy and against literature. It echoes the movement from realistic dialogue to philosophical exposition that occurs in Plato's *Republic*. It also reflects a similar shift that occured in the visual arts during Boethius's lifetime, suggesting that this shift was motivated by an explicit ideology.

Boethius begins by depicting himself as a man whose entire view of the world is subjective and colored by his current personal situation. He is surrounded by the muses of poetry, an art that depicts human experiences subjectively, emotively, and in a temporal, narrative manner. The opening lines of the work present a poem that Boethius has been trying to write. It begins with an allusion to several lines by Rome's greatest poet, Virgil:[57]

> I once tried to sing songs that were blooming with contentment.
> Alas, I must now begin lamentable, sorrowful songs.
> See how the tortured muses compel me to write . . . (I:1m)

So Boethius's thought it limited to the subjective medium of poetry, rather than dispassionate prose. He cannot even directly write about his own condition, but only about how he must write; and his poetry comes not from within, but from the "tortured" muses. In Kantian terms, Boethius is heteronomous, not autonomous and governed by reason. In Platonic terms, he is at least three steps removed from the Forms. But with the arrival of Lady Philosophy, the journey toward reason immediately gets underway. She herself is described in paradoxes that make her impossible to visualize: she seems at times to be human-sized, and at times to reach all the way to heaven. Her dress, made of "imperishible materials," depicts the Greek letters Π (for practical) and Θ (for theoretical), connected by a ladder "with which one could climb from the lower to the higher element" (I:1p). In keeping with the Platonic-Augustinian belief that the essential truth in a work of art is never literal but always allegorical, Philosophy wears on her sleeve "an ostentatious symbolism which alerts us to its status as symbolism"; and this differs markedly from the literal language of Boethius's opening poem.[58]

In describing Lady Philosophy, Boethius renounces the realism that he can handle so effectively elsewhere. Describing the obviously corporeal muses of poetry, he had recalled: "Having been thus chided, the chorus hung their heads sorrowfully, confessing their shame with a bashful blush, and left my dwelling-place" (I:1p). But objectivity and earthly realism, philosophy and poetry, seem to Boethius to be diametrically opposed. That is why Lady Philosophy is said to dwell partly outside of time and partly within it, in touch both with the eternal truth, "so that in no way would she be thought to be of our age" (I:1p), and also with her dejected interlocutor. By contrast, the muses—who are experts in naturalistic representation and are represented naturalistically—turn out to be mere "stage whores" (1:1p).

As a character in his dialogue, Boethius begins with a perspective that is completely subjective and so far removed from the eternal truth that he doesn't even think that he sees corporeal things as evil; he says only that he "seems to see" them so (I:4p). But, as we learn later, man is innately rational, and although Boethius has strayed far from his native home, the realm of philosophy (I:5p), there lies within him the allegedly rational idea that the entire universe is directed by Divine Order. Once this innate idea has been uncovered, Boethius has a new perspective from which to view the world, and he is immediately able to rediscover a number of truths that are "visible" from his more rational vantage point. The fog of false ideas has already begun to disappear.

In the second book of the *Consolation*, Boethius learns to remove himself to some degree from earthbound space and time. From this new and broader temporal perspective, Fortune begins to look entirely predictable and constant, for she is *always* in flux. Boethius invents the image of a wheel of fortune, always revolving, always bringing the illustrious down from their exalted positions and raising the low on high (I:Vm). But from above the face of the earth, Fortune's effects begin to appear almost meaningless, for the whole world seems "to occupy absolutely no space" (II:7p). Boethius's new perceptions are not just different; they are better, because God "wanted the human race to stand above all earthly things" (II:5p). Still, even at the end of Book Three, Boethius realizes that his perspective remains limited: "I seem to look at [the arguments against worldly success] as it were through a narrow crack, but I would prefer to learn them more openly from you," he tells Philosophy (II:9p).

By now the language of the *Consolation* has become far less "poetic." The prose sections have begun to grow significantly in length, and the remaining verse passages are becoming ever more didactic. Lady Philosophy now occupies a good deal of time in purely theoretical discourse. She is willing to concede the "pleasures of poetic song," but she nevertheless has to ask Boethius to "postpone for a little while this ecstasy [*voluptas*], while I weave arguments that are ordered for you in a sequence" (4:6p).[59] At the beginning, Boethius the prisoner is in such a desperate condition that he requires "mild and moderate lotions [of poetry] to remove the darkness of false affections, so that [he] can recognize the splendor of the true light" (I:6p). He is not yet ready to listen to coherent logical arguments. Therefore, Lady Philosophy must "let the persuasiveness of rhetoric's sweetness" do its work; but she notes that rhetoric "only proceeds on the right path when it does not abandon our principles" (2:1p).[60] Poetry is defended only as a propaedeutic, and only when its implicit meaning equals the truth of philosophy. As Boethius's condition improves, Lady Philosophy is able to drop her rhetorical and poetic methods altogether. She must ultimately turn to explicit statements of doctrine, because only these can provide "remedies" for Boethius's ills, rather than the mere anaesthetic provided by rhetoric (2:3p). Furthermore, as the dialogue progresses, there is ever less dialogue, perhaps because the portrayal of a conversation is a narrative form, bound therefore by time and individual personality. Indications of Boethius's emotional state have by now become relatively sparse, because both the text and the characters are growing increasingly "objective."

Boethius's *Consolation*, like Plato's *Republic*, is a rhetorical and poetic work that is aimed against rhetoric and poetry. Both authors claim to expose the essential metaphysical structure of the universe, as opposed to its merely contingent facts. They do not exactly argue that this structure is beautiful and good, but they present it as such. Thus, for example, Plato never proves that the Forms are morally and aesthetically superior to phenomena, but he presents them with glowing praise. Similarly, Boethius gains consolation by looking at the universe from God's perspective, *sub specie aeternitatis*, instead of from an earthly vantage point. If belief in God is interpreted in a philosophical way—to mean the idea that being as a whole is well ordered and rational—then Plato and Boethius offer an argument for the existence of God despite the manifest evils of the empirical world: in other words, a *theodicy.* Their theodicy consists in showing that contingent facts about the empirical world are not really real, that the only truth which deserves this name is supra-empirical and rational. This position necessitates an educational program, an effort to guide the student from knowledge of the empirical—gained through history, poetry, and literature—to knowledge of the really real, which comes from metaphysics. Once students have attained this knowledge, they will see that the absolute truth is more pure, more glorious, and more beautiful than the knowledge held by people who dwell within Plato's "cave" or Boethius's "fog" of opinion.

Boethius's work is persuasive insofar as it tells a plausible and moving story; but the end of the story transcends empirical plausibility, as well as human emotion, in order to enter a realm that cannot be described in narrative but only named in the abstract language of metaphysics: the sempiternal world or the domain of truth-in-itself. It is only because the story terminates in this domain that the empirical descriptions and poetry of the earlier sections are said to be justified; literature is only defensible if it "honey-coats" the truths of philosophy. In that case, however, we are entitled to ask whether the *Consolation* really is persuasive at all. If its mode of persuasion is narrative—and Boethius employs this very effectively at times—then doesn't it fail just when the narrative stops? Having been lured into the game by the promise of beautiful poetry about the predicament of a real human being, we are then offered metaphysics as the final reward. But perhaps this is a kind of swindle, since we entered seeking a good story. Put another way, Boethius *tells* us that philosophy is superior to poetry, but this is a mere assertion. What he *shows* us, by means of his excellent use of poetry and narrative, is that philosophy is actually inferior.

Most medieval critics retained Boethius's view that poetry was only valuable insofar as it encapsulated general truths that could be paraphrased in theoretical language. Indeed, almost all medieval theorists held that texts could simultaneously contain literal, moral, allegorical, and anagogical (or eschatological) truth-claims. The literal meaning of a text told readers what had happened; the allegorical, what the events signified; the moral, what they taught us about how to live; and the anagogical, what they portended about the ultimate fate of the universe.[61] Of these four levels, the literal was the least important; indeed, it was often disparaged as empty of meaning and irrelevent. Hence, perhaps, the widespread indifference to distinctions between fact and fiction in the Middle Ages. For example, a fourteenth-century manual noted about the genre of didactic stories: "Whether it is the truth of history or fiction doesn't matter because the example is not supplied for its own sake, but for its signification."[62] The same thing could perhaps be said if someone complained that Lady Philosophy really did not visit Boethius in his cell: the book is a lie on the literal level, but it contains moral truth. Because of the priority of moral, allegorical, and eschatological meaning to the merely literal, history and literature were valued less than philosophy and theology, which dealt directly with abstract issues. History and literature were valuable only instrumentally, as a means of honey-coating the fundamental insights of philosophy.

On the other hand, much medieval literature eludes easy paraphrase into moral, allegorical, or eschatological propositions. Even Boethius's own *Consolation* may have been read in the Middle Ages primarily as a moving literal story, rather than as an argument for the primacy of philosophy. Pierre Courcelle has collected hundreds of illustrations from medieval editions of the book: these represent the literal facts of Boethius's story in charming and moving ways, but they ignore the anti-mimetic aspects of the original text.[63] For example, according to the text, Lady Philosophy is impossible to visualize; but in medieval illuminated manuscripts, she generally appears as a graceful, elegant courtier. The early scenes of the book are the most frequently illustrated, since they are by far the most dramatic. It is possible that medieval readers concluded upon finishing the book that the illustrations, like Boethius's own mimetic prose, were inferior sources of meaning, transcended by the speculative philosophy of the last chapters. But it is also possible that people primarily enjoyed the book for its early scenes, which they imagined vividly with the help of illustrations.

FROM BOETHIUS TO DANTE

Nevertheless, the pattern of Boethius's work—the movement from mimesis to speculative philosophy—must have embodied a widely held attitude, for the same pattern is repeated in the greatest of medieval literary works, Dante's *Divine Comedy*. Like the *Consolation*, this is a fictionalized autobiography about a man who is awakened from "despair so bitter that death is scarcely better" (*Inferno* 1:7). He is taken on an educational journey, led first by a poet, Virgil; then by a figure representing theology, Beatrice; and finally by a mystic, St. Bernard.[64] As Dante the pilgrim gradually adopts the vantage point of God and learns that the universe is rational and just, the poem progresses from highly emotional, mimetic verse to abstract (although still metrical) language. Dante's poem alludes constantly to the tradition of medieval love poetry, in which knights channel their unrequited, adulterous love into the pursuit of good deeds. Hence the figure of Beatrice, Dante's divine protector, who was also the subject of his secular love poems. However, Beatrice leads Dante beyond the world that can be described in poetry, and also beyond worldly love, pointing him in the direction of that mystical "love which moves the sun and all the other stars." This is a metaphysical vision, an account of the suprasensible principle that justifies the universe, whereas the empirical facts of earth, hell, and purgatory are its mere epiphenomena.

A comparison between two cantos will show the progress that Dante makes from poetry to theology. In canto 5 of the *Inferno*, Dante the pilgrim enters the second circle of hell, reserved for the lustful, which is a place buffetted by terrible storms. In this circle are found those "carnal sinners who subject reason to desire." Among them are Helen, Achilles, Tristan, and other heroes from epic poetry, as well as thousands of anonymous shades. As soon as Dante hears some of their names, "pity took me, and I was like a man led astray." Virgil tells him that if he wants to hear their story, he should appeal to them with love. Accordingly, Dante calls out to them pityingly, and two shades are attracted to him like magnets. They are Paolo and Francesca, a teacher and his student, who were betrayed into kissing adulterously when they read an Arthurian romance together. Thus love poetry was the lure that condemned them to damnation. Dante the pilgrim is so stricken by their story (which is beautifully told), that he faints in pity.

The Dante who passes through hell in the company of a poet is still trapped in the domain of earthly love and human passion. He is described in poetic and emotional terms, and the poem depicts his pity for two figures who were themselves led into carnal love by love poetry. Dante the pilgrim knows, but fails to understand, that hell was made by "divine authority, the highest wisdom, and first love" (*Inferno* 1:3). From the perspective of the divine, even Paolo and Francesca's eternal suffering is part of a divine order that is, in total, ideal. As Dante gradually realized this, he passes from a hell that is graphically and movingly described toward a paradise that is increasingly abstract. In the final canto of the *Paradiso*, Dante beholds the Divine Love itself, but language fails him and he cannot describe it at all. He says:

> Da quinci innanzi il mio veder fu maggio
> che'l parlar mostra, ch'a tal vista cede,
> e cede la memoria a tanto oltraggio. (33:55ff.)

> ("From then on, my vision was greater than speech
> shows—speech which fails at such a sight, and memory
> fails when faced with such superabundance.")

As Dante gazes at the Infinite Goodness, what he sees is a metaphysical theory that is articulated using the vocabulary of scholastic philosophy, although it is paradoxical and beyond the power of human minds to grasp:

> Nel suo profundo vidi che s'interna,
> legato con amore in un volume,
> ciò che per l'universo si squaderna:

sustanze a accidenti e lor costume
　　quasi conflati insieme, per tal modo
　　che ciò che dico è un semplice lume. (33:85–90)

("In its profundity I saw what is gathered together, bound
with love in a single volume, that which in the universe is
disparate: substances and accidents and their dispositions
almost conflated together, in such a way that what I say is
but a crude illumination.")

This vision is the climax of the entire *Divine Comedy*, and the experience
gives Dante his license to write metaphorically. Socrates told myths because
he had one eye on Truth. Augustine permitted rhetoric as a means of
instruction only for those who already knew the word of God. Similarly,
although Dante opposes poetry in general, he allows himself to tell a story
because he has seen the Divine Love, and therefore he can set all of his
concrete experiences in its perspective. Moreover, he *must* write metaphorically if he wants "to leave to future generations a single ember of [God's]
glory" (33:71–72), because his ecstatic vision cannot be literally described. As
he writes in the first canto of the *Paradiso*:

Trasumanar sigificar *per verba*
　　non si poria; però l'essemplo basti
　　a cui esperïenza grazia serba. (1:7off.)[65]

("Transcending the human cannot be signified *in words*;
however, the example can serve for him to whom grace
gives the experience.")

Dante's whole journey is an effort to *trasumanar*, to move beyond the
human. Since he has been graced with an experience of the Empyrean, his
example can help us to transcend the ordinary and the phenomenal. If we
assume that Dante did not actually ascend to heaven as a living man, then we
can interpret the *Divine Comedy* as a metaphorical account of the intellectual
journey that anyone can take who moves from the empirical to the *a priori*.
However, no literal account of this journey could be offered to replace the
metaphor, for its terminus transcends literal speech.

Like the philosopher in the presence of the Forms, Dante in paradise
lacks the language to express what he sees. He says that during his journey
through paradise, he saw "things which he who descends from there knows
not and cannot retell" (1:4). This might seem to contradict the Socratic
theory that all words must correspond to things, and vice versa. If Forms (for
Socrates) and Divine Love (for Dante) are things, then there must be words

to name them. In fact, the words "Form" and "God" do *name* things for Socrates and Dante; and they are meaningful because the things they name exist. But that does not mean that these things can be *described.* Some words, Socrates and Dante believe, refer to things that we cannot portray in representational language or images. To platonists, these things seem better than ordinary objects, and the fact that they cannot be described in our language, nor literally seen by our eyes, is taken as a warrant of their superiority. However, from another perspective, it appears that Socrates, Boethius, and Dante have failed to produce the consolation that they promised, for their systems rely upon so-called truths that actually have no meaning at all.

Dante notes:

> perché appressando sé al suo disire,
> nostro intelletto si profonda tanto,
> che dietro la memoria non può ire. (1:7–9)

> ("for approaching the object of its desire, our intellect sinks
> so deep that memory cannot follow after it.")

But if the object of our intellect's desire is the Ideal, the *a priori*–and yet we can have no memory or perception of what we find in its domain–then perhaps we have found nothing there at all. If words like "Love" are names that have no use, then perhaps they are just ciphers. The *Paradiso* is the least successful part of the *Comedy* as a work of poetry; and the *Inferno* is great precisely because of the moving concrete imagery that Dante employs. Thus Dante's magnificent poem makes exactly the opposite point from the one he intended. Far from convincing us to renounce poetry and concrete love as "infernal," it reveals their power while making *a priori* speculation appear dry and unsatisfactory.[66]

THEOLOGY AND SPIRITUAL EXPERIENCE

Boethius wrote his *Consolation* heroically as he waited in jail, later to be executed by having his skull crushed with a rope. If ever a Socratic, "philosophical" attitude earned anyone peace, it seems to have worked for Boethius, who managed to write a serene book under these conditions. Similarly, Dante wrote the *Divine Comedy* (or so the poem tells us), when he was "in the midst of the dark forest" of a spiritual crisis (*Inferno* 1:1–3). In the twentieth century, the ordinary world of earthly phenomena cannot often have looked more miserable than to the young Ludwig Wittgenstein as he served on the Eastern Front of the First World War, reviled by his fellow soldiers, surrounded by death. Nevertheless, Wittgenstein followed Boethius's and Dante's route to consolation by writing the *Tractatus logico-philosophicus* during his wartime service. In this book, he tries to present the *a priori* structure of the world in total, and not piecemeal as it appears to human beings. "The usual way of looking at things sees objects as it were from the midst of them, the view *sub specie aeternitatis* from outside. In such a way they have the whole world as background. Is this it perhaps–in this view the object is seen *together with* space and time instead of *in* space and time?"[67] This is similar to Boethius's concept of the divine perspective, which is sempiternal; and it also resembles Dante's vision of the Empyrean. Wittgenstein makes the analogy even more obvious when he evokes God explicitly: "*How* things are in the world is a matter of complete indifference for what is higher. God does not reveal himself *in* the world" (6.432).

Like Plato, the early Wittgenstein hopes to create an ideal language of purely propositional claims, and he believes that the world revealed by *a priori* speculation is beautiful and redeeming, unlike the detestable world described in ordinary, concrete language. Like Plato and Boethius, Wittgenstein cannot prove that the formal structure of the world is aesthetically preferable to its content, so he writes his *Tractatus* as a kind of imitation of the world as seen *sub specie aeternitatis*, which is intended to make the world of the *a priori* seem attractive. If Wittgenstein's representation of the cosmos succeeds in presenting it as beautiful and justified, then he has shown that God exists. However, unlike his predecessors, the early Wittgenstein makes no effort to initiate his readers slowly into the mysteries of the universe by presenting truth in a dramatic form. In the *Tractatus*, no concessions are made to the reader, no examples or explanations are ever offered, no transition is made from ordinary to "ideal" language, and the author's personality is entirely effaced. This allows Wittgenstein to represent the universe exactly as it is, and not as it appears to us. He writes in the preface: "Perhaps this book will be understood only by one who has already had the thoughts which are expressed in it."

If we believe that the metaphysical structure of the cosmos is knowable, then we can try to represent it in a beautiful way, thus showing (but not arguing) that the totality of being is justified and beautiful: in other words, that a certain kind of God exists. This technique, employed by Plato, Boethius, Dante, Spinoza, the young Wittgenstein, and numerous other philosophers, is metaphysical, but it manages to be non-metaphysical with respect to the question of God. God is a kind of value-judgment superimposed upon the total structure that metaphysical inquiry reveals. If we doubt that metaphysics can reveal truth, since its propositions are by definition unverifiable, then this route to theodicy becomes impracticable. Nevertheless, another path remains open: namely, to impose a value-judgment upon the whole of existence *without* first interpreting it metaphysically. No effort would be made to uncover the metaphysical structure of what is; but the mere phenomena would be assessed in their totality. If they appeared ordered, justified, beautiful, and so on, then we could assert that the cosmos had a rational and beneficent shape, that is, that there was a God.

John Wisdom has devised a famous parable about two men who come across a long-neglected garden containing both weeds and a few "surprisingly vigorous" plants. They begin to argue about whether or not the garden is being tended by a gardener, although no one has seen anyone at work there.

> The first man says to the other "He must have worked while people slept." The other says "No, someone would have heard him and besides, anybody who cared about the plants would have kept down the weeds." The first man says "Look at the way these are arranged. There is a purpose and a feeling for beauty here. I believe that some-one comes, someone invisible to mortal eyes. I believe that the more carefully we look the more we shall find confirmation of this." They examine the garden ever so carefully and sometimes they come on new things suggesting the contrary and even that a malicious person has been at work. Besides examining the garden carefully they also study what happens to gardens left without attention. Each learns all the other learns about this and about the garden. Consequently, when after all this, one says "I still believe a gardener comes" while the other says "I don't" their different words now reflect no difference as to what they have found in the garden, no difference as to what they would find in the garden if they looked further and no difference about how fast untended gardens fall into disorder. At this stage, in this context, the gardener hypothesis has ceased to be experimental, the difference between one who accepts and one who rejects it is now not a matter of the one expecting something the other does not expect. What is the difference between them? The one says "A gardener comes unseen and unheard. He is manifested only in his works with which we are all familiar," the other says "There is no gardener," and with this difference in what they say about the gardener goes a difference in how they feel towards the garden.[68]

Wisdom's parable is supposed to establish the possibility of theism for people who do not believe in metaphysics, by suggesting that we can rationally see the universe as a kind of tended garden (thus implying the existence of a cosmic gardener). Wisdom argues that the dispute about the garden is one of a class "which though they cannot be settled by experiment are yet disputes in which one party may be right and the other wrong and in which both parties may offer reasons and the one better reasons than the other."[69] This dispute is similar to debates about whether a painting is beautiful, whether someone should continue a personal relationship, or whether an act is right or wrong. The garden, like a painting, is subject to being pictured in a particular light, described from a certain perspective, compared to other cases, and so on. This is precisely how we can argue about all normative questions.

Nevertheless, I do not think that Wisdom's approach to religion works on its own terms, nor that it could possibly vindicate a form of religious faith that would satisfy traditional Jewish or Christian believers. It cannot work, first of all, because discussing the beauty of the universe as a whole is not the same as talking about whether a specific garden is tended, or whether a particular act is moral. A garden, like an act, can be perceived, can be compared to other gardens, and can be placed in a broader context. Indeed, Wisdom's two men consider it important to "study what happens to [other] gardens left without attention." But if we are talking about the universe, then there is no "other garden"; there is no context within which to place the whole of existence; and there isn't even any way to *perceive* the totality of being throughout the vastness of time. The entirety of what exists—treated as a single thing—is a metaphysical concept, an inference that travels past experience into the realm of the infinite. In itself, it cannot be perceived. Thus I do not see how any progress can be made in a dispute between the person who says, "All is justified," and the person who denies this. By contrast, Wisdom's two men—while they cannot solve their dispute about the concrete garden experimentally—can at least make progress in coming to an agreement. They can examine all kinds of other gardens, describe the garden before them comprehensively and eloquently, and possibly achieve a breakthrough of some kind.

Secondly, even if Wisdom's parable worked, the only form of faith that it could justify would be a belief in God as cosmic planner and caretaker. God as lawgiver, judge, Strength of Israel, sacrificer of his son, angry and loving father—these images could never emerge from a mere "thick description" of the cosmic garden. Most religions make specific claims about God's actions and desires; only an Enlightenment-style deist could be satisfied with an abstract view of God as beneficent caretaker.

But if Wisdom's approach to religion fails, it is not the only way to make rational sense of faith after the demise of metaphysics. Luther and a host of religious humanists or naturalists—Protestant, Catholic, and Jewish—have articulated a more satisfactory empirical approach to God. On their view, we must take seriously the possibility that someone could experience God, not as a mere description of the universe, but as a divine *person* whose love, anger, mercy, and (above all) presence can be felt directly. This is the hypothesis that religion makes, and that St. John, Luther, and others have answered affirmatively. In essence, this approach sets aside the problem of theodicy by refusing to characterize "everything" as either evil or good; it avoids such universal judgments and instead concentrates on establishing a relationship with one person who is good, namely, God.

We are accustomed to arguments that attempt to dismiss religious experience by explaining faith, visions, and spiritual sensations as the mere results of neuroses, mental illnesses, objectified superegos, mirages, and so on. But we must be careful, for all human experience can be "explained." For example, if one person, having a body temperature of 98.6° Fahrenheit, observes a test tube in a laboratory, while another person, having a temperature of 104°, observes an angel at his door, then we can equally well "explain" both experiences as the result of the observers' body temperatures. There is no *a priori* reason to assume that 98.6° is the ideal temperature at which to experience the world.[70] We value scientific evidence because it is supposed to be replicable and available to all who follow the established procedures; furthermore, it helps us to predict future events. However, some scientific phenomena take place only intermittently, under extraordinary circumstances (for example, in multibillion-dollar particle accelerators), and after great effort has been expended to achieve them. By the same token, the religious believer maintains that God does not disclose himself casually: spiritual exercises must first be gone through, an appropriate attitude must be achieved, and God's grace must fall upon the sinner. These preconditions, difficult as they may be to achieve, seem to occur for millions of human beings who believe that they experience God. Skeptics have the right to prefer reductive explanations of these experiences, dismissing them by telling stories about human neurosis or physiology. But believers have equally cogent and comprehensive stories of their own to tell. This does not mean that both are right, nor that the truth is permanently mysterious—only that there is no *a priori* reason to reject experiential claims about God.

An advocate of science may oppose religious beliefs on the ground that huge amounts of evidence seem to support the scientific worldview. For example, a scientist might believe that the the universe is a vast arena of impersonal forces acting upon objects in space and time, thus leaving no room for God. But this image is not scientific at all; it is metaphysical. For science requires a pragmatic attitude toward phenomena taken individually; and it allows generalizations only if these are offered cautiously and *ad hoc.* No amount of evidence could ever support a thesis about the fundamental nature of existence, so any such thesis would be a metaphysical doctrine and not a scientific hypothesis. Thus the best scientific spirit requires that we consider all truth-claims that may be supported by directly relevant evidence, including claims that God speaks to the faithful. Belief in God is inconsistent with a materialist picture of the universe, but that picture was never supported by concrete scientific evidence anyway—not because the evidence has supported some other conception, but because a holistic picture of the universe cannot be derived from evidence of any kind.

As William James argued at length, experiences "of direct personal communication with the divine" are the "fundamental" and "primordial" basis of religion; they are much more important to the religious life "than either theology or ecclesiasticism."[71] Despite the idea of religion-as-metaphysics that was promulgated by Hellenistic philosophers, Judaism and Christianity essentially have little to do with metaphysics. Thus George Fox, founder of the Quakers, offers a paradigm case of what religious faith means to the believer:

> When all my hopes . . . in all men were gone so that I had nothing outwardly to help me, nor could tell me what to do, then, Oh then, I heard a voice which said "There is one, even Jesus Christ, that can speak to thy condition" and when I heard it my heart did leap with joy. Then the Lord did let me see why there was none upon the earth that could speak to my condition . . . that Jesus Christ might have the preeminence, who enlightens and gives grace and faith, and power. Thus when God doth work who shall prevent it? And this I knew experimentally.[72]

CHAPTER 6

HUMANISTS AND SCHOLASTICS IN THE RENAISSANCE

HUMANISM VERSUS SCHOLASTICISM

In preceding chapters, I discussed Protagoras's literary approach to ethics, defending it by analyzing works that exemplify his method. Among Protagoras's many successors, none were more loyal to his approach than the humanists of the Renaissance.[1] Like the Greek Sophists, Renaissance humanists were professional rhetoricians, historians, literary critics, poets, and teachers of rhetoric. They opposed philosophy at a time when it was dominant, defending their own disciplines as superior sources of value. And they directed eloquent polemics and satires against philosophers, thus contributing an important chapter to the ancient quarrel between philosophy and rhetoric. Pico della Mirandola was one Renaissance author who defended philosophy, despite his personal links to the humanist movement, but he captured the significance of the issue for everyone in his day when he wrote: "There is so great a contrast between the task of an orator and that of a philosopher that none greater can be imagined."[2]

In medieval and Renaissance terminology, the humanities included grammar, rhetoric, poetry, history, and moral philosophy–the last denoting works of practical advice as much as ethical theory. Although the humanities flourished at times during the Middle Ages, scholasticism gradually became dominant, prompting a revolt by the humanists of the early Renaissance.[3] As

Donald Kelley writes: "Humanism began, then, as an insurrection of the liberal and lowly 'arts'—in which children learned their 'letters'—against the intellectual hegemony of the 'sciences' (theology, law, medicine, and the theoretical parts of philosophy), installed at the top of the *Studium*, which was the term employed both for the medieval hierarchy of learning and for its principle institutional embodiment, the medieval university."[4]

The scholastics held an exalted place in the medieval *Studium*, as the custodians of theology, theoretical philosophy, and jurisprudence. I have described scholasticism as a purely theoretical approach to morality and spirituality. For scholastic theologians, metaphysics, logic, and speculative theology were the fundamental disciplines. Scholastics admired stories, especially Bible stories, but they read them as collections of propositions that could support general metaphysical theories. Although they believed that scripture was literally true, they were much more interested in its moral, eschatological, and allegorical levels of meaning.

For example, in his *Summa theologiae*, Thomas Aquinas presents a systematic treatment of almost all conceivable metaphysical, theological, legal, and moral issues, and every paragraph is adorned with quotations from scripture, patristic authors, or pagans such as Aristotle and Cicero. Aquinas extracts these quotations from their original sources as if the truths that they enunciated were universal and independent of context. For him, neither the original audience nor the circumstances of writing makes any difference; and it is irrelevant whether he is quoting a literary character, a biblical narrator, or a pagan philosopher.

We can get a sense of Aquinas's interpretive methods by selecting one moral question from the *Summa*, more or less at random. For instance, he asks whether "devotion" is an act in its own right (*specialis actus*), or else a state of mind with which we execute acts. In favor of the view that devotion is a state of mind, he first cites a biblical passage: "All the multitude offered victims, and praises and holocausts, with a devout mind" (2 Chron. 29:31). This verse suggests to Aquinas that devotion is a mental state, unlike praises and sacrifices, which are acts. Then he offers several deductive arguments for the same conclusion. First, he argues that devotion is found in many acts, which would be impossible if it were itself an act. He adds the following proof: all acts result either from appetitive or cognitive faculties; devotion results from neither; therefore, devotion is not an act. However, against this argument, he suggests another: all merits are the result of acts; devotion brings merit; therefore, devotion is an act. Faced with these conflicting deductive arguments, Aquinas offers an etymological theory about the word *devotio*: he thinks that it is derived from the word meaning "vowing" (*devovendo*), which suggests that it is an act after all. Then he cites a secular historian, Livy, who said that people were devout who vowed to suffer death for their army's sake—which implies that a vow (an act) is an example of devotion. Finally, Aquinas cites another biblical verse, "everyone offered first fruits to God with a most prompt and ready (*devota*) heart" (Ex. 35:20), arguing that this passage implies that devotion is an act. He concludes that devotion is an act of vowing to do things for the end of serving God, which alters the manner or mode by which other acts are executed. Thus scriptural and secular quotes, etymology, and Aristotelian logic and metaphysics combine to support Aquinas's conclusion.[5]

It is difficult to imagine that Livy or the author of Chronicles had Aquinas's question explicitly in mind; but this does not matter to Aquinas, since he is unconcerned about authorial intentions. In general, the scholastics interpreted literary texts as signifying general meanings ("figures"), and they defended their interpretations with *a priori*, deductive arguments. If the words in an authoritative text could be shown logically to entail a particular meaning, and that meaning was true, then the words contained the suggested meaning.

The scholastics' deductive method of interpretation was not the only approach known in the middle ages; there were also literary and rhetorical traditions. The literary approach, according to Hennig Brinkmann, emphasized "the doctrine of the 'circumstances' [surrounding a work], which could be seen in connection to the *inventio* [intentions]" of the author.[6] And the rhetorical approach was described by Servius in the fourth century A.D. as follows: "In explaining authors one must consider: the life of the poet, the title of the work, the quality of the poetry, the intention of the writer, . . . the explanation."[7] Thus, unlike scholastic critics, Servius and other rhetoricians stressed the biographies of authors as keys to their intentions. Even a scholastic, Nicholas of Lyra (ca. 1270–1349) could write: "One must begin with the intention of the author, for on this depends the understanding of the book."[8] Still, at least during the scholastic ascendancy of the fourteenth century, rhetorical and literary approaches to interpretation were overshadowed by the deductive methods of philosophers.

Medieval exegetes more or less equated authorial intentions with the literal sense of texts, because the literal sense meant (roughly) the concrete images that an author intended his or her audience to envision as they read.[9] The scholastics acknowledged the value of these images, but they pushed far beyond, believing that each passage also implied innumerable figures. If the passage was biblical, then its divine author had deliberately intended all of its infinite meanings, concrete and abstract, literal and figurative. For Saint Bonaventure, this proved the profundity of Scripture.[10]

Humanist Methods of Interpretation

Humanism differed from scholasticism most obviously in its approach to literary interpretation. Erasmus wrote: "Let [the student] not consider it adequate to pull out four or five little words [from scripture]; let him consider the origin of what is said, by whom it is said, to whom it is said, when, on what occasion, in what words, what precedes it, what follows. For it is from a comprehensive examination of these things that one learns the meaning of a given utterance."[11] He realized that a literary or historical character might not speak for the author of a book; that the author might not say the same thing to every audience or in every situation; and that what an author really meant could often be discerned only if one was sensitive to context, irony, narrative structure, ambiguity, audience, and other contingencies that are ideally purged from philosophical discourse. Erasmus and other humanists sometimes found general propositions implicit in narrative texts, but they distrusted "figurative" readings except when they believed that the author had deliberately intended some kind of allegory.

Today the importance of authorial intentions remains hotly debated. Sometimes, this issue is stated as if there were a true answer that could be discovered. For example, literary theorists sometimes assert either that a text is the product of an author's mind, or that "the author" is a fictional construct. They declare either that writers control their texts by means of conscious (or unconscious) thought, or that language always eludes their control. And they claim either that authors' intentions are knowable, or that they are forever obscure. Each of these assertions superficially takes the form of a sentence that could either be true or false; yet it is impossible to see what evidence could support such propositions. Whether we deny the existence of authors or affirm their presence, we have in mind an abstract model, and either model is consistent with all conceivable empirical facts. Thus it is fruitless to debate questions about the existence or freedom of authors as if some kind of true answer could emerge.

Nevertheless, we can discuss how we ought to read books. Each approach to texts raises a different set of questions. We can ask what an author meant to say; what a book says to us; what the author says without meaning to; what the structure of the text implies about how it should be read; what relationship the work bears to its predecessors; what the author's contemporaries thought about the text; what the words logically imply; how the work compares to other texts from the same background; and myriad other questions. Each question begins a kind of "game" with rules of its own. Each game is rational, because it invites particular procedures, leads to further questions, and produces answers that are defensible in the terms of the game. To say that one game is true or false is to make a category mistake, for rules are not truth-claims that can be asserted or denied. As Erasmus remarked, "I know the manna did not taste the same to everyone"; and likewise he thought that people can have legitimately different readings of Scripture.[12] On the other hand, each game may be more or less *useful* within a broader social context. Thus, if we want to decide whether to try to understand an author's intentions, this is not a metaphysical or epistemological matter, but rather a moral or political one. We have to decide how to spend our limited time and resources—whether to use it assessing what authors meant to say, or what they did not mean to say, or what their texts mean to us, or some other matter.

Humanists were particularly interested in authorial intentions; they preferred the "game" of asking what authors meant over all other interpretive games. Further, they recognized that an author's intentions might not be reducible into some kind of moral or lesson that could be precisely paraphrased in general language. When they defended their approach to interpretation, they usually offered ethical or political—rather than metaphysical or epistemological—justifications. It is difficult to find Renaissance texts that discuss literary theory in the modern sense, but it is easy to find moral justifications for reading in particular ways. Specifically, many of the first humanists were civic republicans. Indeed, Hans Baron has argued that the original motivation for the revival of humanism was civic republican ideology.[13] In a republican system, leaders and citizens are obligated to consider the conscious ideas and interests of at least some of their compatriots before they make decisions. Therefore, republicanism places a strong emphasis upon communication, deliberation, and understanding (although the right to participate in political dialogue may not be open to everyone). Humanist critics thought that literary texts were examples of communication; in good books, authors of the past had deliberately said or shown something of value. The purpose of reading books was not to subject oneself to authority (humanists could be hostile critics), but rather to understand an author's intended meaning, just as a good republican sought to understand what his compatriots were trying to say during political debates. Literary criticism was helpful practice for political deliberation; it also provided interesting concrete insights from wise authors of the past.

The humanists' emphasis on authorial intentions entailed a number of consequences. First, as I have noted, they concentrated on the literal sense of stories, as opposed to their allegorical meanings, seeking to visualize the concrete images that the author originally had in mind. At the same time, they were sensitive to irony. Irony implies authorial detachment from the literal meaning of a text, but it does not mean that an author intends some non-literal meaning that could be clearly stated. Thus irony differs both from allegory and from sarcasm (which is the mere *negation* of literal meaning). Third, they recognized that the meanings of words change, so they began to study the history of language, or philology. More generally, they realized that the meaning of a text could be determined in part by the audience for which it was originally intended, and by the practical situation (*circumstantiae*) that had called it forth. Thus, as Kelley writes, humanist "classical and biblical scholars were confronted with questions of anachronism, the instability of meaning, cultural context, and various kinds of linguistic relativity."[14] But despite their growing awareness of cultural change, they still believed that authorial intentions could be perceived, if only we understood the circumstances in which each text was written. Finally, the humanists' interest in original intentions encouraged them to edit texts (seeking to remove copyists' errors), to compare manuscripts, to study original languages, and to read texts as carefully constructed wholes, instead of collections of propositions. In short, their methods of interpretation were historical and empirical, rather than logical and deductive.

Thomas More, Erasmus's friend and fellow humanist, remarked of scholastics that they "judge themselves alone capable of giving a ready interpretation, according to their own whims, of any piece of literature, even of Scripture, . . . although they have never seen the passage, have never looked into the work, and do not know in what context the passage occurs."[15] More described scholastic methods pejoratively, but his opponents could reply that truths are truths, wherever they may appear; and that the appropriate test of validity is reason and interpreted revelation. Just as Socrates wanted to apply dialectic in order to judge the theories that he found implicit in Protagoras's eloquent speeches, so the scholastics interpreted literature and Scripture on the basis of Aristotelian metaphysics. More described this method satirically when he recalled a certain theologian with whom he had once dined: "[N]o matter what statement was made by anybody, no matter how carefully and cautiously modified, or thought out, it had barely left the lips of the speaker when he would promptly tear it apart with a syllogism; even though the subject of the conversation had nothing to do with theology or philosophy."[16] More, like Protagoras, presumably preferred to let people speak at length and rhetorically, using narrative and thick description as well as syllogistic logic to support their views. We can get a sense of his ideal conversation from the dialogue that forms the first part of his *Utopia*.

THE EDUCATIONAL AND POLITICAL IDEALS OF THE HUMANISTS

The humanists' interpretive methods and political ideals went hand-in-hand with a new approach to education: they emphasized literature, languages, rhetoric, and the imitation of classics instead of logic and metaphysics. Lorenzo Valla put the following words into the mouth of Maffeo Vegio, who represents humanism in Valla's dialogue *On Pleasure*. "I have been initiated," says Vegio, "not into the rites of philosophy, but into the more significant and lofty ones of oratory and poetry."[17] For humanists, rhetoric and literature (as well as history) were valuable because they offered concrete, value-laden depictions of human life. From Petrarch to Valla–and on to Erasmus and Ben Jonson–the humanists continually stressed the moral and political value of reading good literature, but they showed little interest in moral theory. For example, Philip Sidney expressed a humanist platitude when he wrote:

> I say the philosopher teacheth, but he teacheth obscurely, so as the learned only can understand him; that is to say, he teacheth them that are already taught. But the poet is the food for the tenderest stomachs, the poet is indeed the right popular philosopher, whereof Aesop's tales give good proof. . . . Truly, I have known men, that even with reading *Amadis de Gaule* (which God knoweth wanteth much of a perfect poesy) have found their hearts moved to the exercise of courtesy, liberality, and especially courage. Who readeth Aeneas carrying old Anchises on his back, that wisheth not it were his fortune to perform so excellent an act?[18]

Sidney's educational ideals recall Protagoras's description of his classroom, in which "the works of the best poets are set before [children], . . . and in these works are displayed many warnings, many detailed narratives and praises and eulogies of good men of ancient times, so that the boy may desire to imitate them competitively and may stretch himself to become like them."[19] Although Sidney closely imitated Aristotle's *Poetics*, his view of moral education was shared by all humanists, and not merely by neo-Aristotelians. It represented a revival of the educational program of Protagoras, Isocrates, Cicero, Quintillian, Aulus Gellius, and other ancients, many of whose works were popular during the Renaissance.

Humanist educators, like Sophists, preferred rhetoric to the traditional source of wisdom: philosophy. When they read moral philosophy, their preferred texts were the literary essays and dialogues of writers such as Plutarch, rather than systematic theoretical treatises. Plato was favorite of the humanists, but what they admired in him was not so much his arguments and doctrines as the personality of Socrates, an important figure for More, Erasmus, Rabelais, and many other Renaissance authors. On the other hand, the humanists' avoidance of theory did not cause them to disparage "wisdom"; rather, most humanists argued that wisdom was intrinsically linked to eloquence. For philosophers in the Socratic tradition, eloquence is a loose cannon: it can just as well destroy truth and justice as falsehood and evil. But Renaissance humanists often identified the good with the results of reasonable discussions: for them, the decisions that a community reached after sufficient debate were the morally right decisions, almost by definition.

This meant that responsible and persuasive rhetoric naturally led to wisdom and virtue. Modern pragmatists and "communications-ethicists" believe that truth is identical to a consensus reached under fair conditions. It may seem anachronistic to attribute the same view to writers of the fifteenth and sixteenth centuries; but if anyone was a communications-ethicist before 1900, it was Erasmus. As I argue in more detail below, Erasmus was skeptical about both deductive arguments and personal experiences, arguing that either could be deployed on both sides of most questions. On the other hand, he believed that an agreement reached by many people was not only a sign of truth, but also a manifestation of God, for Christ was Concord.[20] This view colors passages like the following (Erasmus is addressing Luther):

> Where is a certain criterion, by which in the Church we may by all means prove or disprove dogmas from sacred Literature, a rule which is absolutely certain, a spiritual light clearer than the sun? [If] we grant the possibility that a general council may be corrupt, . . . nevertheless, more probably is the Spirit of God there than in private conventicles. . . . If the Church of God cannot be manifested, and, nevertheless, it is necessary that there be some certain criteria, it is safer in my opinion to follow public authority than the opinion of this or that man.[21]

Similarly, Valla, a radical humanist of the fifteenth century, inverted the Socratic hierarchy, calling eloquence "the queen of truth and perfect wisdom."[22] For him, the ultimate criterion of truth was consensus, and eloquence was especially useful as a means to produce concord. Wisdom was worthy of the name only if it provided helpful support for orators; but the test of truth lay in the *persuasiveness* of facts, doctrines, examples, and methods. In general, he thought, philosophical arguments were unpersuasive because they were too dependent upon linear chains of reasoning—which inevitably had weak links somewhere—whereas orators used numerous, free-standing analogies, examples, and stories to support their views. Besides, logical arguments could be used with equal force by both sides in most debates; and they ignored the prevailing values of the community. Someone might object that rhetoric too can create conflict, and that dialectic can produce agreement. But, in defense of Valla, it should be said that rhetoricians, almost by definition, seek the actual agreement of the people whom they address, whereas the implicit premise of a philosophical argument is that it makes no difference what people think: the goal is abstract truth. Valla denounced philosophers for calling themselves the sole "friends of wisdom," preferring statesmen, rhetoricians, kings, and other political leaders, "whose wisdom governed states before philosophers rose up, and after their appearance as well."[23]

I have argued that each episode in the quarrel between philosophy and rhetoric since classical times has also revived the dispute about the active and contemplative life. It would be too simple to claim that the humanists always favored the *vita activa*: Petrarch condemned it, and Thomas More was highly ambivalent about it.[24] But, despite these and other exceptions, the battle lines generally broke down in the expected way. As Baron writes:

> From the end of the Trecento onward, the ever-recurring themes in the humanistic philosophy of life were the super-iority of the *vita activa* over "selfish" withdrawal into scholarship and contemplation, the praise of the family as the foundation of a sound society, and the argument that the perfect life was not that of the "sage" but that of the citizen who, in addition to his studies, consummates his *humanitas* by shouldering man's social duties and by serving his fellow-citizens in public office.[25]

Although defenders of philosophy (Pico della Mirandola, Marsilio Ficino, and others) often favored the *vita contemplativa* as conducive to speculative thought, proponents of the humanities generally preferred the active life. According to Valla, when Aristotle said that the contemplative life was closest to God, he was just spuriously defending his own useless profession.[26] The alliance of active people with humanists was one of mutual convenience. Rhetoric, not philosophy, was considered the most useful discipline in the political arena; and the humanities were thought to serve the practical needs of courtiers, orators, lawyers, and other active citizens. Francis Bacon, who was not a humanist, nevertheless conceded that "it is eloquence that prevaileth in an active life"—even though "in true value it is inferior to wisdom."[27] Thus believers in an active life promoted humanistic education as a source of eloquence; and, in turn, humanists recommended the active life. They thought that public activity provided experience, which was a basic ingredient of wisdom. If abstract speculation could not reveal truth, then one could better learn wisdom in the political arena. Thus (as Protagoras had argued) a humanistic education continued even after the student left school and entered politics.

Similarly, history—the record of past human *activity*—was thought to convey a store of practical experience greater than anyone could acquire in his or her lifetime. For example, Thomas Elyot emphasized the importance of experience, "whereof cometh wisdom," calling it (in a misquotation of Cicero) "the light of virtue." By observing "acts committed or done by other men," he said, we can be "instructed to apprehend the thing which to the public weal, or to our own persons, may be commodious; and to eschew that thing which . . . appeareth noisome and vicious." Thus the purpose of history was to serve republics and active citizens by collecting and preserving the experience of past commonwealths. Elyot concluded: "The knowledge of this experience is called example and is expressed by history."[28] Similarly, when Thomas North translated Plutarch's *Lives* into English in 1579, he explained that, compared to history, all "other learning is private, fitter for universities than cities, fuller of contemplation than experience, more commendable in the students themselves than profitable to others. Whereas stories are fit for every place, reach to all persons, serve for all times, teach the living, revive the dead, so far excelling all other books as it is better to see learning in noble men's lives than to read it in philosophers' writings."[29] Here North imitated Plutarch's own, Sophist-influenced defense of history.

I have argued that the dispute between philosophy and the humanities parallels, not only the debate about the active and contemplative life, but also the perennial argument about the value of imitative arts. Therefore, it is not surprising that the greatest centers of Renaissance humanism were also places where the visual arts flourished, often under the same patrons. Humanists appreciated the moral value of concrete depictions of reality, and these are precisely what Renaissance artists provided with increasing virtuosity. Thomas Elyot argued: "it is commendable in a gentleman to paint and carve exactly." A gentleman who knew how to draw, he said—"and happeneth to read any noble and excellent history, whereby his courage is inflamed to the imitation of virtue"—might try "to express lively and (as I might say) actually in portraiture, not only the fact or affair, but also the sundry affections of every personage . . . , which might in any wise appear or be perceived in their visage, countenance, or gesture."[30] For Elyot, the plastic arts had the same function as history: they provided inspiring examples of virtue and supported concrete value-judgments. Renaissance art typically presented an imaginary piece of three-dimensional space, filled with human beings, shown *as* it would appear from a particular point of view, and depicted in such a way as to suggest moral judgments. For example, a painting might show, by means of her "visage, countenance, or gesture," that the Virgin Mary was sweet and pure. This conception of the purpose of art was ancient; but it was anathema to Socrates, and it had disappeared during the early Christian period for ideological reasons.

Thus, to sum up, the humanists promoted literature and history, attacked philosophy, defended republicanism and the active life, and enjoyed painting. Early in the history of humanism, Valla wrote: "The scholastic *ratio* [reason, method], which makes use of difficult and harsh syllogistic instruments, must give place to persuasive virtue of eloquence, which arouses sentiments and passions fit to form and transform men, and thus capable of offering—through the reading of Thucyidides, Livy, Demosthenes, and Cicero—an ethical and political teaching, which no cold philosophical treatise could offer."[31] This passage captures all the basic ingredients of humanism:

the attack on syllogistic (i.e., general and deductive) reasoning; the commitment to rhetoric; the near-identification of eloquence and virtue; the defense of history and oratory, especially as contained in ancient texts; and the preference for ethical and political guidance over abstract speculation.

In all of these respects, the humanists believed that they were engaged in a revolutionary movement, which had grown from modest beginnings when Petrarch and a few other Italians had revolted against the authority of the *Studium*, and which ultimately came to dominate public life, the Church, and even the universities. However, many current scholars doubt the humanists' claims to originality, consistency, and influence. They note that the humanists' ideas had mostly been anticipated by medieval writers, and that scholastic philosophy survived the Renaissance despite the humanists' best efforts. Further, they disparage the humanists' claims to broad social and cultural influence. But for my purposes, Renaissance humanists are not interesting primarily because they were original, consistent, or influential–if, indeed, they were any of these things. Rather, they are interesting because their approach is worthy of imitation. They viewed themselves as participants in a countercultural movement that arose in the heyday of scholasticism and that finally won a victory over abstract philosophy. This self-image (even if it was false) encouraged them to write polemics against philosophy and to treat the quarrel between the humanities and theory as a fundamental issue. Today, in an age of analytic philosophy–and also of theory-building in economics and psychology–that issue remains fundamental.

ERASMUS AND CHRISTIAN HUMANISM

The acknowledged leader of sixteenth-century humanists was Erasmus, who was also particularly self-conscious about the dispute between philosophy and literature. Erasmus was educated by the Brethren of the Common Life at Deventer in Holland (1474–84), and then at the Augustinian monastery at Steyn (1486–93). The Brethren's approach to spirituality, known as the *devotio moderna*, offered an early alternative to scholasticism during its period of dominance. The essence of the *devotio moderna* is captured in a work, *The Imitation of Christ*, that is generally attributed to another student at Deventer who also became an Augustinian monk, Thomas à Kempis. This popular book, written in about 1413, begins with strong words against scholastic theology:

> Of what use is it to discourse learnedly on the Trinity, if
> you lack humility and displease the Trinity? . . . I would
> far rather feel contrition than be able to define it. If you
> knew the whole Bible by heart, and all the teaching of the

philosophers, how would this help you without the grace
and love of God? . . . Of what value are lengthy controversies on deep and obscure matters, when it is not by our
knowledge of such things that we shall at length by
judged? . . . [W]hat concern to us are such things as
genera and species?[32]

Erasmus makes similar points in many of his polemical works. For
example, he writes: "anyone should not think himself to be a Christian if
he disputes about instances, relations, quiddities, and formalities with an
obscure and irksome confusion of words, but rather if he holds and
exhibits what Christ taught and showed forth."[33] In short, the good
Christian must *imitate* Christ, and not seek to analyze him philosophically.
Further, Erasmus constantly echoes Thomas à Kempis's view that "All
sacred scriptures should be read in the spirit in which they were written."
Erasmus's most famous book, *The Praise of Folly*, follows Thomas's advice to
"Be content to be accounted a fool for Christ's sake if you wish to be a
Religious."[34]

On the other hand, *The Imitation of Christ* often verges on anti-intellectualism, whereas Erasmus was a tireless defender of education, scholarship,
and erudition. Erasmus adopted the critical side of Thomas à Kempis's
thought—his attack on scholasticism and theory—but he also promoted a
positive alternative to theology. This alternative was the literal interpretation
and moral imitation of literature, especially scripture. Erasmus wanted "even
the lowliest woman," and even "the Turks and Saracens," to read the New
Testament in the vernacular, so that they could imitate Christ's example.
"Would that . . . the farmer sing some portion of [scriptures] at the plow, the
weaver hum some parts of them to the movement of his shuttle, the traveller
lighten the weariness of the journey with stories of this kind!"[35] This was a
populist vision, consistent with Erasmus's view that sophisticated logic was
unnecessary as an aid to reading the Bible—for it was the *story* that counted,
and anyone could understand a story.[36]

What Erasmus called the "philosophy of Christ" was not primarily a
series of doctrines, but rather a practice or activity: the *imitation* of Christ. In
this as in many other respects, Erasmus resembled Protagoras, who had
taught the art of citizenship based upon imitation, and not a theory of the
good. Erasmus wrote: "In this kind of philosophy, located as it is more truly
in the disposition of the mind than in syllogisms, life means more than
debate, inspiration is preferable to erudition, transformation is a more
important matter than intellectual comprehension. . . . Another, perhaps,
even a non-Christian, may discuss more subtly how the angels understand,
but to persuade us to lead here an angelic life, free from every strain, this
indeed is the duty of the Christian theologian."[37]

On the other hand, Erasmus knew that great difficulties would arise before one could establish an accurate version of the original text of the Bible, let alone understand its literal meaning 1,500 years after its composition. The surviving texts were corrupt; the sense of words had changed; and there were obscure references and obvious ambiguities to grapple with. Therefore, far from belittling intellectuals, Erasmus believed that learning and scholarship were valuable aids to faith; but he also thought that the fruits of scholarship could be widely distributed. "Only a few can be learned," he wrote, "but all can be Christian, all can be devout, and–I shall boldly add–all can be theologians."[38] By "theologians," he meant imitators of Christ; and, as someone who was learned, he sought to help devout Christians to practice their "theology." His greatest contribution to Christian faith was a revised edition of the New Testament, a masterpiece of textual and historical scholarship. For similar reasons, he composed scholarly "paraphrases," in which he wrote as if he were an evangelist, explaining the intended meaning of his gospel. Today, no critic would pretend to paraphrase an author's full, authentic, intended meaning; to adopt an authorial voice in this way would seem pretentious. If Erasmus's paraphrases represent his notion of the single, objective meaning of the original texts, then they are authoritarian and arrogant. However, if they are supposed to epitomize a *process* by which each Christian seeks to understand, for him- or herself, what the evangelist originally meant to say (in part by applying historical scholarship), then they are models of humanistic criticism.

Erasmus viewed the New Testament as the ultimate source of moral value. Not only did it have a divine author, but anyone could see that it was uniquely *eloquent.* The words of Jesus, the exhortations of Paul, and the gospel narratives were all primarily examples of persuasive rhetoric; likewise, all good Christians used eloquence and personal behavior to persuade other people to imitate Christ. Erasmus himself wished for "an eloquence which not only captivates the ear with its fleeting delight but which leaves a lasting sting in the minds of its hearers, which grips, which tranforms, which sends away a far different listener than it had received."[39] Such rhetorical ability would make Erasmus a better Christian, he thought; and Christ himself had exemplified the value of eloquence. I have already argued that humanists believed rhetoric and virtue to be closely linked. Erasmus relocated this belief to the religious realm, seeking (as two modern scholars write) "to unite eloquence and piety" into a "rhetorical theology."[40]

Like Protagoras, Erasmus believed that examples of virtue–in his case, Christian virtue–should be imbued "in the very embraces of parents and the caresses of nurses."[41] He also believed that virtue could be imparted through the study of secular literature and history. Students, he argued, should be constantly assigned essay topics to train their rhetorical skills. Every topic that he suggested was moral, and each had a concrete historical or literary reference. So, for example, students were to write essays on the following topics: "it's hard to decide who was more foolish, Crates who threw gold in the sea or Midas who thought there was nothing better than gold. . . . Or: no praise can match the deserts of King Codrus, who thought that his people's safety was worth buying at the cost of his own life."[42] By composing essays on these themes, students would acquire both virtue and eloquence from concrete examples, without any need for a grounded, systematic moral theory.

Despite his commitment to moral education, Erasmus generally resisted theory. At one point, he called for pious and learned men "to draw together in a short statement the whole philosophy of Christ from the most pure sources." He hoped that the results could be transmitted to the Turks so that they would see the evident superiority of Christianity. From this passage, it sounds as if Erasmus thought that Christ's teachings could be reduced to a list of general doctrines or principles. However, he offered no such list himself, which suggests that he considered this kind of interpretation to be beyond him. Furthermore, in the same letter, he emphasized that the best way to impress the infidels would be to imitate Christ, so that they could behold "that which Christ taught and exemplified shining forth in our own lives."[43] Erasmus's failure to provide a list of Christian doctrines seems more characteristic than his call for such a list to be created. He rarely (if ever) offered deductive, exegetical, or empirical arguments for or against specific doctrines. However, in 1519, he drew up a list of the doctrines that all patristic theologians had endorsed, for he could accept theological principles if they had enjoyed orthodox consensus.[44] At the end of his life, after years of being attacked by both Catholics and Protestants, Erasmus remarked: "Yet no one has presented himself, Lutheran or Antilutheran, who can clearly point to any suspect doctrine in my works—though such hordes of them have done their best in this research." It would have been difficult for anyone to state only doctrines that were acceptable to both sides in the Reformation controversy—unless, like Erasmus, one tried never to state doctrines at all, except when they were supported by perfect consensus.[45]

Two modern historians, Anthony Grafton and Lisa Jardine, note that Erasmus's promotion of literary education was "self-evidently part of a systematic programme of spiritual development." But they assert that there was no "explicit link between [his] influential textbooks of Latin eloquence and any moral or devotional meta-system." Thus, they note, "What Erasmus does not explain . . . is how the young theologian can be sure that simple, straightforward reading will produce guaranteed right doctrine." For Erasmus, they suggest, "the mere exercise of reading the text as it really is will make the reader moral and wise in a direct way that no systematic body of doctrine can rival." But they clearly doubt this assumption, arguing that "the welding of profane learning to lay piety requires a certain amount of intellectual sleight-of-hand." They suggest that Erasmus was admired largely because of his somewhat artificial reputation for personal probity, which made people believe that humanism really was linked to morals—a kind of argument from authority. Moreover, Grafton and Jardine provide several examples of *failed* humanistic education, in which students acted immorally despite being exposed to classical texts. They conclude that humanism "offered everyone a model of true culture as something given, absolute, to be mastered, not questioned—and thus fostered in all its initiates a properly docile attitude toward authority." Scholasticism, they claim, died at the hands of humanism because it had "bred too independent an attitude to survive" in the Europe of the Counter-Reformation.[46]

In this critique, we see the lingering legacy of Socrates. For Socrates, morality meant possessing correct doctrines; freedom meant the ability to criticize false doctrines logically; and stories were dangerous because their doctrinal content was not necessarily correct. To anyone who agrees with Socrates, scholasticism seems more liberating than humanism, because humanists revered canonical literature and satirized pure reason. But Erasmus was hardly a slavish follower of authority, nor was he an irrationalist; he was a scholar, a parodist, a scathing critic, and an independent thinker. Grafton and Jardine—like Erasmus's scholastic contemporaries—fail to recognize his position as a defensible alternative to Socratic philosophy. Erasmus did not believe that canonical texts contained implicit moral doctrines, to whose authority students should submit. Rather, he thought that the process of seeing concrete cases from someone else's perspective would teach students how to participate in a dialogue about ethics.

The ultimate goal of this debate was consensus, which was practically the same thing as truth. J. K. McConica writes: "Briefly put, without *consensus* and concord, its social concomitant, no dogmatic certainty could be had about anything, and no problem of faith could be solved. The *consensus*, in Erasmus' thought, is the principle of intelligibility itself."[47] As a strong pacifist, Erasmus believed that any dialogue ought to occur under conditions of peace, even when the Turks and Saracens were one's opponents.[48] Valid arguments worked by reason, example, or eloquence, and not by force. Finally, as a believer in universal education, Erasmus wanted everyone to be included in the debate—women as well as men, commoners as well as nobles—although not necessarily on terms of perfect equality. If students found a particular author's point of view congenial, they could imitate it. If not, they could criticize his work, but by using parody rather than deductive logic, for logic was inappropriate to literary criticism. Meanwhile, Erasmus believed that certain virtues were essential to good criticism, as they were to good citizenship. To be an able scholar, he thought, one had to be intellectually honest, open to foreign perspectives, ready to accept criticism, capable of working collaboratively, committed to achieving consensus, yet intellectually independent. Although Erasmus failed to embody all of these virtues, he did promote them, and it took no "sleight-of-hand" for him to identify them with the virtues of competent scholars.

LUTHER AS HUMANIST

The radicalism of Erasmus's anti-theoretical position can be seen most clearly in his debate with Martin Luther. Like Erasmus and Thomas à Kempis, Luther was an Augustinian monk who was moved by the *devotio moderna*. And, despite his strong distaste for the ostentation of Medici Rome, he was deeply influenced by humanism. In particular, Luther, like the humanists, condemned scholasticism and all forms of religious metaphysics and *disputare de deo* (disputing about God).[49] He preferred close readings of scripture in the original languages or in sensitive vernacular translations, such as the one that he made from Erasmus's Greek edition of the New Testament.

In his *Heidelberg Disputation* of 1518, Luther denounced Aristotle and speculative metaphysics in general, advancing the following suggestive "proofs" for his position:

> XIX. He does not deserve to be called a theologian who observes with his intellect the "invisible" things of God "through the things that have been made."
> XX. But he is a theologian who understands by observing visible things and the "back parts of God" through sufferings and the cross.[50]

Scholastic theologians had attempted to understand God in a theoretical way by analyzing (or "observing with their intellect") what "has been made" (i.e, Scripture, history, and nature) until "invisible things" (theories about the infinite and transcendent God) emerged. But Luther, adopting a similar approach to Erasmus and Thomas à Kempis, advocated observing the literal truth ("visible things") that we know about God in an empathetic spirit. In practical terms, this meant reading, visualizing, and imitating the literal story of the Bible.

In the first of the "proofs" quoted above, Luther alludes to Paul's Letter to the Romans, 1:20, where the apostle writes: "For that which may be known of God is manifest . . . ; for God hath shown it unto them [i.e., the pagans]. The invisible things of him from the creation of the world are clearly seen, being understood by the things that are made, even his eternal power and Godhead." Thus God has manifested himself clearly in concrete, "visible" phenomena, and there is nothing supersensory about him that needs to be known. Although it is a paradox, "the invisible things" are "clearly seen." On the other hand, all that we can see of God are his *posteriora*, for (as Luther reminds us in Proof XX) the Lord said to Moses: "And I will take away mine hand, and thou shalt see my back parts; but my face shall not be seen" (Exodus 33:23). Thus we have to infer from mere glimpses of the divine some greater truths about God. But it is a contingent fact that today we can only see backward glances of God, for the Lord previously "spake unto Moses face to face, as a man speaketh unto his friend" (Exodus 33:11). Thus we human beings have (collectively) experienced *everything* about God, including God's very face; it just happens that some of our experiences must now be vicarious, rather than direct. Luther concludes that we must now understand through "sufferings and the cross," a phrase that probably refers both to our sufferings and those of God. Thus he defines as "true theology" a passionate, experiential, empathetic relationship with an active God, not the effort to understand God by means of abstract reason. Luther's definition of "theology" is idiosyncratic, but it closely resembles Erasmus's notion of a *theologia Christi.*

It is difficult to grapple with the notion that the invisible things of God, "even his eternal power and Godhead," can be clearly seen. But these things have frequently been *represented.* The Bible shows them by telling a long story about God's interventions in human history, through which a picture of His character and power emerges. Similarly, the visual arts depict the divine, for example, by showing Christ enthroned in majesty amid ranks of angels. Music represents God in masses, passions, and oratorios; and so does poetry—think of Dante or Milton. We might say that these depictions, being spatiotemporal, only gesture toward a truth that is metaphysical because it transcends experience. But Luther, Erasmus, and Paul hold that what we see when we contemplate the Bible (or its best re-presentations in other media) *just is* what can be known about God. Moreover, they hold that what we cannot know about God is also empirical; it just so happens that we fallen, post-Mosaic human beings are not now permitted to experience it.

To say that God is fully subject to being experienced is not to assume that God is material. It is possible (at least from a logical point of view) that we can experience what is *not* material; and Luther, as a devout Christian who is also an anti-metaphysician, claims that this is precisely what we ought to do. Our eyes can behold the *posteriora dei*; our hearts can feel God's love; and our minds can develop a portrait of God's will and character from tangible manifestations of the divine. In modern philosophical terminology, Luther is not a materialist with respect to God, but he is a naturalist. Philosophical naturalism is the view that everything can be known by the same means that we know natural objects, namely, by means of experiment, observation, and sensation. Thus naturalism is a form of monism; it asserts that everything is one kind of thing—nature. Naturalism opposes the dualistic theory that there is nature, on one hand—which is subject to experience—and there is also another realm, occupied by the *a priori*, Reason, God, the truths of mathematics and logic, and so forth, which cannot be experienced. Some natural items might be too large, too small, too hot, too far away, or too fast for us to experience directly; but they still lie on a continuum with ordinary objects. God might fall into the category of things that we happen to be too weak to experience without his grace; but he is still natural. Further, although naturalists assert that all is nature, whether nature is wholly or partly material remains open to question; and Luther claims that one very important part of nature is divine rather than earthly or carnal. Luther neither believes that God *is* nature as a whole (a deeply metaphysical view asserted, for example, by Spinoza), nor that God is just an *ordinary* part of nature. On the contrary, God has created everything else and rules the cosmos. Nevertheless, Luther naturalizes God insofar as he treats God as part of what we experience.[51]

ERASMUS VERSUS LUTHER

When Luther attacked scholasticism and adopted an empirical approach to religion, he sounded a great deal like Erasmus. Indeed, during their lifetimes, Erasmus and Luther were widely assumed to be allies: both criticized speculative theology, both sought to reform such corrupt practices as the selling of indulgences and church offices, and both favored universal access to Scripture in the vernacular. But for a long time after Luther left the Church, Erasmus refused either to join him or to criticize him. As a result, Erasmus came under intense pressure to declare himself for Catholicism or for the Protestants. Both sides openly expressed frustration that the most famous scholar in Christendom seemed content to sit on the fence. As Erasmus recalled, "The Lutheran tragedy had burdened [me] with unbearable ill will; [I] was torn apart by each faction, while [I] sought to serve the best interests of each."[52]

As long as Erasmus remained neutral, he ran the risk that his evenhandedness would be mistaken for heresy. However, his commitment to Catholicism was probably sincere. Among other people, Pope Leo X, Pope Adrian VI, the Emperor Charles V, and King Henry VIII of England all specifically implored him to attack Luther.[53] At last, he decided to defend the Church's teaching on a key matter of Reformation controversy: the existence of a free will. His dispute with Luther on this issue is interesting for my purposes because Erasmus outflanks his opponent on the anti-metaphysical, anti-theoretical extreme. He adopts a radically humanistic (or pragmatic) approach to doctrine, stating the humanist attack on theory as clearly as it has ever been stated. In response, Luther criticizes Erasmus for his resistance to theory, using arguments that recall Socrates' attack on the Sophists. Thus the debate reveals the limits of Luther's humanism.

In their pamphlets on the topic of freedom and necessity, Erasmus and Luther explicitly address each other's arguments, but their basic disagreement about method makes it difficult for them to engage on common ground. Like Protagoras, Erasmus protests his ignorance of dialectic: "I am quite aware," he writes, "that I am a poor match in such a contest; I am less experienced than other men, and I have always had a deep aversion to fighting. Consequently I have always preferred playing in the freer field of the muses, than fighting ironclad in close combat" (p. 6).[54] Luther, on the other hand (like Socrates), claims that he is unskilled in rhetoric—he says that he is practically a "barbarian" in that respect—and so he can only offer rigorous logical arguments (p. 97). Despite his earlier attacks on speculative theology, Luther's method in the debate is basically dialectical. If God is omnipotent and knows the future, Luther reasons, then we have no power to alter what God has foreordained. He concludes: "if the foreknowledge and omnipotence of God are admitted, we must be under [total] necessity" (p. 132). Therefore, "the free will is a downright lie" (p. 98). This is the basis of Luther's view that we cannot be saved by good works, but only by God's grace, which we attain by faith alone.

Erasmus begins his criticism of Luther by questioning our ability to know any true general propositions about religious matters. "Men were not wont to intrude upon these concealed, even superfluous questions with irreligious curiosity" (p. 9). Erasmus doubts that we can profitably derive answers to theological problems by interpreting Scripture, for as we press into its thickets in search of general truths, darkness soon envelops us (p. 8). Theological propositions are usually impossible to test against Scriptural or other evidence. Therefore, he writes, "so great is my dislike of [such] assertions that I prefer the views of the skeptics whenever the inviolable authority of Scripture and the decision of the Church permit" (p. 6). In particular, he notes that most biblical passages that discuss an individual's will, choice, or desire are equally consistent with either the theory of free will or the concept of determinism (p. 67). He concludes, "one should be persuaded to waste neither time nor ingenuity in such labyrinths; neither to refute nor to endorse Luther's teachings [regarding the will]" (p. 12).

Erasmus wants to be a good Catholic, so he says that he is willing to affirm the theological propositions that have been endorsed by Church councils and popes. Even if our free will "cannot be proved by clear scriptural testimony, it has been expounded with good foundation by orthodox Church Fathers" (p. 22). Erasmus does not present the fathers' *arguments* for freedom of the will, perhaps because his skepticism about speculative theology would undermine their methods as much as Luther's. It is enough for him to note that they believed in a free will; that they were orthodox thinkers and saints; and that he is an obedient Catholic who accepts their findings.

Erasmus's skepticism about theology enrages Luther, who responds that to avoid making theological assertions is no mark of a Christian spirit. "Indeed, one must delight in assertions to be a Christian at all! . . . Take away assertions and you take away Christianity. . . . That would be to deny at once all piety and religion, like asserting that piety, religion and all dogmas are nothing at all" (p. 100–101). In keeping with the Socratic approach to religion that I discussed in the previous chapter, Luther equates theological propositions with religious faith. To have faith, he argues, means believing in certain assertions of a general character. For example, a person of faith must profess that God is omniscient and omnipotent, and that our actions are completely predetermined.[55]

Addressing Erasmus, Luther remarks: "You seem to look upon the Christian doctrines as nothing better than the opinions of philosophers and men" (p. 102). Luther is right about Erasmus's view of religious doctrines: he does consider them to be mere human opinions. But Erasmus never equates doctrines with Christianity; although he distrusts speculative theology, he nevertheless believes wholeheartedly in the truth of the Bible narrative. Thus Luther accurately calls his opponent an "academic" and a "skeptic," for Erasmus doubts our ability to discover metaphysical truths about moral and spiritual matters (p. 102). Like the ancient Pyrrhonist skeptics, Erasmus doubts that experience or deductive arguments could either prove or rebut theological assertions. Therefore, following Aristotle, Erasmus prefers the concrete particular truths that are contained in stories. But Luther remarks that the "Holy Spirit is no skeptic," for it offers us truths that are like philosophical doctrines, only infallible (p. 103). Thus, according to Luther, Erasmus is impious to treat Christian doctrines as *mere* philosophy.

Offering a familiar argument against skepticism, Luther charges Erasmus with hypocritically *asserting* a "dislike of assertions" (p. 101). Luther believes that Erasmus is in the awkward position of offering general arguments against general arguments—a dilemma that also confronted Protagoras, Aristotle, William James, Wittgenstein, and other opponents of moral theory. He recalls that Erasmus had once wanted scholars to write an "outline guide to Christianity" for the use of infidels—an impossible task if religion cannot be summarized in the form of "assertions" (p. 105). Finally, Luther becomes so exasperated with Erasmus's skepticism, evasiveness, and apparent hypocrisy that he shifts from Latin to his native tongue, saying: "If, as you say, it be irreligious, curious, superfluous to know whether God's foreknowledge is contingent; whether our will can contribute anything pertinent to our eternal salvation; [and other such questions], what then, I ask, is religious, serious, and useful knowledge? This is weak stuff, Erasmus. *Das ist zu viel!* (p. 104)."

Luther may be right to complain that Erasmus cannot consistently assert his opposition to assertions. I believe that Erasmus's best response to this dilemma is contained in his *Praise of Folly*, which I discuss in chapter 7. However, even his work on free will is more complex that Luther concedes. Erasmus calls his book a *diatriba*, which is not a "diatribe" in the modern sense, but rather a genre of dialogue that was employed by Epictetus, Galen, Plurarch, Cicero, and Seneca—all more or less Pyrrhonist and skeptical writers. Epictetus actually wrote a *Diatribe* on freedom, although it is not clear that Erasmus knew the original work. In the ancient diatribe, the participants reached no certain conclusion, because Pyrrhonists doubted the possibility of certainty. Moreover, they set aside metaphysical and speculative questions as unanswerable and irrelevant: Pyrrho and Epictetus called these issues *adiaphora*, a word that Erasmus echoes. In his pamphlet entitled *Hyperaspistes*, Erasmus writes:

> a skeptic is not he who does not care to know what is true
> and what is false, since skeptics derive their name from
> deliberating. Rather, he is a skeptic who does not facilely
> define, nor on behalf of his opinion engage in mortal
> combat. . . . Such, you see, were the orthodox skeptics of
> old regarding the interpretation of Literature, inquiring
> and suspending a decision, deferring to the judgments of
> others. And in many matters for defining, the Church, as
> we have said before, was a skeptic, suspending a decision
> for many centuries [presumably until a consensus of
> human opinion could emerge].[56]

Still, even a Pyrrhonist must decide how to live. Therefore, a diatribe addresses practical, moral issues, such as the best kind of government, the active versus the contemplative life, the morality of suicide, and so on. The participants seek agreement about *probable* truth, which they achieve by weighing rhetorical speeches on either side of each question.

Epictetus writes that his method requires the following steps:

1. A recognition of the conflict between men;
2. A search for the origins of that conflict;
3. A condemnation of mere opinion and
4. An expression of skepticism regarding it;
5. A kind of investigation to determine whether the opinion is rightly held; and
6. The invention of a kind of standard (*canon*) of judgment.[57]

This is exactly what Erasmus offers. He: (1) recognizes that some Christians affirm and others deny the existence of free will; (2) blames the conflict on Luther; (3) condemns the doctrines on both sides as mere opinions; and

(4) expresses his skepticism regarding these opinions. Then he (5) determines that the Catholic position is rightly held, on the basis of (6) a new standard of judgment: namely, consensus within the church over time.

Since Erasmus is writing a diatribe, which can reach no certain conclusion, he wants to join with Luther in a cooperative and peaceful effort to weigh diverse human opinions. This is an extraordinarily gentle way to treat an excommunicated heretic whose ideas had produced schism and open warfare. But Erasmus believes in peaceful discussion as the very embodiment of Christ. Moreover, his methodological views require him to assert his openness to Luther's opinions, whatever the Church may say about them. A genuine consensus does not exist unless everyone has had a chance to express his or her opinions freely, and everyone else has listened. Unfortunately, Erasmus cannot literally write a dialogue in which he and Luther cooperate in the search for probable truth. Their exchange occurs in the real world, with Luther deciding for himself how to play his own part. Since Luther opposes Pyrrhonism and believes in scripture as an absolute criterion of truth, he refuses to engage in a skeptical diatribe. Thus the debate is ultimately unsatisfactory: it is frustrated for precisely the same reasons that blocked agreement in the *Protagoras*.

Erasmus hopes that his arguments against speculative theology may persuade readers to drop the issue of determinism that Luther has raised (p. 20). The best response, he thinks, would be neither to endorse nor to rebut Luther, but (in a Wittgensteinian or Pyrrhonist spirit) to declare the question unanswerable and therefore meaningless. However, knowing that the Lutheran challenge will not be so easily ignored by most readers, Erasmus proceeds—clearly without enthusiasm—to defend the official Church position concerning free will. It is as if he were unilaterally playing the role of a participant in a classical "diatribe," weighing past opinions in search of the probable truth. But freedom of the will is not an appropriate topic for a diatribe, which deals better with practical issues. Erasmus does his best to write a Pyrrhonist dialogue about a metaphysical topic—and the results are not perfectly satisfactory.

As might be expected, several of Erasmus's arguments are pragmatic. Assume, he begins, that Luther is correct and that our actions are completely determined. If people were convinced that they had no free will and that their eternal fate was preordained, then they would sin with abandon. Therefore, "What could be more useless than to publish this paradox to the world? . . . What a loophole the publication of this opinion would open to godlessness among innumerable people!" (p. 11). Further, Erasmus emphasizes that the vast majority of theologians and commentators have affirmed the existence of a free will. He concedes that majority opinion can be mistaken (p. 15); but he doubts that God would have allowed numerous saints, popes, and the holy Church to err on such a basic matter of doctrine for 1,300 years (pp. 17–19).

Thus the fact that the doctrine of free will has persuaded so many people, among them blessed saints and workers of miracles, supports the theory.[58] This is an indirect, pragmatic argument for an assertion that is too abstract in itself to persuade the pragmatic Erasmus.

Having relied on such arguments, Erasmus anticipates the objection that we should not treat religious matters by human lights: "some will say: Erasmus should learn about Christ and disregard human prudence. This nobody understands, unless he has the Spirit of God" (p. 94). Erasmus replies that he wants nothing more than to feel the Spirit of God, but he believes that God's Spirit has been felt, not only by him, but also by all the devout Christians who have believed in the free will for a millennium. So once again, Erasmus turns to human experience as a source of evidence for his opinions about God. He does so because he sees no alternative to human experience, since Scripture is unclear about metaphysical issues.

In response, Luther denounces Erasmus's pragmatism. He writes:

> You make it clear that this peace and tranquility of the flesh [that comes from believing in a free will] are to you far more important than faith, conscience, salvation, the word of God, the glory of Christ and God himself. There-fore, let me tell you, and I beg you to let it sink deep into your mind, I am concerned with a serious, vital and eternal verity, yes such a fundamental one, that it ought to be maintained even at the cost of life itself, and even though the whole world should not only be thrown into turmoil and fighting, but shattered in chaos and reduced to nothing. . . . You say, by our doctrine [of determinism] a floodgate of iniquity is opened. Be it so. (pp. 107–8, 110)

In this passage, Luther states philosophy's side in the quarrel between philosophy and humanism as explicitly as it has ever been stated. Luther believes that our fundamental moral and spiritual task is to understand doctrine, meaning a set of eternal verities that can be discovered, but never created, by human beings. "If we know nothing of these things, we shall know nothing whatsoever of Christianity, and shall be worse off than all the heathens" (p. 106). Salvation comes only by faith, and faith means believing in certain transcendent truths. Thus Luther adopts a version of Socrates' doctrine that knowledge makes us good; for Luther, nothing can make us good, but knowledge can save our souls. Erasmus, on the other hand, doubts that we can know eternal verities, and he worries that Luther's doctrines are not only senseless, but will actually make people bad. As Luther notes, this difference "is the very hinge upon which our disputation turns. It is the crucial issue between you and me" (p. 106).

Luther understands Erasmus's pragmatism as purely prudential or hedonic, as if Erasmus simply wanted to believe whatever made people happy and well-behaved. He also considers his opponent impious and "perverse," because Erasmus "judges of divine things and words according to the customs and things of men" (p. 125). But Erasmus's position is more subtle than this. He does not want to discuss the question of free will at all, because he sees no way to resolve it, and he believes that the issue is irrelevant to morality and to biblical interpretation. If anything is impious, he argues, it is to pursue questions that we are not equipped to answer. But if Erasmus is forced to choose between freedom and determinism, then he prefers to believe the doctrine that has convinced the most Christians and that makes people the most spiritually secure. He does not shun Luther's "serious, vital and eternal verity" because he finds it inconvenient or disconcerting, but because he doubts its truth-value. Cicero (a skeptic) had argued that the appropriate questions to discuss in a dialogue were political or ethical; they involved mere opinions; and their solution could promote honesty and convenience.[59] This is just how Erasmus treats the question of free will. But Luther, not being a skeptic, believes that free will is a meta-physical theory that can be conclusively rebutted; thus it is not a mere matter of opinion to be addressed in the interests of social utility.

Luther exhibits a certain degree of skepticism himself.[60] He attributes to Erasmus the position that human beings are free, yet unable to do right without God's assistance. But in that case, he argues, the will exhibits no trace, no evidence of its power; it is "a sort of mere abstract willing" (p. 124). This anticipates empiricist arguments against free will, causality, essence, and other metaphysical entities that escape human observation. Empiricists argue that if these things cannot be observed, they do not exist. Erasmus agrees, but he believes that determinism is just as untestable as the theory of meta-physical freedom.[61] Luther is an empiricist, but Erasmus is a pragmatist; and this defines their difference. Empiricists reject some doctrines as "meta-physical," and instead they devise allegedly non-metaphysical models of reality. For example, the theory that the world is composed only of sense-data (held by Hume, Ayer, and others) is supposed to be a non-metaphysical alternative to the theory of things-in-themselves. Similarly, Luther's doctrine of determinism is supposed to avoid the metaphysical abstraction of a free will. But pragmatists consider the empiricists' worldview to be just as specu-lative as traditional metaphysics. They prefer not to discuss such abstract questions at all; and this is clearly the essence of Erasmus's position.

Nevertheless, Erasmus has committed himself, as a loyal Catholic and a doctor of theology, to a defense of free will. Therefore, he devotes several chapters to biblical exegesis, trying to show that scripture implies the existence of human freedom. He warns: "Most of the time [biblical passages] can be applied conveniently to an interpretation favorable to free will, or to one against it" (p. 67). But, despite this warning, he tries to weigh the *probable* meaning of scriptural testimony—a Pyrrhonist approach. In particular, he collects numerous examples of moral exhortation from the Bible, and asks why God would exhort us if we had no freedom. He concludes: "whenever the word 'will' is used, it implies free will. Doesn't the reader of such passages ask: why do you [God] make conditional promises, when it depends solely on your will? Why do you blame me, when all my works, good and bad, are accomplished by you, and I am only your tool?" (p. 35).

No doubt this argument is intended as a guess about the probable truth, like one that a participant in a diatribe would offer. However, it is perfectly conceivable that God might admonish us and entreat us even if we were mere material objects, totally subject to mechanical laws of cause and effect. God's exhortations would, after all, have causal power: they would *make* some people act better. Analogously, even if we do not believe that dogs (or hamsters) have free wills, we still scold them. Thus Erasmus's deduction of metaphysics from Scripture is weak—as he seems to recognize. He shows his uneasiness about this kind of argument when he interprets a verse from Paul: "If anyone, therefore, has cleansed himself from these, he will be a vessel for honorable use" (2 Tim. 2:21). Erasmus asks: "How could someone keep clean, if he is totally incapable of doing anything?" (pp. 42–43). Thus he interprets the passage to mean that human beings must possess metaphysical freedom. But Paul has been exhorting Timothy to "shun profane and vain babblings"; he has not been arguing about freedom of the will. Whether or not we possess metaphysical freedom, Paul could still entreat Timothy to shun heresy. In short, the passage is neutral with respect to the question of free will.

Nevertheless, Erasmus's reading ascribes an implicit philosophical meaning to the passage, and one that Paul probably did not intend. This is an interpretive approach that Erasmus criticizes when the scholastics employ it. Since he distrusts figurative readings, there is a ring of defensiveness in his next paragraph: "I know," he writes, "that this is a mode of figurative expression. For the moment I am quite satisfied that it contradicts those who want to ascribe everything to mere necessity" (p. 43). Luther, who agrees with Erasmus's general disdain for figurative interpretation, pounces on this passage, remarking: "it is not enough for you to say there may be a figure. I must inquire whether there need be and must be a figure. And if you do not prove that there must necessarily be a figure, you achieve nothing. . . . The Word of God must be taken in its plain meaning, as the words stand" (p. 128–9).

Luther may be correct to recognize an inconsistency in Erasmus's position, although Erasmus could perhaps explain that he is (of necessity) only discussing probable truths. Erasmus is on firmer ground when he attacks Luther's scriptural exegesis, for Luther also purports to discover metaphysics in the Bible, despite his disclaimers. Luther seems to believe that his doctrine of determinism is the clear, literal, and indubitable meaning of several scriptural passages; but Erasmus accuses him of "forcing" their meaning "to refer to grace and free will" (p. 63). For example, Erasmus discusses the following verse from Paul: "So then neither he who plants is anything, nor he who waters, but God who gives the growth" (1 Cor. 3:7). Erasmus believes, contrary to Luther, that the literal topic of this passage is not free will or determinism. Rather, the point is to exalt God and to belittle his creatures, but without denying (or affirming) that people are free. Erasmus cites numerous biblical passages in which "nothing" is used to mean something of little value or significance. For example, Paul writes, "though I have all faith, [yet] have not charity, I am nothing" (1 Cor 13:2). Paul does not mean that we would disappear off the face of the earth if we lacked charity, only that we would have no *value* without it. Thus, Erasmus concludes, when Paul says that he who plants is nothing, he is not saying that we lack causal responsibility for earthly affairs; he is merely stressing God's much greater power and significance.[62]

Luther believes that he has won the battle of Bible citations by discovering undeniable scriptural support for his theory of determinism. Erasmus undermines these readings, however, and tentatively suggests that other Bible passages imply metaphysical freedom. In the final analysis, Erasmus should be content with a stalemate. If neither writer can use biblical exegesis to demonstrate the certain truth of his doctrine, then Luther's challenge to Catholicism must fail. Absent a water-tight argument against freedom, it is surely better to drop the whole topic—and this is Erasmus's real preference. However, even if we grant Erasmus a narrow kind of victory, all that he has done is to forestall Luther's criticism; he has not yet offered a positive program to guide our lives. In the next chapter, I will discuss the positive ideas of Erasmus and those of another humanist who was in many ways his disciple: William Shakespeare.

THE WISE FOOL

I have argued that Renaissance humanists preferred rhetoric, history, art, and literature to speculative philosophy and theology; and I have quoted passages in which they defended their favored disciplines against the methods of scholastics and other philosophers. But the proof of a humanist approach is in the pudding. So, for example, it is wrong to emphasize a theoretical work like Sidney's *Defense of Poetry* at the expense of his actual verse. Nor should we focus exclusively on Erasmus's dispute with Luther, for in that debate Erasmus was forced to engage in the kind of abstract reasoning that he generally avoided. His scholarly editions, paraphrases, anthologies, and handbooks of eloquence constitute the real substance of his work, and they embody his positive views persuasively. However, they are difficult to summarize in a way that captures their value. Fortunately, his short satirical work, *The Praise of Folly*, is a self-contained piece of literature that shows, rather than tells, the foolishness of philosophy and the superiority of satire as a method of persuasion.

THE PRAISE OF FOLLY

The Praise of Folly is a speech delivered by Folly in praise of herself. As a fool (she wears a court jester's garb), she does not care that one is supposed to deliver an encomium in someone *else*'s praise. "What could be more fitting," she asks, "than for Folly to trumpet her own merits . . . ?"' At first glance, at least, her speech appears to present a set of arguments in favor of folly. She argues that foolishness—especially the foolishness of infancy, senility, and inebriation—makes people happy and shields them from despair. She prefers spontaneity and naturalness to self-control and convention; vanity to self-criticism; and frankness to etiquette. She even defends flattery as a social lubricant.

In the second section of her speech, she demonstrates her own importance by listing all the fools who serve her cause. Prominent among her servants are monks: proponents of the *vita contemplativa* who do no one any good. But the greatest fools of all are theologians and philosophers, who "interpret hidden mysteries to suit themselves: how the world was created and designed; through what channels the stain of sin filtered down to posterity; by what means, in what measure, and how long Christ was formed in the Virgin's womb"—and other hairsplitting questions, all of them lifted from Peter Lombard's scholastic textbook, the *Sentences* (p. 126). Like Erasmus, Folly enjoys recalling the fact that the greatest saints were philosophically naive. "The apostles," she says, "knew personally the mother of Jesus, but which one of them proved how she had been kept immaculate from Adam's sin with the logic [that] our theologians display?" (p. 128).

Folly also attacks the theologians' interpretive methods. When they gloss texts, she says, they combine brief scriptural citations with quotations from secular history and logical arguments ("syllogisms, major and minor, conclusions, corollaries, idiotic hypotheses, and further scholastic rubbish"). The secular history that they cite is usually medieval gossip, she says, and they "interpret it allegorically, tropologically, and anagogically" (p. 134). This sounds like a caricature of Aquinas's method.

In the last section of her book, Folly cites authorities who have defended foolishness, above all Jesus and Paul. For didn't Paul say: "suffer fools gladly," "receive me as a fool," and "we are fools for Christ's sake"? (p. 147). Folly also offers a portrait of the holy fool that recalls Thomas à Kempis. The fool-for-Christ is unconcerned about convention and proper deportment, careless about worldly goods, irreverent toward human authority, ignorant of theory—but ecstatically committed to God.

Almost every reader of *The Praise of Folly* wants to know whether we are to take her arguments seriously. On one hand, Folly's satire of theologians and her praise of holy fools could appear in a straightforward argumentative work by Erasmus, whom she calls her "friend" (p. 141). Like Erasmus, she peppers her speech with classical and biblical quotations, she uses effective Latin oratory, and she shares many of his likes and dislikes. On the other hand, Folly's celebrations of drunkenness, flattery, and senility do not sound very Erasmian. Besides, if her arguments against philosophers and theologians are taken at face value, then they represent just another example of an anti-philosophical *doctrine*, and as such they do not advance the case against philosophers.

However, Erasmus distances himself from Folly's assertions by employing a complex form of irony. His irony is apparent already in the first paragraph of the book, where Folly remarks: "as soon as I stepped forward to address this crowded assembly, every face immediately brightened up with a new, unwonted gaiety and all your frowns were smoothed away" (p. 86). We are supposed to imagine an audience laughing at the very sight of a jester who takes the lectern, dressed in cap and bells, to praise herself. This is the literal image that Erasmus's prose suggests. But if Folly is a fool, she is a learned and clever one, for in her opening remarks she cites Terence, Homer, and a proverb of Italian origin: "By much laughter you know that a fool is present." John Donne made this proverb the theme of one of his "Paradoxes," explaining: "I always did, and shall understand, that *Adage* [that] by much *laughing* thou maist know there is a *fool*, not [to mean] that the *laughers* are *fools*, but that among them there is some *fool*, at whom *wise men* laugh: which moved *Erasmus* to put this as his first *Argument* in the mouth of his *Folly*, that *she made Beholders laugh*; for *fools* are the most laughed at, and laugh themselves the least of any."[2]

This, in fact, seems to be Folly's argument. And since it is a subtle argument, supported by clever allusions to classical authors, perhaps she is not a fool after all. In that case, the audience is foolish to laugh at her for being a fool. But if they are laughing at her even though she is not foolish, then the adage that she has quoted is wrong, for laughter has not proved that a fool is present. And if the adage is wrong, then she is a fool for quoting it. Thus the passage contains a vertiginous paradox.

A similar paradox occurs when Folly recalls that the Delphic oracle had once called Socrates the wisest man in the world. But the oracle, she says, "showed little enough wisdom in its judgment, for once when he tried to do something in public he had to break off amid general laughter" (p. 99). If it is true that "by laughter you may know the fool," then apparently Socrates was a fool. Yet Folly is the true fool, because she has made up this anecdote, which cannot be found in Plato. Or perhaps she is no fool after all, because Socrates explained that he was wise only because he knew that he knew nothing. Thus when people scoffed at Socrates (as Folly claims they did), they were the true fools, because they thought that they had wisdom. Socrates was a self-conscious fool, like Folly—and so he was simultaneously both wise and foolish.

My reading might appear labored, except that similar paradoxes and jokes abound in *The Praise of Folly*. Even the title is a three-way pun, for *Encomium Moriae* can mean "A Praise of Folly," "An Encomium Delivered by Folly," or "A Praise of [Thomas] More"—Erasmus's friend and dedicatee, who was no fool. Further, there is a running joke about the relationship between Erasmus and Folly. She constantly quotes Erasmus's works, suggesting that she admires him. She even says that she "mention[s] his name from time to time by way of a compliment" (p. 144). Yet a compliment from a fool is no honor. Elsewhere, arguing that folly is preferable to wisdom, she draws a satirical portrait of a pedantic scholar that may be a self-deprecating caricature of Erasmus:

> [He is] a man who had frittered away all his boyhood and youth in acquiring learning, has lost the happiest part of his life in wakeful nights, toil and care, and never tastes a drop of pleasure even in what's left to him. He's always thrifty, impoverished, miserable, grumpy, harsh and unjust to himself, disagreeable and unpopular with his fellows, pale and thin, sickly and bear-eyed, prematurely white-haired and senile, worn-out and dying before his time. . . . There you have a splendid picture of a wise man. (p. 110)

But *is* this a wise man? He is learned, but he is also wasting his life, which is not a very wise thing to do. Folly uses her portrait of the scholar as evidence that fools are superior, yet she constantly quotes Erasmus's scholarship—and he is her creator. So is she the creature of a fool or of a wise man? And is *he* joking or is he serious?

When Folly cites Paul's words—"I speak as a fool"—in praise of herself, she concedes that "certain Greek pedants" will attack her for misunderstanding Paul's sense. A leader of these pedants is Erasmus, who is always emphasizing the *intended* meaning of scripture. According to Folly, Erasmus would argue that Paul did not literally call himself a fool; he just wanted to belittle himself for rhetorical purposes. This sounds like an authentically Erasmian reading: it resembles his interpretation of the word "nothing" in Paul, as discussed in chapter 6. But Folly says that she prefers to ignore Erasmus's reading of the text in favor of Nicholas of Lyra's scholastic interpretation, which calls "upon the full forces of dialectic" (p. 145). After all, scholasticism is the authentically *foolish* approach to criticism. But when she quotes Nicholas, his reading turns out to be literal after all, although "a little later he appears to forget himself and slips into another interpretation." Once again, paradoxes abound, and it is impossible to pin down Erasmus's intentions.

Erasmus's irony and humor were lost on some of his contemporaries. For example, Martin Dorp complained that Erasmus really should have written a "Praise of *Wisdom.*" Trying to ward off Dorp's criticism, Erasmus replied: "remember that it is Folly and a woman who has spoken." Here he quotes verbatim Folly's own final words, thus treating the fool as his authority even as he distances himself from her. "You see," he tells Dorp, "that I have continually forestalled any occasion for offense. But the people whose ears are attuned to nothing but propositions, conclusions, and corollaries, do not weigh sufficiently such matters [as who is speaking and whether the text is ironic]."[3] Thus one possible reason that Erasmus wrote in the voice of a fool was to forestall criticism. A court jester can say openly what others would never dare to imply. As Folly argues: "The fact is, kings do dislike the truth, but the outcome of this is extraordinary for my fools. They can speak truths and even open insults and still be heard with positive pleasure" (p. 110). However, if Erasmus's intent was simply to escape accountability for what his fool said, then he failed, because everyone took her satire on clergy, monks, theologians, and kings as Erasmus's own. But Erasmus had a deeper reason to write ironically.

To say that philosophy is pointless is to make a philosophical statement, which is therefore a paradox. However, Erasmus does not say this in *The Praise of Folly*. Instead, he says that a fool, if she gave a foolish speech, would claim that philosophy was pointless. Thus Erasmus does not offer a general proposition about methods of argument, but rather a concrete (albeit fictional) statement about one foolish woman and her silly ideas. The self-refuting quality of her argument becomes just another ironic move in a text that is replete with paradoxes. Nevertheless, the book points in a clear direction—away from theory, and toward oratory. Rhetoric, after all, is shown to be highly effective, especially when it is spiced with irony. Who wants to be the butt of Erasmus's paradoxical wit? Who wants to play Martin Dorp, a true fool? It seems safer to read literature and rhetoric, to drop scholastic logic, and to try to keep up with Erasmus.

The Praise of Folly also suggests that we ought to wrestle with difficult questions about the proper role of wisdom and foolishness, rhetoric and logic, scholarship and ignorance. On many points, Folly sounds like a typical humanist in the tradition of Protagoras. For example, she makes fun of Plato's dictum that philosophers should rule (p. 100); she favors the *vita activa* (p. 110); and she consistently defends pluralism and diversity over conformity to any universal principles. Discussing monastic rules that treat all monks uniformly, she remarks, "But this equality applied to such a diversity of persons and temperaments will only result in inequality, as anyone can see" (p. 131). She asserts that "human affairs are so complex and obscure that nothing can be known of them for certain, as has rightly been stated by my Academicians" (p. 118). However, if we assume that Erasmus agrees with Folly on these points—or even that *she* is being forthright—then we risk ignoring the irony that permeates the text. Any abstract answer to these questions would be unsatisfactory and unconvincing; so Erasmus does not offer such answers. Instead, by discussing these matters through the ironic medium of a fool, he encourages us to reflect for ourselves. And he suggests that it is sometimes wise to think as if one were a fool—that is, without concern for conventions, without pretension, without respect for authority, and (above all) without philosophizing.

SHAKESPEARE AS HUMANIST

The Erasmian figure of the wise fool reappears in *King Lear*. Shakespeare continues Erasmus's attack on speculative philosophy, but he also gives a much more substantial indication of how we might live ethically without theory. Furthermore, in *King Lear*, Shakespeare addresses the most telling argument against humanistic ethics: namely, that rhetoric and fiction can deceive and can serve the interests of the wicked. He responds that narrative offers the best method for telling the difference between good and evil rhetoric; thus fiction can keep its own house in order. At the same time, he shows the inadequacy of moral theory as a means of judging particular cases.

My argument for the significance of *King Lear* depends fundamentally upon a close reading of the play, which I offer below. However, it is relevant to note that Shakespeare lived during a period when the conflict between philosophy and the humanities was being hotly debated; and his works reveal an explicit awareness of that quarrel. In a book that runs to almost 1,500 dense pages, T. W. Baldwin has argued that Shakespeare knew all of the classical texts that were commonly taught in sixteenth-century grammar schools. Even if Shakespeare never attended such a school himself, he somehow acquired an equivalent education.[4] Tudor schools were organized according to the educational ideals of Erasmus and his contemporaries; Erasmus personally had an enormous influence on their curricula.[5] These schools taught very little except the Latin literary classics, but they taught these works quite rigorously—and with moral and civic education as their constant purpose.

Meanwhile, the formal university curriculum was still dominated by scholastic logic, theology, and law; but throughout the Tudor period, efforts were made to introduce humanistic studies. In 1518, a dispute at Oxford between "Greeks" (i.e., humanists) and "Trojans" (scholastics) grew so intense that Thomas More, the Chancellor, had to intervene on behalf of the "Greeks." Corpus Christi College, Oxford, and St. Johns, Cambridge, had progressive charters that provided for literary studies during part of each day.[6] At the same time, a new class of students started arriving at the universities: gentlemen who brought along their own tutors, from whom they received humanistic training so that they could ignore the formal scholastic curriculum.

One such student is Lucentio, a protagonist in *The Taming of the Shrew*. When the action begins, Lucentio has just arrived at Padua, "nursery of arts," which was in fact a great seat of Renaissance humanism (I.i.2).[7] He plans to "institute / A course of learning and ingenious studies" (I.i.9).[8] Addressing his servant and tutor Tranio, Lucentio says:

> for the time I study
> Virtue and that part of philosophy
> Will I apply that treats of happiness
> By virtue specially to be achiev'd.
> Tell me thy mind, for I have Pisa left
> And am to Padua come, as he that leaves
> A shallow plash to plunge him in the deep. (I.i.17–23)

Lucentio's talk of happiness achieved through virtue alludes to Aristotelian ethics, which the scholastics had turned into a formal moral system. But Tranio appears to be a humanist, for he is not pleased with Lucentio's enthusiasm for moral philosophy. He argues on behalf of the unofficial humanistic curriculum that tutors (like himself) then offered in England, as opposed to the formal scholastic curriculum of the universities. He says:

> *Mi pardonato*, gentle master mine;
> I am, in all affected as yourself,
> Glad that you thus continue your resolve
> To suck the sweets of sweet philosophy.
> Only, good master, while we do admire
> This virtue and this moral discipline,
> Let's be no Stoics nor no stocks, I pray,
> Or so devote to Aristotle's checks
> As Ovid be an outcast quite abjur'd.
> Balk logic with acquaintance that you have,
> And practice rhetoric in your common talk,
> Music and poesy use to quicken you,
> The mathematics, and the metaphysics,
> Fall to them as your stomach serves you:
> No profit grows where no pleasure ta'en. (I.i.25–39)

Tranio thinks that a modest acquaintance with logic is sufficient; that philosophy should not crowd rhetoric and poetry out of the curriculum. Later he quotes Terence from a Latin grammar text, as a humanist educator might (I.i.162).

Of course, we cannot assume that Shakespeare endorsed Tranio's humanism. But he certainly understood the humanists' point of view and the nature of their conflict with philosophy. Indeed, one subplot of *The Taming of the Shrew* concerns a contest among suitors for Bianca, the "shrew's" scholarly sister. This turns into a competition between Hortensio—a student of music and mathematics, parts of the scholastic quadrivium—and Lucentio, who is said to be "as cunning in Greek, Latin, and other languages as the other in music and mathematics" (II.i.802). Thus Lucentio is by now a humanist, or at least pretends to be one.

The humanities are not taken very seriously in *The Taming of the Shrew*. When Lucentio actually gets around to "lecturing" Bianca in Latin literature, he uses the opportunity to slip her a love note. She chooses him in the end over Hortensio, but not because of his educational theory. Nevertheless, Shakespeare's understanding of humanism may illuminate one of his most salient qualities: his lack of doctrine. Ideas, perspectives, mores, arguments, dilemmas, and conventions fill his plays; but we can never say that Shakespeare offers an explicit moral or political argument of his own. His works are often recommended for their ethical value, yet they have no thesis. As Lars Engle writes, "Most traditional authorities . . . have praised, or occasionally blamed, Shakespeare for not having a nameable philosophy, seen in traditional terms as a set of essentialist commitments. Thus Coleridge on myriad-mindedness, Keats on negative capability, Arnold on Shakespeare's freedom from our questions, and Eliot on Shakespeare's inferiority to Dante."[9]

The quality that these diverse critics have all discovered in Shakespeare is not his alone; it is typical of the humanists' approach to morals. His plays show us the difference between good and evil in concrete situations, without offering rules or principles. We can learn from his works, but by imitation and not by deriving doctrines. At the same time, he frequently demonstrates that moral theory can stand in the way of acting well. In my view, this is one of the lessons of *King Lear*.

KING LEAR

King Lear presents two parallel tragic plots. In each, a father misinterprets his children, mistaking fluent oratory for sincerity, and flattery for respect, while failing to recognize true love in the one child who actually feels it. Lear designs a formal ceremony in which his daughters are to praise him. His evil older children, Goneril and Regan, play according to his rules, eloquently stating that they love him; and he rewards them with parts of his kingdom. But his youngest daughter, Cordelia, finds herself unable to state in conventional, artificial terms what she simply feels—true love; and Lear mistakes her silence for betrayal.

Everyone who reads or sees *King Lear* knows that Cordelia is Lear's one sincere daughter. So do all of the characters who watch from on stage: not only the loyal Kent and the chivalrous France, but even wicked Goneril, who remarks to Regan: "he hath always lov'd our sister most; and with what poor judgment he hath cast her off appears too grossly" (I.i.289).¹⁰ "Grossly" here means "obviously"; and Lear's misjudgment is indeed obvious. Members of the audience have two advantages in judging Cordelia correctly. First, the actress who plays her invariably tries to suggest sincerity. Second, we can hear her say privately: "What shall Cordelia speak? Love and be silent" (I.i.61). Lear cannot hear this "aside," but he has had many years in which to know his daughters. Besides, Goneril and Regan give speeches that, in their hyperbole, their conventionality, and their crass efforts to outbid each other, simply appear insincere; whereas Cordelia's behavior is guileless and brave.

The literal content of the first scene—the characters' rhetoric and actions—is enough to indicate certain basic ideas. Cordelia is sincere, and it would be almost impossible to play her as the most hypocritical of Lear's children. Nor would it be easy to play Goneril and Regan as loyal, generous daughters. Thus the fact that Lear is wrong is clearly supported by the text. Yet we can disagree about certain subtler points. For example, some people find Cordelia innocent and courageous; others think that she is somewhat self-righteous, and that she should be more tactful toward Lear. Each interpretation can be supported by a reading of the text, and each reading would lead an actress to play Cordelia differently.

On one reading, she can be played as self-possessed, as lecturing her father about the limits of filial piety and the value of candor. In that case, she is not necessarily *wrong*, but she is more than a passive victim. On the other hand, Stanley Cavell suggests that the scene should be played as follows.¹¹ Lear demands formal, public affirmations of respect, which have nothing to do with genuine feelings. Thus he addresses the court in his speeches, using formulaic phrases and a declamatory tone that is appropriate to public rituals; and so do Goneril and Regan. Everyone is satisfied. But Cordelia, being almost a child, does not understand the function of courtly rhetoric; her asides express genuine confusion about what she is to say. When she finally has to speak, she talks directly to Lear, imploring him not to force her to proceed with a ritual that she finds puzzling and inhuman. Thus her famous response, "Nothing, my lord," should be said beseechingly, *sotto voce* to Lear. It means (as Cavell writes) "don't force me, I don't know what you want, there is nothing I can say."

Cavell concedes that the scene can be played otherwise. Nevertheless, his close reading provides a powerful argument in favor of Cordelia; it makes sense of her statements and actions, and it makes her look innocent. What Cavell does not offer is a philosophical argument in favor of honesty. He never addresses the dispute between Kantians, who condemn all lies as violations of moral principle, and consequentialists, who might favor tactful dissembling if it produces better results. It is unnecessary for him to discuss this issue in order to defend Cordelia, because a positive account of her character can emerge from the text itself if it is interpreted as he suggests. Furthermore, to read the play in the light of abstract moral principles would violate the main lesson of the work: namely, that philosophy blinds us to moral truth.

To understand this message, we should ask *why* Lear misjudges his daughters. Kent, his loyal servant, says: "See better, Lear" (I.i.157). Lear sees exactly what we see, but he sees it wrong. Kent, on the other hand, typically tries to observe the particularities of the people around him, in order to judge them fairly. In the opening lines of the play, he is introduced to Edmund, and immediately remarks: "I must know you, and sue to love you better" (I.i.29). Kent's ethic, his approach to all human encounters, is to seek to know people accurately, in the hopes of loving them. There is irony in Edmund's reply— "Sir, I shall study deserving"—for Edmund is a wicked and deceitful man. But Kent's sensitive observation of behavior allows him to recognize evil as well as goodness, even though he always hopes that he may love. By contrast, Lear is not only suspicious, but also blind to the particularities that Kent observes so finely. The most important reason for his blindness is that he thinks in broad abstractions.

A MARKET METAPHOR

One category that Lear employs is economic. He intends to reward each daughter's statement of love with a commensurate grant of land, implying that he believes love to be precisely quantifiable and exchangeable for other values at an appropriate price. "Which of you," he asks, "shall we say doth love us most? / That we our largest bounty may extend" (I.i.50). He envisions a complex market, in which his daughters each have value to their suitors; their speeches have value to him, equivalent to the worth of their love; and the dowries that he bestows on their husbands have appropriate financial value. The purpose of his ceremony is to allow the market to "clear," so that everything receives its due price. Understanding his economic metaphor, Regan and Goneril each offer a catalog of worldly goods as evidence of their love. For example, Regan, trying to outbid Goneril, begins her speech: "I am made of that self metal as my sister / And prize me at her worth. . . . Only she comes too short" (I.i.68).

When Cordelia, instead of offering a speech in her father's praise, says, "Nothing, my lord," Lear interprets this as a bid of zero, indicating that Cordelia's respect for him is nil (I.i.86). "Nothing will come of nothing," he replies. When she refuses to raise her bid (for she does not see love as economic), he struggles to understand her behavior in terms of his market metaphor. In succession, he remarks: "thy truth then be thy dower"; "Let pride . . . marry her"; "But now her price is fallen"; and "[she is] Dower'd with our curse" (I.i.107, 128, 196, 204). Lear assumes that truth, pride, and his malediction are equal in value to her speech, that is, worthless.

Much later in the play, when Lear is mad, Cordelia shows that her love for him is not worthless, but rather priceless. She says: "He that helps him take all my outward worth" (IV.iv.10). In fact, she gives her very life to try to save Lear. In general, she does not see love, worldly renown, and money as measurable on a common scale. When her suitor, Burgundy, refuses her hand because her dowry is now nothing, Cordelia says: "Since that respect and fortunes are his love, / I shall not be his wife" (I.i.247). But Lear views love, public expressions of respect, and money as interchangeable, asking Burgundy, "What, in the least, will you require in present *dower* with her, / Or cease your quest of *love?*" (I.i.190–2).[12] Fortunately for Cordelia, one of her suitors does not believe that love has a measurable price. This is France, who, taken with Cordelia's sincerity, says, "She is herself a dowry" (I.i.239). In other words, he loves her for her inherent worth, which is not fungible for land or praise. Indeed, France finds her "most rich, being poor," for what attracts him to her is the very sincerity that has cost her her dowry (I.i.249). Nor does he care about the market's estimation of her: "'tis strange," he reflects, "that from their colds't neglect / My love should kindle to inflam'd respect" (I.i.254).

In order to love people for their inherent worth, instead of setting a market price for them, one has to observe the irresolvable particularities of their behavior. The market fails to judge Cordelia fairly, assessing her as a "little-seeming substance," whose price has fallen (I.i.197). It cannot judge people appropriately, because it deals in quantities, but human beings cannot be understood adequately with numbers. Nevertheless, members of the audience are able to reach the same conclusion as Kent, who tells Lear the obvious truth: "Thy youngest daughter does not love thee least" (I.i.151). We know that what Kent says is true because we have not been weighing bids, but have rather tried to see the behavior of each character as either virtuous or vicious. This is an exercise in judgment that is aided by our past experience with human beings and by the precision of Shakespeare's language; but no act of measurement is necessary.

Like Kent, France is a careful observer who always hopes to love other people. He is not present when Cordelia says "Nothing" to Lear, but he has observed her behavior in general, and he doubts that she can have sinned so badly—

> which to believe of her,
> Must be a faith that reason without miracle
> Should never plant in me. (I.i.220ff.)

Thus Kent and France exemplify alternatives to Lear's suspicious, mercantile method of judging human worth.

NATURAL LAW

The other abstract category that Lear employs to judge his daughters is "nature." He believes that natural forces determine human behavior. Thus he begins an oath: "By all the operation of the orbs / From which we do exist and cease to be, . . ." (I.i.110). At least before tragedy befalls him, Lear thinks that the omnipotent natural forces are wise and just. In distress, he appeals to them, crying, "Hear, Nature, hear! dear Goddess, hear!" (I.iv.273). According to Lear, when a child does his parent wrong, the child is "disnatur'd" (I.iv.281). Similarly, Lear's courtier, Gloucester, is fond of distinctions between just nature and unnatural evil. "Unnatural," he cries when he hears the (false) news that Edgar has betrayed him: "worse than brutish!" (I.ii.73). When Regan, Goneril, and Cornwall cast the king out into the stormy night, Gloucester cries: "Alack, alack! Edmund, I like not this unnatural dealing" (II.iii.1).

In Western history, a moral appeal to nature has been one of the most common methods of making ethical judgments—as common, perhaps, as economic calculations of value. Philosophers have repeatedly offered theories about the "state of nature," "human nature," and "natural law," in order to ground their ethical theories. This was certainly true in Shakespeare's day, when medieval philosophies of natural law still prevailed, only to be replaced gradually by modern state-of-nature theories. John F. Danby has written: "The idea of Nature, then, in orthodox Elizabethan thought, is always something normative for human beings. It is impossible to talk about Nature without talking also about pattern and ideal form; about Reason as displayed in Nature; about Custom which is the basis of Law and equally with Law as expression of Nature's pattern."[13]

Danby quotes Richard Hooker, Francis Bacon, and other writers as exemplars of the "orthodox" Elizabethan view. Of course, there was also an unorthodox theory: that nature was wicked or chaotic. But even Hobbes (born when Shakespeare was twenty-four), who considered the state of nature to be abominable, still used his understanding of it to secure a theory of justice: for him, nature was a threat that had to be avoided at all costs. Indeed, one might say that the concept of nature is almost inherently normative, because it suggests that creation has a single, inevitable, and universal character before we intervene with our customs and laws. The very distinction between nature and culture (or reason or law) is usually a value-judgment, rather than a matter of fact. If nature is good—Hooker called it God's instrument—then our laws ought to imitate it; but if it is wicked and violent, then we must suppress it with rules and principles.[14]

Both the orthodox and the unorthodox theories of nature were challenged in the 1590s by John Donne. His eighth paradox, entitled "That Nature is Our Worst Guide," may have been a source for Shakespeare, because it combines most of the conspicuous themes of *King Lear*. In the course of a few sentences, Donne discusses foolishness, nature, bastardy, "nothing," the definition of "man," and even the cause of thunder–all topics in *Lear*. Donne argues that we cannot extract normative guidance from nature, because we cannot generalize about it usefully. "If by *Nature* we shall understand our *essence*, our *definition*, our *reasonableness*, then this being alike common to all (the *Idiot* and the *Wizard* being alike *reasonable*) why should not all men having equally all one *nature* follow one course?" But all men do not act alike, so clearly nature cannot explain their actions. Further, Donne argues that "our poore knowledge" is not sufficient to explain the meaning of natural phenomena like rain and thunder in such a way as to offer moral guidance.[15]

Likewise, within the world of *King Lear*, a theory of nature is no better than a market transaction as a means of determining real moral worth. Despite their appeals to "the wisdom of nature" (I.ii.101), Lear and Gloucester have no means of distinguishing a "monster" from a friend–and nature contains both (I.iv.251). At the beginning of the play, the two fathers both believe that natural law, social conventions, and moral values are all in harmony. There-fore, the conventional prerogatives of fathers and kings are natural and just, and the artificial speeches of Goneril and Regan are signs of their natural filial piety. Anyone who violates this harmony (either by turning against her father, or by failing to give a conventional speech) is "unnatural." But an abstract theory of cosmic order cannot help either Lear or Gloucester to predict evil, to recognize goodness, or to act well.

Once tragedy befalls them, both men revise their optimistic concepts of human nature and of nature itself. Initially, Lear thinks that his daughters' highly conventional speeches conform to their "natural" role as respectful children. But once he has lost his power, he sees that there is no necessary connection between natural behavior and social conventions. Lear gradually comes to understand Regan's view: that old men, being weak, have no natural rights. Sarcastically, he suggests that she wants to hear the following speech from him:

> "Dear daughter, I confess that I am old;
> Age is unnecessary: on my knees I beg   [Kneeling.]
> That you'll vouchsafe me raiment, bed, and food." (II.iv.150–153)

Lear wants this might-is-right doctrine to appear vile; he is still trying to appeal to Regan's conscience. But he has glimpsed a vision of nature as immoral–as the dictatorship of the strong–and he gradually begins to believe that this is the truth. When Edgar, beholding the mad Lear, says: "O thou side-piercing sight!", Lear replies: "Nature's above art in that respect" (IV.vi.86). The king is now insane, but presumably he means that nature is even better than art at breaking our hearts. Perhaps this realization is one cause of Lear's madness, for at first he put great stock in the justice of nature.

Just as Lear's initial faith in nature fades, so he grows quickly disenchanted with *human* nature and natural rights. At the beginning of the play, he frequently cites his own nature as a justification for his actions. He is, he thinks, by "nature" a man of his word (I.i.170), a good father (I.iv.264; I.v.31), and someone who is worthy of deference. Because his authority is part of his inherent nature, he does not need his troops to protect him: his daughters will treat him as his identity requires. Likewise, he intends to give the "largest bounty . . . / Where nature doth with merit challenge"–that is, to the daughter whose personal merits are so great as to vie with her natural affections for her father (I.i.52). But when Lear renounces his power, he discovers that his older daughters give him no "natural" respect at all, and that his identity as a man of authority and justice was just an illusion. Recent events have, he now thinks, "like an engine wrenched my frame of Nature / From the fix'd place" (I.iv.265–66).

Minus the trappings of power, Lear seems to be–naturally or essentially–just nothing. As his Fool tells him: "now thou art an O without a figure" (I.iv.189). This estimation echoes Lear's evaluation of Cordelia as "nothing" (I.i.244). But Lear begins to think that *all* human beings, outside of conventional laws, are worthless. On the stormy heath (i.e., in the state of nature), he encounters Edgar, who has disguised himself as a mad, naked beggar in order to escape his own father's death sentence. Lear asks: "Is man no more than this? . . . thou art the thing itself; unaccommodated man is no more but such a poor, bare, forked animal as thou art" (III.iv.100ff.).

When Lear's initial philosophy is shaken by his tragic experiences, his first instinct is to develop a new cosmic theory. In the midst of the terrible storm, he says:

> I tax you not, you elements, with unkindness;
> I never gave you kingdom, call'd you children,
> You owe me no subscription: then let fall
> Your horrible pleasure; here I stand, your slave (III.ii.16–19)

Here Lear tries to establish a new theory of natural right, arguing that what the gods do is justified because they owe him nothing and he is naturally their slave. If the gods are sovereign but arbitrary, then Lear is not morally responsible for the storm (which he could otherwise interpret as fit punishment for his sins). But he is still unsure what constitutes natural justice, now that his initial faith in his own virtue and authority has been shaken. Addressing the elements, he says, "yet I call you servile ministers, / That will with two pernicious daughters join" (III.ii.21–22). Here he suggests that nature is in league with Goneril and Regan, which would imply an intensely pessimistic theory of natural justice.

When Lear sees Edgar, disguised as Poor Tom, he refuses to take shelter, saying instead, "First let me talk with this philosopher. / What is the cause of thunder?" (III.iv.151–52). He may be wondering whether the storm is providential punishment for his mistreatment of Cordelia. A few lines later, he says to Poor Tom, "Noble philosopher, your company" (III.iv.169). In Jacobean England, philosophers were often experts in science or astrology rather than ethics or metaphysics; but (regardless of their specific interests) they all sought general theories of nature. Lear, confused about his own moral situation, seeks a philosophical answer, and so he turns to Poor Tom for a concept of the cosmos.

In his Paradox VIII, Donne criticized the idea that nature, understood metaphysically, could offer the kind of moral guidance that Lear seeks. He wrote: "And that poore knowledge whereby we conceive what *rain* is, what *wind*, what *thunder*, we call *Metaphysicke, supernaturall*; such *small* things, such *no* things do we allow our pliant *Natures* apprehension."[16] Donne did not call human beings "no thing"; he saved that derogatory term for the kinds of superempirical truths that metaphysicians seek. The question that Lear puts to Edgar is a classic example of "Metaphysicke"—the king hopes to understand the cause of thunder in a way that can allay his doubts about the moral essence of nature itself. At the same time, by speculating about the cosmos, he can avoid acknowledging his personal guilt.

Similarly, once inside a humble farmhouse, Lear suggests: "Let them anatomize Regan, see what breeds about her heart. Is there any cause in nature that make these hard hearts?" (III.vi.74–76). Lear has become pessimistic about nature, but he still thinks that understanding its laws can help him to tell whether there is a difference between right and wrong, and where that difference may lie. Even after the storm scene, he persists in drawing moral conclusions from nature. For instance, he promises to pardon adulterers, since "The wren goes to't, and the small gilded fly / Does lecher in my sight" (IV.vi.112–13).

Gloucester's disenchantment with nature and natural rights follows a similar course. When his eyes are being put out, he cries: "O you gods!" (III.viii.84). But the gods offer him no aid; and from then on, his view of providence, nature, and human nature is thoroughly pessimistic. Like Lear, Gloucester sees the disguised Edgar on the heath and concludes that human nature is miserable: "I such a fellow saw, / Which made me think a man a worm" (IV.i.32). Then he utters his famous aphorism about the injustice of existence itself: "As flies to wanton boys, are we to th'Gods; / They kill us for their sport" (IV.i.34–36).

Gloucester tells the animistic gods whom he worships (i.e., nature) that he will kill himself rather than "quarrel with your great opposeless wills"

(IV.vi.38). However, Gloucester's good son Edgar is standing beside him, still concealed as Poor Tom. Edgar tricks the blind Gloucester into thinking that he has thrown himself off a towering cliff and been miraculously saved. Edgar then cites this alleged miracle as evidence that the divine order is just and merciful, saying:

> thou happy father,
> Think that the clearest Gods, who make them honours
> Of men's impossibilities, have preserved thee.

Gloucester agrees, and promises, "henceforth I'll bear / Affliction" (IV.vi.72–76). But the "clearest Gods" have *not* preserved Gloucester; his son has. And a little later, when Edgar tells his father to "pray that right may thrive," the opposite immediately happens: the wicked camp of Regan, Goneril, and Edmund defeats Cordelia's army, leading to her death by hanging (V.ii.2). The gods seem indeed to act like "wanton boys"—by the time they have done their work, Cordelia is murdered; Lear, mad; Gloucester, blind; and the Fool, presumably dead. Meanwhile, Edgar has been forced to run naked through a winter storm. The evil characters are all dead too, but they have suffered much less than the good ones.

Gloucester's theory of nature is more astrological than philosophical, and therefore it might seem irrelevant to my topic. But astrology was considered a serious art, akin to metaphysics; and within the fictional world of *King Lear*, Gloucester's astrology actually makes accurate predictions. At the beginning of the play, Gloucester prophesies: "These late eclipses in the sun and moon portend no good to us: though the wisdom of Nature can reason it thus and thus, yet Nature finds itself scourg'd by the sequent events. Love cools, friendship falls off, brothers divide: in cities, mutinies; in countries, discord; in palaces, treason; and the bond crack'd twixt son and father" (I.ii.100–106).

All of these prophecies come true; and for all we know, the stars actually do exercise control over Lear's kingdom and its inhabitants. It would certainly be anachronistic to assume that astrology is foolish. But Gloucester's mistake is more fundamental, and he would be deluded even if he employed a much more sophisticated theory of nature—a subtle metaphysical system, say, or twentieth-century physics—in order to understand moral questions. Even if Gloucester has understood the general mechanisms of the cosmos in which he lives, such understanding cannot help him to make moral judgments about particular people. The same could be said about any philosophical system that builds an ethical structure on the foundations of physics or metaphysics. For example, Gloucester's references to astrology and the gods' "great opposeless wills" may indicate that he believes in determinism as opposed to free will; but this belief has no relevance to moral issues. As Erasmus argued in his debate with Luther, we cannot decide the issue of free will, and in any case it is an irrelevant and distracting topic.

Lear and Gloucester grow increasingly pessimistic about nature; but some characters in the play remain optimists to the end. Cordelia, for one, seems to have a positive view of nature, asking help from "All bless'd secrets, / All you unpublish'd virtues of the earth" (IV.iv.15–16). Likewise, Albany sees the benign hand of providence practically wherever he looks. When Cornwall is killed by a servant (who is appalled by the blinding of Gloucester), Albany pronounces: "This shows you are above, / You justicers, that these our nether crimes / So speedily can venge!" (IV.ii.78–79). When Goneril and Regan murder each other, Albany calls this a "judgment of the heavens" (IV.iii.230). And at last, when he inherits the kingdom, he declares:

> All friends shall taste
> The wages of their virtue, and all foes
> The cup of their deservings. (V.iii.301–3)

Can Cordelia and Albany be right about the justice of nature? Some critics essentially agree with them, arguing that *King Lear* is a Christian allegory in which a wise and just providence ultimately works its will. Danby goes so far as to say: "*King Lear*, I feel, is at least as Christian as the *Divine Comedy*."[17] Critics who claim that nature and the gods are good in *King Lear* point to the death of all the evil characters, the ultimate victory of Albany and Edgar (both good), and the moral education that Lear and Gloucester receive after their initial sins. In the purgatory of life, these men sin and suffer; but they also repent, presumably readying themselves for a paradise beyond death. Cordelia, it is true, dies horribly without ever having sinned, but she is interpreted as a Christ-figure who sacrifices herself for her repentant father.

On the other hand, opponents of the Christian-allegory thesis note that the gods seem to permit (or even to create) a great deal of indiscriminate suffering and death before they allow the few people who remain alive at the end of Act V to construct a better order. Critics who view the world of *King Lear* as evil share this attitude with several characters in the play, who believe that nature is intrinsically immoral. Freed from the bonds of so-called "natural law," these characters act in their own wicked self-interest. Meanwhile, they fool Gloucester and Lear by using categories like "nature" in a completely cynical and hypocritical way. The most self-conscious and effective of these "Machiavels" is Edmund, Gloucester's illegitimate son, who has been deprived of his inheritance because of a mere cultural convention in favor of marriage. Consequently, he throws his lot in with nature, which, he believes, has no truck with either conventions or moral scruples:

Thou, Nature, art my goddess; to thy law
My services are bound. Wherefore should I
Stand in the plague of custom, and permit
The curiosity of nations to deprive me,
For that I am some twelve or fourteen moonshines
Lag of a brother? (I.ii.1–6)

Edmund believes that nature is a realm of naked, immoral power. He also thinks that human nature—minus social conventions—is part of this cruel cosmic order. Giving instructions to strangle Cordelia and Lear, he says: "Know thou this, that men / Are as time is; to be tender-minded / Does not become a sword" (V.iii.31). Edmund knows perfectly well that his theory of a conscienceless nature clashes with his father's initially rather pious faith in the harmony of social conventions, morality, and the natural order. Edmund forges a letter, allegedly written by his brother, that condemns respect for age as a mere "policy," which keeps "our fortunes from us till our oldness cannot relish them" (I.ii.45). Upon hearing the contents of this letter, Gloucester calls Edgar "unnatural." Thus, for Gloucester, the child who fails to respect his father acts contrary to nature—but for Edmund, nature permits anything.

Edmund, who tries to kill his father, says insincerely that "the revenging Gods / 'Gainst parricides [do] all the thunder bend" (II.i.44–45). Despite this pious remark, he believes that he can get away with murder; and in reality, the only victims of thunder are Lear, Kent, Edgar, and the Fool. Later, Edmund pretends to agree with Gloucester that it is "Most savage and unnatural" to send Lear out into the storm; but then he colludes with Goneril, Regan, and Cornwall in sending his own father, blinded, onto the same heath (III.iii.2).

Although the Machiavels in the play are profoundly unattractive, they seem to understand the fictional world of *King Lear*—better, at least, than naïfs like Cordelia. It is true that all of the wicked characters die in the end, but they *expect* violence and destruction, so their demise does not invalidate their position. Nevertheless, when the Machiavels deny that nature is just, this constitutes a dogmatic assertion in its own right.[18] For example, after Edmund has heard his father make astrological predictions of doom (I.ii.100ff.), he tells the audience:

This is the excellent foppery of the world, that, when we are sick in fortune, often the surfeits of our own behavior, we make guilty of our disasters the sun, the moon, and stars; as if we were villains on necessity, fools by heavenly compulsion. . . . An admirable evasion of whoremaster man, to lay his goatish disposition to the charge of a star!

> . . . Fut! I should have been [rough and lecherous] had
> the maidenliest star in the firmament twinkled on my
> bastardizing. (I.ii.115–25)

According to Edmund's theory of nature, each person has an inherent character (often "goatish") that makes his own actions inevitable, and therefore beyond condemnation. Edmund also believes in a doctrine of might-is-right. When he decides to betray his own father to Regan and Goneril, he says:

> This seems a fair deserving, and must draw me
> That which my father loses; no less than all:
> The younger rises when the old doth fall. (III.iii.23–25)

This, then, is Edmund's "philosophy": he thinks that people's natures cause their actions, and that the strongest person deserves to win. Edmund states that his brother Edgar has a "noble . . . nature"—and therefore deserves to lose his fortune (I.ii.176). Along similar lines, Goneril calls Albany a "moral fool" because he is weak and law-abiding (IV.ii.58). Edmund and Goneril may be right that crime pays in the world of *Lear*. But if they believe that their actions are *justified* because of their theory of nature, then they are just as dogmatic as the pious Albany. When Cornwall puts out Gloucester's eyes (crying "Out, vile jelly!"), no one in the audience thinks that this is appropriate behavior, since nature is essentially cruel and arbitrary (III.viii.81). Although the Machiavels *argue* that their actions are "natural," we *see* them as abhorrent. Thus their philosophy, like the pious theories of Cordelia, Albany, and others, is invalidated by the play.[19]

In the final analysis, it seems to me that it is impossible to say whether nature (or human nature) is inherently good or evil within the world of *King Lear*. Moreover, it is a moral error even to speculate about this question. Albany prophesies that Goneril will come to a bad end because her lack of scruples and self-control is unnatural: she is a "Nature which contemns it[s] origin" (IV.ii.32). Goneril replies: "No more; the text is foolish" (IV.ii.37). Albany's prophecy is literally correct, yet Goneril is equally right to see that his pious optimism is inane. After all, his theory of nature does not prevent him from marrying Goneril, nor does he have the sense to stop her evil plans. Meanwhile, Gloucester's ultimately pessimistic theory of nature is no more helpful to him. Whether nature is just or wicked is an utterly abstract question, similar to Hamlet's "To be or not to be"; and as such it has no certain answer. Philosophical speculation merely blinds us to particulars. The good that is achieved in the play is achieved by characters like Kent—who has no obvious doctrine of nature—and Edgar, who also eschews theorizing.

A Man Pregnant to Good Pity

In several cases, Edgar appears to adopt a view of providence and nature as ultimately good. For example, when he wants to console his father, he tells him that "the clearest Gods . . . have preserved thee." After he wins a duel with Edmund, Edgar wants his suddenly contrite brother to do some good, and says:

> The Gods are just, and of our pleasant vices
> Make instruments to plague us;
> The dark and vicious place where thee he got
> Cost him his eyes. (V.iii.169–73)

Here, Edgar refers to Gloucester's begetting Edmund out of wedlock: this is what made Edmund a "bastard." Edgar implies that the sin of promiscuity is the ultimate cause of Gloucester's blinding, rather than Edmund's wicked deeds. Therefore, Gloucester's suffering was providential. Edgar's argument is successful, for Edmund replies: "This speech of yours hath mov'd me, / And shall perchance do good" (V.iii.198–99). Edmund then tries to revoke his orders to kill Cordelia, but too late—which suggests that a beneficent providence may not be in control after all.

In each of these cases, Edgar appeals to a fair and wise providence. Yet when his father falls into despair because Cordelia's army has been defeated, Edgar cannot again praise the gods, for he has just prayed vainly to them for victory. Instead, he adopts the rhetoric of a stoic:

> EDGAR: What! in ill thoughts again? Men must endure
>   Their going hence, even as their coming hither:
>   Ripeness is all. Come on.
> GLOU.:   And that's true too. (V.iii.9–11)

Although it has an Old-Testament ring, the doctrine that "ripeness is all" does not sound very optimistic or Christian.[20] Thus Edgar adjusts his rhetoric to the occasion: he is intellectually inconsistent, but his motives are consistently honorable. Similarly, he adopts a variety of disguises, dressing first as Poor Tom, then as a Kentish peasant, and finally as a nameless knight. When he approaches his father as a peasant, he explains to the audience: "Why I do trifle thus with his despair / Is done to cure it" (IV.vi.33–34). I suspect that Edgar's occasional statements about the just gods are, like his disguises, "trifles" meant to cure despair.

His real view of nature and providence, if he has one at all, is hard to establish. If he had genuine beliefs, they would most likely appear in his soliloquies, but these mainly reveal bewilderment. For example, at the beginning of Act IV, Edgar makes a somewhat hopeful speech:

> The lowest and most dejected thing of Fortune
> Stands still in esperance, lives not in fear;
> The lamentable change is from the best;
> The worst returns to laughter. Welcome, then,
> Thou unsubstantial air that I embrace (IV.i.3–7)

But right away he sees his blinded father and cries:

> World, world, O world!
> But that thy strange mutations make us hate thee,
> Life would not yield to age. (IV.i.10–12)

Characters in *King Lear*–like spectators and critics of the play–can hardly help theorizing from time to time about whether nature is just or evil. This question is clearly on Kent's mind all along, for when he sees Lear with Cordelia dead in his arms, he asks: "Is this the promis'd end?" (V.iii.262). However, even though Kent fears that life is inherently tragic, he still does the right thing. Likewise, Edgar makes a few pessimistic statements about nature's inherent wickedness, but he does not allow his pessimism to prevent him from trying to make things better. What motivates him, then, is not a secure theory about nature, but rather simple compassion. Despite his relatively modest role in the plot, Edgar has more lines that anyone but Lear, and he is very often present on stage. Like the bystanders who are depicted in the margins of Renaissance paintings, Edgar serves in part as a kind of ideal observer; and what makes him exemplary is his propensity to pity. Disguised as Poor Tom, he sees the hallucinating Lear and remarks: "My tears begin to take his part so much, / They mar my counterfeiting" (III.vi.59–60). The next day, he encounters his father with Lear, and says: "I would not take this from report; it is, / And my heart breaks at it" (IV.vi.139–40). Apparently, the mere sight of the blind Gloucester and the mad Lear is enough to move *many* people to pity, for Regan says:

> It was great ignorance, Gloucester's eyes being put out,
> To let him live. Where he arrives he moves
> All hearts against us. (IV.v.8–10)

Similarly, it is the very sight of the mad king, the murdered Cordelia, and the blinded Gloucester that moves the audience to pity. A philosopher might object that we (and Edgar) need some covert theory of right and wrong in order to judge what we see; but theories seem to blind both Lear and Gloucester, whereas we simply see what is, and our hearts break at it.

When Edgar's blind father asks, "Now, good sir, what are you?" he replies:

> A most poor man, made tame to Fortune's blows;
> Who, by the art of known and feeling sorrows,
> Am pregnant to good pity. (IV.vi.218–20)

It is significant that Gloucester asks "*what* are you?"—for Edgar's identity is constantly being questioned. At various points when he comes on stage, someone asks, "What art thou . . . ?"; "What are you there?"; "Is it a beggar-man?"; "Is that the naked fellow?"; and finally, "What are you? / Your name? your quality?" (III.iv.43,129; IV.i.29,40; V.iii.118–19). At the beginning of the play, everyone knows precisely who Edgar is: he is heir to the Earl of Gloucester, a beloved son, and (in Edmund's words) "A brother noble / Whose nature is so far from doing harms / That he suspects none" (I.ii.176). Thus Edgar's "nature" appears at first to be stable and identifiable.

However, as a result of his brother's plot, Edgar is disinherited, forced to flee for his life in the middle of the night, stripped of his very clothes, and compelled to adopt a variety of disguises and accents. As a result, he could, like Lear, conclude that man is naturally "nothing." Indeed, he says, "Edgar I nothing am" (II.iii.21). Nevertheless, rather than resort to the nihilistic aphorisms that Lear and his own father utter when they realize that there is no comprehensible human nature, Edgar puts aside theorizing and simply responds ethically to what he sees.

SEEING AND BLINDNESS

Edgar's chief virtue, like Kent's, is the ability to see. Metaphors of seeing and blindness recur throughout the play, from the moment when Kent first says, "See better, Lear." For example, Albany, although ultimately a good character, is too taken with moral abstractions to see correctly. When Goneril sends Lear away with only half his men, Albany says: "How far your eyes may pierce I cannot tell: / Striving to better, oft we mar what's well" (I.iv.344–45). The second line in this couplet typifies Albany's merely formal, conventional, and superficial morality.[21] Everyone—Kent, the Fool, Lear, and the audience—can simply see that Goneril has done wrong. It would be impossible to play her as kind or honest; she is hardly "striving to better." Albany's eyes do not, therefore, pierce very far at all.

Similarly, both Lear and Gloucester begin the play in a state of metaphorical blindness. Only when Gloucester's eyes are literally put out, does he at last begin to "see." On the heath, an old man tells him, "You cannot see your way," and he replies: "I have no way, and therefore want no eyes; I stumbled when I saw" (IV.i.18). Likewise, Lear refuses at first to see Cordelia and Kent as honest, but when he begins to understand the truth, he wishes himself blind: "Old fond eyes," he says, "Beweep this cause again, I'll pluck ye out" (I.iv.299). Lear never literally loses his sight, but he begins to hallucinate, seeing stools as daughters. At the beginning of the play, Gloucester and Lear can see (in the literal sense), but they are blinded by theory. As the action progresses, they lose their sight, but they gain moral insight about particulars. To some degree, the old men get better at the kind of "seeing" that Kent and Edgar epitomize—an empathetic and discriminating observation of individual human beings and their motives.

As Gloucester and Lear suffer, both men learn to see better. In extremity, each makes a speech in sympathy with the suffering poor, and castigates himself for not having recognized their plight earlier. In the midst of the storm, Lear cries:

> Poor naked wretches, whereso'er you are,
> . . . .
> How shall your houseless heads . . . defend you
> From seasons such as these? O! I have ta'en
> Too little care of this. Take physic, Pomp;
> Expose thyself to feel what wretches feel (III.iv.28–34)

Similarly, Gloucester gives his purse to his son, whom he mistakes for a peasant, and says:

> Heavens, deal so still!
> Let the superfluous and lust-dieted man,
> That slaves your ordinance, that will not see
> Because he does not feel, feel your power quickly;
> So distribution should undo excess,
> And each man have enough. (IV.i.65–70)

Gloucester thinks that the gods are arbitrary and merciless; but he now understands that wealthy men, like himself, cannot recognize suffering in others until they themselves suffer divine disfavor. Ill fortune, even if it is undeserved, at least has the advantage that it makes us see better.[22] Similarly, Lear tells Gloucester: "If thou wilt weep my fortunes, take my eyes" (IV.vi.174). He says this because he wants Gloucester to feel his anguish, but he also sympathizes with other people. Both the king and the earl know that to see, they must feel. This theme inspires their colloquy when they finally meet near Dover, one blind and poor, the other mad:

LEAR: Your eyes are in a heavy case, your purse in a light: yet you see
           how this world goes.
GLOU.:   I see it feelingly.
LEAR: What! art mad? A man may see how this world goes with no
           eyes. Look with thine ears: see how yond justice rails upon yond
           simple thief. Hark, in thine ear: change places, and handy-
           dandy, which is the justice, which is the thief? (IV.vi.144–52)

By now, Lear and Gloucester can see through the trappings of power
and can sympathize with poverty, to such an extent that Gloucester calls for a
new "distribution" of wealth, and Lear excuses all the crimes of the poor
(IV.vi.163ff.). Lear has given up his economic metaphor, telling Regan: "O!
reason not the need" (II.iv.262). Further, he and Gloucester have both
stopped proclaiming their "natural" rights. Their compassion for the poor is a
commendable improvement in their moral vision, made possible by their
renunciation of the moral theories with which they began the play. It is true
that Gloucester seems to move toward a new theory, a radical critique of
wealth and inequality. This position could be just as general and abstract as
his early embrace of natural law and inherited social status. However, it is
difficult to take his political statements seriously as the elements of a theory:
they are appealing not because they are right in the abstract, but because they
reflect a clearer vision of himself, and they lead him to give his purse to the
blind beggar.

SHAME AND THE CONSOLATIONS OF PHILOSOPHY

Lear's compassion, on the other hand, is rather hypothetical. Gloucester
gives away his purse, but Lear cannot make good on his promises to the
poverty-stricken multitudes, for he is no longer king.[23] The one good deed
that he could still perform would be to reconcile himself to the banished
and disowned Cordelia. But Kent reports that Lear "by no means / Will
yield to see his daughter," because "burning shame / Detains him from [her]"
(IV.iii.40–47).
        When Lear is finally brought before Cordelia, he refuses to believe that
it is she; and when persuaded of her identity, he neither apologizes nor
professes love, but says only, "I know you do not love me. . . . You have
some cause" (IV.vii.73–75). The next and final time that he sees her alive, he
spins his famous fantasy: "Come, let's away to prison; / We two alone will
sing like birds i'th'cage" (V.iii.8–9). As Cavell argues, Lear consistently
avoids the embarrassment of forthrightly stating his shame or his love; he
refuses to acknowledge the realities of his relationship with Cordelia until she
is dead. At that point, he suddenly becomes clear-sighted and literal: "I know

when one is dead, and when one lives; / She's dead as earth" (V.iii.259–60). Lear's embarrassment in the face of his living, loving daughter is surely one reason that he prefers the ceremonious speeches of Goneril and Regan to Cordelia's frankness.

Lear is not alone in fearing embarrassment; Kent conceals himself from the king just as Lear hides from Cordelia. Explaining that he intends to remain disguised, Kent says first, "Some dear cause / Will in concealment wrap me up awhile" (IV.iii.51–52); and later he asks Cordelia to allow him to remain anonymous, "Till time and I think meet" (IV.VII.10). Since Kent never explains his motivation for secrecy, it may be that he mainly wants to avoid embarrassment. Similarly, Edgar conceals himself from his father under several disguises, explaining that this is his method of curing Gloucester's despair. But he later confesses:

> Met I my father with his bleeding rings,
> Led him, begg'd for him, sav'd him from despair;
> Never–O fault!–reveal'd myself unto him,
> Until some half-hour past, when I was arm'd (V.iii.188–92)

Edgar has some reason to fear his father, who has ordered his death. However, Gloucester is now blind, banished, and clearly helpless. Besides, Edgar postpones revealing himself despite his father's most earnest pleas: "Oh! dear son Edgar . . . , / Might I but live to see thee in my touch, / I'd say I had eyes again" (IV.i.21–23). Therefore, Edgar can hardly require weapons before declaring himself to his father. Rather, like Lear and Kent, he is perhaps embarrassed; he needs to "arm" himself emotionally. These three characters avoid openly expressing their love–even to the point of cruelty–in contrast to Cordelia, who says of Lear, "Soon may I hear and see him!" (IV.iv.29).

Cavell has argued that the "avoidance of love" is a basic theme in *King Lear*. He has, further, suggested an analogy.[24] Lear and others in the play refuse to acknowledge the love that simply exists before their eyes. They prefer formal statements to the testimony of their senses, doubting where no doubt is necessary, demanding proof for the obvious, and resorting to theory when no theory is required. In all of these respects, the avoidance of love is like the attitude of philosophers, especially since Descartes. Instead of acknowledging particular facts that they find, philosophers demand proof for the world's existence, and inquire abstractly into the nature of our relationship with being. Even "commonsense" thinkers–Samuel Johnson, kicking the stone to prove that it exists; G. E. Moore, refusing to doubt the existence of his own hand–still believe that skepticism and realism are two competing doctrines, of which one must be correct and the other false. But according to Cavell, Shakespeare shows what cannot be proved: that we are better off leaving such questions behind. Metaphysical theories are screens that we erect between ourselves and particular facts, in order to hide our shame. Rather than demanding proof, especially in the moral realm, we simply ought to act well. And acting well, as Shakespeare shows us, does not require any theory.

Cavell does not argue that Shakespeare was interested in formal epistemology; only that his plays happen to shed light on Cartesian skepticism. It seems unlikely that Shakespeare had Descartes's problems in mind, for the great philosopher was only about seven years old when *Lear* was first performed, and Shakespeare never showed much concern with narrowly epistemological issues.[25] However, the contrast between wisdom and foolishness is an explicit theme in *King Lear*, and wisdom is specifically identified with "philosophy." Two major philosophical theories are available to characters in the play: one is a doctrine of natural justice, the other is nihilism. Both theories are presented as hypotheses about nature in-itself or in general. But the doctrine of natural justice produces no useful results, while nihilism merely offers a spurious justification for actions that we can see are evil. Graham Bradshaw, discussing the feelings of horror and pity that are created by *King Lear*, remarks: "What they affirm is proved upon our pulses, and incompatible with nihilism."[26]

THIS GREAT STAGE OF FOOLS

As well as showing the failure of philosophical wisdom, *King Lear* also offers a positive alternative: a particular kind of foolishness. Both Edgar and Kent are "fools" in the Erasmian sense: they eschew the "wisdom" of philosophy. As Cavell remarks in his essay on *King Lear*, "The seer is not needed. Nothing we can know or need to know is unknown."[27] Edgar and Kent recognize this; they are unaffected by skeptical attacks on morality, because they can see what is right in concrete situations. But the most effective critic of philosophical speculation is the Fool, who simply acknowledges particular facts and refuses either to generalize from them or to seek reasons for them. For example, he says: "The reason why the seven stars are no mo than seven is a pretty reason." Lear, beginning to catch on, says, "Because they are not eight?," to which the Fool replies, "Yes, indeed: thou would'st make a good Fool" (I.v.34–36). If this is foolishness, then it is the same commonsense variety that Folly propounded in Erasmus.

The Fool seems to anticipate Wittgenstein's advice to "leave everything as it is," to accept the world as we find it.[28] For him, the only "reason" that there are seven stars is that there are seven stars. If the Fool were criticizing scientific theories (such as the hypotheses of astronomers), then he would be anti-intellectual. But these are not, I think, the targets of his satire. After all, a modern astronomical theory would never pretend to tell us anything about morality. We believe that there are seven stars in the Pleiades because earlier in the history of the universe matter was in a different arrangement, and natural forces acted according to predictable laws to create the current pattern. One could then ask why the earlier arrangement existed, and a similar answer could be found. But at no point would an *ultimate* answer emerge; for example, there is no reason that the universe runs according to certain laws instead of other ones. Nor can science tell us whether the laws of our universe are just or unjust. Lear, however, believes that natural causes imply something about moral problems; that we can understand what (if anything) is right by comprehending nature. It is for this reason that he asks, "What is the cause of thunder?" He expects an answer such as, "to punish *you*," or, "to inflict cruel and arbitrary harm." But here the Fool disagrees with Lear, for he doubts that physics or metaphysics can help us to know whether anything is morally right.

The Fool is fond of reciting folk wisdom in the form of short rhymed stories, which are often versions of Aesop's fables. But these do not constitute a philosophy. First of all, they are concrete stories or examples that always bear a close resemblance to Lear's immediate situation; they do not offer usable generalizations:

> *FOOL*: Canst tell how an oyster makes his shell?
> *LEAR*: No.
> *FOOL*: Nor I neither; but I can tell why a snail has a house.
> *LEAR*: Why?
> *FOOL*: Why, to put's head in; not to give it away to his daughters, and leave his horns without a case. (I.v.25–30)

Besides, the Fool constantly undermines his own pronouncements, just as Erasmus's Folly does—by reminding us that he is a fool. Thus he tells Kent, "When a wise man gives thee better counsel, give me mine again: I would have none but knaves follow it, since a Fool gives it" (II.iv.79–80). This recalls Folly's warning that her speech should not be taken seriously, since a fool and a woman has spoken. But, as in Erasmus's *Praise of Folly*, Shakespeare's Fool is a sympathetic character.

The Fool does the right thing despite his belief that there is no good reason for being good: he even calls himself a fool for going with Lear onto the heath (II.iv.79–80). Perhaps the reason that he remains loyal is his great capacity for compassion. For instance, a Knight tells Lear, "Since my young Lady's going into France, Sir, the Fool hath much pined away" (I.iv.71–72). It is unclear whether the Fool has grieved for Lear or for Cordelia—perhaps for both—but he certainly has great sympathy for his master. This sympathy is possible, in part, because the Fool sees through Lear's trappings of power to the weak old man beneath. He constantly mocks the king, calling him "Nuncle" when others still use honorifics, and addressing him as "thou" when even the king's daughters call him "my lord." "Nuncle" is a term of endearment as well as disparagement, an apt word to use with someone whom you love in part because you pity him. The Fool even says, "I had rather be any kind o'thing than a fool; and yet I would not be thee, Nuncle; thou hast pared thy wit o'both sides, and left nothing i'th'middle" (I.iv.181–84). He repeatedly chides Lear for banishing Cordelia: a dangerous reproach, given Lear's temper, but a sign of the Fool's sincere concern for the king.

Nevertheless, the Fool does not base his sympathy upon any abstract theory of justice; he does not even think that Lear deserves respect because of his character. Kent explains that he wants to serve Lear because "you have that in your countenance which I would fain call master." When Lear asks what this is, Kent replies: "Authority" (I.iv.27–30). We cannot tell whether Kent really finds Lear a figure of authority, nor whether Lear still looks dignified. But the Fool clearly thinks that the king is a foolish, weak old man, "an O without a figure." Regardless, he follows him loyally onto the heath.

We might interpret this action as a kind of existential embrace of virtue, an arbitrary or irrational decision to act loyally. But I suggest that the Fool's choice is not irrational or arbitrary, although it does lack the kind of reason that could be stated in the form of an argument. If his were an arbitrary choice, then people who watch the play would not applaud it and admire the Fool for what he does. After all, although the king has erred, his error is one that many people might make; and the play shows that we should pity him. The Fool sees Lear in an accurate, unromanticized, yet sympathetic light. In short, the Fool loves the king, despite his faults. Any kind of abstract reasoning would only interfere with his precise understanding and embrace of the concrete man before him.

In *King Lear*, everyone is always calling himself or someone else a fool. Cordelia terms herself a fool because she cannot dissemble; Goneril uses the word of Albany because he is moral; Edmund thinks his father a fool for believing in astrology; and Lear applies the term to everyone: "When we are born, we cry that we are come / To this great stage of fools" (IV.vi.180–81).[29] The king also singles himself out as "the natural fool of fortune" (IV.vi.189). All of these references invite us to ask what really constitutes foolishness in the world of *King Lear*. The same question also arises for readers of *The Praise of Folly*, and in both cases the answer is ambiguous. The Fool calls Kent a "fool" for remaining loyal to the king (II.iv.84); but later, when Kent joins him and Lear on the heath, the Fool says, "Marry, here's grace and a codpiece, that's a wise man and a fool" (III.ii.40). It is impossible to tell from this statement which man is wise and which is foolish. In response to one of the Fool's fables, Lear asks, "Dost thou call me fool, boy?" The Fool replies, "All thy other titles thou hast given away; that thou wast born with." Here is another claim that everyone is a fool by birth; and Kent seems to agree, remarking, "This is not altogether Fool, my Lord." The Fool replies, "No, faith, lords and great men will not let me; if I had a monopoly out, they would have part on't; and ladies too, they will not let me have all the fool to myself; they'll be snatching" (I.iv.145–52).

In this passage, the Fool virtually replicates Erasmus's rhetoric about the ubiquity of folly. But if everyone is a fool, then the characters on Shakespeare's "great stage of fools" at least differ in their varieties of foolishness. The most foolish of all are the people who depend most heavily upon notions of wisdom: Albany, Lear, and Gloucester. Other characters, like Kent and the Fool himself, are fools only because they put themselves in difficult positions, but with good intentions. They lack arguments for what they do in terms of either self-interest or natural law; but we can see that they do right. The Fool explains that he intends to remain with the king, "And let the wise man fly" (II.iv.80). It is foolish, he tells Kent, to take "one's part that's out of favour" (I.iv.97). Yet he also says: "The knave turns Fool that runs away; / The Fool no knave, perdy" (II.iv.81–82). The second line of this couplet seems clear enough: the Fool is no knave, for he is loyal despite his awareness of Lear's faults. The first line is more enigmatic, but it perhaps means that the "wise" man who runs away is also a fool, for he shows himself to be a knave.

The Fool is, in general, an enigmatic figure with unknown motives and uncertain beliefs. He disappears after Act III without explanation, his last line the obscure "And I'll go to bed at noon" (III.vi.83). Stage productions often suggest that he dies of exposure, but this is not specified in the text. His major soliloquy is a prophecy about an age of corruption that can always seem to be a depiction of the present. He ends: "This prophecy Merlin shall make; for I live before his time" (III.ii.95). Thus the Fool seems to step out of the action of the play in order to speak both as a contemporary of the audience and as an ancient sage, with precise knowledge of the future.[30] His reference to Merlin can be taken as a joke, or else as an indication of the Fool's time-transcending wisdom. That ambiguity is again Erasmian: it leads us to ask what constitutes wisdom and what is foolishness; but it does not supply an answer. I suggest that the answer lies in the play itself, which shows us the difference between good and evil without offering the kind of "wisdom" that Lear seeks and that the Fool mocks.

THAT GLIB AND OILY ART

On the other hand, the play seems to end with an explicit moral doctrine, which is stated by Edgar. We should, he says, "Speak what we feel, not what we ought to say" (V.iii.323). Throughout *King Lear*, simple, honest people who speak what they feel are at odds with dissembling orators. Regan and Goneril give carefully constructed speeches that Lear later recognizes as lies: "They flattered me like a dog" (IV.vi.96–97). In contrast, Cordelia says, "my love's / More pondrous than my tongue" (I.i.76); and she adds, "for I want that glib and oily art / To speak and purpose not" (I.i.223–24). Similarly, the Fool regrets that he is plain-spoken and honest: "Prithee, Nuncle," he says, "keep a schoolmaster that can teach thy Fool to lie; I would fain learn to lie" (I.iv.175–76). Nevertheless, he persists in telling the truth to his master. And Kent makes a cardinal virtue out of just such simple honesty. He praises Cordelia–"That justly think'st and hast most rightly said"–while criticizing her sisters' "large speeches" (I.i.182–83).

Kent includes among his own best qualities the fact that he can "deliver a plain message bluntly" (I.iv.33). He gets himself thrown into the stocks for his frank abuse of the smarmy Oswald; and when Cornwall chides him for his "plainness," he offers a parody of courtly rhetoric:

> KENT: Sir, in good faith, in sincere verity
> Under th'allowance of your great aspect,
> Whose influence, like a wreath of radiant fire
> On flick'ring Phoebus' front,–
> CORN.:   What mean you by this?
> KENT: To go out of my dialect, which you discommend so much. I
> know, Sir, I am no flatterer (II.ii.102–7)

These quotations might suggest that the good characters in the play are enemies of rhetoric. Certainly, they are opponents of dishonesty and of false conventionality. They know that people who say they speak "in sincere verity" may actually be liars. On the other hand, the good characters are not enthusiastic about moral theory as a means of telling right from wrong. Nor are they above dissembling in order to do good or to make moral points. Not only does Edgar adopt a variety of disguises in order to help his father, but "honest" Kent *pretends* to be a plain laborer. In fact, when he tells Cornwall that he is so honest that he prefers to go to the stocks rather than dissemble, he is actually pretending to be someone who he is not. But his motivations are good:

> If but as well I other accents borrow,
> That can my speech defuse, my good intent
> May carry through (I.iv.1–4)

Because of their willingness to "fool" other people, Kent and Edgar do more good than Cordelia, who is so plain-spoken that she misleads her father. Lear is more responsible than she for the misunderstanding; but she does not help matters by absolutely refusing to use rhetoric. In contrast, Kent and Edgar are not only good at seeing, but also at showing. When Kent, disguised, wants to show Lear that he is loyal, he trips Oswald. Lear can interpret this visible demonstration accurately, even though he earlier misjudged Kent's speech. Lear correctly says: "I thank thee, fellow; thou serv'st me, and I'll love thee" (I.iv.85). Lear should have been able to see Kent as loyal all along, but Kent now makes the interpretation easier for him, by providing an illustration of his character. Similarly, Edgar demonstrates his love for Gloucester not by an argument, but by actually preventing his suicide.

Kent and Edgar show the truth while lying about their own identities. In this respect, they are like actors—for performers always dissemble, but often in the interests of a higher, moral truth. The point of all the counterfeiting is to help Lear and Gloucester to survive and to "see better." Like actors, Kent and Edgar put on costumes and simulate accents; Edgar even says that he "plays" the fool and that he "cannot daub it further" (IV.i.51). Although both characters shun courtly rhetoric, they are nevertheless capable of making up fictional stories, effective speeches, and visible demonstrations. Thus they are not only actors, but also authors of their own fictional dramas. The villains of the play, meanwhile, are also liars and orators, but they get their just deserts—the drama depicts them as scoundrels. Finally, *King Lear* is itself an exercise in falsehood, deception, and rhetoric, for it is a fictional story, played by dissembling actors, and filled with intensely moving poetry. But Shakespeare's fiction condemns the lies of Goneril and Regan, while applauding the deception of Edgar and Kent. Thus his rhetorical art clearly distinguishes between good and evil rhetoric; and his fiction shows the difference between moral and immoral fiction. The services of philosophy—traditional "Queen of the Sciences"—are not required, for literature can govern in its own realm.

CONCLUSION

THE BELOVED

COMMUNITY

I f everyone who is affected by a policy agrees to it, then it seems pointless
to criticize the plan on moral grounds, especially if the whole community
continues to support it in hindsight. Consensus, at least when it endures
over the long term, is a sufficient test of moral truth.

"Nevertheless," as Reinhold Niebuhr once observed, "only a roman-
ticist of the purest water could maintain that a national group ever arrives at
a 'common mind' or becomes conscious of a 'general will' without the use of
either force or the threat of force. . . . The limitations of the human mind and
imagination, the inability of human beings to transcend their own interests
sufficiently to envisage the interests of their fellow-men as clearly as they do
their own makes force an inevitable part of social cohesion. But the same
force which guarantees peace also makes for injustice."[1]

Niebuhr wrote this passage as part of his lifelong polemic against the
social gospel doctrine. Some proponents of the social gospel believed that
society would be reformed as soon as powerful people were shown the
relevance of the New Testament to modern life. Niebuhr, however, held
what he called a "realist" theory of human nature, which suggested that rich
and powerful people would never seek the advice and consent of the weak.
Individuals could be good, he thought, since we are created in God's image;
but we must also live in society, which is always immoral because it cannot
endure without the use of force. "All social co-operation on a larger scale

237

than the most intimate social group requires a measure of coercion."[2] Niebuhr's theory of (potentially) moral individuals in (invariably) immoral society explained the role of original sin in God's creation.

Niebuhr was guided by a theory of immutable human nature and by abstract theological views that need not persuade us. But he was also a perceptive observer of public affairs, and he was surely right to conclude that most contemporary societies, communities, and organizations operate not on the principle of consensus, but rather according to the dictates of power. In chapter 2, I offered some reasons to support this generalization. For one thing, consensus violates the interests of the powerful. It also requires everyone (no matter how diverse) to join a single conversation with one set of rules. For both of these reasons, some people must be *forced* to participate in consensus-seeking discussions—which violates the consensus ideal. Besides, children, the mentally disabled, animals, and possibly others are not competent to deliberate. If consensus is required as a condition of action, then those who favor the status quo may filibuster. Finally, as a practical matter, it takes too much time for any large group to achieve unanimous consent.

Nevertheless, we can travel some distance on the road to consensus, and the distance we travel is a measure of our moral achievement. Some of the obstacles that we face on this journey are practical. For instance, if our legal and political systems are unfair, then people who enjoy special privileges are unlikely to seek consensus with their less powerful peers. Similarly, if there are no forums in which people can discuss ethical questions freely, then little discussion will take place. These are important matters, but they lie largely beyond the scope of this book.

Instead, I have emphasized the virtues, habits, and methods that either frustrate or assist the creation of consensus. In particular, I have contrasted two archetypal characters: the philosopher and the humanist. Philosophers seek general moral rules that can solve our ethical dilemmas. If we have such rules, then we do not have much need for democracy. Perhaps the public can be allowed to apply abstract principles to particular cases—but casuistry is a limited role, and ambitious moral theorists try to make it utterly mechanical. Furthermore, many philosophers disparage the very tools—rhetoric, narrative, the visual arts—that are most effective in bringing about public agreement. Believing that moral truth is discovered through abstract thought, they do not expect to learn anything important by participating in democratic dialogues, especially when public discourse includes displays of rhetoric and emotion. And because they deal in generalizations, philosophers can be blind to the crucial details of other people's circumstances.

Finally, some moral philosophers deny the possibility of indeterminate or intractable moral problems. When several principles appear to conflict, they either argue that some moral rules "trump" the rest, or else that all values can be measured on a single scale. If they are right, then technical reasoning can solve every apparent dilemma. But if some situations cannot be resolved by moral theory, then we may have to use rhetoric to decide among competing options.

The archetypal humanist is the philosopher's antithesis, favoring democratic deliberation, rhetoric and narrative, attention to particulars, and participation in public life. Protagoras was a humanist because he distrusted metaphysics and technical methods of moral assessment, preferring democratic dialogues in which people described particulars "thickly," often turning to past literature for inspiration. Erasmus, Shakespeare, and Nabokov were humanists because they depicted theorists as blind and foolish, meanwhile drawing human details so finely that their readers could form accurate moral judgments about particulars. Like Protagoras, they imitated and alluded to existing literature to enrich their art. Finally, Edgar and Kent, Erasmus's Fool, and even the Jesus of the New Testament are humanists, because they too eschew theory; but they accurately perceive the details of other people's lives and teach by means of stories and concrete examples.

Given Niebuhr's warning about the immorality of all human societies, we may wonder whether humanists can ever expect much practical success. The young Martin Luther King Jr. read Niebuhr and was deeply influenced by his pessimistic vision. "I became so enamored of his social ethics," King wrote, "that I almost fell into the trap of accepting uncritically everything he wrote."[3] In particular, King accepted Niebuhr's analysis of race relations in America: "It is hopeless," Niebuhr had written, "for the Negro to expect complete emancipation from the menial social and economic position into which the white man has forced him, merely by trusting in the moral sense of the white race." But, he added, "It is equally hopeless to attempt emancipation through violent rebellion"–for the odds against victory were too long.[4] Besides, violence ignored Jesus' message of peace, and it posed inherent risks. Niebuhr wrote: "Since it is impossible to count on enough moral goodwill among those who possess irresponsible power to sacrifice it for the good of the whole, it must be destroyed by coercive methods and these will always run the peril of introducing new forms of injustice in place of those abolished."[5] For example, a violent struggle for African American emancipation would create a black military leadership that might ultimately prove as despotic as the existing segregationist regime.

King therefore faced a dual Niebuhrian paradox. As an African American leader, he wanted to end segregation: but whites would never budge without force, and force would never work against an overwhelming majority. As a Christian minister, King preached peace and harmony, but he knew that people had to live in societies, and societies were always immoral. Niebuhr had suggested that a nonviolent movement for racial justice could achieve some good in America if it followed Gandhian principles of direct action. To King, Gandhian ideas seemed even more promising; they offered a radical solution to both his spiritual and political dilemmas. Nonviolent resistance, he wrote, is "one of the most potent weapons available to oppressed people in their quest for social justice."[6] The successful bus boycott and protests in Montgomery, Alabama, showed, according to King, that "Niebuhr had overemphasized the corruption of human nature."[7] The civil rights movement demonstrated the power of moral rhetoric and democratic principles even in a world where consensus is a utopian ideal.

King's consistent object was the creation of a "beloved community," whose foundation was *agape*–disinterested love–rather than oppression. *Agape*, in King's work, means the absence of coercion and the presence of "understanding good will."[8] Far from passive, it often requires nonviolent direct action, even civil disobedience, the result of which is the "creation of the beloved community" (whereas "the aftermath of violence is tragic bitterness").[9] The connection between *agape* and community is fundamental to King's thought:

> *Agape* is love seeking to preserve and create community. It is insistence on community even when one seeks to break it. *Agape* is a willingness to sacrifice in the interests of mutuality. *Agape* is a willingness to go to any length to restore community. . . . Love, *agape*, is the only cement that can hold this broken community together. When I am commanded to love, I am commanded to restore community, to resist injustice, and to meet the needs of my brothers.[10]

Unlike "sentimental or affectionate" love, *agape* permits us to judge other people critically and dispassionately; King even calls it a "stern love."[11] At the same time, it requires a discerning attention to particular facts, because it treats other people as complex individuals, not abstractions. King writes that *agape* "springs from the *need* of the other person–his need for belonging to the best of the human family. The Samaritan who helped the Jew on the Jericho road was 'good' because he responded to the human need that he was presented with." The Samaritan's capacity for empathy was not blocked by the abstraction of an ethnic category. Like Edgar, he was a man "pregnant to good pity." Only such people can form a beloved community.

As I have argued, grossly unfair political systems encourage powerful people to resort to force; they thereby restrict or destroy *agape*. Thus King and the other civil rights leaders sought voting rights and equal legal protection–not only in the interests of African Americans, but also to make possible a beloved community. Likewise, they sought racial desegregation in part because a segregated society is hostile to *agape*: it prevents people from engaging as equals, and it categorizes individuals under the gross abstraction of race.

If the political goals of the civil rights movement were consistent with a beloved community, the movement also showed by example how such a community would function. Membership was voluntary, participants were highly diverse, yet most decisions were made consensually. Because whites would not willingly abandon their privileges, the movement had to use force. But its tactics—sit-ins, boycotts, and marches—were *minimally* coercive. Civil rights leaders exercised extraordinary vigilance and discipline to keep violent racist resistance from provoking a violent response from their movement.

Since the civil rights movement was nonviolent and consensual, a Niebuhrian "realist" would doubt that it could either cohere or achieve much success against a violent enemy. By the same token, many social scientists might expect the movement to face a fatal problem of collective action. For any single African American, resistance to segregation was dangerous and futile. If everyone acted at once, then they might prevail, to everyone's benefit. But no one could compel (or even expect) everyone else to act, so it was irrational for individuals to defy the racist authorities. Two years after the Montgomery bus boycott began, King recalled: "Many of the Negroes who joined the protest did not expect it to succeed. When asked why, they usually gave one of three answers: 'I didn't expect Negroes to stick to it,' or 'I never thought we Negroes had the nerve,' or 'I thought the pressure from the white folks would kill it before it got started.'"[12] Still, despite reasonable doubts, each of these people took the terrible risk of protesting segregation. Contrary to the social scientist's understanding of "rational" action—and contrary to Niebuhr's theory of human nature—people did act together nonviolently and voluntarily for a miraculous moment that redeemed American democracy.

This was possible, in large part, because of the power of King's rhetoric. King sometimes sought to persuade his audiences by appealing to abstract principles that he hoped they shared. For example, he wrote: "How does one determine when a law is just or unjust? A just law is a man-made code that squares with the moral law or the code of God. An unjust law is a code that is out of harmony with the moral law. To put it in the terms of Saint Thomas Aquinas, an unjust law is a human law that is not rooted in eternal and natural law."[13] But such reasoning cannot have persuaded many of King's opponents, since segregation and racial inequality have often been called "godly" and "natural," and no empirical evidence can disprove this view. Similarly, appeals to constitutional principles of liberty and equality have generally failed to promote racial justice, even though most Americans espouse these principles. After all, the Supreme Court once found segregation consistent with "equal protection"—and "liberty" could mean the freedom to discriminate.

King was far more persuasive when he abandoned abstractions and depicted the harsh particularities of life under segregation. For example, addressing white moderate clergymen who had advised him to "wait" for change, King wrote: "when you suddenly find your tongue twisted and your speech stammering as you seek to explain to your six-year-old daughter why she can't go to the public amusement park that has just been advertised on television, and see tears welling up in her eyes when she is told that Funtown is closed to colored children, and see the depressing clouds of inferiority begin to form in her little mental sky, and see her begin to distort her little personality by unconsciously developing a bitterness toward white people, . . . then you will understand why we find it difficult to wait."[14]

Just as vivid as King's prose were the televised images of African American children being battered by fire hoses, of peaceful marchers being assaulted by vigilantes. Although racist whites bore full moral responsibility for these moments of violence, the civil rights leaders confronted the most intransigent segregationist authorities and used forms of protest guaranteed to provoke a violent response. In this sense, their protests were staged events with an instructive purpose. King explained: "Nonviolent direct action . . . seeks so to dramatize the issue that it can no longer be ignored."[15] Together, the words, images, and music produced by the civil rights movement vividly described oppression and caught the conscience of a nation.

In my terms, King was a "humanist," because he sought to persuade everyone in his society, including bitter racists, to embrace the beloved community; and he used rhetoric and symbolic action (but never violence) to create agreement. Of course, King was also a Protestant minister—but I have argued that Christianity and humanism are fully compatible. King's Christian humanism led him to three important conclusions. First, he treated God not as a metaphysical abstraction (the Prime Mover, the Ultimate Good, or some such concept), but rather as an enormously powerful and good *person* who might intervene to advise or assist the civil rights movement. Indeed, King called himself a theological "personalist," thus embracing a doctrine shared by his namesake, Martin Luther, who had argued that we must treat God as a person who loves us, and avoid theological speculation. "To say God is personal is not to make him an object among other objects or to attribute to him the finiteness and limitations of human personality," King wrote. It simply means that our interactions with God are concrete—like our relationships with people; and it is pointless to discuss divinity in abstract metaphysical terms. "God is a living God. In him there is feeling and will, responsive to the deepest yearnings of the human heart; thus God both evokes and answers prayers."[16]

Even personalism can be interpreted as an abstract theology, as in King's 1958 book, *Stride toward Freedom*, where he writes: "Personalism's insistence that only personality—finite and infinite—is ultimately real strengthened me in two convictions: it gave me metaphysical and philosophical grounding for the idea of a personal God, and it gave me a metaphysical basis for the dignity and worth of all human personality."[17] Perhaps King meant that we could find theoretical support for morality and justice if we viewed human beings and God as fundamentally alike—as persons—and if we held that only persons are ultimately real. All of this sounds rather abstract, and it violates Martin Luther's injunction against metaphysics. The Good Samaritan presumably required no such theory in order to respond to the Jew's need. But King was not satisfied with theoretical personalism; in addition, he held himself open to the intervention of an actual divine personality, and his resulting experiences led him to a far more concrete concept of God.

He recalled: "I had grown up in the church, and the church meant something very real to me, but it was a kind of inherited religion and I had never felt an experience with God in the way that you must . . . if you're going to walk the lonely paths of life." However, late one night in 1956, King sat at his kitchen table worrying about the safety of his family, for he had just received several death threats. "And I discovered then that religion had to become real to me, and I had to know God for myself." So he prayed for help. "And it seemed to me at that moment that I could hear an inner voice saying to me, 'Martin Luther, stand up for righteousness. Stand up for justice. Stand up for truth. And lo I will be with you, even until the end of the world.'"[18]

This experience could not prove the existence of a Prime Mover or a Divine Creator. But it was evidence, for King, that a powerful divine person would come to his aid if he stood for justice. If we are open-minded, we ought to take King's spiritual experience seriously; but this one event would be far too little to convince anyone to accept a whole religious outlook. Even King's faith rested upon several such experiences, and he felt divine grace directly. In essence, his personalism meant a willingness to include God among the beings who formed his community, if God chose to show Himself.

Even after his experience at the Montgomery kitchen table, King still interpreted personalism metaphysically in the section of *Stride toward Freedom* that I quoted above. But, two years later, he adapted the same passage for a journal article on theology, and now he added: "In past years the idea of a personal God was little more than a metaphysical category which I found theologically and philosophically satisfying. Now it is a living reality that has been validated in the experiences of everyday life. . . . Whatever the cause, God has been profoundly real to me in recent months. In the midst of outer dangers I have felt an inner calm and known resources of strength that only God could give."[19] Thus, like George Fox, King could have said: "When God doth work who shall prevent it? *And this I knew experimentally.*"[20]

A second aspect of King's religious humanism was his spiritual interpretation of words like "community." Erasmus, the quintessential Christian humanist, had argued that God commands us to reach peaceful agreement; and that human concord is a sign of spiritual truth. Jesus, according to Erasmus, was a man of peace who sought to persuade others by the unparalleled force of his rhetoric and his personal sacrifice. Similarly, King writes: "The cross is the eternal expression of the length to which God will go in order to restore broken community. The resurrection is a symbol of God's triumph over all the forces that seek to block community. The Holy Spirit is the continuing community creating reality that moves through history."[21] Thus King shared with Erasmus the idea that people *create* moral truth by reaching agreement—and that this reflects God's will. Here Christian humanism implies a strong version of moral pragmatism, with which Protagoras could easily agree. Pragmatists dismiss all general moral principles except the value of human agreement itself.

King was a Christian humanist in a third important sense. Ever since Protagoras, humanists have mined literature for concrete examples of moral action. For instance, Erasmus treated the Bible as a concrete, human narrative, not as a source of implicit theological doctrines. King's methods of biblical interpretation were, in this sense, thoroughly humanistic. For him, the Bible primarily contained stories about people who had found themselves in analogous situations to those that he and other African Americans faced. As a concrete narrative, it was basically no different from the story of American history, which King often used in a similar way.

For example, while King was being held in Birmingham's city jail, he read a newspaper advertisement in which moderate white clergymen criticized the civil rights movement for its allegedly reckless and aggressive methods. In particular, they called King an "extremist." In his "Letter from a Birmingham Jail," King first responds by noting that *he* is not an extremist; he has been outflanked by African nationalist movements, especially the Nation of Islam. Then he changes tack:

> But as I continued to think about the matter I gradually gained a bit of satisfaction from being considered an extremist. Was not Jesus an extremist in love—"Love your enemies, bless them that curse you, pray for them that despitefully use you." Was not Amos an extremist for justice—"Let justice roll down like waters and righteousness like a mighty stream." Was not Paul an extremist for the gospel of Jesus Christ—"I bear in my body the marks of the Lord Jesus."[22]

King then cites Martin Luther, John Bunyan, Abraham Lincoln, and Thomas Jefferson as other great "extremists." At first glance, this seems an odd assortment of references, for many other biblical passages and secular heroes have been more extreme. But King's audience of Christian ministers would have discovered another level of meaning in this paragraph if they had thought about the original context and purpose of each quotation.[23]

The first comes from Jesus' Sermon on the Mount. Jesus has just said that his followers will face slander for accepting his leadership: "Blessed are ye, when men revile you, and persecute you, and shall say all manner of evil against you falsely, for my sake" (Matth. 5:10). Specifically, Jesus and his followers have been accused of disregarding Jewish law. Likewise, the moderate clergymen attacked King and his associates for deliberately violating ordinances and court orders. But Jesus says: "Think not that I am come to destroy the law, or the prophets: I am not come to destroy, but to fulfill" (5:17). He then explains that it is not enough to obey categorical rules and principles, such as the Ten Commandments; one must be motivated by love. For example, "Ye have heard that it hath been said, Thou shalt love thy neighbor, and hate thine enemy. But I say unto you, Love your enemies, bless them that curse you, do good to them that hate you, and pray for them which despitefully use you, and persecute you" (5:44). King too asked his followers to turn their cheeks and to pray for their oppressors; and he argued that rules and laws had no merit except in a beloved community, the only place where laws are "fulfilled."

King's second quotation comes from Amos (5:24). The prophet denounces Israel's rulers for obeying the letter of God's religious commands; but "Your treading is upon the poor, and ye take from him the burdens of wheat. . . . For I know your manifold transgressions and your mighty sins: they afflict the just, they take a bribe, and they turn aside the poor in the gate from their right" (5:11–12). The Southern white ministers whom King addressed were shamefully similar to Amos's priests: they carried out their formal religious duties, but their churches were legally closed to people of color. Here King suggests that they must learn to love *all* of their neighbors, or else "justice [will] roll down like waters and righteousness like a mighty stream."

King's third biblical quotation comes from Paul's "Letter to the Galatians" (6:17). Indeed, King alludes repeatedly to the Pauline epistles, perhaps because Paul had responded to the divisions and doubts within the church of his day.[24] Specifically, Paul wrote to the Galatian Christians to settle their dispute about Jewish law: those who were former Jews demanded that their brethren circumcise their boys, but the gentiles considered circumcision blasphemous. Paul argued that neither obeying nor violating a written law means anything to Jesus. Rather, strife is sinful and love is all that God demands: "For all the law is fulfilled in one word, even this: Thou shalt love thy neighbor as thyself" (5:14).

Jesus and Paul broke the law of their day in order to build a community of greater love and justice. So did Luther, Bunyan, Lincoln, and

Jefferson (Lincoln by suspending habeas corpus; Jefferson by revolting against the British). Thus King's examples of "extremism" all suggest analogies to his own situation. His message is the insignificance of all laws and moral codes, compared to the creation of a beloved community. But he largely avoids a theoretical argument in favor of his position, instead alluding to concrete stories. In short, his methods of persuasion and interpretation are as humanistic as his conclusions.

Writing in 1960, King implied that the civil rights movement had refuted Niebuhr's pessimistic beliefs about human society. People *could* act peacefully and consensually, persuading their fellow citizens with moral rhetoric, and thereby build a political system in which force would be curtailed and love would predominate. But the intense idealism and solidarity of 1960 gradually diminished in the face of violent white resistance. King's peaceful, universalist, democratic ideals looked increasingly irrelevant as Mississippi burned and Northern cities erupted into riots. The civil rights movement itself fragmented into liberal, nationalist, militant, socialist, and neoconservative strands. Even protesters who remained loyal to Gandhian principles turned out to harbor a great deal of rage, which fed their often bitter internal disputes. Alvin Poussaint, a psychiatrist, recalled: "While they were talking about being nonviolent and 'loving' the sheriff that just hit them over the head, they rampaged around the [movement's] project houses beating up each other. I frequently had to calm Negro civil-rights workers with tranquilizers for what I can describe clinically only as acute attacks of rage."[25]

Far more destructive was white rage against the civil rights movement: a bullet ended King's nonviolent crusade, and many of his associates were also slain. So perhaps Niebuhr was right to stress the "limitations of the human mind and imagination," the impossibility of governing by consensus and love alone. Even the great achievements of the movement—civil rights backed by the federal government, integrated schools, millions of new voters, thousands of African American office-holders—did not produce a beloved community. Today, America is still governed by bargaining, litigation, and coercion. Majority tyranny has survived the enfranchisement of black voters; racism continues to distort our moral judgments; and discrimination has taken new and sophisticated forms.

Indeed, because of the impediments to consensus discussed in chapter 2, no truly beloved community is sustainable except on a very small scale. The civil rights movement was prophetic and utopian: it invoked a paradise of love that could only exist on earth after the Apocalypse. (King's "Letter from a Birmingham Jail," like much of his writing, is saturated with millenarian references.) But a permanent solution to Niebuhr's paradoxes is too much to expect. Measured on a more realistic scale, the civil rights movement was a remarkable success. Using peaceful methods, it reformed the American political system so that the results of democratic decisions would more closely resemble true consensus—for now African American voices and votes counted. By example, it showed how a voluntary, consensual movement could function effectively, at least for a time. It taught many people how to view others as complex individuals even across racial lines. Not least, it proved that humanistic methods are a powerful way to build a more moral, more just, and more loving society.

NOTES

INTRODUCTION

1. Rawls, "Reply to Habermas," *The Journal of Philosophy* 109.3 (March 1995): 140–41; cf. Habermas, "Reconciliation through the Public Use of Reason: Remarks on John Rawls' Political Liberalism," ibid., pp. 128–31.

2. James Dreier, "Structures of Normative Theories," *Monist* 76.1 (January 1993): 37.

3. Ibid., p. 38.

4. Rawls, *A Theory of Justice*, 1972 (Oxford, 1989), p. 187; cf. p. 26.

5. Nagel, *The View from Nowhere* (New York, 1986), p. 152.

6. Baier, "Doing without Moral Theory?" in *Postures of Mind: Essays on Mind and Morals* (Minneapolis, 1985), pp. 235–36.

7. *Critique of Pure Reason*, A 476, Norman Kemp Smith translation (New York, 1965).

8. Cora Diamond, "Having a Rough Story about What Moral Philosophy Is," *New Literary History* 15.1 (Autumn 1983): 167–68.

9. Lewis White Beck, *A Commentary on Kant's Critique of Practical Wisdom* (Chicago, 1960), p. 120. See, e.g., *Critique of Practical Wisdom*, BA 55–56.

1. Moral Judgment

1. *Teresa Harris v. Forklift Systems, Inc.*, 976 F.2d 733 (CA 1992), reversed and remanded by the Supreme Court: 114 S.Ct 367 (1993). Petition for Writ of Certiorari, Joint Appendix, at 156, cited in *Brief for Petitioner on Writ of Certiorari to the United States Court of Appeals for the Sixth Circuit* (hereafter: "Joint Appendix").

2. *Teresa Harris v. Forklift Systems, Inc.*, United States District Court for the Middle District of Tennessee, 1990 U.S. Dist. LEXIS 20115; 60 Empl. Prac. Dec (CCH). Findings of Fact, at 5–6 (hereafter cited as "Findings of Fact."); "Joint Appendix" at 47, 51–52.

3. "Findings of Fact," at 7.

4. "Findings of Fact," at 7–8.

5. *Harris v. Forklift Systems*, 976 F.2d 733, *Brief for Respondent on Writ of Certiori*, citing "Joint Appendix" at 72.

6. "Findings of Fact," at 11, 16–17.

7. Ibid., at 18.

8. "Joint Appendix," at 52–53, 56.

9. Locke, *Essay Concerning Human Understanding*, edited by Alexander Campbell Fraser (Oxford, 1894), book III, chapter X, section 34.

10. Roland Barthes, *Le Degré zéro de l'écriture* (Paris, 1953), pp. 108–11. (Barthes believes that there is such a thing as writing degree zero.)

11. *Utilitarianism* (New York, 1987), p. 12.

12. However, for Kant, empirical evidence can never show that people act *because of* their knowledge of the principles of morality.

13. *Meno* 79e.

14. Taylor criticizes the search for such a procedure. See "The Diversity of Goods," in *Philosophy and the Human Sciences: Philosophical Papers 2* (Cambridge, 1985), p. 245.

15. As will become clear later, I agree with Joseph Raz, Michael Stocker, and others that we frequently resolve conflicts among values, using our practical reason (or judgment) to achieve an appropriate balance in particular circumstances. Therefore, a plurality of values is not necessarily a fatal problem for moral agents, but it is a problem for ambitious theorists, because practical reason does not employ rules, principles, or algorithms to balance conflicting values. Thus, either all values are ultimately commensurable, or else philosophy cannot provide guidance when values conflict. See Stocker, *Plural and Conflicting Values* (Oxford, 1990), pp. 1, 149, and passim; and Raz, *The Morality of Freedom* (Oxford, 1986), p. 339.

16. *Die Metaphysik der Sitten, I: Metaphysische Unfangsgründe der Rechtslehre* (*Metaphysics of Morals, Part One: Metaphysical Elements of Justice*), Akademie-Textausgabe (Berlin, 1968), 201–7.

17. Ibid., 224.

18. *Utilitarianism*, pp. 9–10.

19. Ibid., p. 11.

20. William K. Frankena, *Ethics* (Englewood Cliffs, N.J.), p. 25.

21. Kant, *Grundlegung zur Metaphysik der Sitten* (*Groundwork of the Metaphysics of Morals*), edited by Wilhelm Weischedel (Frankfurt am Main, 1991), p. 28.

22. The challenge to moral theory is not logical. Paul M. Pietroski argues that there is no paradox implied by the following propositions: 1. You must do X. 2 You must do Y. 3. It is impossible for you to do both X and Y. We just need to add the words "*prima facie*" or "*ceteris paribus*" to the first two propositions. Analogously, a physical object may be forced downward by gravity, *and* upward by rocket propulsion. Thus the law of gravity only predicts outcomes *ceteris paribus*; and something similar may be said of ethical principles. There remains a challenge, however. Just as the combined effects of two forces can be understood using Newtonian vectors, so we need "compositional principles" to explain what happens when two *prima facie* moral obligations conflict. In other words, we need a general moral theory. See Pietroski, "Prima Facie Obligations, Ceteris Paribus Laws in Moral Theory," *Ethics* (April 1993): 489–515, especially 506.

23. Dancy, "Ethical Particularism and Morally Relevant Properties," *Mind* 92 (1983): 542.

24. *Theaetetus* 146e–147b. All quotations from Plato are my own translations from the Oxford Greek edition by J. Burnet (1958). I use italics to emphasize words for my own purposes, and not to reflect any emphasis that Plato wanted to convey.

25. *Theaetetus* 148d. Cf. *Sophist* 218c.

26. *Meno* 79d.

27. *Phaedrus* 265d. The words that I have translated as "boundary" and "to mark a boundary" (ὁρίζω) later came to mean "definition" and "to define." But in Plato's day, the original, literal meaning would have been uppermost. And Plato does mean that we should mark out a logical territory when we use a word.

28. Ibid.

29. Edmund Wall, "The Definition of Sexual Harassment," *Public Affairs Quarterly* 5.4 (October 1991): 374, 371.

30. Anita M. Superson, "A Feminist Definition of Sexual Harassment," *Journal of Social Philosophy* 24.1 (Spring 1993): 46, 61.

31. F. M. Christensen, "'Sexual Harassment' Must be Eliminated," *Public Affairs Quarterly* 8.1 (January 1994): 2, 1, 5.

32. Mane Hajdin, "Sexual Harassment in the Law: The Demarcation Problem," *Journal of Social Philosophy* 25.3 (Winter 1994): 102, 118.

33. Deborah Wells and Beverly J. Kracher, "Justice, Sexual Harassment, and the Reasonable Victim Standard," *Journal of Business Ethics* 12.6 (1993): 423.

34. This dialogue is the subject of chapter 3.

35. Kant, *Lectures on Ethics*, translated by Louis Infield (Indianapolis, 1963), p. 229; cf. Grunglegung, BA 54.

36. *Lectures on Ethics*, pp. 226–30. Elsewhere, Kant notes that what we call a "lie" (*mendacium*) in moral contexts may not qualify as one in legal terms if it causes no harm; thus a harmless falsehood is legally different from a lie. Further, he states that it is almost impossible to trace a line between moral and legal reasoning in such cases (*Metaphysical Elements of Justice*, p. 238n).

37. *Lectures on Ethics*, p. 229.

38. "*Erfahrung geschärfte Urteilskraft*," Groundwork, BA ix.

39. Cf. Stanley Rosen, *The Limits of Analysis* (New York, 1980), p. 3 and passim.

40. *Kritik der reinen Vernunft* (*Critique of Pure Reason*), ed. Raymund Schmidt (Hamburg, 1956), A 132. See Onora O'Neill, *The Constructions of Reason*, pp. 166–67.

41. *Critique of Pure Reason*, A 134; *Doctrine of Virtue*, 49, 52.

42. *Critique of Pure Reason*, A 134; B 173 (note).

43. *Die Metaphysik der Sitten, II: Tugendlehre* (*Doctrine of Virtue*), 410. Sally Sedgwick defends Kant on this point: "On Lying and the Role of Content in Kant's Ethics," *Kant-Studien* vol. 82 (1991): 42–62, especially 58. See also Jules Vuillemin, "On Lying: Kant and Benjamin Constant," *Kant-Studien* 73 (1982): 413–24.

44. I have found parts of the preceding argument anticipated by Charles E. Larmore, *Patterns of Moral Complexity* (Cambridge, 1987), pp. 1–21, and by Lawrence A. Blum, *Moral Perception and Particularity* (Cambridge, 1994), pp. 30–61. Kant is defended against this line of criticism by Barbara Herman, "The Practice of Moral Judgment," *The Journal of Philosophy* 82.8 (August 1985): 414–36.

45. Cf. *Philosophical Investigations*, 71 (these are not his examples).

46. Ibid., 65, 66.

47. *Webster's Ninth Collegiate Dictionary* (Springfield, Mass., 1988), ad loc.

48. Ibid., 164.

49. Ryle, *Collected Papers* (New York, 1971), 2: 474–81. Ryle's concept of "thick description" has been made famous by Clifford Geertz, *The Interpretation of Cultures* (New York, 1973), p. 6 and passim.

50. *After Virtue* (2nd ed., Notre Dame, 1984), p. 206.

51. Pater, *Studies in the History of the Renaissance* (1873), excerpted in the *Norton Anthology of English Literature*, 4th ed. (New York, 1979), 2: 1579. Pater quotes from 1 Corinthians 10:11. Paul has just mentioned fornicators who were struck dead by the thousand, and tempters who were "destroyed of serpents," and now he concludes: "all these things happened to them for ensamples: and they are written for our admonition, upon whom the ends of the world are come." Knowing all this makes the Mona Lisa's eyelids a little weary.

52. Ibid.

53. "Findings of Fact," at 10, 17.

54. *Philosophical Investigations*, IIxi, p. 213. Cf. Gilbert Ryle, *The Concept of Mind* (London, 1949), p. 246, for the same observation.

55. Quoted by Garth Hallett, *A Companion to Wittgenstein's "Philosophical Investigations"* (Ithaca, N.Y., 1977), p. 771.

56. *Philosophical Investigations*, 518.

57. Cf. ibid, IIxi (p. 196) and Ryle, pp. 248–49.

58. *Philosophical Investigations*, II.xi (p. 200).

59. Ibid., IIxi (p. 195).

60. Cf. ibid., 60: "When I say: 'My broom is in the corner',–is this really a statement about the broomstick and the brush? ... Suppose that, instead of saying 'Bring me the broom,' you said 'Bring me the broomstick and the brush which is fitted on to it'!–Isn't the answer: 'Do you want the broom? Why do you put it so oddly?'–Is [someone] going to understand the further analyzed sentence better?–This sentence, one might say, achieves the same as the ordinary one, but in a more roundabout way."

61. *Meritor Savings Bank, FSB v. Vinson*, 106 S.Ct. 2399 (1986), at 64. Actually, the Supreme Court upheld a definition originally proposed by the Court of Appeals for the District of Columbia: 243 U.S.App.D.C. 444, 641 F.2d 934 (1985). In the *Harris* case, the Supreme Court refined its definition of sexual harassment: *Harris v. Forklift Systems Inc.*, 114 S.Ct. 367.

62. *Harris*, at 10–11.

63. *Harris*, at 9–10, quoting *Meritor*, at 66.

64. Ibid., at 12–13.

65. *Philosophical Investigations*, 31.

66. Stephen A. Dinan, "The Particularity of Moral Knowledge," *The Thomist* 50 (January 1986): 66–84.

67. John Wisdom, "Gods," in Anthony Flew, ed., *Logic and Language*, first series (Oxford, 1955), pp. 195–96 (italics in the original).

68. Dancy, p. 546. See McDowell, p. 342, for similar comments.

69. *Nicomachean Ethics* 1142a24–25.

70. Ibid. 1142a8ff. There is controversy about the last phrase in this quotation, which could mean: "by which we perceive that the triangle is the ultimate mathematical object." In fact, this version more readily fits the Greek. But if practical reason were like the faculty that we use to recognize that a triangle is the foundation of geometry, then it would be a form of abstract reasoning, which Aristotle repeatedly denies. Further, Nancy Sherman notes that the triangle is *not* the ultimate mathematical object for Aristotle: the point is ultimate: see Sherman, *The Fabric of Character: Aristotle's Theory of Virtue* (Oxford, 1989), p. 39. My translation is similar to those of Martha Nussbaum and Richard McKeon. David Wiggins seems to read the Greek differently, however: see Wiggins, "Deliberation and Practical Ethics," in Joseph Raz, ed., *Practical Reasoning* (Oxford, 1978), p. 148.

71. *Philosophical Investigations*, IIxi, p. 203.

72. Ibid., *Philosophical Investigations*, Iixi, p. 227.

73. *The Fragility of Goodness: Luck and Ethics in Greek Tragedy and Philosophy* (Cambridge, 1986), pp. 277–78. For further discussion of the meaning of *phantasia* in Aristotle's thought (a controversial issue), see: R. J. Hankinson, "Perception and Evaluation: Aristotle on the Moral Imagination," *Dialogue* 29 (1990): 41–63; D. A. Rees, "Aristotle's Treatment of Φαντασία," in John P. Anton and George L. Kustas, *Essays in Ancient Greek Philosophy* (Albany, 1971), pp. 491–504; and Malcolm Schofield, "Aristotle on the Imagination," in Jonathan Barnes et al., eds., *Articles on Aristotle* (New York, 1978), pp. 103–32. See also the discussion of understanding (σύνεσις) and right judgment at *Nicomachean Ethics* 1143a10ff.

74. I discuss Aristotle's account of tragedy at greater length in chapter 4.

75. Cf. Wiggins, pp. 144–45: "in the unfortunate fact that few situations come already inscribed with the names of all the human concerns which they touch or impinge on, resides the crucial importance of the minor premiss of the practical syllogism." Wiggins's account of practical reasoning in Aristotle stresses the importance of correctly seeing the salient features of particular cases.

76. Cf. Sherman, *The Fabric of Character*, chapter 2, "Discerning the Particulars," especially pp. 24–50. Sherman argues that judgment (or the evaluative discernment of particulars) is a necessary process at all stages of Aristotle's practical

syllogism, for we use judgment to arrive at major premises as well as minor ones. Larmore (p. 16) endorses the same position, both as a reading of Aristotle and as an accurate account of how we make moral choices.

77. McDowell, p. 343.

78. Baier, "Doing Without Moral Theory?" p. 233.

79. Williams, *Ethics and the Limits of Philosophy* (Cambridge, Mass., 1985), p. 111.

80. Jorge Luis Borges, "Funes, the Memorious," in *Ficciones* (New York, 1962), p. 115 (story translated by Anthony Kerrigan).

81. *Republic* X.604c ff.

82. *Phaedrus* 267a–b, 272d.

83. *Apology* 17c; *Protagoras*, 325b.

84. *Der Wille zur Macht* (*Will to Power*), 387.

85. *Über Wahrheit und Lüge im aussermoralischen Sinn* (*On Truth and Lying in an Extramoral Sense*), in Karl Schlechta, ed., *Nietzsche's Werke* (Frankfurt, 1969), 3: 359.

86. Hume, *A Treatise of Human Nature: Book III: Of Morals*, part ii (Oxford, 1978), 532–32.

87. Aristotle reached the same conclusion about the role of judges in the legal system of his time: *Nicomachean Ethics* 1132a3ff. And Sedgwick (p. 58) argues that Kant held this view as well.

88. W. D. Ross, *Foundations of Ethics* (Oxford, 1939), p. 171.

89. Ibid., p. 130.

90. See also Blum, pp. 44–45; Larmore, pp. 9–10; Rawls, *A Theory of Justice* (Oxford, 1973), pp. 46-53. Sherman plausibly attributes the same position to Aristotle. For criticism of this approach, see Judith Lichtenberg, "Moral Certainty," in *Philosophy* 69 (1994): 183–206, especially 199–203.

91. Hume, *Treatise*, pp. 531, 472, 581, 473 (cf. 531), 585.

92. *Groundwork*, p. 30.

93. Cf. Dancy, pp. 533, 537, and Dinan, pp. 74–79.

94. I am indebted here to an unpublished paper by Margaret Olivia Little.

95. Rawls, *A Theory of Justice*, pp. 19–20, 18, 20, 51.

96. Ibid., p. 48.

97. By "considered judgments," Rawls means fairly general ideas that we sometimes decide to adjust in the light of comprehensive moral theories. But concrete opinions, just like general ideas, can be distorted and may require adjustment.

98. Cf. Nussbaum, *Love's Knowledge*, p. 46 and passim.

99. Kohlberg used this example in his testing, and frequently discussed it. See, e.g., Kohlberg, "Stages of Moral Development as a Basis for Moral Education," in Brenda Munsey, ed., *Moral Development, Moral Education, and Kohlberg* (Birmingham, Ala., 1980), p. 27.

2. AGREEMENT

1. Cf. Jürgen Habermas, "On the Logic of Legitimation Problems," in *Legitimation Crisis* (Boston, 1973), p. 107: "In taking up practical discourse, we unavoidably suppose an ideal speech situation that, on the strength of its formal principles, allows consensus only through *generalizable* interests. A cognitivist linguistic ethics [*Sprachethik*] has no need of principles. It is based only on fundamental norms of rational speech that we must always presuppose if we discourse at all."

2. Kant, *Grundlegung*, BA 11; Jean-Jacques Rousseau, *The Social Contract*, translated by G. D. H. Cole (London, 1993), pp. 195, 206, 203.

3. Young, "Impartiality and the Civic Public: Some Implications of Feminist Critique for Moral and Political Theory," pp. 59, 76, in Seyla Benhabib and Drucilla Cornell, eds., *Feminism as Critique* (Oxford, 1987).

4. See Bernard Manin, "On Legitimacy and Political Deliberation," *Political Theory* 15.3 (August 1987): 355–57, translated by Elly Stein and Jane Mansbridge.

5. These issues are the subject of a book on political reform and deliberation that I am writing with support from the Florence and John Schumann Foundation.

6. See, e.g., Ronald Dworkin, *Life's Dominion: An Argument about Abortion, Euthanasia, and Individual Freedom* (New York, 1994), p. 239.

7. This discussion is based upon Rosalind Hursthouse's article, "Virtue Theory and Abortion," in *Philosophy and Public Affairs*, vol. 20, number 3 (Summer 1991), pp. 223–46.

8. *Harris v. Forklift Systems*, 976 F2d 733, Petition for Writ of Certiori, at 5.

9. "Findings of Fact," at 17.

10. *Philosophical Investigations*, 23, 18.

11. *Moral Reasoning* (London, 1969), pp. 42–43.

12. Ibid., p. 94.

13. Cf. Rhees, "Knowing the Difference between Right and Wrong," in *Without Answers* (New York, 1969), p. 101.

14. *Philosophical Investigations*, 19.

15. *Rabidue v. Osceola Refining Co.*, 805 F.2d at 626 (6th Circuit, 1986), J. Keith, dissenting.

16. On the reasonable victim standard, see, e.g., Wells and Kracher, "Justice, Sexual Harassment, and the Reasonable Victim Standard," and Romona L. Paetzold and Bill Shaw, "A Postmodern Feminist View of 'Reasonableness' in Hostile Environmental Sexual Harassment," *Journal of Business Ethics* 13.9 (September 1994): 681–92.

17. Eric A. Havelock, *Preface to Plato* (Oxford, 1963), pp. 201, 209. I am grateful to an anonymous reader for SUNY Press who referred me to this passage.

18. Williams, *Ethics and the Limits of Philosophy*, pp. 116–17.

19. Michael Walzer, *Thick and Thin: Moral Argument at Home and Abroad* (Notre Dame, Ind., 1994), pp. 50–52.

20. *Toward a Rational Society* (1968), translated by Jeremy J. Shapiro (Boston, 1970), p. 7.

21. See e.g., Dewey, *The Public and its Problems* (New York, 1927), pp. 206–8 and passim; James Fishkin, *Democracy and Deliberation* (New Haven, Conn., 1991); Manin, "On Legitimacy and Political Deliberation"; Joshua Cohen, "An Epistemic Conception of Democracy," *Ethics* 97 (October 1986): 26–38; and Jack Knight and James Johnson, "Aggregation and Deliberation: On the Possibility of Democratic Legitimacy," *Political Theory* 22.2 (May 1994): 277–96.

22. Barbara Herrnstein Smith, *Contingencies of Value: Alternative Perspectives for Critical Theory* (Cambridge, Mass., 1988), p. 110.

23. Ibid., p. 112.

24. Ibid., pp. 144–45.

25. Ibid., p. 99.

26. Ibid., p. 129.

27. Engle, *Shakespeare's Pragmatism: Market of His Time* (Chicago, 1993), pp. 27–53.

28. *An Inquiry into the Nature and Causes of the Wealth of Nations*, 1776 (3rd ed.; Edinburgh, 1814), p. 20.

29. F. H. Knight, "Anthropology and Economics," in M. J. Herkovitz, ed., *Economic Anthropology* (New York, 1941), p. 245.

30. For this terminology, see George Dalton, "Karl Polanyi's Analysis of Long-Distance Trade and His Wider Paradigm," in Jeremy Sabloff and C. C. Lamberg-Karlovsky, *Ancient Civilization and Trade* (Albuquerque, 1975), p. 80.

31. Karl Polanyi, *The Great Transformation: The Political and Economic Origins of Our Time* (Boston, 1960), p. 50.

32. Bronislaw Malinowski describes the system of support for in-laws in *Argonauts of the Western Pacific* (London, 1922), p. 61. He notes that gifts to in-laws and the village chief consume 75 percent of each man's crops, yet men compete to outproduce each other because good providers receive "much praise and renown." Malinowski's findings are largely confirmed by J. P. Singh Uberoi, *Politics of the Kula Ring: An Analysis of the Findings of Bronislaw Malinowski* (Manchester, U.K., 1971). And see other references below.

33. Malinowski, p. 94.

34. Thus Malinowski writes (pp. 95–96):

> The Kula consists in the bestowing of a ceremonial gift, which has to be repaid by an equivalent counter-gift after a lapse of time. . . . But it can never be exchanged from hand to hand, with the equivalence between the two objects discussed, bargained about, and computed. . . . Often, when criticizing an incorrect, too hasty, or indecorous procedure of Kula, they will say: "He conducts his Kula as if it were *gimwali* [barter]." . . . The second very important principle is that the equivalence of the counter-gift is left to the giver, and it cannot be enforced by any kind of coercion.

35. Marcel Mauss claims that failure to give an appropriate reciprocal Kula gift can be avenged by war or magic; but Malinowski, who did the fieldwork, states that there was no coercion. See Mauss, *The Gift: Forms and Functions of Exchange in Archaic Societies*, translated by Ian Cunnison (Glencoe, Ill., 1954), p. 24.

36. E.g., Raymond Firth, "Magnitudes and Values in Kula Exchange," in Jerry Leach and Edmund Leach, eds., *The Kula: New Perspectives on Massim Exchange* (Cambridge, 1983), p. 89. Richard Emerson interprets the Kula ring as a "highly institutionalized exchange system" that can be understood by means of a "social exchange theory," which is a theory that interprets all behavior as rational utility-maximization: "Social Exchange Theory," in Morris Rosenberg and Ralph H. Turner, eds., *Social Psychology: Sociological Perspectives* (New York, 1981), p. 59.

37. Chris Gregory, "Kula Gift Exchange and Capitalist Commodity Exchange: A Comparison," in Leach and Leach, pp. 108–9, 114.

38. *Les structures élémentaires de la parenté* (Paris, 1968), pp. 548 and passim.

39. David Cheal, *The Gift Economy* (London, 1988), p. 12ff.

40. *The New York Times*, December 15, 1993, p. A22, citing the December 1993 issue of *The American Economic Review* and an interview with Dr. Waldfogel.

41. Diane Rothbard Margolis asserts that women have been assigned the sphere of gift-exchange in our society, which is otherwise dominated by commodities: see her *Gifts, Commodities, and the Tribute Factor: A Feminist Reformulation of Sociological Theory*, Wellesley College Center for Research on Women, Working Paper No. 145 (1984). Cheal, p. 8, supports this thesis.

42. See Herrnstein Smith, p. 215n44. Bourdieu, whom she cites, asserts that systems of gift-giving are always disguised market exchanges. The practice of gift-giving "never ceases to conform to economic calculation even when it gives every appearance of disinterestedness by departing from the logic of interested calculation (in the narrow sense) and playing for stakes that are non-material and not easily qualified" (*Outline of a Theory of Practice*, translated by Richard Nice [Cambridge, 1977], p. 177; cf. p. 171).

43. Lewis Hyde discusses the importance of separating art from the sphere of commodities in *The Gift: Imagination and the Erotic Life of Property* (New York, 1979).

44. For historical background, see my *Nietzsche and the Modern Crisis of the Humanities* (Albany, 1995), chapters 1 and 9.

3. A Philosopher Encounters a Humanist

1. On Protagoras's international fame, see, e.g., *Hippias Major* 282d-e.

2. Regarding Protagoras, see Ammonius's Scholium on *Iliad* XXI.240, which quotes Protagoras's opinions regarding this Homeric passage. Cited in Rosamond Kent Sprague, ed., *The Older Sophists* (Columbia, S.C., 1972), a translation of Diels-Kranz, *Die Fragmente der Vorsokratiker*, p. 18.

3. Diogenes Laertius, *Vitae philosophorum* IX.54; Aristotle, *Rhetoric* III.5 (1407b6).

4. *Protagoras* 325e–326a.

5. *The Lives of the Noble Grecians and Romans*, translated by John Dryden and revised by Arthur Hugh Clough (New York, 1932), p. 183.

6. *Phaedrus* 261a4–5.

7. *Groundwork*, BA 29.

8. This work is reconstructed (somewhat speculatively) by Mario Untersteiner in *The Sophists*, translated by Kathleen Freeman (Oxford, 1953), p. 26ff. See also Jacqueline de Romilly, *The Greek Sophists in Periclean Athens*, translated by Janet Lloyd (Oxford, 1992), pp. 75–80.

9. Diogenes IX.52; Philostratus, *Lives of the Sophists* 1.10.1 (Philostratus, however, seems highly unreliable).

10. Diogenes Laertius, IX.51. I translate from the Loeb Greek text in R. D. Hicks, ed., *Diogenes Laertius* (Cambridge, Mass., 1958).

11. *Cratylus* 385e ff.; Aristotle, *Metaphysics* XI.6.1062b13.

12. *Laws* 716 c.

13. *Theaetetus* 151e–152a. Socrates also attributes to Protagoras the view that it is impossible to say anything untrue or to refute anyone: see *Euthydemus* 286b–c; *Cratylus* 429d; and *Sophist* 237a (where Protagoras is not mentioned by name.) Cf. Aristotle, *Metaphysics* IV.4 (1007b18) and XI.6 (1062b13). Aristotle interprets Protagoras exactly as Socrates does in the Theaetetus, but his source may have been Plato's dialogues.

14. *Phaedo* 90c. Protagoras is not mentioned by name in this passage, but he is clearly Socrates' target. I discuss the passage in more detail below.

15. *Outline of Pyrrhonism* 1.217–19. I translate from the Loeb Greek text in R. G. Bury, ed., *Sextus Empiricus* (Cambridge, Mass., 1951).

16. In *Against the Schoolmasters* (*Pros Mathematikos*) VII.389, Sextus specifically cites *Theaetetus* 171a.

17. Letter 88, §43. I translate from the Latin text in C. D. N. Costa, ed., *Seneca: Seventeen Letters* (Warminster, 1988).

18. *Theaetetus* 167c.

19. F. C. S. Schiller, an associate of William James, reads *Theaetetus* 166–68 as proof that Protagoras was a pragmatist and a democrat. See his *Studies in Humanism* (London, 1907), pp. 33–38.

20. Diogenes Laertius, IX.50.

21. *Clouds* 890ff.; cf. 112ff.

22. *Rhetoric* II.24.1402a23.

23. See Romilly, pp. 85–86, 89. See also *Theaetetus* 167e, where Socrates, paraphrasing the absent Protagoras, explains that eristic is not a game but a serious method of seeking truth.

24. Cf. Malcolm Schofield, "Socrates versus Protagoras," in Barry S. Gower and Michael C. Stokes, eds., *Socratic Questions: New Essays in the Philosophy of Socrates and Its Significance* (London, 1992), pp. 122–23.

25. Quoted in ibid., p. 89.

26. Versényi, *Socratic Humanism* (New Haven, Conn., 1963), p. 9.

27. See Patrick Coby, *Socrates and the Sophistic Enlightenment: A Commentary on Plato's Protagoras* (Lewisburg, Pa., 1987), pp. 19–25.

28. Cf. Aristotle, *Nicomachean Ethics* 1164a.

29. Cf. Coby, pp. 34–37.

30. Thus it is possible that Socrates only offers his *technē* of measurement as a solution to life within the economic and political realm of the Sophists; beyond that realm there is still room for love. See Coby, p. 22.

31. Schofield, pp. 128–30; Coby, p. 78.

32. Werner Jaeger, *Paideia: The Ideals of Greek Culture*, translated by Gilbert Highet (New York: 1943), 2:107.

33. Jaeger (2:111) understands Protagoras's speech as an ἐπάγγελμα or standardized advertisement delivered to all prospective students.

34. According to G. B. Kerferd, it was common at the time to call Homer and other classic poets "Sophists": see *The Sophistic Movement* (Cambridge, 1981), p. 24.

35. *Nicomachean Ethics* 1142a13–17; 1143b12–13.

36. It is probably Plato's paraphrase of a book by Protagoras entitled "On the Original State of Man." See W. K. C. Guthrie, *The Sophists* (Cambridge, 1971), p. 63n2; Romilly, p. 162. For analogous myths, see Aeschylus, *Prometheus Bound* 450, and the anonymous work entitled *On Ancient Medicine*.

37. Plato's word is δύναμις, which can mean strength, power, ability, capacity, etc.

38. They literally "divided up speech at the joints" (Φωνὴν διηρθρώσατο). This recalls Socrates' definition of dialectical reason, which is the process of dividing concepts at their natural joints: see *Phaedrus* 265d.

39. Cf. the Sophist Prodicus's remarks at 337a. He says that both Socrates and Protagoras should be heard impartially, but that impartiality does not imply equality. Everyone has a right to the audience's respect, but not to their ultimate agreement.

40. See Michael Gagarin, "The Purpose of Plato's *Protagoras*," *Transactions of the American Philolgical Association* 100 (1969): 140, and Coby, p. 176.

41. See Louis Bodin, *Lire le Protagoras: Introduction à la méthode dialectique de Protagoras*, ed. Paul Demont (Paris, 1975), p. 86. In general, see pp. 79–86.

42. Xenophon attributes a social-contract doctrine to Hippias, a Sophist who is also present in Plato's *Protagoras* (see *Memorabilia* 4.4.13). Antiphon, Lycrophon, and the "Anonymous Iamblichi"—all Sophists—apparently held similar doctrines (see Romilly, p. 167).

43. Aristotle adopts the same position, virtually echoing Protagoras: *Nicomachean Ethics* 1103b34ff. and 1099b9ff.

44. Coby, p. 194n1.

45. The reference to Milton is given in the Benjamin Jowett trans. of the *Protagoras*, as revised by Martin Ostwald and edited by Gregory Vlastos (Indianapolis, 1956), p. 53.

46. I have been influenced here by C. C. W. Taylor, *Plato's Protagoras* (Oxford, 1976), pp. 109–10.

47. See Joseph Raz, *The Morality of Freedom*, p. 358: "widespread incommensurabilities put paid to the hope of developing a general system or technology of calculation for practical reasoning." Note, however, that Socrates' idea of commensurability is only one way to solve moral problems that seem to involve conflicting principles. In the *Protagoras*, Socrates uses the method that we now associate with utilitarians and other consequentialists. But some Kantians agree that all (or most) moral dilemmas can be rationally resolved. They argue that certain purported values, such as pleasure, have no weight whatsoever when they conflict with the demands of duty. Thus, rather than assign comparable weight to all values, Kantians declare that certain principles "trump" the rest. One can reject the idea of commensurability and still believe that all dilemmas have philosophical solutions.

48. The word that I translate here as "making a public speech" (δημηγορεῖν) is related to words meaning "the people," "democracy," and "demagogue." Socrates' anti-democratic attitude is manifest throughout the dialogue, and he consistently interprets Protagoras's humanism as democratic.

49. *Republic* VII.517d.

50. Gagarin disagrees with this "common interpretation," but cites numerous authors who have held it (p. 133).

51. *Tusc. Disp.* I.viii.

52. Coby, p. 89.

53. Coby, p. 96, suggests that Socrates wins the debate about procedure because he, unlike Protagoras, does not care about public opinion. Thus he is willing to walk out in (mock) defeat if Protagoras does not accept his terms.

54. Five lines must be missing from the first stanza, since each stanza would originally have been seven lines long. J. M. Edmonds conjectures that Simonides discussed Skopas in these missing lines. Presumably, he would have described Skopas as imperfect, but still worthy of an encomium. See *Lyra Graeca* II (London, 1924), p. 285n2. Hugh Parry suggests that the missing lines contained a consolation to Skopas for some specific misfortune. See "An Interpretation of Simonides 4 (Diehl)," *Transactions of the American Philological Association* 96 (1965): 298.

55. See, e.g., *Gorgias* 470e: "for the men and women who are noble and good I call happy, but the evil and base I call miserable."

56. *Metaphysics of Morals*, Part One: *Metaphysical Elements of Justice*, 224.

57. Socrates' Kantian theme of morality-as-maturity emerges when he uses "childishness" as the opposite of philosophy, e.g., at *Protagoras* 347d–e and *Republic* X.602b and X.604b–d (these passages are discussed below).

58. Edmonds, *Lyra Graeca*, Simonides, 26.

59. Ibid., 28, 33. C. M Bowra argues that Simonides' Dithyrambs were precursors of tragedy. See *Greek Lyric Poetry from Alcman to Simonides* (Oxford, 1961), p. 319.

60. Quoted by Plutarch, *Life of Aratus*, 45, in Edmonds, 2:263.

61. Prodicus was a Sophist who wrote a treatise *On the Correctness of Names*, in which he apparently tried to reform thought by clarifying what object each word in Greek referred to (see Kerferd, pp. 70–73; Diels-Kranz fragment 84A19). Plato and/or Socrates may have thought that this project was inadequate (because it dealt with words, not ideas) and yet similar to Protagoras's search for the "better *logos*." In that case, the useless results that emerge from Prodicus's method in this dialogue may be intended to reflect badly on Protagoras, a fellow Sophist. But this would be unfair, since Protagoras's method is not a matter of establishing definitions, but of pursuing consensus through "thick description."

62. Cf. another poem, in which Simonides writes:

> There is a story that virtue
> lives on a hard-to-climb rock
> with a chorus of pure goddesses standing guard around it
> nor is it visible to the eyes of mortals
> unless a heart-destroying sweat emerge from one
> and he attain the summit of manliness.
> (Edmonds, Simonides, 65)

63. See Coby, pp. 107–11, mainly using the *Protagoras*.

64. Edmonds, 2:265, citing the Scholiast on Pindar.

65. Aristophanes, *Peace* 695; Scholiast on same; Scholiast on Pindar; *Isthmian* 2.10; Plutarch, *Should Old Men Govern?* 5; Stobaeus, *Anthology* 10.62, Hibeh Papyrus, 17; Introduction to Theocritus, 16; Aristotle, *Rhetoric* II.1391a8; Atheneaus 14.656d—all quoted in Edmonds, 2:250–62. Cf. H. S. Taylor, "Plato's Quarrel with Poetry: Simonides," *Journal of the History of Ideas* 36.1 (1975): 4.

66. Aristotle, *Rhetoric* iii.1405b14.

67. *De oratore* 2.86, in Edmonds, Simonides, 43.

68. Regarding his skepticism, see Edmonds, Simonides, 76: "Appearance even overcomes truth." See also Cicero, *De natura deorum* 1.22: "Simonides . . . , into whose mind came many sharp and subtle things, doubting which of them was true, despaired of all truth" (Edmonds, 2:262). An incription states that he won the prize for teaching when he was eighty years old (ibid., Simonides, 176). He was thought to be the inventor of the letters H, Ω, Ξ, and Ψ. (See Suidas, *Lexicon*, and the Scholiast on Dionysus of Thrace, in Edmonds, 2:248, 266).

69. Taylor, p. 5; Bowra, p. 342. See Thucyides I.128–38 on Pausanias.

70. Hence perhaps his view that "good birth" was simply a matter of having rich ancestors. See Edmonds, 2:258. Bowra (p. 329) calls Simonides' "Ode to Skopas" "a realistic and practical criticism of a code of honour which regarded the born aristocrat as the only 'good' man."

71. Plutarch in *De gloria Atheniensum* 3, Greek text in Edmonds, 2:258. Cf. Taylor, p. 13. Simonides describes particular paintings or painters at Edmonds, Simonides, 191, 192, 198.

72. *Inst. Or.* 10.1.64, in Edmonds, 2:270–72. Suidas claimed that Simonides beat Aeschylus in the competition to compose an elegy for the dead at Marathon, because Simonides was better at rousing sympathy (ibid., 2:250). Cf. Catullus 38.7; and Dionysius of Halicarnassus, *Vet. Script.* 420, in ibid. Bowra, p. 363, agrees with the ancient verdict.

73. Edmonds, Simonides, 95.

74. Simonides is supposed to have invented a new epithet for Zeus: ἀρίσταρχος (best-ruler). See Athenaeus, quoted in Edmonds, Simonides, 221. He also wrote: "Zeus alone has the medicine for everything." Stobaeus, in ibid., 100.

75. Simonides' epithet for Sparta was "breaker of men" (analogous to the word meaning "horse-breaker"). It is impossible to know whether this was a positive or negative term for him. See Edmonds, Simonides, 215 (citing Plutarch).

76. *Groundwork*, BA 108ff.

77. Cf. *Symposium* 176e and passim.

78. John Rawls, *A Theory of Justice* (Cambridge, 1971), p. 555. In general, see sections 83 (Happiness and Dominant Ends) and 84 (Hedonism as a Method of Choice).

79. Contrast *Republic* VI.493a (Socrates is speaking): "Each of these private hirelings, whom the politicians call Sophists and regard as their rivals, teaches nothing other than those dogmas that the multitude declare when they are together in crowds, calling this knowledge wisdom."

80. Cf. Gagarin, p. 162.

81. Aristotle seems to take Protagoras's side in this dispute: *Nicomachean Ethics* 1097a10ff.

82. *Theaetetus* 150d–e.

83. Gagarin, p. 148.

84. *Phaedo* 90b–c.

85. *Theaetetus* 157a–b.

86. *Phaedo* 90c–d.

87. Macrobius, *Commentary on the Dream of Scipio*, translated by William Harris Stahl (New York, 1952), 1.ii.4 (p. 84).

4. Instructive Tragedy, Ancient and Modern

1. Rudolf Kassel, ed., *Aristotelis de arte poetica liber* (Oxford, 1965), 1147a1.

2. *Politics* VII.1338a21–22, as discussed by Elizabeth S. Belfiore, *Tragic Pleasures: Aristotle on Plot and Emotion* (Princeton, 1992), p. 45.

3. Isaiah Smithson, "The Moral View of Aristotle's Poetics," *Journal of the History of Ideas* 44 (1983): 4. See also Wayne C. Booth, *The Rhetoric of Fiction* (Chicago, 1961), pp. 4–6. Booth notes that Homer *does* speak in his own voice, and that his style of "[d]irect and authoritative rhetoric" (p. 6) has largely disappeared from modern fiction, thus making recent literature more "Aristotelian" than Greek poetry. Booth criticizes the modern conviction that novels must show and not tell.

4. *Nicomachean Ethics* (*NE*) 1142a22ff.; 1143b3–5.

5. Belfiore, pp. 55–60.

6. Mark Packer, "The Conditions of Aesthetic Feeling in Aristotle's *Poetics*," *British Journal of Aesthetics* 24.2 (1984): 144.

7. Ibid, pp. 68–69, citing *Parts of Animals* 1.5.

8. *Nicomachean Ethics* 1137b13ff. Cf. 1107a30.

9. Ibid., 1179a19–20.

10. Ibid. 1109b20ff. See Martha C. Nussbaum, *The Fragility of Goodness: Luck and Ethics in Greek Tragedy and Philosophy* (Cambridge, 1986), pp. 299–306; and Nussbaum, "The Discernment of Perception: An Aristotelian Conception of Private and Public Rationality," in *Love's Knowledge* (Oxford, 1990), pp. 55–105.

11. *Rhetoric* II:ii.1378b1 (concerning anger). At (*NE*) 1179b5ff., Aristotle concedes that pure arguments have the capacity to influence certain virtuous youths; but the many need experience and habituation to become good. Tragedy (although he does not say it here) can provide emotionally compelling experiences with ethical/educative value. Even for the few people who are subject to influence by "arguments" (*logoi*), literature may have value, for it too is a form of *logos*. This is not to deny that, for Aristotle, the highest activity is abstract reasoning; but abstract reasoning is not about ethics: *NE* 1139a28–29.

12. Belfiore, p. 99.

13. Cf. Smithson, p. 7: "Since happiness is an activity of the soul in accordance with virtue, and since plot has the responsibility of imitating the actions that lead to and constitute happiness or the reverse, plot, finally, has the function of revealing virtue."

14. Socrates' view is so described by Aristotle, *NE* 1145b25. Cf. Plato, *Protagoras* 351c, and passim.

15. *NE*, 1112a2.

16. Smithson, pp. 13–14; and Nussbaum, *Fragility of Goodness*, p. 388: "For Aristotle, pity and fear will be sources of illumination or clarification, as the agent, responding and attending to his or her responses, develops a richer self-understanding concerning the attachments and values that support the responses."

17. Cf. *Rhetoric* 1385b13ff.

18. Smithson, p. 16.

19. Cf. repeated comments by Aristotle that what matters is not having a particular virtue, but exercising it in the right way, at the right time, and toward the right person (e.g., *Nicomachean Ethics* 1109a27ff., 1115b17ff.)

20. Discussed at *NE* 1155a21ff.

21. *Time* interview of March, 1969, in Nabokov, *Strong Opinions* (New York, 1973), p. 121.

22. Interview of 1962 (with various reporters) in ibid., p. 7. Cf. "The Art of Literature and Commonsense" in Fredson Bowers, ed., *Vladimir Nabokov: Lectures on Literature* (New York, 1980), p. 375.

23. *The Annotated Lolita*, edited with notes by Alfred Appel Jr. (New York, 1991), pp. 6–7.

24. *Playboy* interview of 1964, in *Strong Opinions*, p. 41.

25. Letter of February 29, 1956, *The Nabokov-Wilson Letters*, ed. Simon Karlinsky (New York, 1979), p. 298.

26. On interesting parallels between Lolita, subtitled by Humbert *The Confessions of a White Widowed Male* (p. 3), and Rousseau's *Confessions*, see David Rampton, *Vladimir Nabokov* (New York, 1993), pp. 79–80.

27. Alfred Appel identifies forty-six points in the novel at which Quilty appears, sometimes under more than one alias at a time (*Annotated Lolita*, p. 349n).

28. As an example of a concealed fact about Lolita, Carl Proffer notes that sufficient clues are scattered throughout twenty pages of the novel to indicate that Lolita first sleeps with Humbert less than twenty-four hours after having sex with a boy of her own age. See Carl R. Proffer, *Keys to Lolita* (Bloomington, 1968), pp. 6–7.

29. *Paris Review* interview, 1967, in *Strong Opinions*, p. 94 (italics added).

30. Several that I do not discuss here are analyzed in Nomi Tamir-Ghez, "The Art of Persuasion in Nabokov's *Lolita*" (1979), reprinted in Phyllis A. Roth, ed., *Critical Essays on Vladimir Nabokov* (Boston, 1984), pp. 157–76. See also Brian Boyd, *Vladimir Nabokov: The American Years* (Princeton, 1991), p. 231.

31. On this approach to *Lolita*, see Booth, pp. 390–91.

32. After Humbert experiences a moral epiphany near the end of the novel, he recognizes that Lolita's "world" had become one of "total evil" because of his actions (p. 284).

33. See below, p. 000.

34. Contrast his earlier view: "I succeeded in terrorizing Lo, who despite a certain brash alertness and spurts of wit was not as intelligent a child as her I.Q. might suggest" (p. 151). Richard Rorty points out that Lolita was probably referring to her deceased brother when she mentioned death and loneliness (his argument is based on *Lolita*, pp. 68, 286). Humbert does not reach this conclusion, but it is an excellent example of the kind of fact about Lolita's private concerns that we ought to be able to draw out of the text. See Richard Rorty, "Nabokov on Cruelty," in *Irony, Contingency, and Solidarity* (Cambridge, 1989), p. 163.

35. Boyd, p. 237 (note).

36. Douglas Fowler, *Reading Nabokov* (Ithaca, N.Y., 1974), p. 153.

37. Brian Boyd argues that Humbert does not achieve either self-understanding or redemption in the last pages of the novel. His murder of Quilty

(the crime with which he is actually charged) is yet another selfish effort at immortality and transcendence, this time achieved through revenge instead of erotic passion. Boyd identifies numerous parallels between the murder scene and Humbert's first night with Lolita as evidence that Nabokov wants to condemn the murder as much as the rape (Boyd, pp. 252–55). On the other hand, the pairing could represent a contrast: the murder is justified whereas the rape is not. In the end, Boyd may be right that Nabokov wants to deny Humbert full redemption, but it seems to me that Humbert at least comes to understand the evil nature of his own relationship with Lolita.

38. I am indebted for this insight to my colleague, Arthur Evenchik.

39. In the afterword, Nabokov states that the scene with the barber in Kasbeam is one of the "nerves of the novel," "the secret points, the subliminal co-ordinates by means of which the book is plotted," and that it took him a month to write the one relevant sentence (p. 316)

40. Rorty, p. 164. Rorty may believe that Nabokov affirmed a general moral principle: something like "care about others' suffering." But Lawrence A. Blum has shown that an ethics of care is logically and conceptually distinct from any principle-based ethics. See his "Moral Development and Conceptions of Morality," in *Moral Perception and Particularity*, pp. 183–214.

41. Cf. Nabokov's letter to Edmund Wilson of February 29, 1956 (*Nabokov-Wilson Letters*, p. 298): "at a time when American readers are taught from high school on to seek in books 'general ideas' a critic's duty should be to draw attention to the specific detail, to the unique image, without which . . . there can be no art, no genius, no Chehov [sic], no terror, no tenderness, and no surprise." Note, again, the combination of aesthetic and ethical values that are said to emerge from the "specific detail."

42. See Proffer, p. 17.

43. Cf. Nabokov in the afterword (p. 315): "my creature Humbert is a foreigner and an anarchist, and there are many things, besides nymphets, in which I disagree with him."

44. Proffer, pp. 3–4.

45. Interview of 1962 in *Strong Opinions*, p. 16.

46. Cf. *Strong Opinions*, pp. 157–58: interview with Allene Talmey of Vogue.

47. Ibid., p. 19.

48. See Rorty, p. 157.

49. "The Art of Literature and Commonsense," p. 376.

50. As Rorty does: pp. 150–54.

51. Cf. ibid., p. 167: "Nabokov the theorist and generalizer encourages such a reading [i.e., of his works as purely aesthetic), but that reading ignores the point which I take to be illustrated in Nabokov's best practice: Only what is relevant to our sense of what we should do with ourselves, or for others, is aesthetically useful." Rorty is right to distinguish between what Nabokov says and what his books illustrate. For example, Nabokov called "learning to live" a merely "adolescent purpose" of literature, yet his books teach us something about how to live well (See "L'Envoi," in *Lectures on Literature*, p. 381). However, Rorty is too hasty in accepting at face value Nabokov's theoretical generalizations about the role of art.

52. "Mania for Green Fruit," *Victoria Daily Times,* January 17, 1959, quoted in Boyd, p. 230.

53. Stegner, *Escape into Aesthetics: The Art of Vladimir Nabokov* (New York, 1966), pp. 108–9. See also John Hollander, "Lolita," in *Partisan Review*, August 1956: "[Lolita] is the only plausible modern *femme fatale*. She is elusive, perverse, and above all, *transient*." Reprinted in Norman Page, ed., *Nabokov: The Critical Heritage* (London, 1982), p. 83.

54. *Encounter*, October 1958, reprinted in Page, ed., pp. 94, 94.

55. *Freud and Nabokov* (Lincoln, Nebr., 1988), p. 1.

56. Ibid., p. 19.

57. As F. W. Dupee wrote in the *Anchor Review* (1957): "Mr. Nabokov cultivates the groans and guffaws of the recalcitrant fact, the embarrassment that yields to neither myth nor clinic, the bitter commonplaces of life's indestructible surface" (reprinted in Page, ed., p. 91).

58. *Strong Opinions*, p. 69 (1966 interview with Alfred Appel Jr.).

5. RELIGION VERSUS THEOLOGY

1. Rawls, "Reply to Habermas," *The Journal of Philosophy* 92.3 (March 1995): 137n8.

2. For the statistic, see Garry Wills, *Under God: Religion and American Politics* (New York, 1990), p. 16.

3. Greek text from E. J. Jonkers, ed., *Acta et symbola conciliorum quae saeculo quarto habita sunt* (Leiden, Netherlands, 1954), pp. 38–39.

4. *The Babylonish Captivity of the Church*, quoted in Richard H. Popkin, *The History of Scepticism from Erasmus to Descartes* (Assen, Netherlands, 1960), p. 2.

5. *Grundlegung*, BA 28. Kant cites a biblical passage here to support his position, but his interpretation of the scriptural text may be incorrect. He quotes

Mark 10:17–18 (almost identical to Luke 18:18–19), which is rendered as follows in the standard German Protestant Bible, translated by Martin Luther. "A man asked Jesus: Good master, what shall I do that I may inherit eternal life? And Jesus said to him, Why do you call me good? No one is Good but the one God" (from *Die Bibel . . . nach der deutschen Übersetzung Martin Luthers*, Saint Louis, 1920). This passage could possibly be taken to support Kant's thesis that Jesus is only good insofar as he instantiates the Good per se, which is God. But the standard German edition (like the King James Version in English) translates Matthew 19:16–17 in almost the same words, thus ignoring an important change that Matthew made in the received text. According to the original Greek version of Matthew, the man says, "Master, what good shall I do in order to have eternal life? But [Jesus] said to him: Why do you speak to me about the good? One is good. But if you wish to inherit the life, keep the commandments" (*Synopsis quattuor evangeliorum*, 12th ed., Kurt Aland, ed., Stuttgart, 1982, p. 338). Thus, in Matthew's version, "good" is predicated of works, not of Jesus; and Jesus chides the questioner for asking *about* the good, not for calling him good. Matthew's text implies that one should not inquire about the good, for that knowledge is not available to human beings; rather, one should obey God's law as given to us. This can be read as an attack on the metaphysics of morals, rather than a defense of it. Thus it seems to me that Matthew may have deliberately sought to forestall a misinterpretation, like the one that Kant gives, of the ambiguous text found in Mark and Luke.

   6. *Works*, Pelikan ed., vol. 7: *Lectures on Genesis*, p. 279 (my italics). I discuss Luther's attitude toward metaphysics in more detail in the next chapter. See also Bernhard Lohre, *Martin Luther*, translated by Robert C. Schultz (Philadelphia, 1986), p. 161; and Luther's commentary on *Genesis*, described in Rudolf Bultmann, *Faith and Understanding*, translated by Louise Pettitbone Smith (New York, 1969), p. 54.

   7. Bultmann, p. 54.

   8. Ayer, *Language, Truth, and Logic* (New York, 1946), p. 118.

   9. Ibid., p. 119.

   10. See J. L. Austin's critique of Ayer in *Sense and Sensibilia* (Oxford, 1962), pp. 2–19.

   11. Jaroslav Pelikan, *The Christian Tradition*. Vol.1: *The Emergence of the Catholic Tradition* (Chicago, 1971), p. 22.

   12. See Pelikan, p. 53, for a summary.

   13. Erasmus, who is averse to metaphysics (preferring to read the Bible for its literal meaning), ascribes "a certain mutability" to God on the basis of Jeremias 18:8 "If that nation against which I have spoken, shall repent of their evil, I also will repent of the evil that I have thought to do to them." Erasmus notes: "one only says of God that he has abandoned his anger and become merciful after we have

bettered ourselves and he deigns us worthy of his grace." Thus Erasmus, who treats God as a divine person, is not embarrassed to use "God" as the subject of the verb "to become." See his essay, "The Free Will," II:23, in Erasmus and Luther, *Discourse on Free Will*, trans. Ernst F. Winter (New York, 1961), p. 36.

14. From "seeing" to "understand," this is a quote from Isaiah 8:9-10 (See *The Septuagint*, Zondervan edition, London, 1970). Luke has an almost identical passage at 8:10, although he omits the clause beginning "lest . . . ." However, Matthew's text is different. He has: "Therefore speak I to them in parables: because they seeing see not; and hearing they hear not, neither do they understand." Thus Mark and Luke introduce the Isaiah quotation with ἵνα (lest), whereas Matthew uses ὅτι (because). See *The Greek New Testament*, Kurt Aland et al., eds., 1975.

15. Cf. a similar interpretation by C. H. Dodd, who writes: "the wayside and the birds, the thorns and the stony ground are not . . . cryptograms for persecution, the deceitfulness of riches, and so forth. They are there to conjure up a picture of the vast amount of wasted labor which a farmer must face, and so bring into relief the satisfaction that the harvest gives, in spite of all." Thus Jesus means: "Yes, times have been hard and it has taken the Lord a long time to do His work. But now the ends of His labor is at hand. It's just like a sower who goes out to sow . . . ." *The Parables of the Kingdom* (New York, 1961), p. 3.

16. Raymond E. Brown, "Introduction" to the Anchor Bible edition of John (New York, 1966), p. 18.

17. Ibid., pp. 23-24.

18. The Greek word is ἀπαγέλλω, which can mean "report," "pronounce," "proclaim," etc. (an *angelos* is a messenger or an angel). However, the King James version translates it here as "show," because the content of what Jesus reveals after the resurrection is visual; it is not a proposition.

19. Martin Warner, "The Fourth Gospel's Art of Rational Persuasion," in Warner, ed., *The Bible as Rhetoric* (London, 1990), citing A. E. Harvey, *Jesus on Trial: A Study of the Fourth Gospel* (London, 1976).

20. *Tertulliani liber adversus Hermogenem* xxi, in J. P. Migne, ed., *Tertulliani opera omnia* (Paris, 1844), 2:215-16.

21. *De praescriptione haereticos*, vii, in ibid., 2:19.

22. *De anima* v, in ibid., 2:653.

23. *De anima* ii, in ibid., 2:651.

24. *Tractatus logico-philosophicus*, translated by D. F. Pears and B. F. McGuiness (London, 1972), 7.

25. *De anima* iii.

26. Ibid. By "sophists," Tertullian means devious logicians, not humanists like Protagoras.

27. *Metaphysics* vii.1074a38-b14.

28. Werner Jaeger, *Early Christianity and Greek Paideia* (Cambridge, Mass., 1961), pp. 47–49. Plotinus, *Enneads* 1.6.8, reads the *Odyssey* as an allegory of the soul's progress.

29. David Dawson, *Allegorical Readers and Cultural Revision in Ancient Alexandria* (Berkeley, 1992), p. 73.

30. Jaeger, p. 53, describing Gregory's commentary on the Song of Songs.

31. St. Gregory of Nyssa, *Commentary on the Song of Songs*, trans. Casimir McCambley (Brookline, Mass., 1987), p. 49. On the basis of Migne's *Patrologiae graeca* (Paris, 1858), I have changed McCambley's "wire" to "wine." The last phrase could mean, "the likeness *of* what is truly beautiful *to* the truly good."

32. *De doctrina christiana* II.vi.8, in *Patrologiae cursus completus*, J. P. Migne, ed. (Paris, 1887), 34:59.

33. Ibid. I.ii.2.

34. *De magistro* V.15.

35. *De doctrina christiana* III.xxxviii.56. Cf. *De Magistro* IX.27.

36. *De doctrina christiana* II.vi.7.

37. Ibid. III.x.14. Philo had pioneered this test: see Karlfried Froehlich, "Introduction," in *Biblical Interpretation in the Early Church* (Philadelphia, 1984), p. 7.

38. *De doctrina christiana* III.v.9.

39. Ibid. II.xxxvi.54.

40. Ibid. II.vi.8.

41. Ibid. IV.xxviii. 64.

42. Ibid. IV.28.

43. See J. N. D. Kelly, *Jerome: His Life, Writings, and Controversies* (New York: 1975), pp. 11–13, 16.

44. Ibid., pp. 59-60.

45. Epistle 17, para. 3, in *Sancti Eusebii Hieronymi opera omnia*, in *Patrologiae cursus completus*, vol. 22, ed. J-P. Migne (Paris, 1877).

46. See, e.g., his letter of ca. 410 to Marcellinus and Anapsychia.

47. Both the Iconoclastic controversy and the early debates about monasticism and asceticsm were intellectually complex. Images were used for prayer, intercession, and instruction; and one could violently oppose some of these uses but approve of others. (For example, Pope Gregory I opposed the worship of images but approved of their use as a means of instructing the unlettered.) Similarly, there were many types and degrees of asceticism to be defended or attacked. The Iconclasts and the ascetics were often on opposite sides, as when the Byzantine emperor Constantine V destroyed icons but also persecuted monks. And in many cases, defenders of religious art were just as metaphysical as their enemies, praising icons for "participating" in the Being of God. Finally, some partisans in these debates had hidden agendas that were unrelated to theology, such as the defeat of political enemies. Thus my paradigm of a contemplative, abstract, and anti-mimetic culture only applies to a strand in early Christian society. See: Moshe Barasch, *Icon: Studies in the History of an Idea* (New York, 1992); Daniel J. Sahas, ed., *Icon and Logos: Sources in Eighth-Century Iconoclasm* (Toronto, 1986); and Joseph Gutmann, ed., *The Image and the Word: Confrontations in Judaism, Christianity, and Islam* (Missoula, Mont., 1977).

48. This was probably a false and malicious rumor: see Pierre Riché, *Éducation et culture dans l'occident barbare, VIe–VIIIe siècles* (Paris, 1962), p. 96. But the fact that it was plausible indicates how low culture had fallen.

49. *Art and Illusion* (Washington, D.C., 1951), p. 145.

50. *Art in the Early Church* (New York, 1947), p. 24.

51. Cf. Friedrich Ohly, "Vom geistigen Sinn des Wortes im Mettelalter," in *Schriften zur mittelalterlichen Bedeutungsforschung* (Darmstadt, Germany, 1977), p. 15: "The allegedly perspectiveless middle ages have their own appropriate kind of perspective, consisting in the spiritual transparency of what exists. This perspective shows itself in the upward gaze that loosens from the earthly and peers through to the spiritual meaning of the sign that is present in the creaturely. It is perspective in the truest sense, in that it looks through the manifest to the invisible, through the signifying to the signified. It leads from the fundament to the vault, from the earthly to the heavenly. Its essence is not foreshortening, but extension to the sublime. It does not relativize to an earthly vanishing point but aligns with the absolute, making the created transparent to the eternal. It is not a physiological, visual kind of perspective but a theological-spiritual kind, and it defines as such the art of the sublime."

52. For the role of rhetoric in education, see Pierre Riché, *Les écoles et l'enseignement dans l'occident Chrétien de la fin du Ve siècle au mileu du XIe siècle* (Paris, 1979), p. 25. For the conflict between the active and contemplative life in Boethius's time, see Seth Lerer, *Boethius and Dialogue* (Princeton, 1985), p. 21, citing Cassiodorus, Boethius's commentary on Aristotle's *De Interpretatione*, and senatorial letters

of the period. These sources reveal the need to choose between civic humanism and political leadership, on one hand, and philosophical/theological contemplation, on the other.

53. In order to argue that Boethius was not a Catholic, one would have to claim either: (1) that the theological works that traditionally bear his name were not actually written by the author of the *Consolation of Philosophy*; or (2) that he became disillusioned with Christianity at the end of his life. Both views have been argued, but current scholarship generally denies them.

54. Boethius: *The Consolations of Music, Logic, Theology, and Philosophy* (Oxford, 1981), p. 249.

55. Platonic philosophy was equated with true theology in Boethius's immediate milieu. See Cassiodorus, *Variae* I.45 (reproducing a letter from Theodoric to Boethius, drafted by Cassiodorus), in which Theodoric praises Boethius's translations of "Plato the theologian." Quoted by Edmund Reiss, *Boethius* (Boston, 1982), p. 11.

56. Ludwig Bieler, ed., *Boethii Philosophiae consolatio*, in *Corpus Christianorum, series latina*, xviv (Turnhout, Belgium, 1957). References are to book and section number, with "p" denoting prose and "m," meter.

57. The allusions are traced by Gerard O'Daly in *The Poetry of Boethius* (Chapel Hill, N.C., 1991), pp. 36–37.

58. Lerer, p. 102.

59. Cf. Socrates' comment to Protagoras: "I was under the impression that there was a difference between coming together to have a dialogue, and making a public speech" (336b). Dialogue, for Socrates, means laying out well-ordered logical arguments; rhetoric and poetry, while more beguiling than logic, are obfuscating. For Boethius, a more immediate source for the same distinction may have been Cicero's *Tusculan Disputations* 1.iv.8 and 1.viii.16. Here Cicero's questioner plays the role of Protagoras, demanding continuous speeches (*oratio*), but Cicero prefers dialectic (*disputatio*).

60. According to O'Daly, p. 35, this metaphor is drawn from Lucretius. In the *De rerum natura* 1.945ff., Lucretius writes: "I wanted to expound our [i.e., the Epicureans'] doctrine in a softly eloquent Pierian song, and almost to touch it with the sweet honey of the muses" (my trans.).

61. Henri de Lubac, *Exégèse médiévale: Les quatre sens de l'Écriture* (Paris, 1959). This four-volume work is devoted to showing that the doctrine of the four senses was all but universal in medieval exegesis.

62. Bromyard's *Summa predicantum* (ca. 1390), in William Nelson, *Fact or Fiction: The Dilemma of the Renaissance Storyteller* (Cambridge, Mass., 1973), p. 28.

63. Courcelle, *La Consolation de philosophie dans la tradition littéraire: Antécédents et postérité de Boèce* (Paris, 1967). See also the cover art to this volume.

64. Dante's device of using Virgil as a guide comes from an early Christian dialogue about philosophy—not the *Consolation*, but Fulgentius's *De Continentia Virgiliana*, also a sixth-century work. See Lerer, p. 58ff.

65. Just four lines later, Dante alludes to Boethius. In prayer, he speaks of "the wheel [of fortune] which you make sempiternal."

66. Cf. Erich Auerbach, *Dante: Poet of the Secular World* (1929), translated by Ralph Manheim (Chicago, 1961).

67. Wittgenstein, *Notebooks 1914–1916*, edited and translated by G. H. von Wright and G. E. M. Anscombe (New York, 1963), note dated October 7, 1916; cf. *Tractatus*, section 6.45.

68. "Gods," in Flew, *Logic and Language*, p. 193.

69. Ibid., p. 194.

70. I owe the example to William James, *The Varieties of Religious Experience* (London, 1982; first published, 1902), p. 15.

71. Ibid., p. 30.

72. Fox, *Journal*, ed. J. Nickalls (Cambridge, 1952), p. 11; emphasis in the original.

6. HUMANISTS AND SCHOLASTICS

1. On the resemblance between humanists and Sophists, see: W. K. C. Guthrie, *The Sophists* (Cambridge, 1971), pp. 15–16; Bernard Knox, *The Oldest Dead White European Males* (New York, 1993), p. 104; Paul Oskar Kristeller, *Renaissance Thought: The Classic, Scholastic, and Humanist Strains* (New York, 1961), pp. 11–12; Werner Jaeger, *Paideia: The Ideals of Greek Culture*, translated by Gilbert Highet (New York, 1943), p. 301; Jerrold E. Seigel, *Rhetoric and Philosophy in Renaissance Humanism* (Princeton, 1968), pp. xii, 9, and passim; Nancy Struever, *The Language of History in the Renaissance: Rhetoric and Historical Consciousness in Florentine Humanism* (Princeton, 1970), esp. pp. 46, 58–59, 80n, 88, 97, 108, 116, and 132; Charles Trinkaus, "Protagoras in the Renaissance: An Exploration," in Edward P. Mahoney, ed., *Philosophy and Humanism: Renaissance Essays in Honor of Paul Oskar Kristeller* (New York, 1976), pp. 190–213; and Mario Untersteiner, *The Sophists*, translated by Kathleen Freeman (Oxford, 1954), p. xv.

Humanists mostly derived their Sophistic ideas via Latin intermediaries. The Renaissance attitude toward the original Sophists was complicated by the fact that humanists were initially quite ignorant of Greek culture: thus Petrarch confused Socrates with Isocrates (a Sophist) and identified Protagoras with the speculative philosopher Pythagoras (Trinkaus, pp. 192, 198). The word "Sophist" was generally derogatory, but it described people who suffered from an excessive commitment to arcane logical rules–just the opposite of Protagoras's actual attitude. Erasmus, Luther, and others used "Sophist" to mean "scholastic." Likewise, despite Aristotle's emphasis on the ethical value of rhetoric and poetry, the adjective "Aristotelian" connoted abstract theorizing.

2. Letter to Ermolao Barbaro, defending philosophy, in *Renaissance Philosophy*, vol. 1: *The Italian Philosophers*, edited and translated by Arturo B. Fallico and Herman Shapiro (New York, 1967), p. 107. Pico adds: "We [philosophers] seek to present some matter so thoroughly researched that there remains no room for doubt, and so solidly presented the there remains no need for further discussion."

3. During the Middle Ages, writes Kristeller (p. 7), "there was a conflict between the representatives of the *artes*, that is, of the liberal arts and the scientific and philosophical disciplines, and the followers of the *authores*, that is, of the great books, and by the thirteenth century the latter tendency had suffered a decisive, although perhaps temporary, defeat." R. W. Southern states: "I believe the period from about 1100 to about 1320 to have been one of the greatest ages of humanism in the history of Europe: perhaps the greatest of all" (*Medieval Humanism* [New York, 1970], p. 31). However, Southern first distinguishes "scientific" humanism (which prefers human experience to divine law) from "literary" humanism (which emphasizes literature and the humanities as sources of meaning). The latter form of humanism is my topic in this book; but Southern notes that medieval humanism was "much nearer to the type I have described as 'scientific'" (p. 32).

4. Kelley, *Renaissance Humanism* (Boston, 1991), p. 5. Cf. *Protagoras* 318e: Protagoras, who is a grammarian and literary critic, attacks Hippias, whose subjects are mathematics, astronomy, geometry, and music. These are theoretical "quadrivium" sciences, which Protagoras distrusts compared to the "trivium" disciplines that he teaches. He also attacks Socrates' philosophical method. Thus the humanists of the Renaissance were in many ways Protagoras's heirs, defenders of the trivium against the quadrivium. Trinkaus writes (p. 213): "What is very certain . . . is that the Renaissance did not discern in [Protagoras] its predecessor, however much we today are inclined to see a resemblance." But Protagoras's Great Speech is cited approvingly in Baldesar Castiglione, *Il libro del cortegiano*, edited by Giulio Einuadi (Turin, 1960), IV.xi (p. 367); and in Thomas Elyot's *The Book Named the Governor* (London, 1962), I.xiii (p. 45). Trinkaus focuses too narrowly on Renaissance philosophers, who naturally ignored or disliked Protagoras: it was the rhetoricians who found him appealing.

5. *Summa theologiae*, 2a2a.82.2, Latin/English edition by Kevin D. O'Rourke (London, 1964), 39: 35–37.

6. Hennig Brinkmann, *Mittelalterlichen Hermeneutik* (Tübingen, Germany, 1980), p. 5.

7. Servius Grammaticus, *In Vergilii carmina comentarii*, edited by Georg Thilo and Hermann Hagen (Hildesheim, 1961), 1:1.

8. Cited in John B. Gleason, *John Colet* (Berkeley, 1989), p. 136.

9. See Brinkman, p. 158: "That which *littera* and *sensus* signify consists in an *intentio*, which stands ready to be observed by means of an *explanatio*."

10. St. Bonaventure, *Breviloquium*, prologue, §4.

11. Erasmus, *Methodus*, ed. G. B. Winkler, in *Ausgewählte Schriften*, edited by W. Welzig (Darmstadt, Germany, 1967), III.64, quoted and trans. in Anthony Grafton and Lisa Jardine, *From Humanism to the Humanities: Education and the Liberal Arts in Fifteenth- and Sixteenth-Century Europe* (London, 1986), p. 147.

12. Erasmus, "Disputatiuncula" ("A Small Debate" with Colet), from *Opera omnia* (Leiden, Holland, 1703–6), V.1267, translated in Gleason, p. 96.

13. *The Crisis of the Early Italian Renaissance: Civic Humanism and Republican Liberty in an Age of Classicism and Tyranny* (Princeton, 1966). Baron coined the term "civic humanism" in 1928.

14. Kelley, p. 79.

15. Letter to Martin Dorp, from Bruges (October 21, 1515), in Elizabeth Frances Rogers, ed., *St. Thomas More: Selected Letters* (New Haven, Conn., 1961), p. 29.

16. More to Dorp, p. 30.

17. Valla, *On Pleasure* (*De voluptate*, later retitled *De vero bono*), translated by A. Kent Hieatt and Maristella Lorch (New York, 1977), p. 75.

18. *An Apology for Poetry*, ed. Geoffrey Shepherd (New York, 1973), pp. 109, 114. According to Shepherd's note, *Amadis de Gaule* was a "late chivalric prose romance, of Spanish origin, which . . . had a great European success."

19. *Protagoras* 325e–326a.

20. Cf. Marjorie O'Rourke Boyle, *Erasmus on Language and Method in Theology* (Toronto, 1977), p. 138: "To be gathered concordantly in Christ's name is to invite the disclosure of that eloquent reality which his name promises: *oratio*, the revelation of God. . . . And so Christ is fulfilled by charity and learning." Boyle bases her conclusion on the ideal discussion that Erasmus presents in his dialogue *Convivium religiosum* of 1522.

21. *Hyperaspistes*, quoted in Marjorie O'Rourke Boyle, *Rhetoric and Reform: Erasmus' Civil Dispute with Luther* (Cambridge, Mass., 1983), p. 135.

22. *Elegantiae* IV, preface, Latin and English translation in Seigel, p. 140

23. *Dialogo intorno alla professione dei religiosi*, in ibid., p. 141.

24. See Petrarch's *De vita solitaria* and More's *Utopia*, book 1. Chapman makes a confusing statement about the contemplative life. He says that, just as Plato had rightly favored the contemplative life, so he (Chapman) prefers "divine Poesie to all worldly wisdome." But this is an odd analogy, since Plato had distrusted poetry, and especially Homer, for presenting mere worldly knowledge. See Chapman's "Preface to the Reader," in Allardyce Nicoll, ed., *Chapman's Homer* (Princeton, 1967).

25. Baron, p. 7. See also Kenneth Charlton, *Education in Renaissance England* (London, 1965), pp. 21–40, 58, 66–74. Charlton virtually equates the defense of the *vita activa* with humanism.

26. Valla makes this remark several times: references appear in Seigel, p. 141n12.

27. *The Advancement of Learning*, edited by William Aldis Wright (Oxford, 1880), II.xviii.1.

28. Elyot, III.xxv, section entitled, "Of experience which have preceded our time, with a defence of histories" (p. 227).

29. Anthologized in Martindale, p. 220.

30. Elyot, I.viii. Kristeller writes that a "characteristic feature [of Renaissance humanism] is the tendency to express, and to consider worth expressing, the concrete uniqueness of one's feelings, opinions, experiences, and surroundings, a tendency which appears in the bibliographical and descriptive literature of the time as well as in its portrait painting, [and] which is present in all the writings of the humanists" (p. 20).

31. Quoted in Maristella de Panizza Lorch, "Introduction" to Valla's *On Pleasure*, p. 24.

32. Thomas à Kempis (attrib.), *The Imitation of Christ*, translated by by Leo Sherley-Price (Baltimore, 1968), chapters 1 and 3 (pp. 27, 30).

33. *The Paraclesis* (Erasmus's introduction to his 1516 translation of the New Testament), in Erasmus, *Christian Humanism and the Reformation: Selected Writings*, edited by John C. Olin (New York, 1965), p. 101.

34. *Imitation of Christ*, chapters 5 and 17 (pp. 33 and 45.)

35. *Paraclesis*, p. 97.

36. Luther complained that Erasmus called the Drama of Redemption a *fabula* (story, tale, narrative, or fable). But for Erasmus, a *fabula* was an ideal source of meaning. See Margaret Mann Phillips, "Some Last Words of Erasmus," in John

C. Olin, James D. Smart, and Robert E. McNally, eds., *Luther, Erasmus, and the Reformation: A Catholic-Protestant Reappraisal* (New York, 1969), p. 101. See also Boyle, *Erasmus on Language and Method*, pp. 129–41 for a discussion of *con-fabulatio* (discussion or consensus).

37. *Paraclesis*, pp. 100, 98.

38. Ibid., p. 100.

39. Ibid., p. 93.

40. James F. Brady and John C. Olin, introduction to volume 61, *Collected Works of Erasmus* (Toronto, 1992), p. xxxiv.

41. *Paraclesis*, p. 105.

42. *De ratione studii ac legendi interpretandique auctores liber*, translated and excerpted in Martindale, p. 70.

43. Erasmus to Paul Volz, August 14, 1518, in Olin, ed., pp. 114, 113.

44. Letter to John Slechta, quoted and discussed in James Kelsey McConica, "Erasmus and the Grammar of Consent," in J. Coppens, ed., *Scrinium Erasmianum* (Leiden, Netherlands, 1969), 2:97.

45. Letter quoted in Phillips, p. 91.

46. Grafton and Jardine, pp. 139, 148, 144, xiv.

47. McConica, p. 89. See also Phillips (p. 100): Erasmus "often found truth in human consensus." Cf. Boyle, *Rhetoric and Reform* (p. 26): "Although Erasmus does not essay the question of how the consensus may be formed if scripture is unclear, by implication it is the very act of consensus which interprets or clarifies—that is, decides—the truth of the text."

48. Erasmus, "The Complaint of Peace" (*Querela pacis*), translated by Thomas Paynell (1559), in *The 'Adages' of Erasmus and the Complaint of Peace* (New York, 1972), p. 45.

49. Luther's commentary on Genesis, described in Rudolf Bultmann, *Faith and Understanding*, translated by Louise Pettitbone Smith (New York, 1969), p. 54.

50. Erich Vogelsang, ed., *Luthers Werke*, 5:388. This is usefully discussed in Alister McGrath, *Luther's Theology of the Cross* (Oxford, 1985), p. 148ff. Cf. Luther's *Disputation against Scholastic Theology* (1517), theses 44–46.

51. Given Luther's emphasis on the distinction between nature and grace, it may seem paradoxical for me to read him as a naturalist and a monist. But here I use "nature" to mean the world that is known to experience, not creation minus divine grace.

52. *Compendium vitae*, translated by Olin, pp. 29–30.

53. Boyle, *Rhetoric and Reform*, pp. 34–35.

54. In the following pages, unless otherwise noted, I quote from Ernst F. Winter, trans. and ed., *Discourse on Free Will [by] Erasmus [and] Luther* (New York, 1961). Cf. Erasmus's letter to Barbier, quoted in Boyle, *Rhetoric and Reform*, p. 36.

55. Cf. a letter by Luther to Amsdorf, in which he writes of Eramsus: "Not that he is ignorant of our doctrines, those of Christians, but consciously and with forethought he refuses to know them ... that is, the Trinity, the divinity and humanity of Christ, sin and the redemption of the human race, the resurrection of the dead, life eternal and so on." Quoted in Phillips, p. 97.

56. Quoted in Boyle, p. 23.

57. Epictetus, *Diatribe*, as reported by Arrian, Greek/English ed. of W. A. Oldfather (London, 1936), 2.11.13. I have altered the translation to make it more literal, and have added the numbers.

58. For similar reasons, More exempted Aquinas from his general critique of scholastics. More emphasized the fact that Aquinas was responsible for a miracle and had been canonized; but he did not defend the method of the *Summa*. See More's *Confutation of Tyndale*, quoted in Edward L. Surtz, "'Oxford Reformers' and Scholasticism," *Studies in Philology* 47.4 (October 1950): 551–52.

59. Boyle, *Rhetoric and Reform*, p. 15. See, e.g., Cicero's *Ad C. Herennium de ratione dicendi*, Latin/English edition by Harry Caplan (Cambridge, Mass., 1968), I.i.II: "The task of the public speaker is to discuss capably those matters which law and custom have fixed for the uses of citizenship, and to secure as far as possible the agreement of his hearers." Cf. *De Inventione* I.v.6.

60. On the different kinds of skepticism exhibited by Erasmus and Luther, see Richard Popkin, *The History of Scepticism from Erasmus to Descartes* (Assen, Netherlands, 1960), pp. 1–8.

61. Erasmus told Henry VIII that, in attacking Luther, he was opposing the "new dogmas" of Protestantism. (Letter of May 8, 1524, cited in Boyle, *Rhetoric and Reform*, p. 36.)

62. Likewise, in his *Adages*, Erasmus collects passages from Euripides, Plato, Homer, and other authors in which someone says hyperbolically, "I am nothing." See *Adages* I:iii:44, translated by Margaret Mann Phillips in *The Collected Works*, 31:274

7. THE WISE FOOL

1. *Praise of Folly*, translated by Betty Radice in the *Collected Works of Erasmus*, vol. 27 (Toronto, 1978), p. 86. Hereafter, references are given in parentheses.

2. Donne, Paradox X, "That a Wise Man is Known by Much Laughing," in John Hayward, ed., John Donne, *Complete Poetry and Selected Prose* (London, 1930), p. 343. Folly's adage does not appear in Erasmus's *Adagia*, his published collection of proverbs. However, the expression "*Dal riso molto, conosci lo stulto*" ("by much laughing, you know the fool") appears in Torriano, *Piazza universale di proverbi Italiani or a Common Place of Italian Proverbs* (1666), according to Helen Peters's commentary on Donne's *Paradoxes and Problems* (Oxford, 1980), p. 83. Donne also treats this proverb as a commonplace. Some years later, Thomas Hobbes used it in *Leviathan* (London, 1985), 1:6, p. 125: "And therefore much Laughter at the defects of others, is a signe of Pusillanimity. For great minds, one of the proper workes is, to help and free others from scorn; and compare themselves onely with the most able." Nietzsche makes fun of this aphorism in *Beyond Good and Evil*, 294, arguing that gods and true philosophers love to laugh mockingly. And in a particularly hallucinogenic passage of *Ulysses* (London 1960), Joyce has Shakespeare's head appear in a mirror to say "*(In dignified vintriloquy)* 'Tis the loud laugh bespeaks the vacant mind" (p. 508).

Walter Kaiser identifies Folly's allusions to Terence and Homer in his *Praisers of Folly: Erasmus, Rabelais, Shakespeare* (Cambridge, Mass., 1963), p. 41.n.17. He also cites parallels in Erasmus's *Adagia* (J. Leclerc, ed. *Opera omnia* II.316e; II.292f–294b); but these do not seem conclusive to me.

3. Erasmus to Dorp, p. 78.

4. Baldwin, *William Shakspere's Small Latine and Lesse Greeke* (Urbana, Ill., 1974), 2:662.

5. Ibid., 1:77. Shakespeare's numerous specific debts to Erasmus are noted in commentaries to his individual plays, and many are collected by Baldwin. See also: F. G. Butler, "Erasmus and the Deaths of Cordelia and Lear," *English Studies* 73.1 (February 1992): 10–21; and Barbara J. Baines, "Shakespeare's Plays and the Erasmian Box," *Renaissance Papers* (1981): 33–44.

6. See Joseph M. Levine, "Natural History and the New Philosophy: Bacon, Harvey, and the Two Cultures," in *Humanism and History: Origins of Modern English Historiography* (Ithaca, N.Y., 1987), pp. 126, 131.

7. I have quoted passages from *The Taming of the Shrew* from *The Riverside Shakespeare* (Boston, 1974), but I have altered punctuation in places.

8. This may be an allusion to Ovid's *De ponto*, which was a famous defense of the humanities. Ovid wrote, "to study the liberal arts [*ingenues artes*] faithfully makes behavior [*mores*] gentle and permits people not to act savagely." Ovid, *De ponto* II.ix.47–48, my translation from *P. Ovidi Nasonis tristium libri quinque, Ibis, ex ponto libri quatuor . . .* , ed. S. G. Owen (Oxford, 1915). Although Baldwin does not cite this passage from *The Taming of the Shrew*, he shows that Ovid's *De ponto* was part of the Elizabethan curriculum and known to Shakespeare (see Baldwin, 1:387, 512; 2:382, 422, 611–12).

9. Engle, *Shakespearean Pragmatism* (Chicago, 1993), p. 55.

10. I quote *King Lear* from the Arden edition, edited by Kenneth Muir (London, 1972).

11. Cavell, "The Avoidance of Love: A Reading of *King Lear*," in *Disowning Knowledge in Six Plays of Shakespeare* (Cambridge, 1987), pp. 64–65.

12. Italics added.

13. Danby, *Shakespeare's Doctrine of Nature: A Study of "King Lear"* (London, 1949), p. 21.

14. Danby, p. 26, cites Hooker, *Ecclesiastical Polity*, Everyman edition, part I, chapter viii.

15. Paradox VIII, in Hayward, ed., pp. 341–42. Hayward places the phrase "our reasonableness" in brackets to suggest that its authenticity is doubtful, but Peters accepts it.

16. Paradox VIII, "That Nature is Our Worst Guide."

17. Danby, p. 205. The literature on providence in *King Lear* is huge. For works that discuss this topic and cite numerous authorities, see Muir's introduction to the Arden edition, pp. l–lviii; William R. Elton, *"King Lear" and the Gods* (San Marino, 1966), pp. 3–8; and Barbara Everett, "The New King Lear" (1960), in Harold Bloom, ed., *King Lear* (New York, 1992), pp. 119–31.

18. Graham Bradshaw argues that Shakespeare (or at least the character of Ulysses in Shakespeare's *Troylus and Cressida*) "makes the crucial distinction between *dogmatic* scepticism, as represented by the terminal, materialistic nihilism of a Thersites, Iago, or Edmund, and *radical* scepticism, which turns on itself–weighing the human need to affirm values against the inherently problematic nature of all acts of valuing." *Shakespeare's Scepticism* (Ithaca, N.Y., 1987), p. 39. This is roughly the same as my distinction between dogmatic and Pyrhhonist skepticism.

19. Cf. Bradshaw, p. 89: "Nor can the accident of [Cordelia's] death invalidate our earlier responses to everything that has moved us so deeply–in the reconciliation scene, as in all those other scattered, precious moments of tenderness and simple solicitude when characters care for each other or poignantly invoke a 'Grace' which exists in the *Lear*-world only as it is actualised in their own responses and needs."

20. Elton, who doubts the Christian interpretation of Edgar's "ripeness is all," nevertheless cites parallels in Job 14:1–2, Wisdom 7:6, and the *Booke of Common Prayer* (1590).

21. In addition to his natural-law doctrine, Albany seems to employ an economic method of evaluation. Just as Lear calls Cordelia "nothing," Albany–

when he finally judges Goneril—says of her: "You are not worth the dust which the rude wind / Blows in your face" (IV.ii.30–31).

22. The fact that Gloucester *prays* to the Heavens may suggest that he still believes that providence is just and responsive. It is difficult to make Gloucester's speeches entirely consistent, because he is often guilty of waffling and wishful thinking.

23. Jonathan Dollimore, offering a "materialist" reading of *King Lear*, makes much of the king's failure to help the poor. "Insofar as Lear identifies with suffering," he writes, "it is at the point when he is powerless to do anything about it. This is not accidental: the society of *Lear* is structured in such a way that to wait for shared experience to generate justice is to leave it too late. Justice, we might say, is too important to be trusted to empathy. . . . Pity, like kindness, seems in *Lear* to be precious yet ineffectual": "*King Lear* and Essentialist Humanism" (1984), in Harold Bloom, ed., *William Shakespeare's "King Lear"* (New York, 1987), p. 74. For Dollimore, presumably, the solution to the tragedy of *Lear* is not empathy, but rather an objectively better social order, understood by means of a science of history. But surely the play indicates that Lear should have felt more pity earlier. Empathy may be rare, but it is precious, and tragedy can help to encourage it. Thus the solution urged by the play is the play (or others like it).

24. Cavell, pp. 39–123, especially pp. 94–95.

25. Some critics have asserted that Shakespeare consciously anticipated the Cartesian themes of doubt and certainty. See, e.g., Lee A. Jacobus, *Shakespeare and the Dialectic of Certainty* (New York, 1992), p. 2.

26. Bradshaw, p. 90.

27. "The Avoidance of Love," p. 89.

28. *Philosophical Investigations*, 124.

29. Explaining that she cannot give a speech in Lear's praise, Cordelia tells her father, "Unhappy that I am, I cannot heave / My heart into my mouth" (I.i.90–91). This alludes to Ecclesiasticus 21:26, "The heart of fooles is in their mouth: but the mouth of the wise is in their heart." Thus Cordelia implies that her sisters are fools for being insincere. But Goneril, referring to her moralistic husband Albany, says "a fool usurps my bed" (IV.ii.28). Then, when Albany argues that it goes against "wisdom and goodness" to banish Lear and Gloucester, Goneril replies: "Fools do those villains pity who are punish'd / Ere they have done their mischief" (IV.ii.38, 54–55). For Goneril, believers in wisdom and goodness are the true fools. Edmund, meanwhile, thinks that his father is a "fop" for believing in astrology. But Gloucester considers himself a fool for misjudging Edgar: "O my follies! Then Edgar was abus'd" (III.vii.89). Later, when Edgar adopts a disguise to deceive his father, he says, "Bad is the trade that must play fool to sorrow"

(IV.i.37)—thus calling himself a deliberate fool. Kent, picking a fight with Oswald, cries, "Smoile you my speeches, as I were a Fool?" (II.ii.79).

30. I wonder, therefore, whether the Fool disappears because he knows what will happen to Lear and Cordelia, and he cannot stand to see it. The fact that he is not wholly of Lear's time suggests that he can vanish from the action of the play when he wants to.

CONCLUSION

1. Niebuhr, *Moral Man and Immoral Society* (New York, 1932), p. 6.

2. Ibid., p. 3.

3. King, *Stride toward Freedom: The Montgomery Story* (New York, 1958), p. 97.

4. Niebuhr, p. 252. King makes the same point: see "The Social Organization of Nonviolence," *Liberation* (October 1959), reprinted in James M. Washington, ed., *I Have a Dream: Writings and Speeches That Changed the World* (Glenview, Ill., 1992), p. 51.

5. Niebuhr, p. 21.

6. *Stride toward Freedom*, p. 101.

7. Ibid., p. 100.

8. "Facing the Challenge of a New Age," *Phylon* 18 (April 1957): 30.

9. *Stride toward Freedom*, p. 102.

10. Ibid., pp. 105, 106.

11. Ibid., p. 104; "My Trip to the Land of Gandhi," *Ebony* (July 1959), in Washington, p. 44.

12. "Our Struggle," *Liberation* 1 (April 1957): 3–6, in Washington, p. 6.

13. "Letter from a Birmingham Jail" (1963), in Washington, p. 89.

14. Ibid.

15. Ibid., p. 86.

16. King, "Pilgrimage to Nonviolence," *Christian Century* 77 (April 13, 1960): 441.

17. *Stride toward Freedom*, p. 100.

18. Quoted in David J. Garrow, *Bearing the Cross: Martin Luther King, Jr., and the Southern Christian Leadership Conference* (New York, 1988), pp. 57–58. King refers to the same incident in *Stride toward Freedom*, pp. 134–35.

19. King, "Pilgrimage to Nonviolence," p. 441.

20. Fox, *Journal*, ed. J. Nickalls (Cambridge, 1952), p. 11; emphasis in the original.

21. *Stride toward Freedom*, pp. 105–6.

22. "Letter from a Birmingham Jail," p. 94.

23. In the following discussion, I am indebted to David Luban, "Difference Made Legal: The Court and Dr. King," chapter 5 of his *Legal Modernism* (Ann Arbor, 1994), especially pp. 251–59 ("King's Biblical Allusions").

24. King: "Never before have I written a letter this long . . . but what else is there to do when you are alone for days in the dull monotony of a narrow jail cell?" ("Letter," p. 100). Cf. Paul: "Ye see how large a letter I have written unto you with mine own hand" (Gal. 6:11). King: "I hope this letter finds you strong of faith" ("Letter," p. 100). Cf. Paul: "Brethren, the grace of our lord Jesus Christ be with your spirit" (Gal. 6:18). And so on.

25. Poussaint, writing in the *New York Times Magazine* (August 20, 1967), quoted in Robert Weisbrot, *Freedom Bound: A History of America's Civil Rights Movement* (New York, 1991), p. 188.

INDEX

abortion, 65–66, 146, 256 *n* 7
active life: 106–7, 162–63, 187, 206, 209
agape, 240
Agathon, 127
Alcibiades, 89, 93, 102, 112
Alighieri, Dante, 170–173
Amos, 245
Apollinarus of Laodicea, 161
Appel, Alfred, Jr., 135
Aquinas, Thomas, Saint, 147, 180–81, 241
Aristophanes, 88
Aristotle: against moral theory, 4, 42–46, 132–33; circularity in, 128, 198; on contemplation, 187; on God, 152, 158; on judges, 255 *n* 87; Luther on, 194; on moral judgment, 42–46, 94–95, 141, 254–55 *n* 70–76; on narrative and tragedy, 8, 123–28, 138; on phantasia, 254 *n* 73; on Protagoras, 88, 260 *n* 13; on rhetoric, 266 *n* 11; on Simonides, 104

aspect-seeing, 34–38
Augustine of Hippo, Saint, 159–161, 172
Ayer, A. J., 150

Bacon, Francis, 187, 216
Baier, Annette, 3, 46
Baldwin, T. W., 210
Baron, Hans, 183, 187
Barthes, Roland, 250 *n* 10
Beardsmore, R. W., 69–70
Benedict, Saint, 165
Blum, Lawrence A., 252 *n* 44, 268 *n* 40
Boethius, Anicius Manlius Severinus, 165–170, 173, 274 *n* 53
Bonaventure, Saint, 181
Booth, Wayne, 265 *n* 3
Borges, Jorge Luis, 47
Bourdieu, Pierre, 77, 259 *n* 42
Boyd, Brian, 267–68 *n* 37
Boyle, Marjorie O'Rourke, 277 *n* 20, 279 *n* 47